UNITED NATIONS CONFERENCE ON TRADE AND DEVELOPMENT

REVIEW
OF MARITIME TRANSPORT
2013

UNITED NATIONS
New York and Geneva, 2013

NOTE

The Review of Maritime Transport is a recurrent publication prepared by the UNCTAD secretariat since 1968 with the aim of fostering the transparency of maritime markets and analysing relevant developments. Any factual or editorial corrections that may prove necessary, based on comments made by Governments, will be reflected in a corrigendum to be issued subsequently.

*

* *

Symbols of United Nations documents are composed of capital letters combined with figures. Use of such a symbol indicates a reference to a United Nations document.

*

* *

The designations employed and the presentation of the material in this publication do not imply the expression of any opinion whatsoever on the part of the Secretariat of the United Nations concerning the legal status of any country, territory, city or area, or of its authorities, or concerning the delimitation of its frontiers or boundaries.

*

* *

UNCTAD/RMT/2013

UNITED NATIONS PUBLICATION

Sales no. E. 13.II.D.9

ISBN 978-92-1-112872-7

e-ISBN 978-92-1-054195-4

ISSN 0566-7682

ACKNOWLEDGEMENTS

The Review of Maritime Transport 2013 was prepared by the Trade Logistics Branch of the Division on Technology and Logistics, UNCTAD, under the coordination of Jan Hoffmann with administrative support and formatting by Florence Hudry and Wendy Juan, the supervision of José María Rubiato, and the overall guidance of Anne Miroux. The authors were Regina Asariotis, Hassiba Benamara, Jan Hoffmann, Azhar Jaimurzina, Anila Premti, José María Rubiato, Vincent Valentine and Frida Youssef.

The publication was edited by John Rogers, Lucy Annette Deleze-Black and Maritza Ascencios. The cover was designed by Sophie Combette and Nadège Hadjemian. The desktop publishing was carried out by Nathalie Loriot.

The considered comments and valuable input provided by the following reviewers are gratefully acknowledged:

Chapter 1:   Clarkson Research Services, Tracy Chatman, Socrates Leptos-Bourgi, Jan-Willem Vanhoogenhuizen.

Chapter 2:   Clarkson Research Services, Yann Duval, Thomas Pawlik.

Chapter 3:   Hannes Finkenbrink, Robert Piller, Jan-Willem Vanhoogenhuizen.

Chapter 4:   Mary R. Brooks, Ki-Soon Hwang, Dong-Wook Song.

Chapter 5:   Mahin Faghfouri, Stephen Fevrier, André Stochniol, Matthew Wilson.

Chapter 6:   Thanattaporn Rasamit, Gordon Wilmsmeier.

Thanks are also due to Vladislav Chouvalov for reviewing the publication in full.

TABLE OF CONTENTS

LIST OF TABLES, FIGURES AND BOXES

Tables

Figures

Boxes

ABBREVIATIONS

AEO	authorized economic operator
ASYCUDA	Automated System for Customs Data
BIMCO	Baltic and International Maritime Council
bpd	barrels per day
BRICS	Brazil, Russian Federation, India, China and South Africa
BWM Convention	International Convention for the Control and Management of Ships' Ballast Water and Sediments
CBP	United States Customs and Border Protection
CO_2	carbon dioxide
C–TPAT	Customs Trade Partnership against Terrorism
DIS	Danish International Ship Register
dwt	dead-weight ton(s)
ECA	Emission Control Area
ECLAC	Economic Commission for Latin America and the Caribbean
EEDI	Energy Efficiency Design Index
Exim	export-import
FEU	40-foot equivalent unit
FPSO	floating production storage and offloading unit
FSU	floating storage unit
GDP	gross domestic product
GEF	Global Environment Facility
GHG	greenhouse gas
GRIs	general rates increases
GT	gross tonnage
HNS	hazardous noxious substances
HNS Convention	International Convention on Liability and Compensation for Damage in Connection with the Carriage of Hazardous and Noxious Substances by Sea
IAPP	International Air Pollution Prevention (certificate, IMO)
ICS	International Chamber of Shipping
ILO	International Labour Organization
IMO	International Maritime Organization
IOPC Fund	International Oil Pollution Compensation Fund
ISO	International Organization for Standardization
ISPS	International Ship and Port Facilities Security
ITCP	Integrated Technical Cooperation Programme (IMO)
KG	Kommanditgesellschaft
km	kilometre(s)
KOICA	Korean International Cooperation Agency
LDC	least developed country
LNG	liquefied natural gas
LPG	liquefied petroleum gas

LSCI	Liner Shipping Connectivity Index
MARPOL	International Convention for the Prevention of Pollution from Ships
MBM	market-based measure
MEPC	Marine Environment Protection Committee (IMO)
MLC	Maritime Labour Convention
MOU	memorandum of understanding
MRA	mutual recognition agreement
MSC	Mediterranean Shipping Company
NATO	North Atlantic Treaty Organization
NIS	Norwegian International Ship Register
NOx	nitrogen oxides
ODA	official development assistance
OECD	Organization for Economic Cooperation and Development
OHRLLS	Office of the High Representative for the Least Developed Countries, Landlocked Developing Countries and Small Island Developing States
OPEC	Organization of the Petroleum Exporting Countries
PAL	Athens Convention relating to the Carriage of Passengers and their Luggage by Sea
PAL PROT	Protocol to the PAL
PCASP	privately contracted armed security personnel
ppm	parts per million
PPP	public–private partnership
SAFE	Framework of Standards to Secure and Facilitate Global Trade
SCR	selective catalytic reduction
SDR	special drawing right(s)
SEEMP	Ship Energy Efficiency Management Plan
SOLAS	International Convention for the Safety of Life at Sea
SOx	sulphur oxides
SRI	Seafarers' Rights International
STCW	International Convention on Standards of Training, Certification and Watchkeeping for Seafarers
TACB	technical assistance and capacity-building
TEU	20-foot equivalent unit
TPP	Trans-Pacific Partnership
UNFCCC	United Nations Framework Convention on Climate Change
UNICRI	United Nations Interregional Crime and Justice Research Institute
UNODC	United Nations Office on Drugs and Crime
VLCC	very large crude carrier
WCO	World Customs Organization
WTO	World Trade Organization

EXPLANATORY NOTES

- The *Review of Maritime Transport 2013* covers data and events from January 2012 until June 2013. Where possible, every effort has been made to reflect more recent developments.

- All references to dollars ($) are to United States dollars, unless otherwise stated.

- Unless otherwise stated, "ton" means metric ton (1,000 kg) and "mile" means nautical mile.

- Because of rounding, details and percentages presented in tables do not necessarily add up to the totals.

- n.a. Not available

- A hyphen (-) signifies that the amount is nil.

- In the tables and the text, the terms "countries" and "economies" refer to countries, territories or areas.

- Since 2007, the presentation of countries in the *Review of Maritime Transport* has been different from that in previous editions. Since 2007, the new classification is that used by the Statistics Division, United Nations Department of Economic and Social Affairs, and by UNCTAD in its *Handbook of Statistics*. For the purpose of statistical analysis, countries and territories are grouped by economic criteria into three categories, which are further divided into geographical regions. The main categories are developed economies, developing economies and transition economies.

Vessel groupings used in the *Review of Maritime Transport*

Review Group	Constituent Ship Types
Oil tankers	Oil tankers
Bulk carriers	Bulk carriers, combination carriers
General-cargo ships	Multi-purpose and project vessels, roll-on roll-off (ro-ro) cargo, general cargo
Container ships	Fully cellular container ships
Other ships	Liquefied petroleum gas carriers, liquefied natural gas carriers, parcel (chemical) tankers, specialized tankers, reefers, offshore supply, tugs, dredgers, cruise, ferries, other non-cargo ships
Total all ships	Includes all the above-mentioned vessel types

Approximate vessel-size groups referred to in the Review of Maritime Transport, according to generally used shipping terminology

Crude oil tankers
Very large crude carrier	200,000 dwt* plus
Suezmax crude tanker	120,000–200,000 dwt
Aframax crude tanker	80,000–119,999 dwt
Panamax crude tanker	60,000–79,999 dwt

Dry bulk and ore carriers
Capesize bulk carrier	100,000 dwt plus
Panamax bulk carrier	60,000–99,999 dwt
Handymax bulk carrier	40,000–59,999 dwt
Handysize bulk carrier	10,000–39,999 dwt

Container ships
Post-Panamax container ship	beam of >32.3 m
Panamax container ship	beam of< 32.3 m

Source: Clarkson Research Services.
Note: Unless otherwise specified, the ships covered in the *Review of Maritime Transport* include all propelled seagoing merchant vessels of 100 gross tonnage and above, excluding inland waterway vessels, fishing vessels, military vessels, yachts and offshore fixed and mobile platforms and barges (with the exception of floating production storage and offloading units and drillships).
* Dwt, deadweight tons.

FOREWORD

In today's interdependent and globalized world, efficient and cost-effective transportation systems that link global supply chains are the engine fuelling economic development and prosperity. With 80 per cent of global merchandise trade by volume carried by sea and handled by ports worldwide, the strategic economic importance of maritime transport as a trade enabler cannot be overemphasized. The trade competitiveness of all countries – developed and developing alike, and including landlocked countries – depends heavily on effective access to international shipping services and port networks.

The 2013 edition of the *Review of Maritime Transport* estimates global seaborne trade to have increased by 4.3 per cent, with the total reaching over 9 billion tons in 2012 for the first time ever. Driven in particular by growing domestic demand in China and increased intra-Asian and South–South trade, seaborne trade nevertheless remains subject to persistent downside risks facing the world economy and trade. Freight rates have remained low and volatile in the various market segments (container, liquid and dry bulk).

Maritime transport is facing a new and complex environment that involves both challenges and opportunities. Of all the prevailing challenges, however, the interconnected issues of energy security and costs, climate change, and environmental sustainability are perhaps the most unsettling. Climate change in particular continues to rank high on the international policy agenda, including that of shipping and port businesses. Turning to the opportunities, these include – to name but a few – deeper regional integration and South–South cooperation; growing diversification of sources of supply; and access to new markets, facilitated by cooperation agreements and by improved transport networks (for example the Panama Canal expansion).

In view of recent research that suggests that containerization has been a stronger driver of globalization than trade liberalization has, the Review discusses global developments in container trade flows and containership deployment. It also presents trends over 10 years in liner shipping connectivity in developing regions, building upon UNCTAD's Liner Shipping Connectivity Index which was published in 2013 for the tenth year.

The special chapter on "Landlocked countries and maritime transport" provides an overview of recent progress made in understanding impediments to accessing sea-shipping services, for the trade of goods between landlocked territories and overseas markets. The Review proposes a new paradigm for transit based on a conveyor-belt concept, which aims at achieving a continuous supply of transit transport services, supported by institutional frameworks and infrastructure. The argument proposed here is that a regular, reliable and secure transit system is the simple, straightforward goal to pursue in order to guarantee access for landlocked developing countries to global shipping networks on the basis of non-penalizing conditions. Given the review of the Almaty Programme of Action that is to take place in 2014, this proposal could be part of the actions within a new agenda for landlocked and transit developing countries.

As with all previous issues published since 1968, the *Review of Maritime Transport 2013* contains a wealth of analysis and unique data. The Review is the acknowledged United Nations source of statistics and analysis on seaborne trade, the world fleet, freight rates, port traffic, and the latest trends in the legal and regulatory environment for international maritime transport.

Mukhisa Kituyi

Secretary-General of UNCTAD

EXECUTIVE SUMMARY

International seaborne trade grows in 2012, but remains vulnerable to downside risks facing the world economy

While the reorientation in global production and trade continues, with developing countries contributing larger shares to world output and trade, the performance of the global economy and merchandise trade in 2012 is a reminder of the high level of global economic integration and interdependence. During the year, growth in world gross domestic product decelerated to 2.2 per cent from 2.8 per cent recorded in 2011. In tandem, and reflecting a simultaneous drop in import demand of both developed and developing economies, the growth of global merchandise trade volumes also decelerated to 1.8 per cent year-on-year.

The knock-on effects of the problems in the European Union on developing economies are tangible, while the slowdown in larger developing countries, notably China and India, is resonating in other developing regions and low-income countries. Meanwhile, and driven in particular by a rise in China's domestic demand as well as increased intra-Asian and South–South trade, international seaborne trade performed relatively well, with volumes increasing by 4.3 per cent during the year. The performance of international seaborne trade remains, nevertheless, vulnerable to downside risks as well as the uncertainty affecting the world economy and trade. It is also unfolding against a background of an operating landscape for maritime transport that is evolving and that entails some potentially game-changing trends and developments.

Evolving trends affecting international shipping and seaborne trade

Some key trends currently affecting international shipping and its operating landscape include the following elements:

(a) Continued negative effect of the 2008/2009 crisis on global demand, finance and trade

(b) Structural shifts in global production patterns

(c) Changes in comparative advantages and mineral resource endowments, in particular oil and gas

(d) Rise of the South and shift of economic influence away from traditional centres of growth

(e) Demographics, with ageing populations in advanced economies and fast-growing populations in developing regions and with related implications for global production and consumption patterns

(f) Arrival of container megaships and other transport-related technological advances

(g) Climate change and natural hazards

(h) Energy costs and environmental sustainability.

In this context, a number of challenges and opportunities with implications for international seaborne trade are also arising. Of all the prevailing challenges, however, the interconnected issues of energy security and costs, climate change and environmental sustainability are perhaps the most unsettling. Climate change in particular continues to rank high on the international policy agenda. Emerging opportunities, on the other hand, include for example:

(a) Deeper regional integration and South–South cooperation

(b) Growing diversification of sources of supply enabled by technology and efficient transportation

(c) Emergence of new trading partners and access to new markets facilitated by growing trade and cooperation agreements

(d) Expansion/opening of new sea routes (for example, expansion of the Panama Canal and Arctic routes)

(e) Increasing involvement of other developing economies, notably in Africa and South-East Asia, in lower added value and labour-intensive sectors as China moves up the value chain and rebalances towards higher value added sectors

(f) Growth in global demand induced by a growing world population and a rise in the middle class/ consuming category

(g) Emergence of developing-country banks (for example, the proposed BRICS bank – Brazil, the Russian Federation, India, China and South Africa) with the potential to raise funding to meet the significant needs for investment in transport infrastructure.

The turn of the largest shipbuilding cycle in history

The year 2012 saw the turn of the largest shipbuilding cycle in recorded history. Between 2001 and 2011, year after year, newbuilding deliveries reached new historical highs. Only in 2012, for the first time since 2001, was the fleet that entered into service during the year less than that delivered during the previous 12 months. In spite of this slowing down of new deliveries, the world tonnage continued to grow in 2012, albeit at a slower pace than in 2011. The world fleet has more than doubled since 2001, reaching 1.63 billion deadweight tons in January 2013.

Since the historical peaks of 2008 and 2009, the tonnage on order for all major vessel types has decreased drastically. As shipyards continued to deliver pre-ordered tonnage, the order books went down by 50 per cent for container ships, 58 per cent for dry-bulk carriers, 65 per cent for tankers and by 67 per cent for general-cargo ships. At the end of 2008, the dry-bulk order book was equivalent to almost 80 per cent of the fleet at that time, while the tonnage on order as of January 2013 is the equivalent of just 20 per cent of the fleet in service.

Chapter 2 of this year's *Review of Maritime Transport* presents unique fleet profiles for major ship-owning developing countries. From these fleet profiles, it can be seen that several oil- and gas-exporting countries are also important owners of oil- and liquefied-gas tanker tonnage, both under their respective national flags (such as Kuwait) as well as under foreign flags (such as ships owned by Oman registered abroad). By the same token, countries with important offshore investments also tend to own offshore supply ships. Dry-bulk ships are less often controlled by the cargo-owning countries than is the case of the oil-exporting nations. Most container ships are foreign flagged as they engage in international trade, serving routes that connect several countries at the same time. Many of the general-cargo fleets are nationally flagged and serve the coastal or inter-island cabotage trades.

Larger ships and fewer container carriers

This year's *Review* also presents a special focus on 10 years of UNCTAD's Liner Shipping Connectivity Index and the related analysis of container ship deployment.

The last 10 years have seen two important trends, which represent two sides of the same coin. On the one hand, ships have become bigger, and on the other hand the number of companies in most markets has diminished. As regards the number of companies, the average per country has decreased by 27 per cent during the last 10 years, from 22 in 2004 to just 16 in 2013. This trend has important implications for the level of competition, especially for smaller trading nations. While an average of 16 service providers may still be sufficient to ensure a functioning competitive market with many choices for shippers for the average country, on given individual routes, especially those serving smaller developing countries, the decline in competition has led to oligopolistic markets.

Freight rates remained suppressed by oversupply of newbuildings

In 2012, the maritime sector continued to experience low and volatile freight rates in its various segments because of surplus capacity in the global fleet generated by the severe downturn in trade in the wake of the 2008 economic and financial crisis. The steady delivery of newbuildings into an already oversupplied market, coupled with a weak economy, has kept rates under heavy pressure.

The overall low freight rates observed in 2012 reduced carriers' earnings close to, and even below operating costs, especially when bunker oil prices remained both high and volatile. As a result, carriers tried to apply various strategies to remedy the situation, in particular by reducing bunker consumption. The trend of maximizing fleet efficiency, slow steaming, postponing newbuilding deliveries, scrapping and idling some ships observed in 2011 persisted in 2012.

In this difficult shipping context, many private equity funds have seized the opportunity created by tight credit markets and historically low vessel values to invest in ships and shipping companies. Between 2011 and 2012, private equity funds financed no less than 22 shipping transactions with an aggregate magnitude of more than $6.4 billion.

The role of private equity funds appears fundamental for the growth of the sector and could affect its development in several ways, including through the consolidation and vertical integration of transport services.

World container port throughput surpassed 600 million 20-foot equivalent units in 2012

World container port throughput increased by an estimated 3.8 per cent to 601.8 million 20-foot equivalent units in 2012. This increase was lower than the estimated 7.3 per cent increase of 2011. This growth is also reflected in a strong port finance sector as investors look to infrastructure to provide long-term stable returns. This is paramount as a recent study forecast that developing countries will need annual investment of $18.8 trillion in real terms by 2020 to achieve even moderate levels of economic growth.

Investments within ports will lead to increases in efficiency which could help to lower transport costs by enabling goods to get to and from markets in a more timely and cost-effective manner. Recognizing the role of ports in reducing a country's transport costs and working on the back of numerous mandates (Accra Accord paragraphs 57, 121, 165, 166 and Doha Mandate paragraphs 45, 47 and 48) from its member countries, UNCTAD has a long history of working on port reform in developing countries. Whereas previously much focus was given to helping ports identify efficiency indicators to measure and record, the next logical step is for countries to share their data to identify lessons learned and best practices. Yet, despite all the activity on record keeping, it is rare that the information is published at a port or national level, let alone on a global basis. However, external pressure to publish data came in 2013 when a leading journal printed its ranking of container ports using data obtained from liner operators. Thus efforts to assess port performance by port customers are leading towards an era of increased transparency in port operations which could spur greater interport competition, increased port performance and lower transport costs.

Legal issues and regulatory developments

Important legal developments include the entry into force of the 2006 Maritime Labour Convention (effective 20 August 2013) and of the 2002 Athens Convention relating to the Carriage of Passengers and their Luggage by Sea (effective 23 April 2014), as well as a range of regulatory measures to strengthen the legal framework relating to ship-source air pollution, port reception facilities and garbage management. Moreover, different sets of guidelines have been developed with a view to facilitating the widespread adoption of the 2010 Protocol to the International Convention on Liability and Compensation for Damage in Connection with the Carriage of Hazardous and Noxious Substances by Sea, known as the 2010 HNS Convention, and of the 2009 Hong Kong International Convention for the Safe and Environmentally Sound Recycling of Ships. Progress has also been made in respect of technical matters related to the implementation of the 2004 International Convention for the Control and Management of Ships' Ballast Water and Sediments.

To assist in the implementation of a set of technical and operational measures to increase energy efficiency and reduce greenhouse gas emissions from international shipping, which entered into force on 1 January 2013, additional guidelines and unified interpretations were adopted by the Marine Environment Protection Committee of the International Maritime Organization in October 2012 and May 2013. In addition, a resolution on promotion of technical cooperation and transfer of technology relating to the improvement of energy efficiency of ships was adopted in May 2013, and an agreement was reached that a new study be initiated to carry out an update to the estimate of greenhouse gas emissions for international shipping. The issue of possible market-based measures for the reduction of greenhouse gas emissions from international shipping remained controversial, and discussion was postponed.

In relation to maritime and supply-chain security, main areas of progress include enhancements to regulatory measures on maritime security and safety, primarily under the auspices of the International Maritime Organization, as well as implementation and mutual recognition of authorized economic operator programmes.

Implementing trade facilitation reforms

In the area of trade facilitation intensive work on a global agreement continues under the auspices of the World Trade Organization. In this context, results from UNCTAD's research on national trade facilitation implementation plans illustrate that trade facilitation remains a challenge but is also seen as a priority area for national development by developing countries themselves. By identifying the major areas of non-compliance with a future World Trade Organization trade facilitation agreement, the *Review of Maritime Transport* offers insights into the range of time and resource requirements and the needs for technical assistance and capacity-building for developing countries.

Access of landlocked countries to seaports

The passage of trade of landlocked countries through coastal territories to access shipping services is generally governed by a standard principle: goods in transit and their carriage are granted crossing free of fiscal duties and by the most convenient routes. In practice, however, the implementation of this basic norm suffers from numerous operational difficulties, resulting in high transport costs and long travel times, which undermine trade competitiveness and ultimately the economic development of landlocked countries. Over the past decade, under the Almaty Programme of Action launched in 2003, new analytical tools and extensive field research have brought fresh valuable knowledge about the mechanisms explaining detected inefficiencies. Among other things, analysis has revealed that rent-seeking stakeholders may play against improvements, making transit operations unnecessarily complex and unpredictable, to the detriment of governmental and traders' efforts. Thus, by exposing conflicting forces at play along transit chains, the analysis shows that trade of landlocked countries primarily suffer from unreliability resulting from a lack of cooperation among stakeholders and is a main reason behind high transport costs and long transit times.

Chapter 6 of the *Review of Maritime Transport 2013* provides an overview of these findings and, based on them, explores a new paradigm that should allow for a radical transformation of transit transport systems, thereby enabling landlocked countries reliable access to global value chains and allowing them to act in ways other than as providers of primary goods. The proposed approach of a transit belt system would consist of a system open to all transit cargo, based on a trusted transit operator scheme guaranteeing uninterrupted transit from seaport to hinterland and vice versa. The transit belt system aims at making predictability of transit logistics chains a priority that Governments of both landlocked and transit countries should lead, in partnership with traders, port operators and shipping lines, as main beneficiaries of the improvement. Such a reliability model solution could be made part of the priorities of the new development agenda for landlocked and transit developing countries to be adopted in 2014.

1

DEVELOPMENTS IN INTERNATIONAL SEABORNE TRADE

While the reorientation of global production and trade continues, with developing countries contributing larger shares to world economic output and trade, the performance of the global economy and merchandise trade in 2012 is a reminder of the high level of global economic integration and interdependence. In 2012, growth in world gross domestic product (GDP) decelerated to 2.2 per cent from 2.8 per cent recorded in the previous year. In tandem, and reflecting a simultaneous drop in import demand of both developed and developing economies, the growth of global merchandise trade volumes also decelerated to 1.8 per cent year-on-year. The knock-on effects of the problems in the European Union on developing economies are tangible, while the slowdown in larger developing economies, notably China and India, is resonating in other developing regions and low-income countries. Meanwhile, and driven in particular by a rise in China's domestic demand as well as increased intra-Asian and South–South trade, international seaborne trade performed relatively well, with volumes increasing by 4.3 per cent during the year. The performance of international seaborne trade remains, nevertheless, vulnerable to downside risks and uncertainty affecting the world economy and trade. It is also unfolding against a background of an evolving maritime transport operating landscape that entails some potentially game-changing trends and developments.

Chapter 1 covers developments from January 2012 to June 2013. Section A reviews the overall performance of the global economy and world merchandise trade. Section B considers developments in world seaborne trade, including by market segment. Section C highlights selected topical trends that are unfolding on the international shipping arena and are affecting international seaborne trade.

A. WORLD ECONOMIC SITUATION AND PROSPECTS

1. World economic growth

The world economy slowed down in 2012 with GDP increasing by 2.2 per cent, down from 2.8 per cent in 2011. As shown in table 1.1, figures for the world economy and country groupings conceal uneven individual performances. Growth in GDP decelerated in all three country groupings, namely to 1.2 per cent in developed countries, to 4.6 per cent in developing economies and to 3.0 per cent in economies in transition. For comparison, equivalent growth rates in 2011 were 1.5 per cent, 5.9 per cent and 4.5 per cent, respectively.

The United States of America GDP picked up speed in 2012, growing at a rate nearly double (2.2 per cent) the developed country group's average (1.2 per cent). Growth in the European Union came to a standstill (–0.3 per cent), while in Japan it accelerated to 1.9 per cent, reflecting, in particular, post-March 2011 reconstruction efforts.

While still growing at a reasonable rate, developing economies and the economies in transition are increasingly being affected by the problems in Europe and the fragile recovery in the United States. Spillover effects have filtered down through various channels, including through trade by depressing the demand for the exports of developing countries and the economies in transition. Countries such as the Russian Federation, Brazil and China are, in addition

Table 1.1. World economic growth, 2008–2013 (Annual percentage change)

Region/country	2008	2009	2010	2011	2012	2013 [a]
WORLD	1.5	-2.2	4.1	2.8	2.2	2.1
Developed economies	0.0	-3.8	2.6	1.5	1.2	1.0
of which:						
United States	-0.3	-3.1	2.4	1.8	2.2	1.7
Japan	-1.0	-5.5	4.7	-0.6	1.9	1.9
European Union (27)	0.3	-4.3	2.1	1.6	-0.3	-0.2
of which:						
Germany	1.1	-5.1	4.2	3.0	0.7	0.3
France	-0.1	-3.1	1.7	2.0	0.0	-0.2
Italy	-1.2	-5.5	1.7	0.4	-2.4	-1.8
United Kingdom	-1.0	-4.0	1.8	0.9	0.2	1.1
Developing economies	5.3	2.4	7.9	5.9	4.6	4.7
of which:						
Africa	5.2	2.8	4.9	1.0	5.4	4.0
South Africa	3.6	-1.5	3.1	3.5	2.5	1.7
Asia	5.8	3.9	8.9	7.1	5.0	5.4
China	9.6	9.2	10.4	9.3	7.8	7.6
India	6.2	5.0	11.2	7.7	3.8	5.2
Republic of Korea	2.3	0.3	6.3	3.7	2.0	2.3
Developing America	4.0	-1.9	5.9	4.3	3.0	3.1
Brazil	5.2	-0.3	7.5	2.7	0.9	2.5
Least developed countries (LDCs)	7.6	5.4	6.2	3.3	4.8	5.0
Transition economies	5.2	-6.6	4.5	4.5	3.0	2.7
of which:						
Russian Federation	5.2	-7.8	4.5	4.3	3.4	2.5

Source: UNCTAD, Trade and Development Report 2013, table 1.1.
[a] Forecast.

to falling export volumes, facing internal problems and some structural challenges.

Economic growth in China slowed from 9.3 per cent in 2011 to 7.8 per cent in 2012, the lowest rate in more than a decade. Weaker demand for Chinese exports, especially in Europe, and a sharp decline in investment growth in China dampened its overall output growth. The deceleration is also indicative of China's efforts to slow down the pace of its economic growth, mainly to reduce inflationary pressures. It also reflects its changing growth patterns involving moving away from an export-oriented and investment-driven path to a more balanced growth based on higher domestic demand and consumption. Growth in India was cut by more than half in 2012 (3.8 per cent) while growth in newly industrialized economies such as the Republic of Korea also decelerated, owing to a large extent to a reduced European demand for these countries' exports. In Western Asia, robust growth experienced in most oil-exporting countries was matched with weakened economic activity in oil-importing countries. Social unrest and political instability, notably in the Syrian Arab Republic, remain major concerns for the entire region and its economic growth prospects.

Underpinned by the performance of oil-exporting countries, continued fiscal spending on infrastructure projects and greater Africa–Asia investment and trade linkages, Africa recorded the fastest growth among all regions (5.4 per cent). Meanwhile, developing countries in America recorded slower growth (3.0 per cent) compared to the two preceding years as the stagnation in the advanced economies and the slowdown in China affected exports from the region, especially in South America. Some countries such as Brazil and Argentina have, in addition, faced domestic problems that undermine growth (United Nations Department of Economic and Social Affairs, 2013a).

Economies in transition continued to grow in 2012, albeit at a moderate pace of 3 per cent. Strong energy prices supported growth in the energy-exporting economies (for example, Kazakhstan and the Russian Federation), while the adverse effects of the crisis in Europe hampered economic expansion in countries and regions such as the Republic of Moldova, Ukraine and Eastern Europe.

Growth in low income countries has generally been more resilient, but is now also being affected by the slowdown in both developed and developing economies. Least developed countries (LDCs) increased their GDP by 4.8 per cent in 2012, up from

3.3 per cent in 2011, albeit more slowly than the two previous years (2009 and 2010). This trend reflects, among other things, continued weakness in the world economy, lower commodity demand, including from large developing economies, and reduced levels of official development assistance (United Nations Department of Economic and Social Affairs, 2013b).

World industrial production – a measure of economic activity which includes two sectors that are highly sensitive to consumer demand, namely manufacturing and mining – increased by 3 per cent in 2012, despite remaining flat in the advanced economies, in particular the European Union and Japan (Danish Ship Finance, 2013). As shown in figure 1.1, industrial production as measured by the industrial production index of the Organization for Economic Cooperation and Development (OECD), world GDP, merchandise trade and seaborne shipments continue to move in tandem. With demand for shipping services being "derived", the performance of maritime transportation and seaborne trade is largely determined by developments in the world economy and international trade. However, it has been observed that over the years, the world merchandise trade has grown about twice as fast as the world GDP due to the multiplier effect resulting from, among others, the globalization of production processes, increased trade in intermediate goods and components, and the deepening and extension of global supply chains.

UNCTAD expects GDP growth to remain flat in 2013 with the global economy still struggling to return to a strong and sustained growth path. A number of factors are undermining a sustained global economic recovery, including the continued impacts of the financial and economic crises that started in 2008, as well as of the unsustainable financial processes and domestic and international imbalances that have led to the crises. In several countries weaker growth may also be partly due to macroeconomic policy choices (UNCTAD, 2013).

The attention-grabbing news about developing economies fuelling global growth does not lessen the continued interdependence among the world economies. As has been noted in previous editions of the Review of Maritime Transport, a reorientation of global production, economic expansion and trade has been unfolding over the years. Certainly, the 2008/2009 crisis deepened this trend, with developing countries increasingly gaining greater influence and contributing larger shares to global GDP and merchandise trade. And undoubtedly developing

Figure 1.1.   The OECD industrial production index and indices for world gross domestic product, merchandise trade and seaborne shipments (1975–2013), (1990 = 100)

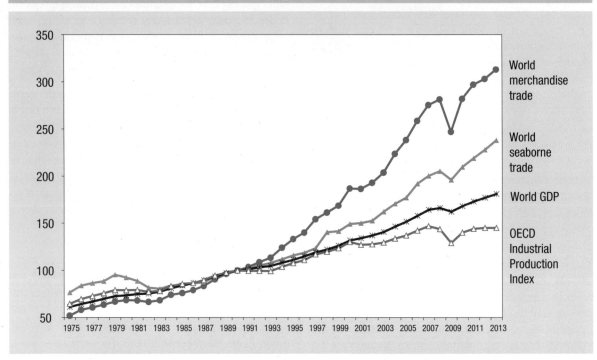

Sources: UNCTAD secretariat, on the basis of OECD *Main Economic Indicators*, May 2013; UNCTAD, The Trade and Development Report 2013; UNCTAD *Review of Maritime Transport*, various issues; World Trade Organization (WTO) (table A1a); the WTO press release 688, 10 April 2013, "World trade 2012, prospects for 2013". The value of the index measuring growth in world seaborne trade for 2013 is calculated on the basis of the growth rate forecast by Clarkson Research Services in *Shipping Review and Outlook*, spring 2013 (Clarkson Research Services, 2013a).

countries are playing a bigger role globally as well as regionally, with deeper South–South linkages and trade integration. However, the performance of the world economy in 2012 is a reminder of the high level of global integration and interdependence. For the foreseeable future, the United States is projected to remain the largest economy in the world (in monetary terms) and developments there and in Europe will continue to have knock-on effects on developing regions (United Nations Development Programme, 2013). In addition to the overspill effects of the problems facing advanced economies, other indicators, such as export flows of the United States, are also pointing to a continued global interconnectedness. Since 2007, exports from the United States to OECD country partners increased by 20 per cent, while its exports to developing America and China expanded by over 50 per cent.

2.   World merchandise trade

For the second year in a row and in line with developments in the global economy and aggregate demand, growth in international trade slowed notably in 2012, averaging 1.8 per cent (table 1.2). This figure refers to merchandise trade in volume terms, that is, in value terms but adjusted to account for inflation and exchange-rate movements. However, trade flows in nominal terms display a similar trend. In 2012, the dollar value of world merchandise exports only increased by 0.2 per cent to reach $18.3 trillion, practically remaining unchanged due to falling prices of commodities such as coffee (–22 per cent), cotton (–42 per cent), iron ore (–23 per cent) and coal (–21 per cent) (WTO, 2013).

Slower global trade growth resulted from a simultaneous deceleration in import demand in both developed and large developing economies. Constrained, among other things, by austerity measures and rising unemployment, Europe's import demand contracted while demand in the United States and Japan remained subdued. Consequently, the global demand for exports of developing countries and economies in transition weakened while – with the exception of Africa – imports destined for developing countries and economies in transition declined markedly.

Exports from developed economies decelerated sharply from 4.9 per cent in 2011 to 0.4 per cent in 2012 due to a contraction in export volumes in the European Union (−0.2 per cent) and Japan (−1.0 per cent). In Japan, exports dropped 11 per cent in the last two quarters of the year, presumably owing to the territorial dispute with China and its adverse effect on the trade between the two countries (WTO, 2013). Exports from the United States fared better, with shipments increasing by 4.1 per cent, albeit at a slower pace than 2011.

After falling by 8.3 per cent in 2011 due to the civil war in Libya, Africa rebounded in 2012 to record the fastest export growth of all regions at 5.7 per cent. Despite export growth rates of 6.9 per cent in Western Asia and 7.2 per cent in China, developing Asia only managed a 3.7 per cent export growth due, in particular, to falling shipments from India (−2.5 per cent). In line with lower economic growth in the region, exports in developing America grew at the slowest rate (2.2 per cent), although the European Union continues to record the worst performance. On the import side, growth in world volumes slowed down significantly in 2012 (1.6 per cent) with imports into

developed countries dropping by 0.5 per cent (3.4 per cent in 2011). Imports into developing countries and the economies in transition recorded a rapid deceleration estimated at 4.5 per cent and 3.9 per cent, respectively.

Reflecting expectations of a moderate pickup in import demand in developed economies and most developing regions, the WTO expects global merchandise trade to grow by 3.3 per cent in 2013, a rate below the average rate of the last 20 years (5.3 per cent) (WTO, 2013). Export and import volumes of developed economies are expected to increase at the same rate of 1.4 per cent. Together, exports of developing economies and the economies in transition are projected to increase by 5.3 per cent, while their imports are predicted to expand by 5.9 per cent.

In addition to the downside risks facing the world economy, projected growth in world merchandise trade could also be undermined by increased protectionism and greater shortage in trade finance. Reports by the WTO and the European Commission have highlighted an increase in protectionist measures

Table 1.2. **Growth in the volume of merchandisea trade, by country groups and geographical region, 2009–2012 (Annual percentage change)**

Exports				Countries/regions	Imports			
2009	2010	2011	2012		2009	2010	2011	2012
-13.3	13.9	5.2	1.8	**WORLD**	-13.6	13.8	5.3	1.6
-15.5	13.0	4.9	0.4	**Developed economies**	-14.6	10.8	3.4	-0.5
				of which:				
-24.8	27.5	-0.6	-1.0	Japan	-12.2	10.1	4.2	3.7
-14.0	15.4	7.2	4.1	United States	-16.4	14.8	3.8	2.8
-14.9	11.6	5.5	-0.2	European Union (27)	-14.5	9.6	2.8	-2.8
-9.7	16.0	6.0	3.6	**Developing economies**	-10.2	18.8	7.4	4.5
				of which:				
-9.5	8.8	-8.3	5.7	**Africa**	-6.2	8.4	2.8	8.0
-7.4	8.3	4.6	2.2	**Developing America**	-17.9	22.5	10.8	2.5
-9.9	18.3	7.8	3.7	**Asia**	-9.1	19.3	3.5	4.6
				of which:				
-14.1	29.1	13.0	7.2	China	-1.1	25.4	10.3	5.9
-6.8	14.0	14.2	-2.5	India	-0.9	13.8	9.1	5.8
3.2	14.7	9.7	1.5	Republic of Korea	-2.3	17.3	4.1	1.2
-4.8	5.7	6.5	6.9	Western Asia	-14.2	8.4	8.1	5.8
-14.4	11.3	4.2	1.0	**Transition economies**	-28.2	15.9	15.7	3.9

Sources: UNCTAD secretariat calculations, based on UNCTADstat.
Note: Data on trade volumes are derived from international merchandise trade values deflated by UNCTAD unit value indices.

since 2008 (Economist Intelligence Unit, 2013), with new trade restrictions continuously being implemented and with nearly 3.0 per cent of world trade estimated to be affected by trade restrictions introduced since the beginning of the crisis (United Nations, 2012). Meanwhile, shortage in trade finance continues to stir some debate, including in view of Basel III regulations and the associated potential restrictions to financing trade (Economist Intelligence Unit, 2013). Since 2011, trade finance originating from European banks and destined for developing economies declined. A survey in the fourth quarter of 2012 by the Asian Development Bank reveals that the trade finance gap in Asia, for example, amounted to $425 billion.

On the upside, some developments may help boost trade, including the expected positive impact of Japan's fiscal stimulus package and expansionary monetary policy; relatively strong GDP growth in China; increased shipments from China to the United States as the latter replaces the European Union as China's largest trading partner; and proliferating trade liberalization arrangements. In this regard, worth noting is the November 2011 commitment by nine countries, including the United States, Mexico, Canada and Japan to a broad agreement called the Trans-Pacific Partnership (TPP) (Economist Intelligence Unit, 2013). Other relevant initiatives include the proposed European Union–United States Free Trade Agreement; the USASEAN Expanded Economic Engagement to create further links between the ASEAN economies and the TPP; a new Regional Comprehensive Economic Partnership to be launched by the ASEAN Plus 6 group (Australia, China, India, Japan, New Zealand and the Republic of Korea); current negotiations on a trilateral trade agreement between China, Japan and the Republic of Korea; and current free-trade agreement negotiations between the European Union and Japan. Meanwhile, at the time of writing, negotiations of the European Union–India agreement were reported as being at the finalization stage. Although trade deals, if successful, can lift international trade flows, some concerns nevertheless remain as to their potential to also divert trade from countries that are not party to the deal, especially when a global trade agreement is not yet in place.

In conclusion, the knock-on effects of the crisis in the European Union on developing economies through reductions in trade, private capital flows, remittances and aid are tangible, while the slowdown in Chinese and Indian economies is resonating in other developing regions and low-income countries.

Despite the current challenging market conditions and the weakened prospects in Europe in particular, global growth is expected to continue, driven mainly by developing countries, including China. Other countries in Asia, Africa and developing America are also expected to offer significant opportunities, not only in terms of economic growth and trade expansion but also as regards maritime business and seaborne shipments.

B. WORLD SEABORNE TRADE

1. General trends in seaborne trade

Driven in particular by a rise in China's domestic demand as well as increased intra-Asian and South–South trade, international seaborne trade performed better than the world economy, with volumes increasing at an estimated 4.3 per cent in 2012, nearly the same rate as 2011. About 9.2 billion tons of goods were loaded in ports worldwide, with tanker trade (crude oil, petroleum products and gas) accounting for less than one third of the total and dry cargo being responsible for the remaining lion's share (tables 1.3 and 1.4, figure 1.2 and Annex I).

Strong growth (5.7 per cent) in dry-cargo shipments remained the mainstay of the expansion in 2012, driven in particular by continued rapid growth in dry-bulk volumes. Fuelled by growing Asian demand for iron ore and coal and in line with the long-term trend, major dry-bulk shipments expanded at the rate of 7.2 per cent. China, which has contributed significantly to the growth of seaborne trade in recent years, continues to generate impressive import volumes. Although iron-ore import growth has moderated compared with high previous levels, coal has stepped in to fill the gap.

Growth in containerized trade measured in 20-foot equivalent units (TEUs) slowed significantly in 2012, with volumes increasing by 3.2 per cent, down from 13.1 per cent in 2010 and 7.1 per cent in 2011. The slump in Europe's import demand and the consequent ripple effect on global export volumes, in particular from Asia, have contributed significantly to the deceleration.

During the year, volumes of crude oil and refined petroleum products have grown marginally at 1.5 per cent in 2012. It should be noted, however, that while the economic slowdown, high oil price levels and new

Table 1.3.	Development in international seaborne trade, selected years (Millions of tons loaded)			
Year	Oil and gas	Main bulks [a]	Other dry cargo	Total (all cargoes)
1970	1 440	448	717	2 605
1980	1 871	608	1 225	3 704
1990	1 755	988	1 265	4 008
2000	2 163	1 295	2 526	5 984
2005	2 422	1 709	2 978	7 109
2006	2 698	1 814	3 188	7 700
2007	2 747	1 953	3 334	8 034
2008	2 742	2 065	3 422	8 229
2009	2 642	2 085	3 131	7 858
2010	2 772	2 335	3 302	8 409
2011	2 794	2 486	3 505	8 784
2012	2 836	2 665	3 664	9 165

Sources: Compiled by the UNCTAD secretariat on the basis of data supplied by reporting countries as well as data obtained from relevant government, port-industry and specialist sources. Data for 2006 onwards have been revised and updated to reflect improved reporting, including more recent figures and better information regarding the breakdown by cargo type. Figures for 2012 are estimated based on preliminary data or on the last year for which data were available.

[a] Iron ore, grain, coal, bauxite/alumina and phosphate rock. Data from 2006 onwards are based on various issues of the *Dry Bulk Trade Outlook*, produced by Clarkson Research Services.

technologies have dampened demand for crude oil, petroleum-product trade fared better in comparison. As regards gas trade, minimal additions of liquefaction installations during the year have constrained volumes, which increased by a moderate 1.6 per cent.

Reflecting to a large extent their increased participation in the world trading system, developing countries continued to contribute larger shares to international seaborne trade. In 2012, they accounted for 60 per cent of global goods loaded and 58 per cent of goods unloaded in 2012 (figure 1.3(a)). However, while the group's share has been on the rise, contributions by individual countries have been uneven, reflecting their respective varying levels of integration into global trading networks and supply chains.

While, in line with previous trends, cargo volumes loaded in the ports of developing countries exceeded the volumes of goods unloaded (figure 1.3(b)), their shares have nevertheless evolved over the past four decades to reach near parity in 2012. Driven by the fast-growing import demand in developing regions – fuelled by their industrialization process and rapidly rising consumer demand – for the first time ever the share of goods unloaded in developing countries is likely soon to surpass their share of goods loaded.

Figure 1.2.	International seaborne trade, selected years (Millions of tons loaded)

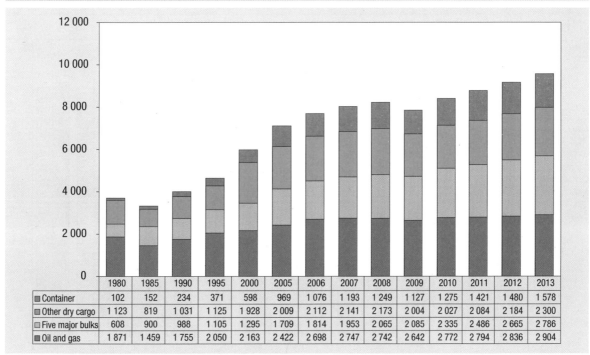

	1980	1985	1990	1995	2000	2005	2006	2007	2008	2009	2010	2011	2012	2013
Container	102	152	234	371	598	969	1 076	1 193	1 249	1 127	1 275	1 421	1 480	1 578
Other dry cargo	1 123	819	1 031	1 125	1 928	2 009	2 112	2 141	2 173	2 004	2 027	2 084	2 184	2 300
Five major bulks	608	900	988	1 105	1 295	1 709	1 814	1 953	2 065	2 085	2 335	2 486	2 665	2 786
Oil and gas	1 871	1 459	1 755	2 050	2 163	2 422	2 698	2 747	2 742	2 642	2 772	2 794	2 836	2 904

Sources: UNCTAD Review of Maritime Transport, various issues. For 2006–2013, the breakdown by type of dry cargo is based on Clarkson Research Services' Shipping Review and Outlook, various issues. Data for 2013 are based on a forecast by Clarkson Research Services (2013a).

Figure 1.3 (a). World seaborne trade, by country group, 2012 (Percentage share in world tonnage)

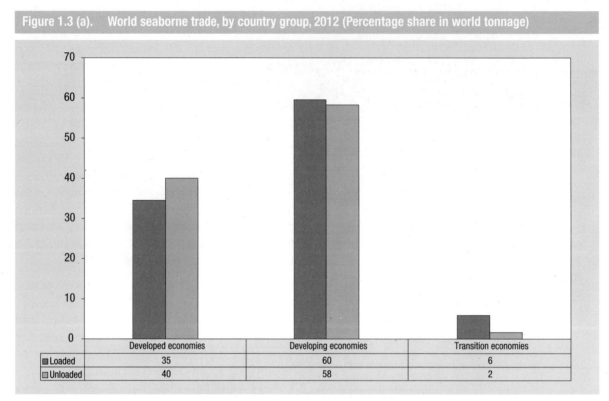

	Developed economies	Developing economies	Transition economies
■ Loaded	35	60	6
□ Unloaded	40	58	2

Sources: Compiled by the UNCTAD secretariat on the basis of data supplied by reporting countries, as well as data obtained from relevant government, port industry and specialist sources. Estimated figures are based on preliminary data or on the last year for which data were available.

Figure 1.3 (b).   Participation of developing countries in world seaborne trade, selected years (Percentage share in world tonnage)

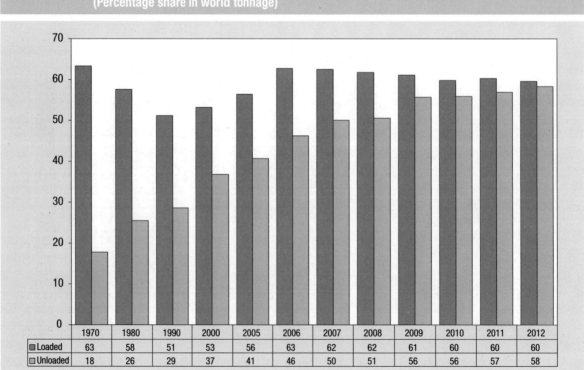

	1970	1980	1990	2000	2005	2006	2007	2008	2009	2010	2011	2012
■ Loaded	63	58	51	53	56	63	62	62	61	60	60	60
□ Unloaded	18	26	29	37	41	46	50	51	56	56	57	58

Source: UNCTAD *Review of Maritime Transport*, various issues.

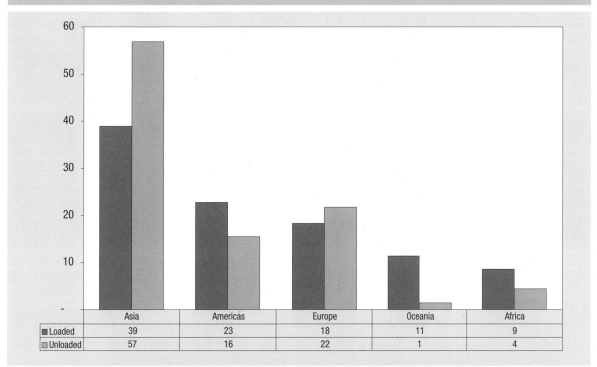

Figure 1.3 (c). World seaborne trade, by geographical region, 2012 (Percentage share in world tonnage)

	Asia	Americas	Europe	Oceania	Africa
Loaded	39	23	18	11	9
Unloaded	57	16	22	1	4

Sources: Compiled by the UNCTAD secretariat on the basis of data supplied by reporting countries as well as data obtained from relevant government, port-industry and specialist sources. Figures are estimated based on preliminary data or on the last year for which data were available.

A regional breakdown indicates that in 2012, Asia still dominated as the main loading and unloading region. Other major loading and unloading areas included, in descending order, the Americas, Europe, Oceania and Africa on the loading side, and Europe, the Americas, Africa and Oceania on the unloading side (figure 1.3 (c)).

Africa is increasingly attracting attention as a region with significant potential for maritime transport and seaborne trade. Although Africa's impact on shipping is still comparatively small, it is poised to expand as the continent sets out to exploit its vast resources and as consumption demand increases in tandem with improved income levels. Africa is becoming increasingly attractive, in particular to Asia, with the value of trade between the regions steadily rising (*Fairplay*, 2013a). While the European Union remains Africa's biggest trading partner, China has now overtaken the United States as Africa's largest single trading partner. Trade flows between the United States and Africa were valued at about $123 billion in 2011, while China–Africa flows stood at about $133 billion (*Fairplay*, 2013a).

Recently, China and the United Republic of Tanzania have signed an agreement to build a major port and industrial zone in the country at an estimated cost

of up to $10 billion (United Nations Department of Economic and Social Affairs, 2013c). Following another discovery of natural gas off the coast of the United Republic of Tanzania, an oil company is now planning the construction of a liquefied natural gas (LNG) facility worth $14 billion (United Nations Department of Economic and Social Affairs, 2013c). Maritime business in Africa could thrive on such developments, with Africa increasingly moving away from being a niche market for shipping operators to gaining mainstream status (*Fairplay*, 2013b). According to the African Development Bank, port throughput in Africa will rise from 265 million tons in 2009 to more than 2 billion tons in 2040, while transport volumes will increase six- to eightfold, with a particularly strong increase of up to 14 times for some landlocked countries (*Fairplay*, 2013a). Reflecting the expected growth, investments in the free zones of Nigeria are reported to have reached $9.4 billion, with six out of the total 25 free zones in the country said to be under construction and four at the design stage (*P.M. News Nigeria*, 2013).

The infrastructure gap remains a challenge that undermines maritime transportation and seaborne trade of many developing regions, including in Africa. Global transport infrastructure needs have been estimated at $11 trillion over the 2009–2030 period (OECD, 2011). To close the gap on the large infrastructure deficit in developing countries, including in transportation, existing estimates indicate that spending must reach $1.8 trillion–$2.3 trillion per year by 2020 compared with the current levels of $0.8 trillion–$0.9 trillion a year (United Nations Development Programme, 2013). For Africa, scaling up investment in transport infrastructure is key, especially as the continent increasingly positions itself as an important area for maritime business and trade. In this context, an emerging "South" provides an opportunity for innovative new structures and partnerships to unfold, including with a view to financing transport infrastructure development and maintenance. Incidentally, at their annual summit held in March 2013, Brazil, the Russian Federation, India, China and South Africa (the BRICS countries) agreed to establish a BRICS Development Bank that would finance projects in developing countries, including those aimed at building infrastructure (*Voice of America News*, 2013).

Looking ahead, some analysts are predicting that the value of world merchandise trade will more than double between 2010 and 2020 and that China's exports to Europe will be valued at almost twice those of the United States' exports to Europe (Ernst and Young, 2011). They are also expecting that intraregional Asian trade will grow rapidly to reach $5 trillion and that Europe's exports to Africa and Western Asia will be around 50 per cent larger than its exports to the United States. In terms of sectoral contribution, trade in machinery, transport equipment, consumer electric products (for example, computers, televisions and washing machines) and industrial goods are expected to make the largest contribution to global merchandise trade over the next ten years (Ernst and Young, 2011). Some observers are projecting that by 2025, annual consumption in developing economies will rise to $30 trillion and that developing economies can be expected to contribute over half of the 1 billion households whose annual earnings surpass the $20,000 mark (United Nations Development Programme, 2013). If these projections do materialize, trade growth patterns and dynamics will likely be affected. For seaborne trade, existing forecasts are also pointing to continued growth, with one estimate for 2013 indicating a projected growth of 4.2 per cent (Clarkson Research Services, 2013a).

Against a background of booming business opportunities in emerging developing economies and projected growth in the world merchandise trade, and bearing in mind the prevailing risks and uncertainties, the maritime transport industry will need to adjust its business strategies to reflect changes in the world economy and patterns of trade, which are expected to intensify in the future.

2. Seaborne trade in ton-miles

Developments in the world economy and changes in trade growth and patterns are shaping the demand for commodities and determining the distances over which cargo travels. Final demand for shipping services, measured in ton–miles, offers better insight into maritime transport activity and demand for ship capacity.

In 2012, growth in ton–miles performed by maritime transportation increased by 4.2 per cent, down from 4.9 per cent in 2011. Bulk commodities, namely minerals and raw materials, accounted for nearly three quarters of the total ton–miles performed in 2012 (figure 1.4). The five major dry bulks (that is, coal, iron ore, grain, bauxite/alumina and phosphate rock) are the main engine of growth, with ton–miles increasing by 6.6 per cent, as compared with 6.1 per cent for minor bulks, 3.9 per cent for other dry cargo including containerized trade, 2.4 per cent for oil and petroleum products, and 0.7 per cent for gas. Much of the growth was driven by a rapid (11.8 per cent) increase in coal ton–miles, followed by growth generated by grain and iron-ore trades with ton–miles growing by 6.2 per cent and 4.1 per cent, respectively.

Interestingly, with much talk about the changing geography of world trade and the growing need to diversify sources of supply often involving shipments over longer journeys, average distances travelled by global seaborne trade appear to have remained steady over time. Between 1970 and 2008, the average distance travelled by cargo remained stable at an average of 4,100 nautical miles (Crowe, 2012). This trend reflects in particular the growing importance of intraregional trade and, to a lesser extent, some of the production moving closer to markets, although in the latter case, the debate on "nearsourcing" remains rather inconclusive.

Much of the increase in average distances travelled during 1970–2008 was generated by trade in the major five bulk commodities, with the average distance increasing from 4,600 to 5,400 nautical miles due to sharp increases in import demand in fast-growing developing regions, in particular China (Crowe, 2012). Robust coal and iron-ore import demand from Asia have contributed significantly to the growth in dry-bulk trade

Table 1.4. World seaborne trade in 2006–2012, by type of cargo, country group and region

Country group	Year	Goods loaded				Goods unloaded			
		Total	Crude	Petroleum products and gas	Dry cargo	Total	Crude	Petroleum products and gas	Dry cargo
		Millions of tons							
World	2006	7 700.3	1 783.4	914.8	5 002.1	7 878.3	1 931.2	893.7	5 053.4
	2007	8 034.1	1 813.4	933.5	5 287.1	8 140.2	1 995.7	903.8	5 240.8
	2008	8 229.5	1 785.2	957.0	5 487.2	8 286.3	1 942.3	934.9	5 409.2
	2009	7 858.0	1 710.5	931.1	5 216.4	7 832.0	1 874.1	921.3	5 036.6
	2010	8 408.9	1 787.7	983.8	5 637.5	8 443.8	1 933.2	979.2	5 531.4
	2011	8 784.3	1 759.5	1 034.2	5 990.5	8 797.7	1 896.5	1 037.7	5 863.5
	2012	9 165.3	1 785.4	1 050.9	6 329.0	9 183.7	1 928.7	1 054.9	6 200.1
Developed economies	2006	2 460.5	132.9	336.4	1 991.3	4 164.7	1 282.0	535.5	2 347.2
	2007	2 608.9	135.1	363.0	2 110.8	3 990.5	1 246.0	524.0	2 220.5
	2008	2 715.4	129.0	405.3	2 181.1	4 007.9	1 251.1	523.8	2 233.0
	2009	2 554.3	115.0	383.8	2 055.5	3 374.4	1 125.3	529.9	1 719.2
	2010	2 865.4	135.9	422.3	2 307.3	3 604.5	1 165.4	522.6	1 916.5
	2011	2 982.5	117.5	451.9	2 413.1	3 632.3	1 085.6	581.3	1 965.4
	2012	3 162.9	121.6	447.3	2 594.0	3 678.8	1 097.7	573.7	2 007.5
Transition economies	2006	410.3	123.1	41.3	245.9	70.6	5.6	3.1	61.9
	2007	407.9	124.4	39.9	243.7	76.8	7.3	3.5	66.0
	2008	431.5	138.2	36.7	256.6	89.3	6.3	3.8	79.2
	2009	505.3	142.1	44.4	318.8	93.3	3.5	4.6	85.3
	2010	515.7	150.2	45.9	319.7	122.1	3.5	4.6	114.0
	2011	505.0	132.6	42.0	330.5	156.7	4.2	4.4	148.1
	2012	542.1	136.6	41.1	364.4	149.2	3.8	4.0	141.4
Developing economies	2006	4 829.5	1 527.5	537.1	2 765.0	3 642.9	643.6	355.1	2 644.3
	2007	5 020.8	1 553.9	530.7	2 932.6	4 073.0	742.4	376.3	2 954.3
	2008	5 082.6	1 518.0	515.1	3 049.6	4 189.1	684.9	407.2	3 097.0
	2009	4 798.4	1 453.5	502.9	2 842.0	4 364.2	745.3	386.9	3 232.1
	2010	5 027.8	1 501.6	515.6	3 010.5	4 717.3	764.4	452.0	3 500.9
	2011	5 296.8	1 509.4	540.4	3 247.0	5 008.8	806.7	452.1	3 750.0
	2012	5 460.3	1 527.2	562.5	3 370.6	5 355.7	827.3	477.2	4 051.2
Africa	2006	721.9	353.8	86.0	282.2	349.8	41.3	39.4	269.1
	2007	732.0	362.5	81.8	287.6	380.0	45.7	44.5	289.8
	2008	766.7	379.2	83.3	304.2	376.6	45.0	43.5	288.1
	2009	708.0	354.0	83.0	271.0	386.8	44.6	39.7	302.5

Table 1.4.   World seaborne trade in 2006–2012, by type of cargo, country group and region *(continued)*

		Goods loaded				Goods unloaded			
Country group	Year	Total	Crude	Petroleum products and gas	Dry cargo	Total	Crude	Petroleum products and gas	Dry cargo
	2010	754.0	351.1	92.0	310.9	416.9	42.7	40.5	333.7
	2011	723.7	338.0	68.5	317.2	378.2	37.8	46.3	294.1
	2012	787.3	370.1	72.6	344.6	407.7	35.9	51.7	320.1
America	2006	1 030.7	251.3	93.9	685.5	373.4	49.6	60.1	263.7
	2007	1 067.1	252.3	90.7	724.2	415.9	76.0	64.0	275.9
	2008	1 108.2	234.6	93.0	780.6	436.8	74.2	69.9	292.7
	2009	1 029.8	225.7	74.0	730.1	371.9	64.4	73.6	234.0
	2010	1 172.6	241.6	85.1	846.0	448.7	69.9	74.7	304.2
	2011	1 239.2	253.8	83.5	901.9	508.3	71.1	73.9	363.4
	2012	1 287.2	250.7	91.6	944.9	538.5	77.5	79.4	381.6
Asia	2006	3 073.1	921.2	357.0	1 794.8	2 906.8	552.7	248.8	2 105.3
	2007	3 214.6	938.2	358.1	1 918.3	3 263.6	620.7	260.8	2 382.1
	2008	3 203.6	902.7	338.6	1 962.2	3 361.9	565.6	286.8	2 509.5
	2009	3 054.3	872.3	345.8	1 836.3	3 592.4	636.3	269.9	2 686.2
	2010	3 094.6	907.5	338.3	1 848.8	3 838.2	651.8	333.1	2 853.4
	2011	3 326.7	916.0	388.2	2 022.6	4 108.8	697.8	328.0	3 082.9
	2012	3 376.7	904.7	397.5	2 074.5	4 396.2	713.8	341.5	3 340.9
Oceania	2006	3.8	1.2	0.1	2.5	12.9	0.0	6.7	6.2
	2007	7.1	0.9	0.1	2.5	13.5	0.0	7.0	6.5
	2008	4.2	1.5	0.1	2.6	13.8	0.0	7.1	6.7
	2009	6.3	1.5	0.2	4.6	13.1	0.0	3.6	9.5
	2010	6.5	1.5	0.2	4.8	13.4	0.0	3.7	9.7
	2011	7.1	1.6	0.2	5.3	13.5	0.0	3.9	9.6
	2012	9.0	1.6	0.8	6.6	13.3	0.0	4.6	8.6
Percentage share									
World	2006	100.0	23.2	11.9	65.0	100.0	24.5	11.3	64.1
	2007	100.0	22.6	11.6	65.8	100.0	24.5	11.1	64.4
	2008	100.0	21.7	11.6	66.7	100.0	23.4	11.3	65.3
	2009	100.0	21.8	11.8	66.4	100.0	23.9	11.8	64.3
	2010	100.0	21.3	11.7	67.0	100.0	22.9	11.6	65.5
	2011	100.0	20.0	11.8	68.2	100.0	21.6	11.8	66.6
	2012	100.0	19.5	11.5	69.1	100.0	21.0	11.5	67.5
Developed economies	2006	32.0	7.4	36.8	39.8	52.9	66.4	59.9	46.4
	2007	32.5	7.5	38.9	39.9	49.0	62.4	58.0	42.4
	2008	33.0	7.2	42.3	39.7	48.4	64.4	56.0	41.3
	2009	32.5	6.7	41.2	39.4	43.1	60.0	57.5	34.1
	2010	34.1	7.6	42.9	40.9	42.7	60.3	53.4	34.6
	2011	34.0	6.7	43.7	40.3	41.3	57.2	56.0	33.5
	2012	34.5	6.8	42.6	41.0	40.1	56.9	54.4	32.4
Transition economies	2006	5.3	6.9	4.5	4.9	0.9	0.3	0.3	1.2
	2007	5.1	6.9	4.3	4.6	0.9	0.4	0.4	1.3
	2008	5.2	7.7	3.8	4.7	1.1	0.3	0.4	1.5

Table 1.4.   World seaborne trade in 2006–2012, by type of cargo, country group and region *(continued)*

Country group	Year	Goods loaded				Goods unloaded			
		Total	Crude	Petroleum products and gas	Dry cargo	Total	Crude	Petroleum products and gas	Dry cargo
	2009	6.4	8.3	4.8	6.1	1.2	0.2	0.5	1.7
	2010	6.1	8.4	4.7	5.7	1.4	0.2	0.5	2.1
	2011	5.7	7.5	4.1	5.5	1.8	0.2	0.4	2.5
	2012	5.9	7.7	3.9	5.8	1.6	0.2	0.4	2.3
Developing economies	2006	62.7	85.6	58.7	55.3	46.2	33.3	39.7	52.3
	2007	62.5	85.7	56.9	55.5	50.0	37.2	41.6	56.4
	2008	61.8	85.0	53.8	55.6	50.6	35.3	43.6	57.3
	2009	61.1	85.0	54.0	54.5	55.7	39.8	42.0	64.2
	2010	59.8	84.0	52.4	53.4	55.9	39.5	46.2	63.3
	2011	60.3	85.8	52.2	54.2	56.9	42.5	43.6	64.0
	2012	59.6	85.5	53.5	53.3	58.3	42.9	45.2	65.3
Africa	2006	9.4	19.8	9.4	5.6	4.4	2.1	4.4	5.3
	2007	9.1	20.0	8.8	5.4	4.7	2.3	4.9	5.5
	2008	9.3	21.2	8.7	5.5	4.5	2.3	4.7	5.3
	2009	9.0	20.7	8.9	5.2	4.9	2.4	4.3	6.0
	2010	9.0	19.6	9.4	5.5	4.9	2.2	4.1	6.0
	2011	8.2	19.2	6.6	5.3	4.3	2.0	4.5	5.0
	2012	8.6	20.7	6.9	5.4	4.4	1.9	4.9	5.2
America	2006	13.4	14.1	10.3	13.7	4.7	2.6	6.7	5.2
	2007	13.3	13.9	9.7	13.7	5.1	3.8	7.1	5.3
	2008	13.5	13.1	9.7	14.2	5.3	3.8	7.5	5.4
	2009	13.1	13.2	7.9	14.0	4.7	3.4	8.0	4.6
	2010	13.9	13.5	8.7	15.0	5.3	3.6	7.6	5.5
	2011	14.1	14.4	8.1	15.1	5.8	3.7	7.1	6.2
	2012	14.0	14.0	8.7	14.9	5.9	4.0	7.5	6.2
Asia	2006	39.9	51.7	39.0	35.9	36.9	28.6	27.8	41.7
	2007	40.0	51.7	38.4	36.3	40.1	31.1	28.9	45.5
	2008	38.9	50.6	35.4	35.8	40.6	29.1	30.7	46.4
	2009	38.9	51.0	37.1	35.2	45.9	34.0	29.3	53.3
	2010	36.8	50.8	34.4	32.8	45.5	33.7	34.0	51.6
	2011	37.9	52.1	37.5	33.8	46.7	36.8	31.6	52.6
	2012	36.8	50.7	37.8	32.8	47.9	37.0	32.4	53.9
Oceania	2006	0.0	0.1	0.01	0.0	0.2	–	0.7	0.1
	2007	0.1	0.1	0.01	0.0	0.2	–	0.8	0.1
	2008	0.1	0.1	0.01	0.0	0.2	–	0.8	0.1
	2009	0.1	0.1	0.02	0.1	0.2	–	0.4	0.2
	2010	0.1	0.1	0.02	0.1	0.2	–	0.4	0.2
	2011	0.1	0.1	0.02	0.1	0.2	–	0.4	0.2
	2012	0.1	0.1	0.08	0.1	0.1	–	0.4	0.1

Sources: Compiled by the UNCTAD secretariat on the basis of data supplied by reporting countries as well as data obtained from government, port-industry and specialist sources. Data from 2006 onwards have been revised and updated to reflect improved reporting, including more recent figures and better information regarding the breakdown by cargo type. Figures for 2012 are estimated on the basis of preliminary data or on the last year for which data were available.

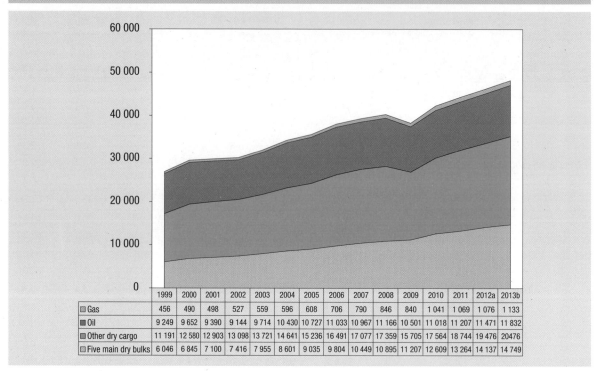

Figure 1.4. World seaborne trade in cargo ton–miles by cargo type, 1999–2013 (Billions of ton–miles)

	1999	2000	2001	2002	2003	2004	2005	2006	2007	2008	2009	2010	2011	2012a	2013b
Gas	456	490	498	527	559	596	608	706	790	846	840	1 041	1 069	1 076	1 133
Oil	9 249	9 652	9 390	9 144	9 714	10 430	10 727	11 033	10 967	11 166	10 501	11 018	11 207	11 471	11 832
Other dry cargo	11 191	12 580	12 903	13 098	13 721	14 641	15 236	16 491	17 077	17 359	15 705	17 564	18 744	19 476	20476
Five main dry bulks	6 046	6 845	7 100	7 416	7 955	8 601	9 035	9 804	10 449	10 895	11 207	12 609	13 264	14 137	14 749

Source: UNCTAD secretariat based on data from Clarkson Research Services (2013a).

[a] Estimated.

[b] Forecast.

volumes. Apart from China, iron-ore and coal demand from other fast-growing economies, in particular India and the Republic of Korea, have also been significant. Iron-ore shipments from Brazil contributed the most ton–miles growth given distances involved on the Brazil–China trade. The average distance travelled by iron-ore trade has risen by 6.7 per cent between 2000 and 2012 while, during the same period, the average distance travelled by coal trade fell by 13.1 per cent to 4,002 miles, reflecting, in particular, the shorter distances between China, Australia and Indonesia (Crowe, 2012). More recently, the shale revolution in the United States has meant that there is now more coal available to be exported, including to Europe and Asia. As a result, coal ton–mile exports from the United States are trending upwards. In 2011, its coal exports were 127 per cent higher than in 2007, while in ton–miles the growth averaged 152 per cent (Clarkson Research Services, 2012a). In a separate development affecting dry-bulk trade, some observers are predicting that if new regulation in Indonesia – a major supplier of minerals such as coal, bauxite and nickel destined for China – effectively constrains exports from the country, China will likely look for substitute sources, including from relatively distant locations such as Australia. As

a result, dry-bulk shipments and mileage are likely to increase. As regards grain trade, its share in the total ton–miles increased from 4.2 per cent in 2000 to 5.4 per cent in 2012, with the sharp drop in exports from the United States being, in ton–mile terms, offset by a surge in Brazilian exports. Over 2000–2012, the average distance travelled by grain cargo increased by 17.8 per cent and reached 6,807 miles, owing to fast-growing flows originating in developing America and destined for China (Crowe, 2012).

In 2012, containerized trade ton–miles increased by 3.0 per cent, compared with 8.8 per cent in 2011. Between 2000 and 2012, the average distance travelled by containerized trade dropped by 1.2 per cent, with the drop in long-haul Asia–Europe and trans-Pacific trade being offset by rapid growth in shorter-distance intra-Asian flows. The continued rise in the longer-haul North–South trade volumes is however likely to increase the average container haul (Crowe, 2012).

Tanker cargo, including crude oil, petroleum products and gas accounted for over one quarter of total ton–miles in 2012, down from over one third in 2000. Within tanker trade, crude oil held the lion's share (19.1 per cent), followed by petroleum products (5.7 per cent) and gas (2.3 per cent). The average distance travelled by crude oil declined marginally (–1.2 per cent) between 2000 and 2012. In contrast, and reflecting growing long-haul imports into Asia and flows from the United States to developing America, average distances travelled by petroleum products increased by 6.4 per cent.[1] This growth will likely continue in view of, inter alia, the following elements: (a) refinery closures in Europe which will create a shortage of middle distillates that will require increasing imports, including long-haul shipments from Western Asia, India and the United States; (b) the need to meet growing demand for distillates in Asia, in particular through increased imports from Western Asia; (c) the intensified exports from the United States to developing America and potentially to other regions, including Africa where demand for middle distillates is on the rise.

Another factor that will influence the ton–miles generated by oil trade is the structure of oil production in the United States, which is such that crude oil ton–miles will not necessarily drop with the evolving energy profile of the country. Refineries in the United States will continue to import heavy crude oil from Western Asia as well as from developing America in view of the fact that the light crude oil produced in West Africa is similar in its structure to the crude oil produced in the United States. Therefore, imports from West Africa to the United States are already declining, with much of the new surplus cargo now being shipped to Asia and with associated crude oil ton–miles increasing (*Financial Times*, 2013). Finally, as pricing differentials also affect demand between regions, additional trade in the direction of higher-priced Asia could also likely to boost tanker ton–miles. Meanwhile, with pipelines extending from Kazakhstan, the Russian Federation and soon Myanmar to China, crude oil ton–miles could be constrained in the future, which would entail some implications for tanker demand, the global tanker fleet and tanker trade patterns

3. Seaborne trade by cargo type

(a) Tanker trade

Tanker trade is greatly determined by global energy production and aggregate demand, the world economy, demographics, urbanization, industrialization and, more importantly, by the "geography" of global energy surpluses and deficits. To put in perspective some of the key developments affecting tanker trade, it is important to highlight at the outset the profound structural transformation that is currently underway.

The global energy map is being redrawn amid, in particular, a rise in oil and gas production in the United States, reports of new finds of mineral resources in various regions (for example, East Africa and the Mediterranean), as well as advances in extraction technology. The recent surge in the shale oil and gas production in the United States – the largest world oil consumer – is probably the single most game-changing trend, with implications extending beyond national borders and having a strong bearing on tanker trade. The International Energy Agency expects the United States to become a net exporter of natural gas by 2020 and to overtake Saudi Arabia as the largest global oil producer by the same year, before becoming nearly self-sufficient in energy by 2035 (International Energy Agency, 2012). Looking ahead, this may result in a new world energy map, with fewer crude volumes traded internationally, more refined products exported from the United States, and China and India potentially emerging as large importers of crude oil and exporters of refined petroleum products. Demand by type of petroleum product will also evolve, with middle distillates such as diesel used in transport growing rapidly (*Lloyd's List*, 2012a).

(i) Crude oil: Production and consumption

In 2012 and for the third year in a row, oil recorded the slowest growth among fossil fuels. In line with weaker global economic growth, in particular in Europe, global oil consumption increased by less than 1.0 per cent, a rate below the historical average (British Petroleum, 2013). As consumption in OECD countries fell by 1.3 per cent in 2012, the marginal growth in the global oil demand, which reached 89.8 million barrels per day (bpd) during the year, was driven by non-OECD countries. On the supply side, global production expanded by 2.2 per cent, with total volumes reaching 86.2 bpd and with members of the Organization of the Petroleum Exporting Countries (OPEC) accounting for most of the growth. An overview of global consumers and producers of crude oil is presented in table 1.5.

(ii) Crude oil: Shipments

Reflecting oil supply and demand dynamics, global crude-oil shipments grew by 1.3 per cent in 2012 with total volumes reaching 55.3 million bpd. Crude oil carried on board tankers accounted for two thirds of this total and increased by an estimated 1.5 per cent taking the total volume to 1.78 billion tons. Growth was particularly boosted by increased global production and inventory-building ahead of the embargo involving

Table 1.5.	**Major producers and consumers of oil and natural gas, 2012 (World market share in percentage)**		
World oil production		**World oil consumption**	
Western Asia	33	Asia Pacific	33
Transition economies	16	North America	23
North America	15	Europe	15
Developing America	12	Developing America	10
Africa	11	Western Asia	9
Asia Pacific	10	Transition economies	6
Europe	4	Africa	4
World natural gas production		**World natural gas consumption**	
North America	25	North America	25
Transition economies	23	Asia Pacific	19
Western Asia	16	Transition economies	18
Asia Pacific	15	Europe	14
Europe	8	Western Asia	12
Developing America	7	Developing America	8
Africa	6	Africa	4

Source: UNCTAD secretariat on the basis of data published in the British Petroleum Statistical Review of World Energy 2013.

Note: Oil includes crude oil, shale oil, oil sands and natural gas liquids (the liquid content of natural gas where this is recovered separately). The term excludes liquid fuels from other sources, such as biomass and coal derivatives.

oil trade with the Islamic Republic of Iran. Major crude-oil loading areas included Western Asia, Africa, developing America and transition economies, while main unloading ports were located in Japan, North America, Europe and developing Asia.

Crude oil imports into the United States declined by 4.3 per cent in 2012, reflecting in particular increased domestic production and pipeline shipments from Canada (British Petroleum, 2013). While in 2007, crude oil imports into the United States stood at 10.1 million bpd, volumes declined to 9.2 million bpd in 2010 and to 8.5 million bpd in 2012. As its production ramps up and imports fall, oil from traditional suppliers such as Angola, Nigeria and the Bolivarian Republic of Venezuela is being directed towards new markets and customers. India is expected to soon overtake the United States as the main destination for Nigerian crude exports, while its imports from the Bolivarian Republic of Venezuela have increased threefold since 2011 (*Financial Times*, 2013). Meanwhile, and pending requisite regulatory approvals, the United States can be expected to export its light sweet crude oil and potentially emerge as a crude oil exporter (*Lloyd's List*, 2012b). This development may further redefine the tanker trade map and, as tanker demand increases in the United States, will probably

entail some implications for the application of the Merchant Marine Act of 1920 (the Jones Act).

In Europe, as production in the North Sea declined, crude oil was mainly sourced from Libya. Europe's imports are expected to eventually shift away from the long-haul Western Asian exports to short-haul African shipments. As weak economic conditions continue to affect European refineries, a shift away from imports of crude oil towards imports of petroleum products can also be expected (Danish Ship Finance, 2013).

In 2012, crude oil import volumes increased by 7.4 per cent in China and over 4.0 per cent in India (British Petroleum, 2013). As these countries continue to build local refineries, their crude oil imports will also increase, including from sources in West Africa and Latin America. This trend is likely to alter the direction of cargo flows, raise demand for tankers and increase ton–miles. However, a potentially offsetting pattern is that a growing proportion of imports into China are likely to be delivered through pipelines from Kazakhstan, the Russian Federation and Myanmar.

As international sanctions prohibit imports of crude oil from the Islamic Republic of Iran, top importers such as China, India and the Republic of Korea are forced to reduce their import volumes to qualify for the 180-day waiver which allows these countries to continue importing Iranian crude oil (United States Institute of Peace, 2012). Consequently, the routing of tanker trade has shifted as more Iranian cargo travels eastward to Asia and as Europe replaces Iranian exports by shipments from the Russian Federation and West Africa (Danish Ship Finance, 2013). This trend is likely to intensify with the duration of the sanctions.

(iii) Refined petroleum products: Supply and refinery developments

Global refinery capacities increased by 0.4 per cent in 2012 and reached a total of 92.5 million bpd. Over 50 per cent of this capacity is located in non-OECD countries driven primarily by expansion in China, India and Western Asia (British Petroleum, 2013). Global capacity is expected to further increase with worldwide refining investments required by 2035 estimated at around $1.3 trillion. Of this total around $230 billion will be needed for existing projects, while $300 billion will be required for additions and around $750 billion will be dedicated for maintenance and replacement (OPEC, 2012). In line with capacity developments, global refinery throughput increased by 0.6 per cent in 2012 with much of the growth being generated by refineries in Africa, Canada, China, India and Mexico. Refineries are increasingly being closed down in Europe and Japan in view of the growing environmental constraints in the OECD region and the heightened competition from refineries in Western Asia and the Far East (Danish Ship Finance, 2013).

(iv) Refined petroleum products: Demand and shipments

Demand for refined petroleum products is closely tied to industrial production, driving and power generation. Thus, reflecting weak industrial production and reduced naphtha demand during the year, growth in petroleum product shipments decelerated to 2.1 per cent in 2012 (Clarkson Research Services, 2013a). UNCTAD estimates this growth at 1.6 per cent; a rate that also includes the performance of gas trade. Global shipments of petroleum products and gas totalled 1.05 billion tons in 2012 (Clarkson Research Services, 2013a), with rising import volumes into Asia, in particular China, Japan and the Republic of Korea offsetting the drop in shipments destined for North America. Strong demand from Asia, in particular for light (for example, gasoline and naphtha) and middle distillates (for example, diesel and kerosene) was met by supply from Europe, India and Western Asia. Meanwhile, demand has been weakening in North America – the second largest importing region of refined oil products.

As gasoline imports into the United States were traditionally met by European supply, the drop in demand and falling imports into the United States are likely to affect the transatlantic product trade. In contrast, exports from the United States have increased – a relatively new phenomenon – driven by the surplus created by declining oil demand internally as well as by the growing demand from developing America induced by the region's industrialization and infrastructure development process. In the meantime, gasoline will increasingly be shipped from Western Asia to the Far East and from Africa to Europe (Danish Ship Finance, 2013).

In 2012, demand for increasingly popular middle distillates was subdued as jet fuel and diesel requirements weakened in line with the global economic situation. However, demand is expected to resume growth as the world economy recovers. Driven mainly by transportation needs (expansion of car fleets) and to a lesser extent industrial requirements, growth in future demand for middle distillates is expected to outpace that of light distillates, with Asia and, in particular, China being in the lead, followed by developing America.

Looking ahead, oil will likely continue to move closer to markets, with the marginal barrel of production moving west to North America and the refining capacity moving to Asia (*Financial Times*, 2013). Demand for refined petroleum products is expected to continue to grow driven by increasing requirements in non-OECD economies from Asia and South America, in particular as they continue to industrialize and as existing refining capacity remains insufficient (Clarkson Research Services, 2012b). Growth in petroleum product trade is expected to be firm on long-haul routes from India and Western Asia in the direction of the Far East (that is, the Republic of Korea, and Asia other than China and Japan). As regards China, its growing domestic production is likely to result in lesser import volumes of petroleum products (Clarkson Research Services, 2013a). Imports into the European Union are expected to remain weak, in line with the current challenging economic situation, while in the United States lower demand for petroleum products and growing refinery capacity are likely to boost exports of petroleum products, particularly in the direction of developing America (Clarkson Research Services, 2013a).

To sum up, new trading lanes both for refined petroleum products and crude oil are emerging in tandem with changes in production, volume and structure of demand as well as the location of global refineries. These changes are likely to be further influenced by other developments, including, for example, the "60/66 programme" of the Russian Federation, which cuts taxes on exports of crude oil and raises them for refined products as a way to help expand and modernize capacity, and the loan agreement between the Bolivarian Republic of Venezuela and China, which will raise oil exports destined for China.

(v) Natural gas: Liquefied gas shipments

Global natural gas consumption increased by 2.2 per cent in 2012 – a rate below the historical average of 2.7 per cent (British Petroleum, 2013). During the same year, production grew by 1.9 per cent, with the United States remaining the world's largest producer (British Petroleum, 2013). An overview of global consumers and producers of natural gas is presented in table 1.5.

In line with supply and demand developments, growth in global gas trade, including land-based and seaborne shipments, remained flat in 2012, growing at an annual rate of less than 1 per cent. Growth in liquefied petroleum gas (LPG) and LNG came to a standstill in 2012. Together, LNG and LPG volumes totalled 289 million tons, the same level as 2011, with a drop in LNG shipments being offset by a rise in LPG cargo.[2] Accounting for some 85 per cent of total gas trade carried by sea, LNG shipments fell at an annual rate of 1.2 per cent in 2012, due to falling imports in Europe and the limited global liquefaction capacity expansion recorded during the year (Clarkson Research Services, 2013a). Falling import demand in the United States is having ripple effects both within and beyond national borders. Lower import volumes are making the highly capital-intensive regasification facilities in the United States obsolete. Meanwhile, the relatively cheaper gas is displacing coal as a source of power generation. In 2012, Europe, where more expensive gas has been used for power generation, increased its coal import volumes sourced from the United States (Clarkson Research Services, 2013a). Qatar remained the largest world exporter with a share of over 32.1 per cent of global LNG exports (British Petroleum, 2013). Increased export volumes were recorded not only in Qatar but also in Australia, Malaysia, Nigeria and the United Arab Emirates, while shipments from Algeria, Egypt and Indonesia contracted (British Petroleum, 2013).

The outlook for LNG trade is positive as global consumption is set to increase in view of:

(a) Surging production and exports in the United States;

(b) New gas finds worldwide (for example, Cyprus, Israel, Mozambique and the United Republic of Tanzania);

(c) The projected growth in Asian LNG imports sustained, in particular, by China's strategic commitment to promote gas use;

(d) The decline in nuclear power use;

(e) The attractiveness of gas as a "greener" alternative to other fossil fuels.

Investments in building supporting infrastructure for LNG trade continue unabated and provide a further positive outlook for gas trade and carriers, operators and builders. As of November 2012 there were 94 liquefaction installations in 19 countries (Clarkson Research Services, 2012c). While there has been little expansion in terms of liquefaction capacity in 2012, some 12 liquefaction projects are reported to be under construction globally, including five in Australia. Papua New Guinea and Colombia are likely to become exporters after the completion of some 20 projects that are reported to be at the design or final investment decision stage (Clarkson Research Services, 2012c). On the import front, there are around 93 import facilities at locations in 26 countries and

these numbers are expected to continue to increase with many countries lining up for their first cargoes (Clarkson Research Services, 2012c). Given recent gas discoveries in Africa, and assuming all projects currently being pursued come on line according to schedule, the region could emerge as the fourth major supplier of LNG, after Australia, Western Asia and the United States (Drewry Shipping Consultants, 2013).

Unlike LNG trade, and accounting for only 16 per cent of global gas trade carried by sea, LPG demand continued to grow in 2012, with total LPG volumes increasing by 7.1 per cent and reaching 45 million tons (Clarkson Research Services, 2013a). During the year, large quantities were shipped from Western Asia in the direction of India and the Far East as part of stock building motivated by relatively lower prices and ample supply. The use of LPG for cooking purposes, car gas consumption and as an input into the petrochemical industry is driving demand in developing regions. With growing production, the United States is projected to emerge as a key supplier of LPG with more and more of its exports currently heading in the direction of developing America.

(b) Dry-cargo trades: Major and minor dry bulks and other dry cargo

Despite the weakness of the global economy, dry-cargo trade volumes continued to grow at a healthy rate of 5.7 per cent in 2012, taking total volumes above the 6 billion tons mark. Judging by historic standards and bearing in mind the global economic situation, this performance is rather impressive (Clarkson Research Services, 2013a).

The volume of dry-bulk cargo including the five major bulk commodities (iron ore, coal, grain, bauxite/alumina and phosphate rock) and minor bulks (agribulks, fertilizers, metals, minerals, steel and forest products) increased by 6.7 per cent in 2012 (Clarkson Research Services, 2013a). A breakdown of this total indicates that much of the growth was generated by the expansion in the five major bulk commodities (7.2 per cent) and to a lesser extent by growth in the minor bulks (4.6 per cent), which in volume terms have added nearly 500 million tons to world seaborne trade between 2002 and 2012 (Clarkson Research Services, 2013a). During the year the five major bulk commodities totalled about 2.7 billion tons while the volume of minor dry bulks reached 1.4 billion tons. Together, major and minor dry bulks accounted for nearly two thirds of global dry-cargo volumes.

On the import side, Asia, and in particular China, is the leading source of import demand for dry bulks, while on the export side the landscape is less clear cut as market shares continue to evolve. Indonesia, for example, is increasingly emerging as an important player with respect to more than one commodity, including coal, bauxite and metals. Its strategic geographical position, as well as its abundance in several raw materials, most notably coal, is now making Indonesia the fastest-growing exporter to Asian countries (Danish Ship Finance, 2013). Other smaller actors are also expanding their shares including, for example, Liberia, Peru and Sierra Leone. Table 1.6 provides an overview of major players in the dry-bulk commodities market.

The main caution, however, to growth in dry-bulk trade is the continued high dependence on the Asian demand and on only two key commodities, namely iron ore and coal. While growth is still strong in China, the recent moderated growth in the country and a shift away from an infrastructure-based investment growth pattern, entail, nevertheless, some implications as to the strength of future demand.

On the positive side however, some projections indicate that the dry-bulk sector is set to emerge as a winner from growth in the world population and urbanization. Some observers maintain that by 2025 urban consumers are likely to inject around $20 trillion annually in additional spending into the world economy, which in turn will trigger a boom in commodity trade (*Shipping and Finance*, 2013). With 1 billion people due to enter the consuming category, rapid growth in urbanization and infrastructure development will entail an increased demand for resources and raw materials. The requisite infrastructure needs in the port sector alone are estimated to be over 2.5 times the current port infrastructure level.

(i)   Coal shipments

Coal is the fastest-growing fossil fuel, accounting for 30 per cent of global primary energy consumption in 2012. Driven by non-OECD countries, global consumption expanded by 2.5 per cent in 2012 while production increased by 2 per cent (British Petroleum, 2013). During the year, the total volume of coal shipments (thermal and coking) increased at an annual rate of 12.3 per cent and surpassed the 1.06 billion tons mark for the first time. Thermal-coal trade, which accounted for 78 per cent of the total, increased at a strong rate of 14.2 per cent in 2012, partly driven by the relative recovery in European imports (following the downturn) and the continued growth in Asian import demand as well as the availability

Table 1.6.   Some major dry bulks and steel: main producers, users, exporters and importers, 2012 (World market shares in percentages)

Steel producers		Steel users	
China	46	China	46
Japan	7	European Union	10
United States	6	North America	9
India	5	Transition economies	4
Russian Federation	5	Western Asia	3
Republic of Korea	5	Developing America	3
Germany	3	Africa	2
Turkey	2	Others	22
Brazil	2		
Ukrain	2		
Others	18		

Iron ore exporters		Iron ore importers	
Australia	45	China	65
Brazil	29	Japan	12
South Africa	5	European Union	10
India	3	Republic of Korea	6
Canada	3	Others	7
Sweden	2		
Others	13		

Coal exporters		Coal importers	
Indonesia	33	European Union	18
Australia	30	Japan	17
United States	10	China	17
Colombia	8	India	15
South Africa	7	Republic of Korea	12
Russian Federation	7	China, Taiwan Province of	5
Canada	3	Malaysia	2
Others	4	Thailand	2
		Others	13

Grain exporters		Grain importers	
United States	20	Asia Pacific	31
Argentina	12	Developing America	21
European Union	10	Africa	20
Australia	10	Western Asia	18
Canada	9	Europe	7
Ukraine	8	Transition economies	3
Others	31		

Sources: UNCTAD secretariat on the basis of data from the World Steel Association (2013a), Clarkson Research Services (2013b) and the International Grains Council (2013).

of cargo from the Atlantic. Unlike iron-ore trade and to a lesser extent coking coal, demand for thermal coal is more diversified, with the European Union accounting for about 18 per cent of imports, followed by Japan, China, India and other smaller importers such as Hong Kong (China), the Republic of Korea, Malaysia, the Philippines and Taiwan Province of China. Coking-coal trade grew 5.4 per cent in 2012 driven by increases in import volumes of 43.7 per cent and 8 per cent in China and India, respectively. Elsewhere, imports into Europe and the Republic of Korea were constrained by limited growth in steel production.

In 2012, increased coal exports from the United States due to the shale-gas production dampened coal prices and boosted imports into Europe, India and also China, which overtook Japan as the largest thermal-coal importer during the year. China's coal imports absorbed the equivalent of around 430 Supramaxes in 2012 (Clarkson Research Services, 2013c).

Coal trade is set to grow in tandem with growing import demand from China and as Indian installations of coal-fired power stations expand. However, growing environmental regulation, including in Europe, together with the upside potential of China given its large domestic coal resources, may have an offsetting effect and result in a much moderated growth (Clarkson Research Services, 2013a). There remains uncertainty as to whether the Chinese imports, which have surged since 2008, can continue to grow at the strong rate observed so far. In a separate development, it should be noted that new coal power plants are expected to come on stream between 2012 and 2020 in Europe. These plants should reach a capacity nearly double the existing capacity during the preceding eight-year period and result in approximately 80 power plant units being newly built or replaced (Research and Markets, 2012). These developments are likely to affect demand for coal and further shape the flows and patterns of coal trade.

(ii) Iron ore shipments and steel production and consumption

As iron ore is a key ingredient used in steel production, its trade is largely determined by developments in the steel sector. According to data from the World Steel Association, global apparent steel use and steel production each increased by 1.2 per cent during 2012 (World Steel Association, 2013a, 2013b). China continued to increase its production with its market share rising from 45.4 per cent in 2011 to 46.3 per cent in 2012. Against this background, iron-ore trade

expanded by 5.4 per cent in 2012, taking the total volumes to 1.11 billion tons. Major iron-ore exporters were Australia, Brazil, Canada, India, South Africa and Sweden. Together, Australia and Brazil account for 73.5 per cent of global exports. Australia, the largest world exporter (44.5 per cent share), increased its shipments by 12.8 per cent. Similarly, other exporters such as Canada, South Africa and Sweden have also increased their shipments, while in India, mining bans and taxes on iron-ore exports have significantly constrained the country's export volumes (−52.8 per cent). As a result, India's market share declined and a structural shift unfolded, whereby India has moved from being a major exporter to a net importer and its import demand is likely to increase over the next few years. Australia has been increasing its market share, while Brazil recorded a decline due to the mine- and infrastructure-expansion projects being completed in Australia and expansion projects in Brazil being delayed. Output from South Africa and smaller suppliers such as Liberia, Peru and Sierra Leone has also been growing.

In 2012, China remained the main destination for iron ore shipped out of Australia and Brazil, driven by large investments in construction and infrastructure. China's economic development, infrastructure investment and increasing per-capita steel consumption are crucial for iron-ore trade. Apart from China, there seems to be no other significant contributors to iron-ore trade growth, as imports into Europe and Japan are stagnating or declining and the import-demand growth in the Republic of Korea is still relatively small scale. The remaining concern is the over-excessive concentration and dependency on the economy of one country (Clarkson Research Services, 2012d). That said and while any cut in China's steel output remains a downside risk, some factors could contribute to further support growth in China's iron-ore imports, at least in the short term. These include low iron-ore stocks and the need for restocking, low prices and higher Australian supply (Clarksons Shipping Services, 2013).

(iii) Grain shipments

Economic growth and population expansion have generated new grain trade patterns, with the share of developing regions in world imports increasing over time. While supply-side factors (for example, weather conditions and arable land) are clearly fundamental for grain markets and trade, demand-side considerations (demographics, consumption patterns and food/feed/industrial usage) are also important factors shaping the structure, size and direction of trade flows.

Total grain production in the crop year 2012/2013 fell by 3.5 per cent to 1.78 billion tons, while for the crop year 2013/2014 the production is forecast to grow by 7.4 per cent and take the total volume to 1.92 billion (International Grains Council, 2013). On the demand side, global grain consumption dropped by 1.7 per cent in 2012/2013 to 1.82 billion tons, but is expected to recover and grow again by 3.6 per cent in 2013/2014 to reach 1.88 billion tons. The significant drop in global grain consumption is the first since 1995, caused by high prices and their dampening effect on ethanol production and livestock feed (Larsen, 2013).

The year 2012 was a negative year for grain trade as the record harvest of 2011 was followed by a significant contraction in output due to severe droughts affecting crops in major producing and exporting countries, namely the United States, the Russian Federation, Kazakhstan, Ukraine and Australia (Larsen, 2013). World grain shipments by sea (wheat, coarse grain and soybean) fell by 1.1 per cent and totalled 357 million tons for the crop year 2012/2013. Volumes are forecast to increase by 2.8 per cent in the crop year 2013/2014. Wheat and coarse grains continue to account for over two thirds of the overall grain trade, with the remaining share being accounted for by soybean.

Global wheat exports fell by 4.4 per cent in the crop year 2012/2013 while coarse grains dropped by 1.9 per cent and soybean trade was the main area of growth (5.5 per cent) (Clarksons Shipping Services, 2013). Japan remained the world's largest importer of wheat and coarse grains with a total of 23.8 million tons, followed by Egypt (14.2 million tons), the Republic of Korea (12.5 million tons), Mexico (12.1 million tons), Saudi Arabia (11.7 million tons) and China (9.1 million tons) (Clarksons Shipping Services, 2013). After achieving self-sufficiency for many years, China is increasingly emerging as an important source of grain import demand.

Although the United States is by far the world's largest grain exporter, its share of the world market is shrinking. The 52 million tons of grain exported in 2012/2013 (down from 72.6 million tons shipped out in 2011/2012) was the smallest volume since 1971 (Larsen, 2013). Export volumes dropped from Australia but increased from Canada, Ukraine and the European Union, while they remained unchanged from Argentina.

One concern facing grain production and entailing implications for seaborne trade is the levelling off of returns for some key crops (for example, rice in Japan

and wheat in Europe) in addition to the potentially devastating effect of climate change-induced weather extremes (for example, drought and flooding). In view of these risks, the traditional 70-days worth of grain stocks is now considered inadequate to ensure food security and a larger buffer is said to be required to avoid food price shocks (Larsen, 2013). While food prices have eased from recent highs, grain markets remain tight due to historically low stock levels and the pressure on food prices resulting from more expensive inputs (fuel and fertilizer) (International Monetary Fund, 2013).

(iv) Bauxite/alumina and phosphate rock

Over the years, growth in bauxite trade has been boosted by higher Indonesian exports, with China accounting for most of global bauxite trade growth between 2002 and 2012. Bauxite trade grew from 30 million tons in 2002 to 82 million tons in 2011 (Clarkson Research Services, 2012e). However, in 2012, bauxite and alumina total volumes fell by 5.3 per cent from the 2011 levels and volumes totalled 107 million tons. The contraction reflected the new export rules introduced in May 2012 by the Indonesian government, which dampened export volumes from the country. There are now concerns about the future of bauxite trade as Indonesia is a crucial supplier of bauxite in addition to other key commodities, including coal and nickel ore – a metal used in many industrial and consumer products such as stainless steel. A measure that would limit exports could in the long term induce a shift in trade patterns as China might be able to source more bauxite from other locations such as Australia or Guinea. The latter country accounted for 25 per cent of world exports in 2011 and has the largest bauxite reserves in the world (Clarkson Research Services, 2012e). The effect on ton–miles is likely to be positive.

As to phosphate rock, global production capacity is projected to increase from 220 million tons per year in 2012 to 256 million tons (United States Geological Survey, 2013). Over half of the growth is expected to originate in North Africa, with Morocco the largest producer. Phosphate rock mines and expansions are underway in a number of other countries, including Angola, Australia, Brazil, Canada, China, the Congo, Egypt, Ethiopia, Guinea-Bissau, Kazakhstan, Namibia, Mali, Mauritania, Mozambique, New Zealand, Senegal, South Africa, Togo, Tunisia, Uganda, and Zambia. A growing world population and rising food, feed and industrial requirements require extensive use of phosphate fertilizer as part of the planting and agricultural production process. As there are no substitutes for phosphorous, its global use in fertilizer is projected to increase from 41.9 million tons in 2012 to 45.3 million tons in 2016. Reflecting continued demand for fertilizers, phosphate rock shipments increased by 3.4 per cent in 2012, up from 29 million to 30 million tons.

(v) Dry cargo: Minor bulks

In 2012, minor-bulks trade increased at a slower annual rate than in the previous year, growing by 4.6 per cent and taking the total volumes to 1.4 billion tons. Metals and minerals accounted for 45.6 per cent of this total followed by manufactures (33.0 per cent) and agribulks (21.3 per cent). The largest growth was recorded in the metals and minerals segment (for example, cement, nickel ore, anthracite) with volumes growing by 6.0 per cent year-on-year. Expansion in nickel-ore exports mainly destined for China (33.8 per cent) fuelled the growth. This robust increase occurred while the new export restrictions introduced in May 2012 (until November 2012) in Indonesia were still in force. This is because nickel-ore shipments from the Philippines helped offset the lower Indonesian availability (Clarkson Research Services, 2013a). The next largest contributor to growth was the manufactures sector (for example, steel and forest products) with 3.6 per cent annual growth. Recently, trade patterns have been shifting in the manufactures sector owing to the surge in Chinese exports with flows destined mainly for other Asian countries, Africa and developing America. Ample supply of the more affordable Chinese steel, supported by a strong global demand, has boosted trade in steel products. Finally, agribulks (soymeal, oilseed/meal and rice) also expanded at 3.5 per cent, despite a drop in sugar and potash volume.

To sum up, dry-bulk commodities, including in particular major bulks such as iron and coal, are the backbone of international seaborne trade and have been the major engine of growth reflecting in particular the fast-growing demand from emerging developing regions. Exporters of dry-bulk commodities are rather diversified, with suppliers spanning different regions and with smaller new players increasingly emerging on the market. On the import side however, there seems to be a greater concentration, with demand emanating mainly from emerging developing regions, namely in Asia, in particular China. Another feature is the high concentration in the structure of the global import demand, as much of global growth is being

entirely driven by iron-ore and coal shipments. Dependence on one market, in particular China and to a lesser extent India, as well as on two single commodities can be problematic in the long run, as growth patterns in these countries change and their import demand moderates or slackens. In this context, and in the absence of significant growth in import demand from other markets that could offset the decline in China and India, the futur of the dry-bulk shipping market remains uncertain. For now however, existing indicators are pointing to continued growth in dry-bulk commodity trade, including in that of minor bulks in tandem with current growth patterns, urbanization trends and population expansion in developing regions.

(vi) Other dry cargo: Containerized trade

For many decades, containerized trade has been the fastest-growing market segment accounting for over 16 per cent of global seaborne trade by volume in 2012 and more than half by value (in 2007). With containerization being closely associated with globalization and fragmentation of global production, a recent study considering 157 countries over the 1962–1990 period provided empirical evidence that containerization is the driver of the twentieth century economic globalization (Bernhofen et al., 2013). In the 22 industrialized countries examined, containerization explains a 320 per cent rise in bilateral trade over the first five years after adoption and 790 per cent over 20 years. By comparison, and over a 20-year period, a bilateral free-trade agreement raises trade by 45 per cent while membership of the General Agreement on Tariffs and Trade adds 285 per cent. Over the period 1962–1990, containerization appears to have had a lesser effect on North–South and South–South trade, probably reflecting the role of port and transport infrastructure availability and efficiency (Bernhofen et al., 2013).

For a long time, containerized trade flows could be predicted by looking at the performance of world GDP with the multiplier effect of the container volume growth ranging between three to four times the GDP growth. This ratio is currently being questioned with some observers arguing that it is no longer a precise predictor of container-demand growth since other factors are also at play (Containerisation International, 2013a). These factors include the rate of offshoring of manufacturing, the extent of containerization of bulk cargoes, the goods-versus-services composition and the manufactured-versus-commodities share of countries. Some analysts maintain that the GDP multiplier has fallen from an average of 3.4 times over 1990–2005 to only 1.5 times in 2012. The reduced value of the multiplier has implications for future growth in demand and for containerized trade, a fact that is being increasingly acknowledged at the industry level. According to a large container carrier, current growth rates should be seen as the "new normal" for the container industry and the 2008/2009 crisis has moved the industry away from the 9–10 per cent growth recorded over the past three decades (*Containerisation International*, 2013a).

Against this background, and while growth decelerated significantly, containerized trade volumes expanded in 2012 to reach 155 million TEUs (figure 1.5(a)) (Clarkson Research Services, 2013b). Containerized trade, which accounted for 65 per cent of "other dry cargo" in 2012 (that is, nearly two thirds of the 2.28 billion tons of dry cargo that remain after removing dry-bulk commodities), increased by 3.2 per cent in 2012, down from 13.1 per cent in 2010 and 7.1 per cent in 2011. The sharp deceleration resulted from the depressed volumes

on the mainlane East–West trade, in particular, the Asia–Europe trade route.

Data from *Containerisation International* indicate that European import volumes have once again fallen back below the pre-crisis level with volumes on the head-haul route from Asia to Europe dropping by 2.6 per cent in 2012, compared with a 6 per cent positive growth in 2011 (table 1.7 and figure 1.5(b)). Falling volumes affected almost all goods, including electrical machinery, metal manufactures, travel goods and handbags, telecom and recording equipment, textiles and miscellaneous manufacture (*Containerisation International*, 2013b).

The contraction is indicative of the severe pressure weighing down on European economies, especially in the Mediterranean. In addition to lower demand, overcapacity is another challenge facing operators on the Asia–Europe lane. In 2012, a number of measures have been taken to manage the demand and supply imbalance and control capacity, including among others suspending or cancelling services, dropping voyages, slow steaming and idling of ships (Clarkson Research Services, 2013a).

Figure 1.5 (a).   Global container trade, 1996–2013 (Millions of TEUs and percentage annual change)

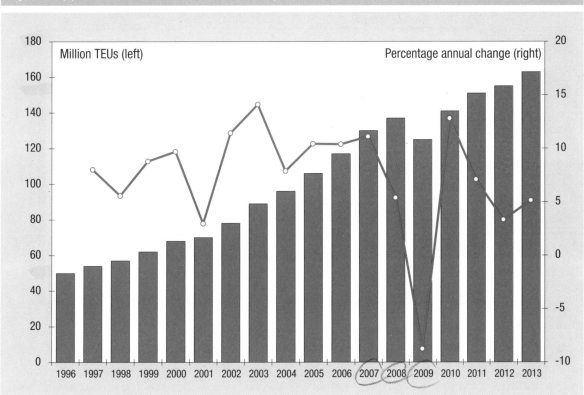

Source: Based on Drewry Shipping Consultants, *Container Market Review and Forecast* 2008/2009, and Clarkson Research Services, *Container Intelligence Monthly*, various issues.

Table 1.7.	Estimated containerized cargo flows on major East–West container trade routes, 2009–2012 (Millions of TEUs and percentage annual change)					
Year	Transpacific		Europe Asia		Transatlantic	
	Asia–North America	North America–Asia	Asia–Europe	Europe–Asia	Europe–North America	North America–Europe
2009	10.6	6.1	11.5	5.5	2.8	2.5
2010	12.3	6.5	13.3	5.7	3.2	2.7
2011	12.4	6.6	14.1	6.2	3.4	2.8
2012	13.3	6.9	13.7	6.3	3.6	2.7
Percentage change 2011–2012	7.4	5.2	-2.6	0.4	5.9	-6.9

Sources: MDS Transmodal data as published in Data Hub Trade Statistics, *Containerisation International*, www.containershipping.com, April, May and June 2013.

The North America–Asia trade showed more resilience and performed better than the previous year as North American imports were relatively more robust. In 2012, trade on the head-haul route from Asia to North America expanded by 7.4 per cent while traffic in the opposite direction expanded by 5.2 per cent. On the transatlantic route, depressed European import demand caused a 6.9 per cent contraction on the North America–Europe leg, while flows into North America increased by 5.9 per cent, sustained by relatively stronger demand in the United States.

Figure 1.5 (b).	Estimated containerized cargo flows on major East–West container trade routes (Millions of TEUs)

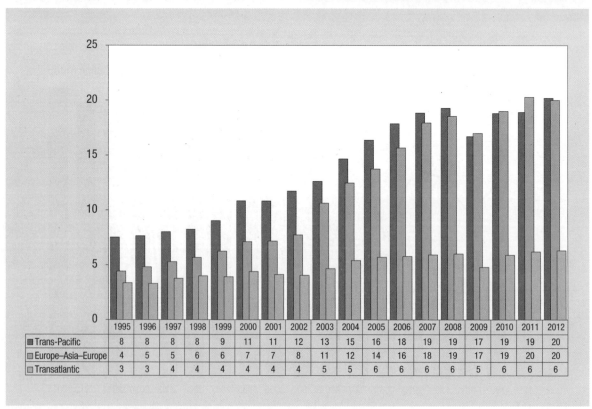

Source: Based on the Global Insight Database as published in *Bulletin FAL*, issue number 288, number 8/2010 ("International maritime transport in Latin America and the Caribbean in 2009 and projections for 2010"), United Nations Economic Commission for Latin America and the Caribbean (ECLAC). Data for 2009, 2010, 2011 and 2012 are based on table 1.7.

Away from the mainlanes, containerized trade flows continued to grow at a rapid pace, albeit slower than in 2011. North–South trade expanded by 3.9 per cent in 2012, while intra-Asian and trade on non-mainlane East–West routes grew by 6.2 per cent and 3.7 per cent respectively (Clarkson Research Services, 2013b). Containerized trade linking Asia, developing America, Africa and Oceania has been growing over the past few years, highlighting the deepening of South–South ties. Reflecting intensified interregional trade volumes the average size of ships deployed on these routes increased markedly. With consumer demand in developing regions set to grow, markets in the "South" will continue to drive global container trade growth (Clarkson Research Services, 2013b). While as noted above the impact of containerization on North–South and South–South trade during the 1962–1990 period appeared to have been relatively smaller than that on the advanced regions, the rapid growth in non-mainlane containerized trade observed over recent years highlights to some extent the growing importance of containerization in promoting trade within and among developing regions.

The weak market fundamentals and the growing deployment of increasingly larger ships have forced operators to continue cascading their ships to secondary and regional routes. Nevertheless, during the year the market saw the arrival of the largest ships to date (+16,000 TEU and Triple-E container ships of 18,300 TEU). In addition to the arrival of these megaships, 2012 saw some operational restructuring with the decision by the largest world carriers Maersk Line, Mediterranean Shipping Company (MSC) and CMA CGM to form the P3 alliance, a large vessel-sharing alliance affecting the three major East–West trade routes (*Lloyd's List*, 2013a). If approved, the initiative will likely affect not only carriers and their bottom line but also ports, shippers, and smaller operators (*Lloyd's List*, 2013b).

Another trend that is unfolding is the continued penetration of containerization into the bulk trade, in particular on the backhaul routes of imbalanced trades. Regulatory developments in the commodity sector are supporting this trend as shown in the case of Australian grain. Since 2008, when grain trading was deregulated in Australia, the country's containerized wheat shipments increased tenfold. Similarly, recent deregulation in Canada's grain market is likely to result in greater containerization of grain trade (Dynamar B.V., 2013).

Finally, an issue that is being increasingly mentioned relates to the "nearsourcing" whereby a number of firms are reported to be relocating closer to home markets given production cost increases in China. Some observers argue, however, that nearsourcing affects limited areas of business and is therefore overrated (*Lloyd's List*, 2013c). In addition, it was observed that there was more than one factor to take into account when making decisions about where to locate production and that there was no one-size-fits-all solution, as in some cases – depending on the product – nearsourcing can generate significant savings while in others it could prove to be expensive (*Lloyd's List*, 2013c).

C. SELECTED EMERGING TRENDS AFFECTING INTERNATIONAL SHIPPING

Despite the positive growth in 2012, international seaborne trade remains vulnerable to many downside risks and exposed to some potentially game-changing trends that could redefine the maritime transport operating landscape. International shipping is facing a new and complex environment that involves both challenges and opportunities, including as noted above the demand and supply mismatch, continued global economic uncertainty and geopolitical tensions. Of all the prevailing challenges however, the interconnected issues of energy security and costs, climate change and environmental sustainability are perhaps the most unsettling. Climate change in particular continues to rank high on the international policy agenda, including of shipping and port business. Despite positive developments on a number of fronts, the world is not yet on track to limit the average global temperature rise to 2°C (above pre-industrial levels) that would ensure that climate change remains manageable (International Energy Agency, 2013). With climate change effects already being felt globally and in the absence of adequate climate change mitigation and adaption action, shipping and ports and therefore international seaborne trade are likely to be severely affected by the potentially devastating impacts of this change (for example, extreme weather events and rising sea levels). For a more detailed discussion on the climate change challenge and maritime transport, see previous first chapters of the *Review of Maritime Transport*, 2009–2012.

Opportunities are, on the other hand, also arising in connection with some of the following trends:

(a) Deeper regional integration and South–South cooperation;

(b) Growing diversification of sources of supply enabled by technology and efficient transportation;

(c) Emergence of new trading partners and access to new markets facilitated by growing trade and cooperation agreements;

(d) The expansion/opening of new sea routes (for example, Panama Canal expansion and arctic routes);

(e) Structural change in the world energy map and consequent ripple effects on tanker trade;

(f) Moving-up of economies' value chains from labour intensive manufacturing to higher skilled production (for example, China) and related implications for other developing regions (Viet Nam, Bangladesh, Africa);

(g) Growth in global demand induced by a growing world population and a rise in the middle-class consuming category;

(h) The emergence of developing-country banks (for example, BRICS) with the potential to raise funding to meet the significant transport infrastructure investment needs.

Against this background, the following section focuses on developments affecting three closely interrelated topics, namely:

(a) Fuel costs and slow steaming;

(b) Lower-sulphur fuels and air emissions;

(c) Innovative ship design (eco-ships).

While these issues have been considered to different extents in the previous editions of the *Review of Maritime Transport*, providing an update on how they are further unfolding is important, especially as related debates are in some cases polarizing the industry (for example, concerning eco-ships). Together, these issues have one element in common, namely fossil fuels, a strategic factor that can significantly determine the competitiveness of shipping and its long term sustainability.

A fourth issue addressed in this section is the expansion of the Panama Canal and some related potential implications. Dealing with this issue at this juncture is particularly topical given, in particular the fast-approaching 2015 deadline set for the completion of the expansion work.

1. Fuel costs and slow steaming

Higher oil prices impact on trade and maritime transport through both their dampening effect on growth and the upward pressure on the cost of fuel used to propel ships. From 2005, oil prices started to rise with some acceleration observed since 2007, and with 2008 recording a historic high of $150 per barrel. For comparison, the spot price of European Brent averaged around $29 in 2000, $55 in 2005, $73 in 2007 and $112 in 2012 (2013 data from the United States Energy Information Administration). This means that oil prices more than doubled between 2005 and 2012 and have increased by more than half since 2007. Marine fuel prices (bunkers) as illustrated by the Rotterdam 380 centistoke increased by nearly threefold between 2005 and 2012. The Rotterdam 380 centistoke averaged $138.4 per ton in 2000, $234 per ton in 2005, $345.1 per ton in 2007 and $639.6 per ton in 2012 (Clarkson Research Services, 2012d). While oil prices and bunkers are correlated, their relationship has evolved over recent years indicating that bunker fuel prices not only depend on oil price movements but are also determined by other factors, such as growing demand for bunkers resulting from an expanding world fleet and the tendency of refineries to produce more distillates (Clarkson Research Services, 2012f).

With fuel costs reported to account for larger shares of operating costs (as much as 50–60 per cent) (World Shipping Council, 2008), a rise in bunker fuel costs cuts significantly into the earnings of shipowners, especially when freight markets are depressed. As container ships operate at relatively higher speeds than bulkers and tankers, rising bunker prices have a special resonance among liner operators. It has been estimated, for example, that the daily cost of bunker fuel averaged 85 per cent of the daily ship cost between 2003 and 2006, while since 2008 bunker fuel cost has increased significantly and represents over three times the daily cost of chartering a ship (Clarkson Research Services, 2012f). A recent industry survey revealed that fuel efficiency is a top priority for shipping with 69 per cent of businesses indicating that efforts should focus on developing more cost-effective means of fuel consumption (*Lloyd's List*, 2013d).

Since 2007, and while it started on the Asia–Europe trade, slow steaming as a fuel-saving measure is being implemented across shipping sectors and routes, including on the North–South trajectory (Clarkson Research Services, 2013b). While rising fuel costs remain the main driver of slow steaming, sailing at lower speed, especially at the worst of the economic downturn, also helped absorb some of the prevailing excess container ship carrying capacity.

However, views about the long-term sustainability of slow steaming vary. Some expect the practice to be transitional and therefore disappear with economic recovery and less volatile oil prices, while others maintain that slow steaming is here to stay. In this regard, trend setters such as Maersk Line are reported to be retrofitting ships to allow for slow steaming and looking to extend the practice further into all trades as well as introducing extra-slow steaming (15–18 knots) into selected trade (*Lloyd's List*, 2013e). For large container carriers, slow steaming at 18–20 knots would bring fuel consumption from 125–175 tons per day to less than 100 tons per day. With bunker pricing approaching $700 per ton, these reductions would generate significant daily overall fuel-cost savings (*Lloyd's List*, 2013e).

One recent study concludes that mandatory slow steaming is legally feasible either under a global agreement or unilaterally as a condition of entry to a port and that it entails both benefits and costs (Faber et al., 2012). Another study analysing four maritime routes finds that the cost of slow steaming for shippers and consignees (inventory costs, waiting time, interest, insurance and depreciation) does not make slow steaming viable at the supply chain level (*Lloyd's List*, 2013f). For shippers, the long-term acceptability and sustainability of slow steaming rest on their ability to adapt their global supply chains, production and distribution to longer transit times while preserving reliability and predictability of services. Adapting to slow steaming can be more challenging for shippers that are operating lean and just-in-time techniques and who may need to reconfigure their production and distribution (*Lloyd's List*, 2013g). Another concern relates to the technical requirements associated with slow steaming and the need to retrofit engines on existing ships which generates additional costs (Wiesmann, 2010).

2. Lower-sulphur fuels and air emissions

Fuel costs are also being affected by the requirement of the International Maritime Organization (IMO) International Convention for the Prevention of Pollution from Ships (MARPOL) Annex VI, governing air pollution and Emission Control Areas (ECAs) in the European Union and North America (for additional information see chapter 5). In 2020, the amount of sulphur allowed in marine fuels will be lowered from 3.5 per cent to 0.5 per cent globally and from a current 1.0 per cent to 0.1 per cent in 2015 for ships sailing though ECAs.

Restricting sulphur content in marine fuels and requiring less-polluting fuels, namely distillate grade, is crucial to reducing air pollution and its adverse effects on human health and the environment. In this respect, it is worth noting that the 7 per cent (or €58.4 billion) contribution of shipping emissions to the total health costs in Europe in 2000 is likely to increase to 12 per cent (€64.1 billion) in 2020, while in the ECAs of the Baltic Sea and North Sea, a drop in the sulphur dioxide emissions will likely cause a 36 per cent reduction in Europe's public health costs arising from international shipping. In value terms this implies a cost reduction from €22 billion in 2000 to €14.1 billion in 2020 (European Commission, 2013).

While the benefits of using less-polluting fuels are not called into question, by affecting the quality and the cost of fuel, the requirement to reduce air emissions entails, nevertheless, some implications for the future of residual fuel, oil refineries, technologies such as exhaust cleaning systems and alternative fuels. Switching fuels could also raise transport costs as shown by a study commissioned by the European Community Shipowners' Association (Dynaliners, 2013). The study forecasts that a switch in fuel types would result in a 11.5 per cent to 20 per cent increase in the average freight rates along 16 Baltic trade routes. One concern facing the industry is whether lower-sulphur fuels will be available at sufficient levels and at affordable rates. While some argue that fuels will be produced to meet the demand, the costs are expected to be significant with the price differential with residual fuels currently estimated at 50 per cent (*Lloyd's List*, 2013h). Bearing in mind the varied concerns, the IMO proposed to conduct a fuel-availability study for 2018 that may suggest postponing the 2020 global reduction by four years. In Europe however, the requirement will be mandatory by 2020 with no fuel-availability study being envisaged; in the meantime, it would appear that the shipping industry remains somewhat hesitant to invest heavily in scrubbers given outstanding concerns over their cost-efficiency and their fitness for use on ocean-going ships (*Lloyd's List*, 2013h).

A potential side effect of lower-sulphur regulations in shipping is the rise in road-transport fuel prices as ships, trucks and cars compete for distillates (*Lloyd's*

List, 2013h). Another factor that could potentially affect bunker demand is the use of natural gas as fuel. Although limited so far, recent contracting includes two gas-powered container ships for use in the United States ECAs (Clarkson Research Services, 2012f). The availability of gas at relatively lower prices makes natural gas an economically and environmentally attractive proposition (*Seatrade*, 2013). However, it may take time for gas-powered ships to be widely used, especially on the mainlane container trade. As far as containerized trade is concerned, gas-powered ships are not thought to be viable for the next two or three decades (*Seatrade*, 2013). At present there seems to be a "chicken and egg" situation whereby carriers are reluctant to invest in gas-powered ships as requisite bunkering infrastructure is yet to be made available, while ports remain uncertain about the benefits of developing bunkering facilities when there is no global gas-powered fleet (*Ports & Harbors*, 2013).

3. Innovative ship designs and eco-ships

By all standards the era of cheap oil is probably over and combined with depressed market fundamentals, high fuel costs and rising environmental regulation, demands for more fuel-efficient and eco-friendly maritime transportation systems are set to intensify. In this context, innovative ship designs are increasingly being sought by industry as the answer to the fuel costs/revenue/environmental sustainability conundrum.

The term "eco-ship" is currently a buzzword in the shipping industry. While an established definition of the concept is yet to emerge, eco-ships can be described as ships that, through the process of hull, engine design and new technologies, make significant savings on costs, with the main savings being on the engine fuel consumption (Roussanoglou, 2013). An additional feature of these ships is their environmental friendliness as reduced fuel consumption generates lower air emissions, including greenhouse gas (GHG) emissions and air pollutants. Many experimental designs and concepts for eco-friendly ships (for example, wind and solar power) are being reported, but their application in the near future remains doubtful (Haider et al., 2013). The standards provided by the Energy Efficiency Design Index (EEDI) adopted in July 2011 under the auspices of IMO – which became mandatory on 1 January 2013 for all newbuildings of 400 gross tonnage (GT) and above – will no doubt significantly influence the design of the first generation of eco-ships (Haider et al., 2013).

The emergence of eco-ships is causing a serious dilemma for shipowners, especially in the context of depressed freight markets, lower earnings, excess ship capacity, finance shortage, stricter environmental regulation and expanding slow-steaming practice. Shipowners are struggling to determine whether to invest in new eco-ships or make the requisite adjustments and improvements to a relatively young large existing fleet to ensure its optimization (Haider et al., 2013). These considerations are dividing the industry and raising many questions which amplify the prevailing uncertainties and financial risks. What heightens this dilemma is the potential market segmentation that may result depending on decisions made today. With the arrival of eco-ships it is possible that a gap between eco-ships and existing ships – considered less efficient – will further deepen and split the shipping market into tiers (Haider et al., 2013). Eco-ships are expected to be almost 30 per cent more fuel-efficient than the current generation of ships (Haider et al., 2013). For example, the new Triple-E ships are reported to consume approximately 35 per cent less fuel per container than the 13,100-TEU ships being delivered to other container shipping lines. The E-class ships are also expected to reduce CO_2 emissions by more than 50 per cent per container moved, compared to the industry average CO_2 performance on the Asia–Europe trade (Building the world's biggest ship, 2013). The division in the industry is tangible with proponents of eco-ships promising significant improvements in relation to the existing fleet (Roussanoglou, 2013) and with sceptics arguing that the claimed benefits of these new ships are yet to be verified (Haider et al., 2013).

Although the importance of cutting the cost of fuel and reducing emissions of all kinds is never called into question, there remains the need to bring more clarity about some outstanding issues including, for example, whether eco-ships constitute a good investment for the future and whether they will provide a more competitive solution in the market. This being said, the deciding factor will be fuel costs, which are set to remain elevated (BIMCO, 2013).

4. Panama Canal expansion

Operational for nearly one century, the Panama Canal is a critical node in international trade and a key asset which connects the East Coast of the United States and Gulf ports with Asia, Oceania, and developing America. The Panama Canal serves more than 144 maritime routes connecting 160 countries and reaching some 1,700 ports in the world (Maritime Services - PanCanal.com, 2013). Total crossings in the Panama Canal reached 12,862 in 2012. Of this total, 3,331 crossings were attributed to container ships (*Bloomberg*, 2013). During the year, more than 300 million tons (Panama Canal/Universal Measurement System (PC/UMS)) of cargo were handled at the canal.

Large-sized ships are increasingly dominating the international shipping networks and the limitations of the Panama Canal's lock system prevent the waterway from accommodating the operation of ships surpassing the Panamax standard, that is, of a capacity of up to 5,100 TEUs. In view of this, and of the rapidly growing international trade flows causing severe capacity constraints, a major expansion project worth $5.25 billion was launched in 2006 to expand the capacity of the canal. The expansion project, which is set to conclude in 2015, will add a third set of locks to the canal system as well as deepen and widen existing channels.

In addition to allowing the passage of an ever-growing number of "post-Panamax" ships with an estimated cut-off point of around 13,500 TEUs, the expansion aims to reduce delays and costs. The Panama Canal Authority estimates the cost savings that will accrue to shippers from economies of scale to range between 7 per cent and 17 per cent (Mid-America Freight Coalition, 2011). Probably the first direct impact of the upgraded canal will be felt by the West Coast ports of the United States and the intermodal land bridge (rail connections using double-stacked rail transport) linking the Pacific and the Atlantic coasts. As the land bridge provides a slightly faster connection, the competition with the Panama Canal is an important consideration and the way in which the West Coast ports and railroads prepare to respond to the canal expansion will determine the extent of the competition. Rail companies in the United States are already engaged in corridor development and inland terminal initiatives (Lower, 2013).

Another overall likely impact is a change in the shipping dynamics of various traded goods induced by a change in not only the economies of scale, but also the toll structure and reduced transit times. While the expansion initially aimed to attract shipments from Asia to the East Coast of the United States, other goods and regions are emerging as potentially important users of the new canal. By allowing larger tonnage to pass, a number of markets, commodities and goods can be expected to benefit. Examples include the following: (a) grain moving from the United States East Coast/Gulf ports to Asia (Mid-America Freight Coalition, 2011); (b) soybean moving from developing America to Asia; (c) coal and iron-ore shipments from Colombia, the Bolivarian Republic of Venezuela and Brazil with destinations in Asia; (d) coal shipments from the East Coast of the United States to Asia, in particular China; (e) oil flowing from Ecuador to the East Coast of the United States; (f) gas cargo originating from Trinidad and destined for consumption in Chile; (g) gas exports from the United States to Asia. Other important potential impacts of the canal modifications include the development of large trans-shipment capacity and points for relay services in the Caribbean area (Rodrigue and Notteboom, 2012), and the reduction of carbon emissions from shipping, a side effect that remains largely unacknowledged (Stott and Wright, 2012).

In addition to the physical expansion, a number of considerations could affect the ability of the expanded Panama Canal to position itself as a key strategic maritime route and international trade asset. These include, among others:

- Developments in fuel prices;
- Sourcing decisions;
- Delivery times;
- The redistribution of manufacturing base to other locations;
- Shifts in the source of global demand towards developing regions and away from traditional locations and partners (Rodrigue and Notteboom, 2012);
- The extent to which ports will be able to handle efficiently the loading and unloading operations involving the larger post-Panamax ships;
- The effect of port investments on both coasts of the United States and the underlying competition;
- The canal fees and how they will affect its competitiveness (*Bloomberg*, 2013).

How other routes such as the Suez Canal respond to the Panama Canal expansion will also be important. It should be noted, however, that while these two passages are considered to be competitors to some extent, they also share complementarity given a renewed development of round-the-world equatorial liner services which benefit both canals (*Bloomberg*, 2013).

While the expansion of the Panama Canal entails numerous implications, these remain nevertheless, difficult to assess with any great degree of certainty. An expansion project of the scale of the Panama Canal involves multiple players and is subject to many unknowns given, in particular, global economic uncertainties and rapid advances in technology, including in ship size and design.

In conclusion and as noted in the present chapter and reiterated in previous editions of this *Review*, a number of trends are unfolding globally and are likely to shape the future of maritime transportation and deeply redefine its operating landscape. By way of recapitulation and while not intended as an exhaustive list, key trends currently at play and requiring further monitoring and assessment include the following:

(a) Continued negative effect of the 2008/2009 crisis on global demand, finance and trade;

(b) Structural shifts in global production patterns;

(c) Changes in comparative advantages and mineral resource endowments;

(d) Rise of the South and shift of economic influence away from traditional centres of growth;

(e) Demographics, with ageing populations in advanced economies and fast-growing populations in developing regions, with related implications for global production and consumption patterns;

(f) The arrival of container megaships and other transport-related technological advances;

(g) Climate change and natural hazards;

(h) Energy costs and environmental sustainability.

By redefining production, consumption, growth and trade patterns and dynamics, and by altering shipping networks and configurations, these trends are likely to also deeply transform international shipping and ports that, respectively, carries and handle 80 per cent of the volume of global merchandise trade and a significant share of its value.

REFERENCES

Bernhofen DM, El-Sahli Z and Kneller R (2013). Estimating the effects of the container revolution on world trade. CESifo Working Paper Series 4136. CESifo, Center for Economic Studies and Ifo Institute. Munich.

BIMCO (2013). Reflections 2013. Available at https://www.bimco.org/About/Press/Reflections.aspx.

Bloomberg (2013). Maersk line to dump Panama Canal for Suez as ships get bigger. 11 March.

British Petroleum (2013). Statistical review of world energy 2013. June.

Building the world's biggest ship – Maersk (2013). Maersk. See http://www.maersk.com/innovation/leadingthroughinnovation/pages/buildingtheworldsbiggestship.aspx (accessed 29 July 2013).

Clarkson Research Services (2012a). *Dry Bulk Trade Outlook.* 18(5).

Clarkson Research Services (2012b). *Oil and Tanker Trades Outlook.* 17(9).

Clarkson Research Services (2012c). *LNG Trade and Transport.* ISBN: 978-1-903352-87-8. London.

Clarkson Research Services (2012d). *Shipping Review and Outlook.* Autumn 2012.

Clarkson Research Services (2012e). *Dry Bulk Trade Outlook.* 18(11).

Clarkson Research Services (2012f). *Container intelligence monthly.* 14(5).

Clarkson Research Services (2013a). *Shipping Review and Outlook.* Spring 2013.

Clarkson Research Services (2013b). *Container Intelligence Monthly.* 15(6).

Clarkson Research Services (2013c). *Dry Bulk Trade Outlook.* 19(4).

Clarksons Shipping Services (2013). *Dry Bulk Trade Outlook.* 19(6).

Containerisation International (2013a). Peaks and troughs. June.

Containerisation International (2013b). Stuck in the Slow Lane. May.

Crowe T (2012). Seaborne trade: The long and the short of it. Clarkson Research Services. 7 September.

Danish Ship Finance (2013). Shipping market review. April. Available at http://www.shipfinance.dk/~/~/media/Shipping-Market-Review/Shipping-Market-Review---April-2013.ashx (accessed 10 September 2013).

Drewry Shipping Consultants (2013). Can Africa do it? March.

Dynaliners (2013). Trade review 2013. Dynamar B.V.

Dynamar B.V. (2013). *Dynaliners weekly.* 26(13).

Economist Intelligence Unit (2013). Global outlook. Country forecast, May 2013. Available at http://gfs.eiu.com/FileHandler.ashx?issue_id=1750391159&mode=pdf (accessed 17 September 2013).

Ernst and Young (2011). *Trading Places: The Emergence of New Patterns of International Trade.* Ernst Young and Oxford Economics. EYG No. AU1000. Available at http://emergingmarkets.ey.com/wp-content/uploads/downloads/2011/11/TBF_212__International_trade_white_paper_v24_Low_Res2.pdf (accessed 9 September 2013).

European Commission (2013). Science for environmental policy. Public health costs of air pollution fall in Europe but remain high for maritime shipping. Issue 324. European Commission. 27 June. Available at http://ec.europa.eu/environment/integration/research/newsalert/pdf/334na4.pdf (accessed 16 September 2013).

Faber J, Nelissen D, Hon G, Wang H and Tsimplis M (2012). Regulated slow steaming in maritime transport: An assessment of options, costs and benefits. CE Delft. Delft.

Fairplay (2013a). Africa's maritime structural transformation. 30 May.

Fairplay (2013b). Energized Africa powers shipping. 9 May.

Financial Times (2013). Oil tanker trade growth is fastest in a decade. 12 May.

International Energy Agency (2012). *World Energy Outlook 2012.* Paris.

International Energy Agency (2013). *World Energy Outlook Special Report: Redrawing the Energy-Climate Map.* Available at www.worldenergyoutlook.org/energyclimatemap (accessed 12 September 2013).

International Grains Council (2013). *Grain Market Report.* 436, 30 August. Available at http://www.igc.int/en/downloads/gmrsummary/gmrsumme.pdf (accessed 17 September 2013).

International Monetary Fund (2013). *World Economic Outlook: Hopes, Realities and Risks*. International Monetary Fund. ISBN 978-1-61635-555-5. Washington.

Larsen J (2013). Global grain stocks drop dangerously low as 2012 consumption exceeded production. Earth Policy Institute. 17 January. Available at http://www.earth-policy.org/indicators/C54/grain_2013 (accessed 11 September 2013).

Lloyd's List (2012a). Get ready for a new world oil map. 12 October.

Lloyd's List (2012b). Washington faces growing pressure to export the US crude. 13 May.

Lloyd's List (2013a). Maersk made the first move to form P3 alliance. 20 June.

Lloyd's List (2013b). Another lost year? 3 July.

Lloyd's List (2013c). Nearsourcing: Homespun yarn or material change? 13 June.

Lloyd's List (2013d). Fuel efficiency is shipping's top concern. 15 March.

Lloyd's List (2013e). Bunker Quarterly: Full slow steaming ahead. 6 June.

Lloyd's List (2013f). Shippers lose out in slow steaming. 7 January.

Lloyd's List (2013g). Lower speeds boost box schedule reliability. 7 January.

Lloyd's List (2013h). Owners opt for scrubbers as SOx emissions deadlines loom. July.

Lower J (2013). Panama Canal expansion fueling US investments. 13 June. Available at http://bizmology.hoovers.com/2013/06/13/panama-canal-expansion-fueling-us-investments/ (accessed 11 September 2013).

Maritime Services – PanCanal.com (2013). Panama Canal Authority. See http://www.pancanal.com/eng/op/transit-stats/index.html (accessed 29 July 2013).

Mid-America Freight Coalition (2011). The far reaching effects of canal expansion. 16 March. Available at http://midamericafreight.org/2011/03/panama-canal-expansion/ (accessed 16 September 2013).

OECD (2011). Strategic transport infrastructure needs to 2030. OECD publising. Paris. Available at http://dx.doi.org/10.1787/9789264114425-en (accessed 9 September 2013).

OPEC (2012). *World Oil Outlook 2012*. ISBN 978-3-9502722-4-6. OPEC secretariat. Vienna.

P.M. News Nigeria (2013). Nigeria's free trade zones attract $9.4b investment. 3 July.

Ports and Harbors (2013). European Commission sets LNG bunkering target. International Association of Ports and Harbors. *Ports and Harbors*. 58(3).

Research and Markets (2012). The market for coal power plants in Europe (analyst version) – market volumes – projects – strategies – trends.

Rodrigue J-P and Notteboom T (2012). The Panama Canal expansion: business as usual or game-changer? *Port Technology International*. 51:10–12.

Roussanoglou N (2013). Eco-ships growing in numbers, could undermine value of older ships. Hellenic Shipping News Worldwide. June.

Seatrade (2013). Gas fuel going mainstream. March.

Shipping and Finance (2013). Boom in commodities trade by 2025, due to one billion people entering consuming class. May.

Stott P and Wright P (2012). The Panama Canal expansion: business as usual or game changer for ship design? *Port Technology International*. 53:27–28.

UNCTAD (2013). *Trade and Development Report, 2013*. United Nations publication. UNCTAD/TDR/2013. New York and Geneva.

United Nations (2012). *The Global Partnership for Development: Making Rhetoric a Reality*. MDG Gap Task Force Report 2012. United Nations publication. Sales No. E.12.I.5. New York.

United Nations Department of Economic and Social Affairs (2013a). World economic situation and prospects. Monthly briefing, January.

United Nations Department of Economic and Social Affairs (2013b). World economic situation and prospects. Update as of mid-2013.

United Nations Department of Economic and Social Affairs (2013c). World economic situation and prospects. Monthly briefing, April.

United Nations Development Programme (2013). *Human Development Report 2013. The Rise of the South: Human Progress in a Diverse World*. United Nations publication. ISBN 978-92-1-126340-4. New York.

United States Geological Survey (2013). *Mineral Commodity Summaries 2013*. United States Geological Survey. ISBN 978–1–4113–3548–6. Washington DC.

United States Institute of Peace (2012). U.S. renews Iran sanctions waivers December. Available at http://iranprimer.usip.org/blog/2012/dec/10/us-renews-iran-sanctions-waivers (accessed 10 September 2012).

Voice of America News (2013). BRICS leaders optimistic about new development bank. 27 March.

Wiesmann A (2010). Slow steaming – a viable long-term option? *Wärtsila Technical Journal*. February.

World Shipping Council (2008). Record fuel prices places stress on ocean shipping. May.

World Steel Association (2013a). World crude steel output increases by 1.2% in 2012. January.

World Steel Association (2013b). Short Range Outlook. April.

WTO (2013). World trade 2012, prospects for 2013. WTO press release 688. 10 April.

ENDNOTES

[1] Average distances and rates of change are calculated on the basis of more recent data published in Clarkson Research Services (2013a).

[2] Based on data from Clarkson Research Services. Data on LPG trade covers OECD only.

2

STRUCTURE, OWNERSHIP AND REGISTRATION OF THE WORLD FLEET

This chapter presents the supply side of the shipping industry. It covers the vessel types, age profile, ownership and registration of the world fleet. The chapter also reviews deliveries, demolitions and tonnage on order.

The year 2012 saw the turn of the largest shipbuilding cycle in recorded history. Between 2001 and 2011, year after year, newbuilding deliveries reached new historical highs. Only in 2012, for the first time since 2001, was the fleet that entered into service during the year less than that delivered during the previous 12 months. In spite of this slowing down of new deliveries, the world tonnage continued to grow in 2012, albeit at a slower pace than in 2011. The world fleet has more than doubled since 2001, reaching 1.63 billion deadweight tons (dwt) in January 2013.

Since the historical peaks of 2008 and 2009, the tonnage on order for all major vessel types has decreased drastically. As shipyards continued to deliver pre-ordered tonnage, the orderbooks went down by 50 per cent for container ships, 58 per cent for dry-bulk carriers, 65 per cent for tankers and by 67 per cent for general-cargo ships. At the end of 2008, the dry-bulk order book was equivalent to almost 80 per cent of the fleet at that time, while the tonnage on order as of January 2013 is the equivalent of just 20 per cent of the fleet in service.

Chapter 2 of this year's Review presents unique fleet profiles for 48 major ship-owning developing countries. Several oil- and gas-exporting countries are also important owners of oil- and liquefied-gas tanker tonnage, both under their respective national as well as under foreign flags. By the same token, countries with important offshore investments also tend to own offshore supply ships. Dry-bulk ships are less often controlled by the cargo-owning countries than is the case of the oil-exporting nations. Most container ships are foreign flagged as they engage in international trade, serving routes that connect several countries at the same time. Many of the general-cargo fleets are nationally flagged and serve the coastal or inter-island cabotage trades.

This year's chapter 2 also presents a special focus on 10 years of UNCTAD's Liner Shipping Connectivity Index (LSCI) and the related analysis of container ship deployment. The last 10 years have seen two important trends, which represent two sides of the same coin. On the one hand, ships have become bigger, and on the other hand the number of companies in most markets has diminished. As regards the number of companies, the average per country has decreased by 27 per cent during the last 10 years, from 22 in 2004 to just 16 in 2013. This trend has important implications for the level of competition, especially for smaller trading nations. While an average of 16 service providers may still be sufficient to ensure a functioning competitive market with many choices for shippers for the average country, on given individual routes, especially those serving smaller developing countries, the decline in competition has led to oligopolistic markets.

A. STRUCTURE OF THE WORLD FLEET

1. World fleet growth and principal vessel types

The growth of the world fleet [1]

The year 2012 saw the turn of the largest shipbuilding cycle, in terms of GT, in recorded history. Between 2001 and 2011, year after year, newbuilding deliveries reached new historical highs. Even after the economic downturn of 2008, the dead-weight tonnage delivered annually continued to increase for three more years due to orders that had largely been placed prior to the crisis. Only in 2012, for the first time since 2001, was the fleet that entered into service during the year less than that delivered during the previous 12 months.

In spite of this slowing down of new deliveries, the world tonnage continued to grow in 2012, albeit at a slower pace; year-on-year growth amounted to 6 per cent, compared to a 10 per cent increase the previous year. The world fleet more than doubled since 2001, reaching 1.63 billion dwt in January 2013 (figure 2.1 and table 2.1).

The turning point in the shipbuilding cycle is further evidenced in figure 2.3, which illustrates the age structure of the existing fleet. There was more tonnage built in 2011 (that is, 2 years old in figure 2.3) than tonnage built in 2012. Such a large weakening has not been seen since the mid-1990s. The turning point is also visible in figure 2.10, which shows that the order book had already started to regress in 2009.

The numbers in the shipping fleet react only slowly to a changing economic environment. While the downturn in demand became clear in 2008, the order book showed a decline in 2009, new deliveries went down in 2012, and the existing fleet still continues to grow in 2013. The order book, however, is rapidly decreasing, and the current schedule only provides for output of close to recent levels for this year and a little less so for 2014.

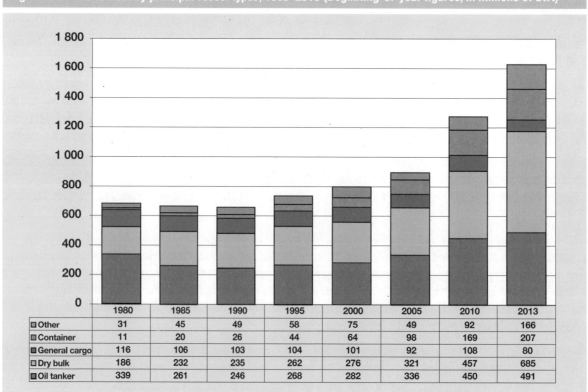

Figure 2.1. World fleet by principal vessel types, 1980–2013 (Beginning-of-year figures, in millions of dwt)

	1980	1985	1990	1995	2000	2005	2010	2013
Other	31	45	49	58	75	49	92	166
Container	11	20	26	44	64	98	169	207
General cargo	116	106	103	104	101	92	108	80
Dry bulk	186	232	235	262	276	321	457	685
Oil tanker	339	261	246	268	282	336	450	491

Source: Compiled by the UNCTAD secretariat, on the basis of data supplied by Clarkson Research Services and previous issues of the *Review of Maritime Transport*.

Note: All propelled seagoing merchant vessels of 100 GT and above, excluding inland waterway vessels, fishing vessels, military vessels, yachts, and offshore fixed and mobile platforms and barges (with the exception of floating production storage and offloading units (FPSOs) and drillships).

The world fleet in January 2013 consists of 42 per cent dry-bulk tonnage (in dwt), a historical record for this vessel type. General-cargo tonnage, on the other hand, continued its decline; its share of the world total is now less than 5 per cent, down from a 15 per cent share 20 years ago. Oil tankers, too, saw their share decline, from almost half of the world tonnage in 1980, to 30 per cent in January 2013 (table 2.1 and Annex II).

Table 2.1.	World fleet by principal vessel types, 2012–2013 (Beginning-of-year figures, thousands of dwt; percentage share in italics)		
Principal types	2012	2013	Percentage change 2013/2012
Oil tankers	469 516	490 743	4.5%
	30.6%	*30.1%*	*-0.4%*
Bulk carriers	623 006	684 673	9.9%
	40.5%	*42.0%*	*1.5%*
General cargo ships	80 825	80 345	-0.6%
	5.3%	*4.9%*	*-0.3%*
Container ships	196 853	206 577	4.9%
	12.8%	*12.7%*	*-0.1%*
Other types:	166 667	166 445	-0.1%
	10.8%	*10.2%*	*-0.6%*
Gas carriers	44 060	44 346	0.6%
	2.9%	*2.7%*	*-0.1%*
Chemical tankers	23 238	23 293	0.2%
	1.5%	*1.4%*	*-0.1%*
Offshore	70 767	69 991	-1.1%
	4.6%	*4.3%*	*-0.3%*
Ferries and passenger ships	5 466	5 504	0.7%
	0.4%	*0.3%*	*0.0%*
Other/n.a.	23 137	23 312	0.8%
	1.5%	*1.4%*	*-0.1%*
World total	1 536 868	1 628 783	6.0%
	100%	*100%*	*0.0%*

Source: Compiled by the UNCTAD secretariat, on the basis of data supplied by Clarkson Research Services.
Note: Propelled seagoing merchant vessels of 100 GT and above.

Oil tankers

Following heavy scrapping and conversions of single-hull ships in recent years, most oil tankers are now double hulled, in compliance with relevant IMO environmental and safety regulations, as well as the Oil Pollution Act of the United States of America, which phased out single-hull tankers from United States waters in 2010. After the renovation of the fleet, today only 14 per cent of tanker tonnage is 15 years or older.

When the last single-hulled very large crude carrier (VLCC) was delivered in 1996, there were 376 in service. In early 2013, there are only three. Only 243, however, were actually scrapped. Sixty were converted into floating oil production and storage facilities and 70 were converted into dry-bulk carriers. Some of the older VLCCs are deployed as FPSOs (*Shipping Intelligence Weekly, 2013*).

Bulk carriers

The largest existing ships in operation for ocean transport are dry bulkers owned and operated by the Brazilian iron-ore conglomerate Vale, called "Vale-max". In April 2013, the latest vessel of this series, the *Vale Korea*, entered into service, with a capacity of 402,303 dwt. While initially built to call in Chinese ports, Vale is now developing trans-shipment hubs in Malaysia and the Philippines as the ships are not allowed to enter ports in China fully loaded. Due to regulatory limitations in China, Vale-max ships that entered Chinese ports in early 2013 were registered as just under 300,000 dwt.

In 2012, seven times more tonnage of bulk carriers was delivered than 10 years earlier. At the same time, the order book is dwindling, amounting today to just one fifth of the existing fleet (Clarkson Research Services, 2013a).

General-cargo ships

General-cargo vessels – sometimes also referred to as "break-bulk" ships – have seen their importance decline over the last decades, largely to the benefit of container ships. As more and more goods are containerized, the market for carriage by break-bulk cargo ships has dropped.

Nevertheless, some goods, in particular dry cargo that is too large for containers, will always require transport as break-bulk. The specialized break-bulk fleet has been modernized in recent years, as most older ships were demolished. According to a recent report by Dynamar (Dynamar, 2013), among the almost 800 ships deployed by the 25 largest specialized operators, fewer than 100 are older than 25 years, with only a small number still dating from the 1970s. With over 500 units built since 2000, the majority of the specialized fleet consists of modern, highly productive and multi-employable ships that carry a wide range of cargoes, from forest products to bags and project cargoes.

Container ships

Container ships carry an estimated 52 per cent of global seaborne trade in terms of value (World Shipping Council, 2013). Their share of the world fleet has grown almost eightfold since 1980, as goods are increasingly containerized for international transport. Apart from manufactured goods, more and more commodities (such as coffee) as well as refrigerated cargo (fruit, meat, fish) are today largely transported in standardized sea containers.

Most new container ships today are gearless, that is, they are no longer equipped with their own container-handling cranes, but depend on the seaports to provide specialized handling equipment. This trend goes hand-in-hand with the delivery of larger vessels, as these are less often equipped with their own cargo-handling equipment. This poses a challenge for smaller ports, especially in developing countries, which may not have enough volume to justify investment in specialized and costly ship-to-shore cranes in their container terminals.

The share of gearless ships among the total deliveries of container vessels keeps increasing. In 2005, there were four times more gearless ships delivered than ships with their own handling equipment, while in 2012 the proportion was 6 to 1 (table 2.2 and figure 2.2). Gearless container ships are on average more than twice the size than geared vessels, and the average size of both types of ships has gone up by almost 80 per cent since 2005.

The year 2013 also saw the delivery of the first "Triple E" container ships by Daewoo in the Republic of Korea to Maersk in Denmark. The Triple E stands for energy efficiency, economies of scale and environmental improvements. For a short period these ships, with a declared container-carrying capacity of 18,000 full TEUs, were the largest container ships, taking over from the 16,000-TEU vessels of CMA CGM, which were the largest container vessels until early 2013. In 2013, CSCL from China placed orders for even larger container ships, also in shipyards in the Republic of Korea, scheduled to carry 18,400 TEU and to be delivered in 2014.

Other types

Chemical tankers have seen a trend towards larger vessels, aiming at economies of scale. The share of ships above 36,000 dwt has increased from 23 per cent in 2005 to 28 per cent today, while the share of the smallest units (below 10,000 dwt) went down from 47 per cent to 40 per cent during the same period (*Fairplay, 2013*).

Table 2.2.	Container ship deliveries								
	Gearless			Geared			Total		
Year built	Ships	TEU	Average vessel size (TEU)	Ships	TEU	Average vessel size (TEU)	Ships	TEU	Average vessel size (TEU)
2005	217	847 530	3 906	55	96 010	1 746	272	943 540	3 469
2006	285	1 237 630	4 343	86	142 104	1 652	371	1 379 734	3 719
2007	297	1 166 968	3 929	102	148 268	1 454	399	1 315 236	3 296
2008	321	1 319 897	4 112	114	181 322	1 591	435	1 501 219	3 451
2009	204	978 900	4 799	72	127 394	1 769	276	1 106 294	4 008
2010	217	1 297 291	5 978	48	92 117	1 919	265	1 389 408	5 243
2011	159	1 126 977	7 088	32	83 728	2 617	191	1 210 705	6 339
2012	172	1 161 695	6 754	29	89 476	3 085	201	1 251 171	6 225

Source: Compiled by the UNCTAD secretariat, on the basis of data supplied by Clarkson Research Services.
Note: Fully cellular container ships of 100 GT and above.

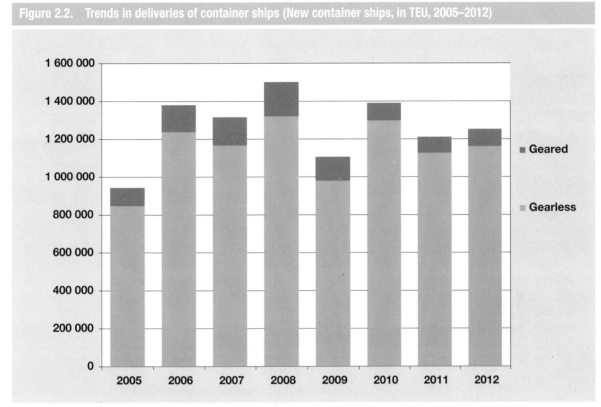

Figure 2.2.   Trends in deliveries of container ships (New container ships, in TEU, 2005–2012)

Source: Compiled by the UNCTAD secretariat, based on data provided by Clarkson Research Services.

2. Age distribution of the world merchant fleet

In January 2013, 20 per cent of all seagoing merchant ships were younger than 5 years, representing 40 per cent of the world's deadweight tonnage (see table 2.3 and figure 2.3). Ships delivered in more recent years are on average larger than older ships. New container ships are on average three times the size of those built 20 or more years ago, and only 5 per cent of the container ship tonnage is older than 20 years. Oil tankers, too, tend to be replaced relatively early; only 4 per cent of the existing oil-tanker tonnage was built more than 20 years ago.

The average age (per ship) in January 2013 was highest for general-cargo ships (25 years), followed by other types (22.6 years), oil tankers (16.7 years), container ships (10.8 years) and dry-bulk carriers (9.9 years). Following

the surge of newbuildings in the dry-bulk segment, almost half of the dry-bulk dead weight tonnage is only 4 years old or younger, overtaking for the first time container ships as the youngest vessel category.

As a reflection of most recent ships being larger than older ones, the global average age per ship shows an age of 20.3 years, while the average age by dwt is 9.6 years. Their geographical distribution is also well balanced and ships registered in developing countries are now only slightly older (two years) than those flying the flag of developed countries. Among the 10 major flag states, Greece has the oldest fleet, followed by Panama and China. The youngest fleets are those registered in the Marshall Islands, Hong Kong (China) and Singapore. On average, foreign-flagged ships are slightly younger than nationally flagged ones. This situation and its rationale are discussed below.

Figure 2.3.   Age structure of world fleet, national and foreign flags

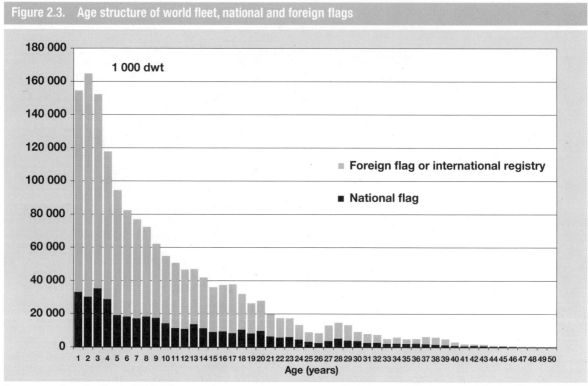

Source: Compiled by the UNCTAD secretariat, on the basis of data from Clarkson Research Services.
Note: For vessels of 1,000 GT and above.

**Table 2.3.   Age distribution of the world merchant fleet, by vessel type, as of 1 January 2013
(Percentage of total ships and dwt)**

Country grouping Types of vessels		0–4 years	5–9 years	10–14 years	15–19 years	20 years and +	Average age (years) 2013	Average age (years) 2012	Percentage change 2013/2012
WORLD									
Bulk carriers	**Bulk carriers Ships**	44	15	12	13	16	9.94	11.57	-1.63
	Dwt	49	16	11	13	11	8.36	9.71	-1.35
	Average vessel size (dwt)	81 514	75 173	65 405	71 528	48 211			
Container ships	**Ships**	23	29	18	20	10	10.81	10.73	0.08
	Dwt	34	32	16	13	5	8.25	8.24	0.01
	Average vessel size (dwt)	59 547	43 782	37 049	26 750	19 962			
General cargo	**Ships**	12	11	7	12	58	24.99	24.58	0.41
	Dwt	22	13	10	10	44	19.10	19.61	-0.51
	Average vessel size (dwt)	7 396	5 237	6 845	3 705	3 081			
Oil tankers	**Ships**	24	20	10	12	34	16.74	16.50	0.25
	Dwt	37	28	20	10	4	8.14	8.01	0.13
	Average vessel size (dwt)	69 029	64 212	87 809	35 925	5 921			
Others	**Ships**	17	13	10	10	50	22.57	22.29	0.28
	Dwt	23	20	13	10	34	16.07	15.84	0.23
	Average vessel size (dwt)	6 985	8 251	6 898	5 119	3 968			
All ships	**Ships**	20	15	10	12	44	20.34	20.30	0.03
	Dwt	40	22	14	12	12	9.60	10.19	-0.59
	Average vessel size (dwt)	40 664	32 047	31 610	21 098	6 267			

Table 2.3.	Age distribution of the world merchant fleet, by vessel type, as of 1 January 2013 (Percentage of total ships and dwt) *(continued)*								
Country grouping Types of vessels		0–4 years	5–9 years	10–14 years	15–19 years	20 years and +	Average age (years) 2013	Average age (years) 2012	Percentage change 2013/2012
DEVELOPING ECONOMIES									
Bulk carriers	Ships	41	10	9	16	24	11.77	13.99	-2.22
	Dwt	48	10	8	17	16	9.76	11.76	-2.00
	Average vessel size (dwt)	80 772	65 854	60 514	75 693	47 053			
Container ships	Ships	21	23	15	25	17	12.83	13.06	-0.23
	Dwt	36	28	12	17	7	8.63	9.18	-0.55
	Average vessel size (dwt)	56 530	41 481	28 210	22 545	13 619			
General cargo	Ships	11	12	5	8	63	25.38	24.95	0.43
	Dwt	19	12	6	9	53	21.02	21.79	-0.78
	Average vessel size (dwt)	6 396	4 194	5 808	4 342	3 102			
Oil tankers	Ships	24	14	7	12	43	18.69	18.61	0.08
	Dwt	43	23	15	12	8	8.42	8.51	-0.09
	Average vessel size (dwt)	64 176	59 987	74 818	37 046	6 404			
Others	Ships	20	15	9	11	45	20.19	20.01	0.18
	Dwt	24	16	9	9	42	17.85	17.91	-0.06
	Average vessel size (dwt)	5 122	5 269	4 909	4 265	4 224			
All ships	Ships	20	14	8	11	46	20.21	20.28	-0.07
	Dwt	41	16	11	14	18	10.75	11.88	-1.13
	Average vessel size (dwt)	35 193	22 382	25 060	23 249	6 856			
DEVELOPED ECONOMIES									
Bulk carriers	Ships	46	19	14	12	9	8.31	9.28	-0.98
	Dwt	50	20	13	11	6	7.24	8.03	-0.79
	Average vessel size (dwt)	82 751	79 903	68 206	68 126	51 940			
Container ships	Ships	24	33	19	17	6	9.60	9.39	0.22
	Dwt	33	33	18	12	4	8.07	7.86	0.21
	Average vessel size (dwt)	61 076	44 622	40 797	30 302	30 536			
General cargo	Ships	16	12	11	19	41	20.89	20.57	0.32
	Dwt	28	16	16	12	29	15.38	15.65	-0.27
	Average vessel size (dwt)	8 690	6 825	7 618	3 319	3 751			
Oil tankers	Ships	26	28	15	14	17	12.59	12.13	0.46
	Dwt	34	32	24	8	2	7.88	7.59	0.29
	Average vessel size (dwt)	74 911	66 936	94 955	35 850	7 199			
Others	Ships	15	13	12	11	49	23.36	22.96	0.40
	Dwt	23	23	15	10	28	14.63	14.17	0.47
	Average vessel size (dwt)	9 764	11 817	8 684	6 534	4 971			
All ships	Ships	22	17	13	14	34	18.20	18.10	0.11
	Dwt	39	26	17	10	8	8.61	8.82	-0.21
	Average vessel size (dwt)	47 299	40 209	36 065	20 843	7 594			

Table 2.3.   Age distribution of the world merchant fleet, by vessel type, as of 1 January 2013 (Percentage of total ships and dwt) *(continued)*

Country grouping Types of vessels		0–4 years	5–9 years	10–14 years	15–19 years	20 years and +	Average age (years) 2013	Average age (years) 2012	Percentage change 2013/2012
COUNTRIES WITH ECONOMIES IN TRANSITION									
Bulk carriers	Ships	29	13	7	13	39	15.64	18.68	-3.04
	Dwt	31	11	7	13	38	15.07	18.16	-3.09
	Average vessel size (dwt)	45 120	35 203	43 734	42 427	40 694			
Container ships	Ships	13	3	17	30	37	18.20	17.27	0.93
	Dwt	30	4	15	26	25	14.59	13.66	0.94
	Average vessel size (dwt)	27 602	13 760	11 201	10 566	8 560			
General cargo	Ships	4	4	1	7	83	30.33	29.65	0.68
	Dwt	7	7	2	10	74	26.39	25.97	0.42
	Average vessel size (dwt)	6 144	6 124	5 299	4 403	2 985			
General cargo	Ships	17	14	5	5	60	22.69	22.88	-0.18
	Dwt	34	34	17	6	9	9.46	8.89	0.57
	Average vessel size (dwt)	48 168	58 518	81 964	31 915	3 636			
Oil tankers	Ships	7	5	3	5	80	28.57	27.92	0.65
	Dwt	18	13	3	3	63	21.88	21.27	0.61
	Average vessel size (dwt)	3 378	3 655	1 237	815	916			
Others	Ships	8	6	3	6	77	27.92	27.49	0.42
	Dwt	27	22	11	9	32	14.96	15.46	-0.50
	Average vessel size (dwt)	23 192	25 073	26 839	8 930	2 758			
All ships	Ships	8	6	3	6	77	27.92	27.49	0.42
	Dwt	27	22	11	9	32	14.96	15.46	-0.50
	Average vessel size (dwt)	23 192	25 073	26 839	8 930	2 758			

Source: Compiled by the UNCTAD secretariat, on the basis of data supplied by Clarkson Research Services.
Note: Propelled seagoing merchant vessels of 100 GT and above.

B.   OWNERSHIP AND OPERATION OF THE WORLD FLEET

1.   Ship-owning countries

The national concentration of fleet ownership is illustrated by the fact that owners from five countries – in order of decreasing tonnage, Greece, Japan, China, Germany and the Republic of Korea – together account for 53 per cent of the world tonnage. Among the top 35 ship-owning economies, 17 are in Asia, 14 in Europe, and 4 in the Americas (table 2.4).

In terms of vessel numbers, the largest ship-owning country is China, with 5,313 ocean-going merchant ships, out of which about half fly the national Chinese flag. This makes more nationally flagged Chinese-owned ships than nationally flagged ships from Greece, Japan and Germany combined.

Another way to consider fleet ownership is in terms of ship value. Container vessels and gas carriers, for example, are more expensive than dry and liquid bulkers. The market value of a vessel also depends on its age and maintenance. Estimates for January 2013 (Clarkson Research Services, 2013b) suggest that the Japanese-owned fleet currently reaches the highest value, amounting to almost $100 billion, followed by the United States ($92 billion), Greece ($72 billion), China ($61 billion) and Germany ($60 billion). The total of the world fleet being estimated to be worth $809 billion, the top five ship-owning countries by fleet value thus would control almost 48 per cent of the world fleet; the top 10 owner countries under this criteria would have a market share in value terms of 67 per cent.

From a registration perspective, most of the top 35 ship-owning countries have more than half of their tonnage under a foreign flag. Exceptions include

| Table 2.4. | The 35 countries and territories with the largest owned fleets, as of 1 January 2013 (Dwt) | | | | | | | |

Country or territory of ownership [a]	Number of vessels			Deadweight tonnage				
	National flag	Foreign and internat. flag [b]	Total	National flag [c]	Foreign and international flag [b]	Total	Foreign and international flag as a percentage of total [b]	Total as a percentage of world
Greece	825	2 870	3 695	69 644 624	175 205 954	244 850 578	71.56	15.17
Japan	738	3 253	3 991	17 216 128	206 598 880	223 815 008	92.31	13.87
China	2 665	2 648	5 313	66 936 002	123 142 833	190 078 835	64.79	11.78
Germany	396	3 437	3 833	16 641 757	109 136 771	125 778 528	86.77	7.79
Republic of Korea	764	812	1 576	16 624 445	58 471 361	75 095 806	77.86	4.65
Singapore	1 090	798	1 888	32 711 136	31 441 668	64 152 804	49.01	3.98
United States	768	1 175	1 943	8 671 669	49 606 395	58 278 064	85.12	3.61
United Kingdom	415	822	1 237	10 447 630	39 857 066	50 304 696	79.23	3.12
Norway	414	1 494	1 908	2 190 036	43 802 209	45 992 245	95.24	2.85
Taiwan Province of China	102	712	814	3 311 133	40 948 712	44 259 845	92.52	2.74
Denmark	45	946	991	68 724	40 646 119	40 714 843	99.83	2.52
Bermuda	4	206	210	209 778	32 686 529	32 896 307	99.36	2.04
Turkey	645	935	1 580	9 619 689	19 470 911	29 090 600	66.93	1.80
Italy	673	211	884	19 097 635	6 245 330	25 342 964	24.64	1.57
Hong Kong (China)	269	297	566	15 768 670	8 556 599	24 325 269	35.18	1.51
India	584	158	742	15 063 983	7 377 303	22 441 287	32.87	1.39
United Arab Emirates	82	617	699	700 914	18 772 655	19 473 569	96.40	1.21
Russian Federation	1 195	532	1 727	5 495 653	13 888 598	19 384 251	71.65	1.20
Malaysia	472	142	614	9 520 599	7 593 951	17 114 550	44.37	1.06
Netherlands	757	450	1 207	6 100 843	10 571 723	16 672 566	63.41	1.03
Brazil	202	108	310	2 837 889	13 314 666	16 152 555	82.43	1.00
Switzerland	39	291	330	1 144 359	14 506 537	15 650 896	92.69	0.97
Islamic Republic of Iran	108	121	229	1 748 219	13 568 542	15 316 761	88.59	0.95
Indonesia	1 383	147	1 530	11 910 441	3 390 980	15 301 421	22.16	0.95
Cyprus	183	192	375	6 178 327	7 745 606	13 923 933	55.63	0.86
France	179	230	409	3 862 058	7 144 805	11 006 863	64.91	0.68
Canada	206	145	351	2 650 551	6 571 778	9 222 329	71.26	0.57
Monaco		126	126		9 157 769	9 157 769	100.00	0.57
Belgium	90	155	245	4 008 509	4 720 024	8 728 533	54.08	0.54
Viet Nam	758	83	841	6 422 675	1 540 097	7 962 772	19.34	0.49
Saudi Arabia	62	125	187	1 036 358	6 771 973	7 808 332	86.73	0.48
Kuwait	40	36	76	4 037 837	2 862 528	6 900 365	41.48	0.43
Sweden	114	225	339	1 323 946	5 120 753	6 444 699	79.46	0.40
Oman	3	31	34	5 332	6 133 802	6 139 134	99.91	0.38
Thailand	336	79	415	4 444 401	1 652 413	6 096 814	27.10	0.38
Total top 35 countries	16 606	24 609	41 215	377 651 950	1 148 223 839	1 525 875 789	75.25	94.55
Other owners	2 655	2 522	5 177	29 703 524	52 879 452	82 582 976	64.03	5.12
Total of known country of ownership	19 261	27 131	46 392	407 355 474	1 201 103 291	1 608 458 765	74.67	99.67
Others, unknown country of ownership			730			5 297 140		0.33
World total			47 122			1 613 755 905		100

Source: Compiled by the UNCTAD secretariat, on the basis of data supplied by Clarkson Research Services.

Note: Vessels of 1,000 GT and above, ranked by deadweight tonnage.

[a]   The country of ownership indicates where the true controlling interest (that is, the parent company) of the fleet is located. In several cases, determining this has required making certain judgements. Thus, for instance, Greece is shown as the country of ownership for vessels owned by a Greek national with representative offices in New York, London and Piraeus, although the owner may be domiciled in the United States.

[b]   "Foreign and international flag" in this table includes vessels registered in second/international registers such as the Danish or Norwegian International Ship Registers (DIS or NIS respectively).

countries with a large cabotage fleet, such as India, Indonesia or Viet Nam, and countries where the national register provides a competitive flag that is also used by many foreign owners, as is the case for example for Singapore, which thus effectively become an open register.

Figure 2.4 provides 48 maritime fleet profiles, illustrating the type of ships controlled by the main developing ship-owning countries, including the share of nationally and foreign-flagged tonnage for each main vessel type.

Several oil- and gas-exporting countries are also important owners of oil and liquefied-gas tanker tonnage, both under their respective national as well as under foreign flags. Algeria, for example, has a high share of oil and liquefied-gas tankers; Argentina's fleet consists of mostly foreign-flagged oil tankers; Ecuador's oil tankers include the nationally flagged cabotage fleet (for example, to the Galapagos Islands) as well as foreign-flagged tankers servicing the international transport of Ecuador's oil exports. Other countries with a high share of oil and gas tankers are Egypt, the Islamic Republic of Iran, Kazakhstan, Kuwait, Libya, Malaysia, Mexico, Nigeria, Oman, Peru, Qatar, the Russian Federation, Saudi Arabia, the United Arab Emirates and the Bolivarian Republic of Venezuela.

By the same token, countries with important offshore investments also tend to own ships providing offshore supply services. Angola's fleet, for example, largely specializes in the oil and offshore business; Brazil, too, owns an important fleet of offshore vessels, in addition to its dry-bulk and oil-tanker fleet. Cameroun's entire fleet consists of nationally flagged offshore supply and storage vessels, as do most of Nigeria's and Tunisia's fleets. The offshore fleet of the Democratic Republic of the Congo, on the other hand, is fully foreign flagged.

Dry-bulk ships are less often controlled by the cargo-owning countries than is the case of the oil-exporting nations. Nevertheless, important owners of dry-bulk tonnage include major importers and exporters of iron ore and other dry commodities, such as Brazil (exports) and China (imports). Other economies with a high share of dry-bulk tonnage include Hong Kong (China), Taiwan Province of China, Croatia, the Republic of Korea, Lebanon, Pakistan, the Philippines, Singapore, South Africa, Thailand, Turkey, and Ukraine.

Most container ships are foreign flagged. They engage in international trade, serving routes that connect several countries at the same time. On such routes,

cargo reservation regimes have in practice shown to be difficult to enforce. Countries/territories with a share of foreign-flagged container fleets include Chile, Hong Kong (China), Kuwait, Morocco, Singapore and South Africa.

Many of the nationally owned fleets serve the national (coastal or inter-island) cabotage trades or benefit from other cargo-reservation regimes. These ships tend to be nationally flagged as foreign ships are excluded from certain markets by the national legislation. Examples here include parts of Bangladesh's bulk and general-cargo ships, some of Chile's dry- and liquid-bulk fleet, an important share of China's bulk and general-cargo ships, part of Cuba's general-cargo carriers, India's general-cargo and tanker fleet, and a wide range of different vessels engaged in Indonesia's inter-island transport. Other countries with important nationally flagged general-cargo fleets include Ethiopia, Myanmar, the Russian Federation, the Philippines and Viet Nam.

Panama, which is mostly known for its open register, also comprises of some national shipowners, mostly, albeit not exclusively, using the national Panama flag. The largest part of the Panamanian-owned fleet consists of general-cargo ships, and about half of them do not use the flag of Panama. Owners from Singapore also use both the national flag and foreign flags.

2. Container ship operators

The largest container ship operators in 2013 continued to be Maersk Line (Denmark), MSC (Switzerland) and CMA CGM (France). Together, these three European companies operate one third of the global container-carrying capacity (TEU; table 2.5). On the main East–West route between Asia and Europe these same three carriers also deploy the largest ships and they cooperate with each other through slot-sharing arrangements, with plans to enhance their cooperation through a P3 alliance (*International Transport Journal, 2013*). This combination of larger ships and cooperation allows them to achieve important economies of scale, which smaller competing lines on this route cannot match.

Among the top 20 operators, 14 are from Asia, 5 from Europe, and one, Chilean CSAV, from South America, which has a market share of 2 per cent. From a continental origin angle, one could note that the European companies, including the three world largest carriers, gather a combined market share of 49 per

Figure 2.4. Fleet profiles of the major 48 ship-owning developing countries/territories and countries/territories with economies in transition (Dwt, by country of ownership, 1 January 2013)

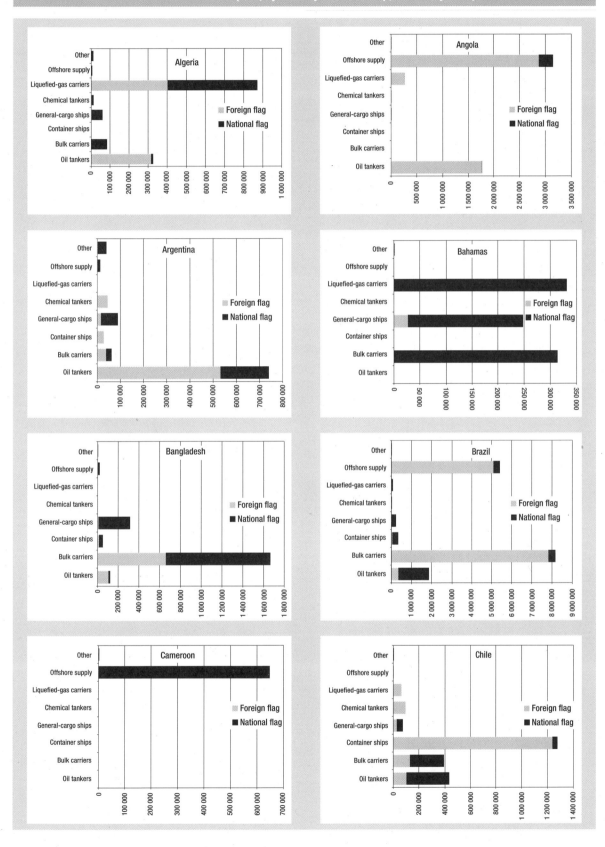

Figure 2.4. Fleet profiles of the major 48 ship-owning developing countries/territories and countries/territories with economies in transition (Dwt, by country of ownership, 1 January 2013) *(continued)*

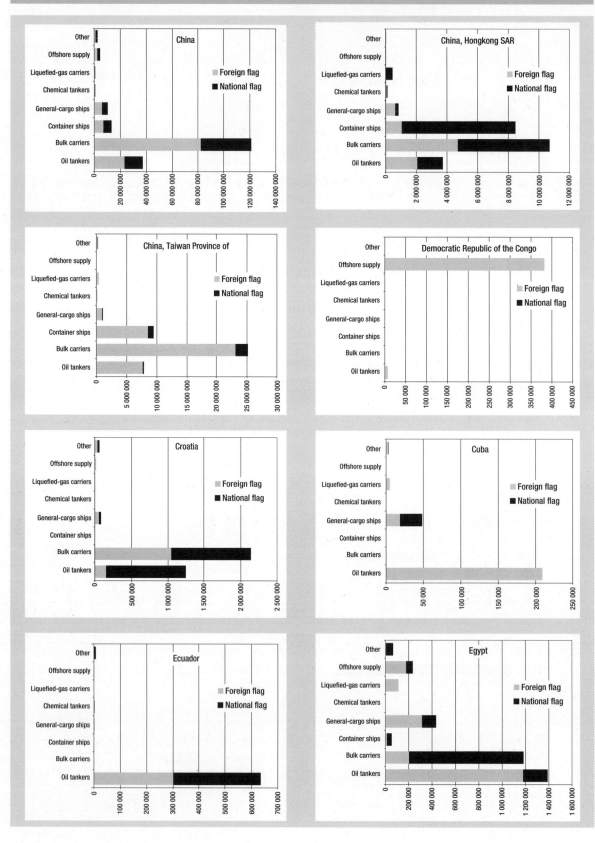

Figure 2.4. Fleet profiles of the major 48 ship-owning developing countries/territories and countries/territories with economies in transition (Dwt, by country of ownership, 1 January 2013) *(continued)*

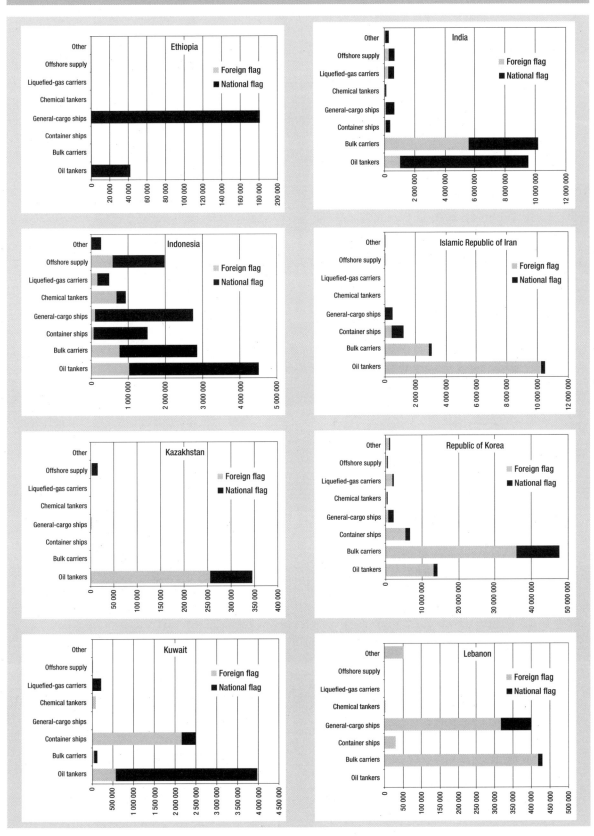

Figure 2.4. Fleet profiles of the major 48 ship-owning developing countries/territories and countries/territories with economies in transition (Dwt, by country of ownership, 1 January 2013) *(continued)*

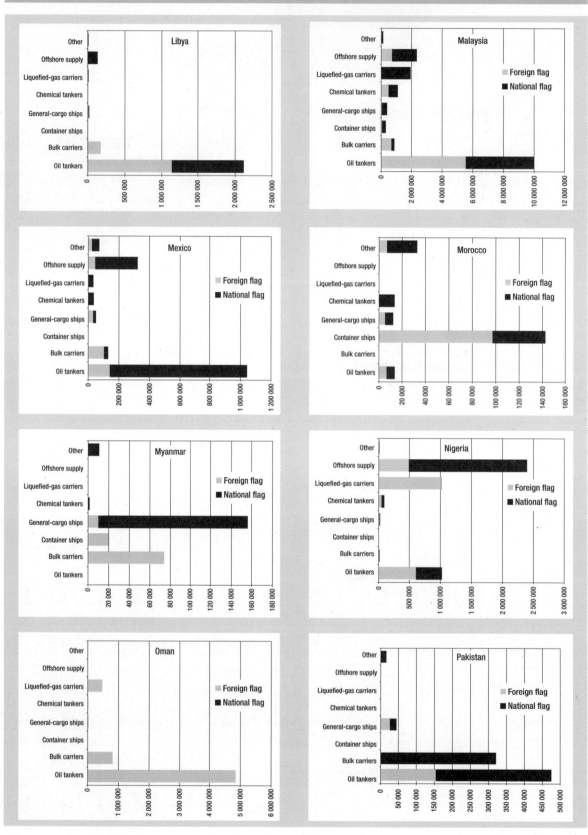

Figure 2.4. Fleet profiles of the major 48 ship-owning developing countries/territories and countries/territories with economies in transition (Dwt, by country of ownership, 1 January 2013) *(continued)*

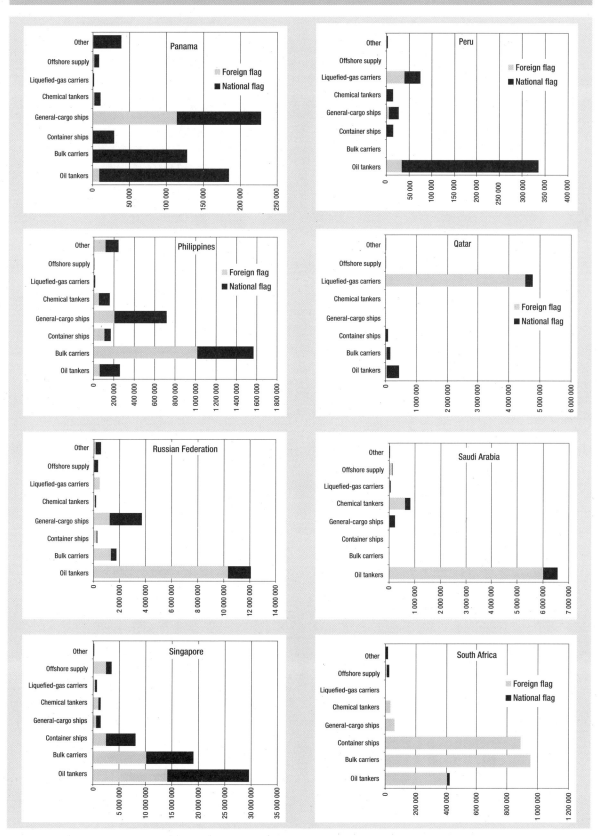

Figure 2.4. Fleet profiles of the major 48 ship-owning developing countries/territories and countries/territories with economies in transition (Dwt, by country of ownership, 1 January 2013) *(continued)*

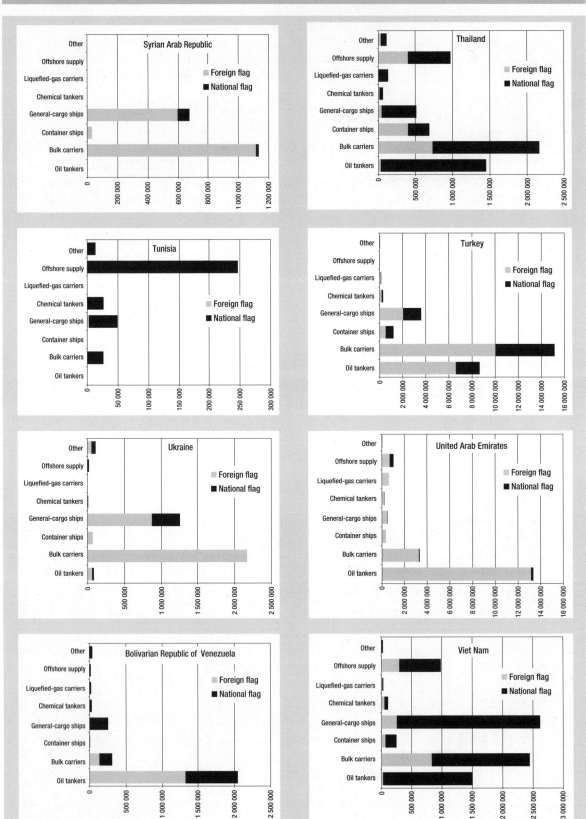

Source: UNCTAD secretariat, based on data provided by Clarkson Research Services.
Note: Propelled seagoing merchant vessels of 1,000 GT and above.

cent, equivalent to the combined Asian participation. It is also worth noting here that about half of the ships operated by the shipping lines are chartered-in, that is, the owners do not operate their container ships. Many of these owners are based in Germany. Moreover, the ships owned by the operators themselves tend to be larger than the charter-owner fleet. In particular, ships of 8,000 TEU and above are twice as often owned by liner companies such as Maersk, MSC and CMG CGM than by the charter-owners.

Table 2.5.	The 20 leading liner companies, 1 January 2013 (Number of ships and total shipboard capacity deployed, in TEUs)							
Ranking (TEU)	Operator	Country/ territory	Number of vessels	Average vessel size	TEU	Share of world total, TEU (percentage)	Cumulated share, TEU (percentage)	Growth in TEU over 2012 (percentage)
1	Maersk Line	Denmark	453	4 745	2 149 524	13.4%	13.4%	2.1%
2	MSC	Switzerland	398	5 186	2 064 118	12.9%	26.2%	1.9%
3	CMA CGM Group	France	288	4 004	1 153 088	7.2%	33.4%	-0.7%
4	COSCO	China	155	4 614	715 219	4.5%	37.9%	14.6%
5	Evergreen Line	Taiwan Province of China	187	3 795	709 702	4.4%	42.3%	24.3%
6	Hapag-Lloyd Group	Germany	141	4 533	639 148	4.0%	46.3%	-1.5%
7	APL	Singapore	127	4 492	570 497	3.6%	49.8%	-4.9%
8	CSCL	China	124	4 550	564 151	3.5%	53.3%	1.3%
9	Hanjin	Republic of Korea	107	5 190	555 279	3.5%	56.8%	11.6%
10	MOL	Japan	111	4 576	507 894	3.2%	60.0%	13.2%
11	OOCL	Hong Kong (China)	102	4 442	453 044	2.8%	62.8%	14.0%
12	NYK	Japan	93	4 334	403 030	2.5%	65.3%	28.0%
13	Hamburg Sud	Germany	93	4 132	384 293	2.4%	67.7%	4.1%
14	HMM	Republic of Korea	67	5 438	364 373	2.3%	70.0%	15.8%
15	Yang Ming	Taiwan Province of China	86	4 222	363 057	2.3%	72.2%	5.7%
16	K Line	Japan	75	4 558	341 848	2.1%	74.3%	-0.2%
17	Zim	Israel	71	3 978	282 411	1.8%	76.1%	-7.1%
18	UASC	Kuwait	41	6 361	260 818	1.6%	77.7%	36.5%
19	CSAV	Chile	55	4 716	259 391	1.6%	79.3%	-25.5%
20	PIL	Singapore	98	2 426	237 776	1.5%	80.8%	0.3%
Total top 20 liner companies			2 872	4 519	12 978 661	80.8%		
Others			2 957	1 041	3 079 572	19.2%		
Total all liner companies			5 829	2 755	16 058 233	100.0%		

Source: UNCTAD secretariat, based on data provided by Lloyd's List Intelligence, available at www.lloydslistintelligence.com.
Note: Includes all container-carrying ships known to be operated by liner shipping companies.

C. CONTAINER SHIP DEPLOYMENT AND LINER SHIPPING CONNECTIVITY

1. Container shipping and international trade

The importance of containerization for global trade has recently been re-emphasized. As *The Economist* put it, "Containers have been more important for globalization than freer trade" (*The Economist*, 2013). A new study (Bernhofen et al.,

2013) covering the introduction of containerization until 1990 concluded that containerization had a stronger impact on driving globalization than trade liberalization, especially for developed countries and North–North trade. At the same time, the study concluded that during the early stages of containerization, for trade involving developing economies the impact of the gradual goods boxing process had been relatively small.

On a related matter, and recalling that container trade remains largely serviced by regular liner shipping services, it appears worth noting that a recent study by the Economic and Social Commission for Asia and the Pacific and the World Bank (Arvis et al., 2013), covering more recent data, found that liner shipping connectivity – measuring the capacity of a country to carry its containerized foreign trade using liner shipping – had a stronger impact on trade costs than the indicators for "logistics performance", "air connectivity", "costs of starting a business" and "lower tariffs" combined.

Annex V of this *Review* includes UNCTAD's LSCI in its tenth year. Since 2004, the LSCI has provided an indicator of each coastal country's access to the global liner shipping network. The complete time series is published in electronic format on UNCTADstat (UNCTADStat – Statistical Database, 2013). The underlying data is provided by Lloyds List Intelligence (Lloyd's List Intelligence – Containers, 2013); the LSCI is generated from five components which capture the deployment of container ships by liner shipping companies to a country's ports of call as follows: (a) the number of ships; (b) their total container-carrying capacity; (c) the number of companies providing services with their own operated ships; (d) the number of services provided; (e) the size (in TEU) of the largest ship deployed.

Making use of the 10-year time series of the LSCI and its underlying data, this section discusses, first, key global developments in vessel deployment, and then looks at trends in the LSCI in selected regions in Latin America, Africa and Asia.

2. Bigger ships deployed by fewer companies

The last 10 years have seen two important trends, which represent two sides of the same coin. On the one hand, ships are becoming bigger, and on the other hand the number of companies in most markets is diminishing (figure 2.5).

As regards vessel sizes, since 2004 the average container-carrying capacity of the largest ship in the 159 countries covered by UNCTAD's database has almost doubled, from 2,812 TEU 10 years ago to 5,540 TEU in 2013. The size of the largest existing ships has also almost doubled during these 10 years (from 8,238 TEU to 16,020 TEU), and although the new ultra-large container carriers are only deployed on a small number of routes (mainly Europe–Asia), they have pushed the previously used ships out of this market, which have had to find cargo on other routes,

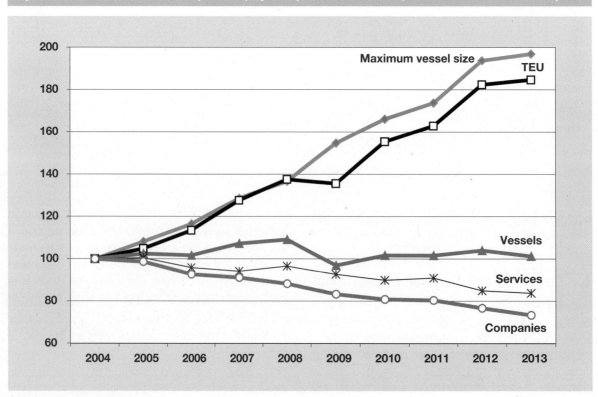

Figure 2.5.   Trends in container-ship fleet deployment (Index =100 for 2004, data for mid-2004–mid-2013)

Source: UNCTAD, based on data provided by Lloyds List Intelligence.

including North–South and intraregional trade lanes. In other words, although the largest 15,000+ TEU ships are not deployed in Latin America, Africa or South Asia, their deployment still has an important impact on these regions, as the cascading effect forces the 8,000+ TEU ships – the biggest in 2004 – to find new markets. This trend can be expected to continue. For the time being, the container ship order book is dominated by post-Panamax ships, which account for 92 per cent of the container-carrying capacity on order (Clarkson Research Services, 2013c).

As regards the number of companies, the average per country has decreased by 27 per cent during the last 10 years, from 22 in 2004 to just 16 in 2013. This trend has important implications for the level of competition, especially for smaller trading nations. While an average of 16 service providers may still be sufficient to ensure a functioning competitive market with many choices for shippers for the average country, on given individual routes, especially those serving smaller developing countries, the decline in competition has led to oligopolistic markets. For example, in 2004 there were 22 countries served by three or fewer carriers, while in 2013, 31 countries were facing such a less-than-desirable situation. Even on the main East–West routes, analysts have expressed concerns that shippers will be confronted with less choice, as medium-sized carriers are squeezed out of the market (*Journal of Commerce, 2013*).

Rather than increasing the number of vessels deployed, the carriers response to the growing demand has been the use of larger ships. As of 2004, the average number of ships deployed per country has remained almost constant, while the total container-carrying capacity increased by more than 80 per cent.

From the shippers' perspective, larger ships and more total TEU carrying capacity bring overall good news. Both a comfortable available carrying capacity for the growing trade in containerized goods, and the doubling of ship sizes to achieve economies of scale should lead to lower freight costs. However, lower operational unit costs achieved by shipping lines thanks to newer, larger and more fuel-efficient ships may not necessarily be passed on to the shippers, that is, the importers and exporters. The very process of concentration of cargo in larger ships may also lead to the same capacity now offered by fewer providers, hence less competition and, in some oligopolistic markets, a situation where shippers may in fact be confronted with higher freight rates and less choice of services.

3. Regional trends

Overall, thanks to larger ships and more container-carrying capacity deployed from and to the world's ports, the average LSCI in most countries shows that their connectivity has increased. Since 2004, 120 countries recorded an improved LSCI, while the LSCI in 39 countries went down. Figure 2.6 illustrates trends in some selected developing countries in Latin America, Africa and Asia.

On the west coast of South and Central America, Panama appears best connected to global liner shipping networks, largely thanks to its canal. Although Panama has less trade than its Southern neighbours, its container terminals provide trans-shipment services for practically all of North, Central and South America, connecting East–West and North–South liner services. In South America, Ecuador has not been able to accommodate the same LSCI growth as its neighbours, partly because its main port, Guayaquil, has been confronted with limitations in the dredging of the access channel and insufficient investment in specialized container handling cranes. On South America's east coast, Brazil shows the highest LSCI, closely followed by Argentina and Uruguay. Although much smaller than its neighbours, Uruguay has been able to attract liner services for transit and trans-shipment cargo. The Bolivarian Republic of Venezuela, whose main export is crude oil, has not recorded any increase in container ship deployment during the last 10 years.

In West Africa, Nigeria has seen the highest growth of its LSCI, mostly fuelled by growing demand for imports. In general, the LSCI of the West African countries move largely in parallel to each other, as the same companies deploy the same ships to call at most ports along the coast. The LSCI of the Côte d'Ivoire has seen important drops in 2006 and 2010, when political turmoil and economic embargoes discouraged liner companies to serve the port of Abidjan. In Eastern Africa, Djibouti has overtaken its neighbours and became an important trans-shipment centre, connecting East–West services with feeder services from Eastern and Southern Africa. It also serves as a gateway for neighbouring landlocked Ethiopia and increasingly caters for cargo destined for South Sudan.

In South Asia, the LSCI of Bangladesh, India and Pakistan almost exclusively reflects the vessel deployment for these countries' national foreign trade. In Sri Lanka on the other hand, large container ships are deployed to connect to feeder services, including to India, thus benefiting from cabotage restrictions which continue to limit the attractiveness of Indian ports for trans-shipment operations to the different ports of this large country.

Malaysia, in South-East Asia, has seen its LSCI grow much faster than its neighbours Indonesia and Thailand, almost reaching the LSCI of Singapore. Comparing the developments in Singapore and Malaysia, it is interesting to note that the two countries' LSCI moves largely in parallel, as the same companies and ships provide the same services passing through the Strait of Malacca. The data for 2007 and 2008, however, also illustrate a certain competition, when one country's ability to attract additional liner companies may be to the detriment of the other's LSCI.

In East Asia, the Republic of Korea and Japan started out with the same LSCI in 2004. Since then, Japan has remained relatively stagnant, its rank slipping from ninth in 2004 to fifteenth in 2013. During the same period, the Republic of Korea has attracted more and bigger ships, partly to cater for its own trade, but also to provide trans-shipment services for cargo to and from ports of neighbouring countries. For the last 10 years China has the highest LSCI not only in its region but also among all countries covered by LSCI.

D. REGISTRATION OF SHIPS

1. Flags of registration

The five largest fleets by flag of registration in January 2013, and in terms of dwt, were Panama (21.5 per cent of the world total dwt), Liberia (12.2 per cent), the Marshall Islands (8.6 per cent), Hong Kong, China (8 per cent) and Singapore (5.5 per cent) (see table 2.6 for details of the 35 flags of registration with the largest registered fleets). The latter two were also those with the highest year-on-year growth, increasing their tonnage by more than 16 per cent. As regards vessel types, Liberia caters largely for oil tankers, while Panama flags a high number of dry-bulk carriers. The Bahamas has many "other" vessels, including a large number of cruise ships.

The traditional distinction between "national" flagged fleets and "open registers" is becoming increasingly blurred. Among the top 35 fleets, there are 11 that could be considered purely open as less than 2 per cent of the ships flying their flags belong to owners from the same country. At the other end of the spectrum, there are 8 flags that are used almost

Figure 2.6. Trends in the LSCI (Index =100 for the maximum value in 2004)

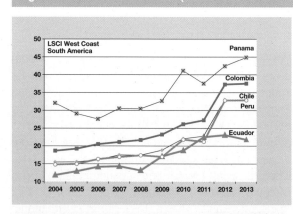

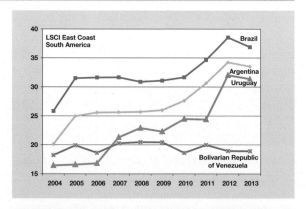

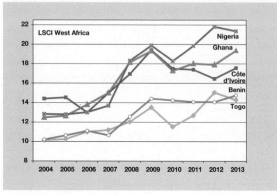

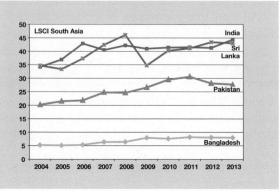

Figure 2.6. Trends in the LSCI (Index =100 for the maximum value in 2004) *(continued)*

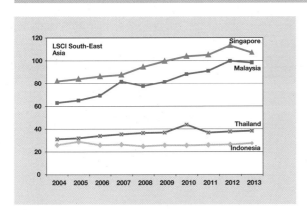

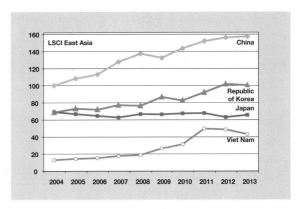

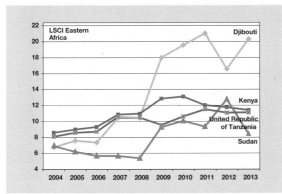

Source: UNCTAD. The LSCI is generated from data provided by Lloyds List Intelligence. The LSCI for 159 countries is available on-line under (http://stats.unctad.org/lsci).

exclusively (more than 95 per cent of the total) by owners from the country; these could be called purely national flags. In between, 16 of the top 35 flags are used by both national and foreign owners. The flag of the Philippines, for example, is used three times more by foreigners than Philippine nationals. For Singapore, the proportion of foreign to national ownership is about 2:1, and for the United Kingdom it is about 50:50 (not including here the flag of the Isle of Man).

In January 2013, a new historical record share of 73 per cent of the world fleet was "flagged out", that is, the nationality of the vessel's owner was different from the flag under which the vessel was registered (figure 2.7). In other words, for almost three out of every four dwt, shipowners chose a flag different from their own nationality. The remaining 27 per cent are kept under the national flag because either the owner considered the national flag competitive in terms of costs and services provided, or he may not have had a choice, as is often the case for government cargo and cabotage traffic.

In the past, important reasons to choose a foreign flag were the tax regimes and the possibility to employ foreign seafarers. The latter reason was particularly important for countries with higher labour costs, that is mostly developed countries (Cullinane, 2005). Today, the responsibilities of flag States in ensuring compliance with international regulations and in providing 24/7 services to shipowners are increasingly important, and many developing countries' owners also choose to register their fleets under foreign flags that offer a solid institutional framework and enjoy a good compliance reputation.

The regional shares by vessel type and flag of registration are provided in table 2.7 (see Annex II for the national shares). In total, developing countries register more than three quarters of the world fleet, including the world's major open registers (Panama, Liberia, and the Marshall Islands), but also important national fleets employed in coastal and inter-island cabotage trades (for example, China, India and Indonesia), as well as mixed registers with national and foreign owners (for example, Hong Kong (China), Singapore and the Philippines). The fleets registered in developed countries/overseas territories also include major open registers (for example, Malta, the Isle of Man and Bermuda), flags used by both nationals and foreigners (for example, Cyprus, the United Kingdom and France), and flags that are almost exclusively used by national owners (for example, Germany and Japan). The Danish (DIS) and Norwegian (NIS) international ship registers are these countries' second registers; they provide better conditions to shipowners than the same countries' first registers in terms of taxes and possibilities to employ foreign seafarers. DIS and NIS are still today mostly used by Danish and Norwegian nationals respectively (see Annex III).

Among the developing regions, Africa's share is determined largely by the register of Liberia, which

Table 2.6.	The 35 flags of registration with the largest registered fleets, as of 1 January 2013 (Dwt)						
Flag of registration	Number of vessels	Share of world total, vessels	Deadweight tonnage (thousands dwt)	Share of world total (percentage dwt)	Cumulated share (percentage dwt)	National ownership (percentage) [a]	Dwt Growth 2013/2012 (percentage)
Panama	8 580	9.87	350 506	21.52	21.52	0.14	5.03
Liberia	3 144	3.62	198 032	12.16	33.68	0.01	5.83
Marshall Islands	2 064	2.37	140 016	8.60	42.27	0.11	11.08
Hong Kong (China)	2 221	2.55	129 806	7.97	50.24	12.15	16.87
Singapore	3 339	3.84	89 697	5.51	55.75	36.60	16.62
Greece	1 551	1.78	75 424	4.63	60.38	92.60	5.13
Bahamas	1 446	1.66	73 702	4.52	64.91	1.18	1.44
Malta	1 794	2.06	68 831	4.23	69.13	0.35	8.18
China	3 727	4.29	68 642	4.21	73.35	98.18	9.83
Cyprus	1 030	1.18	31 706	1.95	75.29	19.51	7.61
Isle of Man	422	0.49	22 629	1.39	76.68	0.00	9.32
United Kingdom	1 343	1.54	21 095	1.30	77.98	49.88	6.99
Italy	1 506	1.73	20 612	1.27	79.24	93.46	2.44
Japan	5 379	6.19	20 409	1.25	80.50	99.32	11.04
Norway (NIS)	536	0.62	18 093	1.11	81.61	82.33	5.37
Republic of Korea	1 894	2.18	17 720	1.09	82.69	96.47	-10.74
Germany	781	0.90	17 128	1.05	83.75	97.59	2.30
India	1 385	1.59	15 876	0.97	84.72	96.16	-3.45
Indonesia	6 293	7.24	14 267	0.88	85.60	90.28	0.17
Antigua and Barbuda	1 302	1.50	14 142	0.87	86.47	0.00	4.27
Denmark (DIS)	482	0.55	13 739	0.84	87.31	92.53	1.24
Bermuda	168	0.19	12 378	0.76	88.07	1.69	0.45
United States	3 452	3.97	12 321	0.76	88.83	73.93	-1.18
Malaysia	1 539	1.77	10 508	0.65	89.47	92.82	-3.15
Turkey	1 365	1.57	10 215	0.63	90.10	96.94	3.30
United Republic of Tanzania	198	0.23	8 815	0.54	90.64	0.30	10.45
Netherlands	1 250	1.44	8 712	0.53	91.17	70.90	6.73
France	543	0.62	7 431	0.46	91.63	52.40	-0.22
Viet Nam	1 772	2.04	7 284	0.45	92.08	97.55	1.52
Belgium	216	0.25	6 913	0.42	92.50	58.35	0.46
Russian Federation	2 324	2.67	6 784	0.42	92.92	84.57	-2.14
Philippines	1 383	1.59	6 417	0.39	93.31	26.36	-2.41
St. Vincent and the Grenadines	1 046	1.20	4 919	0.30	93.61	0.08	-18.09
Thailand	755	0.87	4 811	0.30	93.91	97.95	-6.63
Cayman Islands	174	0.20	4 310	0.26	94.17	0.00	2.12
Top 35 total	66 404	76.38	1 533 889	94.17	94.17	24.30	6.71
World total	86 942	100.00	1 628 783	100.00	100.00	23.00	5.98

Source: Compiled by the UNCTAD secretariat, on the basis of data supplied by Clarkson Research Services.

Note: Propelled seagoing merchant vessels of 100 GT and above; ranked by deadweight tonnage.

[a]   The estimate of national ownership is based on available information of commercial seagoing vessels of 1,000 GT and above.

Figure 2.7. Global share of foreign-flagged fleet (Beginning-of-year figures, percentage of world total dwt, 1989–2013)

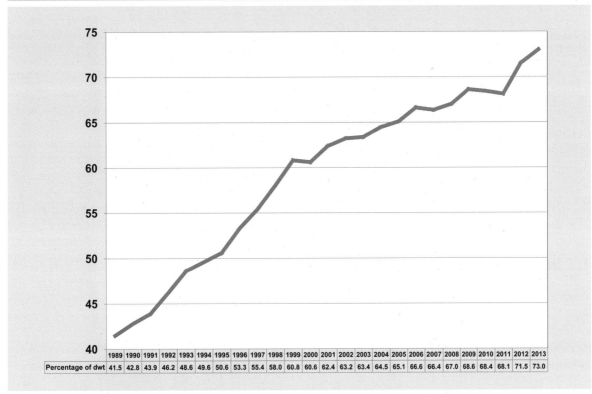

	1989	1990	1991	1992	1993	1994	1995	1996	1997	1998	1999	2000	2001	2002	2003	2004	2005	2006	2007	2008	2009	2010	2011	2012	2013
Percentage of dwt	41.5	42.8	43.9	46.2	48.6	49.6	50.6	53.3	55.4	58.0	60.8	60.6	62.4	63.2	63.4	64.5	65.1	66.6	66.4	67.0	68.6	68.4	68.1	71.5	73.0

Source: UNCTAD, Review of Maritime Transport, various issues.
Note: Estimate based on available information of seagoing merchant vessels of 1,000 GT and above.

caters above all for container ships and oil tankers. For the Latin American and Caribbean fleets, the flag of Panama explains the region's high share among bulk carriers. Almost one quarter of the world fleet is registered in developing countries in Asia, with a particularly high share among the general-cargo ships (almost 33 per cent of the world total). The share of Oceania reflects to a large extent the register of the Marshall Islands, with its specialization in oil tankers and dry-bulk carriers.

Table 2.7. Distribution of dwt capacity of vessel types, by country group of registration, 2013 (Beginning-of-year figures, percentage of dwt)

	Total	Oil tankers	Bulk carriers	General cargo ships	Container ships	Other types
Developing economies	75.49	72.23	81.13	65.07	72.26	70.92
... of Africa	13.55	16.87	10.07	5.37	23.11	10.17
... of America	28.57	21.08	34.95	24.74	23.24	32.86
... of Asia	24.42	21.94	27.46	32.80	21.64	18.61
... of Oceania	8.95	12.35	8.66	2.15	4.27	9.28
Developed economies	23.36	26.80	18.55	28.64	27.68	25.13
Transition economies	0.72	0.77	0.26	5.21	0.04	1.17
Unknown and other flags	0.42	0.19	0.06	1.08	0.01	2.78
World total	**100.00**	**100.00**	**100.00**	**100.00**	**100.00**	**100.00**

Source: Compiled by the UNCTAD secretariat, on the basis of data supplied Clarkson Research Services.
Note: Propelled seagoing merchant vessels of 100 GT and above.

2. Nationality of controlling interests

Vessel registers often specialize in different ship types and countries of ownership. Annex III provides a detailed overview of the countries of ownership that register their ships under the main flags of registration. The flag of Antigua and Barbuda is mostly used by owners from Germany; the Bahamas registers, above all, ships from Canada, Greece and Norway; Greek and German owners are the main clients for the registers of Cyprus and of Liberia; and 47 per cent of the Panamanian deadweight tonnage is Japanese owned.

E. SHIPBUILDING, DEMOLITION AND NEW ORDERS

1. Deliveries of newbuildings

Three countries (China, the Republic of Korea and Japan) together built 92 per cent of the world's new tonnage (GT) in 2012, with China alone accounting for more than 40 per cent. Almost 57 per cent of the tonnage delivered in 2012 was on dry-bulk ships,

followed by oil tankers (18.4 per cent) and container ships (14.4 per cent) (figure 2.8 and table 2.8). This is a significantly different picture from just six years ago. In 2006, the Republic of Korea was the largest shipbuilder, followed by Japan. China and Europe each had a market share of about 15 per cent.

Shipbuilders also specialize in different vessel types. While China and Japan have mostly built dry-bulk carriers, the Republic of Korea had a far higher share in container ships and oil tankers, and European and other regions' yards had a somewhat higher share among the offshore and passenger vessels. In addition to bulk carriers, Japan is also focusing on other specialized ships, including gas and car carriers. The four largest individual shipbuilding groups are from the Republic of Korea; shipbuilding in China is spread among a larger number of individual shipbuilders.

Even more so than ships, sea containers are almost exclusively built in China. Low production costs and the need for empty boxes to transport Chinese exports made China the natural location for setting up factories for the construction of containers. Interestingly, at the end of 2013, a new factory for reefer containers is scheduled to open in San Antonio, Chile. Maersk

---

Figure 2.8. Deliveries of newbuildings, major vessel types and countries where built, 2012 (Thousands of GT)

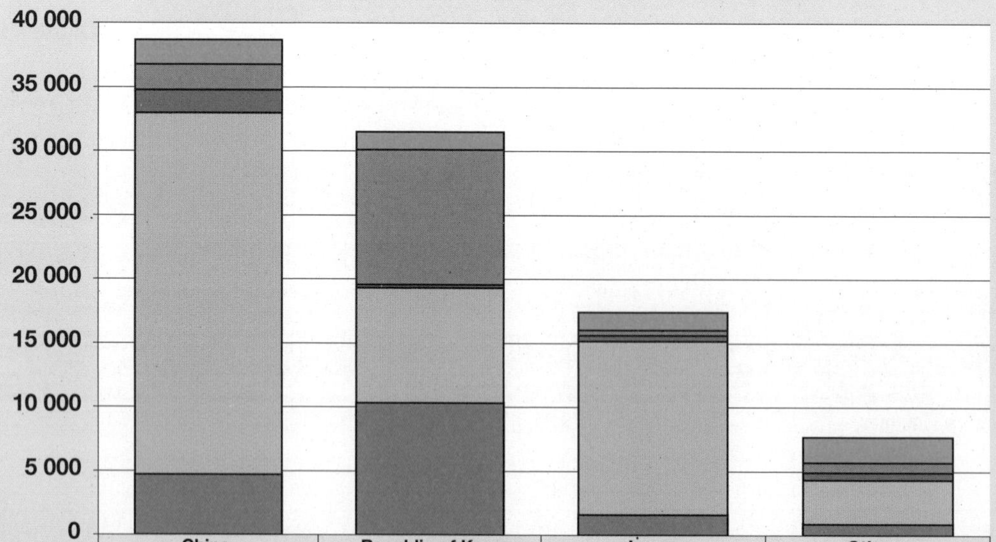

	China	Republic of Korea	Japan	Others
Other	1 914	1 391	1 406	1 989
Container	1 984	10 540	390	773
General cargo	1 833	260	472	583
Dry bulk	28 217	8 988	13 571	3 468
Oil tanker	4 729	10 311	1 592	877

Source: UNCTAD secretariat, on the basis of data supplied by Clarkson Research Services.

Note: Propelled seagoing merchant vessels of 100 GT and above.

Table 2.8.	Deliveries of newbuildings, major vessel types and countries where built, 2012 (Thousands of GT)					
	China	Republic of Korea	Japan	Philippines	Rest of world	World total
Oil tankers	4 729	10 311	1 592	251	626	17 510
Bulk carriers	28 217	8 988	13 571	2 342	1 126	54 244
General cargo	1 833	260	472	–	583	3 147
Container ships	1 984	10 540	390	–	773	13 687
Gas carriers	179	173	152	–	18	522
Chemical tankers	68	188	200	–	44	499
Offshore	967	506	108	102	819	2 502
Ferries and passenger ships	100	71	36	–	875	1 082
Other	600	453	910	–	131	2 094
Total	**38 677**	**31 491**	**17 429**	**2 696**	**4 994**	**95 287**

Source: Compiled by the UNCTAD secretariat on the basis of data provided by Clarkson Research Services.
Note: Propelled seagoing merchant vessels of 100 GT and above.

Container Industry San Santonio is going to be the first reefer container factory in South America (MCI San Antonio, 2013). The company is scheduled to produce 40,000 reefer containers per year. South America is among the regions with the highest demand for empty reefer containers for export. The new factory will thus help correct a reefer trade imbalance and reduce repositioning costs as fewer empty reefer containers will need to be moved from Asia to South America (*World Cargo News, 2013*).

2. Demolition of ships

The Indian subcontinent continued to be the major ship-breaking region in 2012, accounting for more than 70 per cent of the tonnage (GT) reported sold for breaking. Within the subcontinent, Bangladesh was the largest ship-breaking country, followed by India and Pakistan. Chinese breakers demolished 21.6 per cent and the rest of the world the remaining 11.7 per cent (table 2.9).

Table 2.9.	Tonnage reported sold for demolition, major vessel types and countries where demolished, 2012 (Thousands of GT)						
	China	India	Bangladesh	Pakistan	Unknown Indian Subcontinent	Turkey	Others/ unknown	World Total
Oil tankers	1 459	369	1 197	2 711	191	21	200	6 149
Bulk carriers	5 533	5 446	6 064	1 959	205	365	720	20 293
General cargo	316	393	1 166	28	–	291	471	2 665
Container ships	316	553	2 954	7	216	124	76	4 246
Gas carriers	4	89	30	–	–	77	38	238
Chemical tankers	7	11	333	–	21	–	27	399
Offshore	154	4	44	649	156	75	100	1 182
Ferries and passenger ships	12	4	82	–	–	139	66	303
Other	55	158	386	17	–	146	56	817
Total	**7 855**	**7 027**	**12 256**	**5 372**	**790**	**1 239**	**1 755**	**36 293**

Source: Compiled by the UNCTAD secretariat, on the basis of data from Clarkson Research Services.
Note: Propelled seagoing merchant vessels of 100 GT and above.

As illustrated in figure 2.9, oil tankers tend to be sold for breaking at a much younger age than dry-bulk carriers. Environmental regulations often do not allow older tankers to be deployed beyond two decades, while dry bulkers often trade to carry cargo for three or more decades. General-cargo and passenger ships (included under "other" in figure 2.9) tend to be deployed the longest; they are often trading on inter-island and coastal cabotage services, which are not bound by the international regulations of IMO.

Figure 2.9.   Tonnage reported sold for demolition in 2012, by age (Years and dwt)

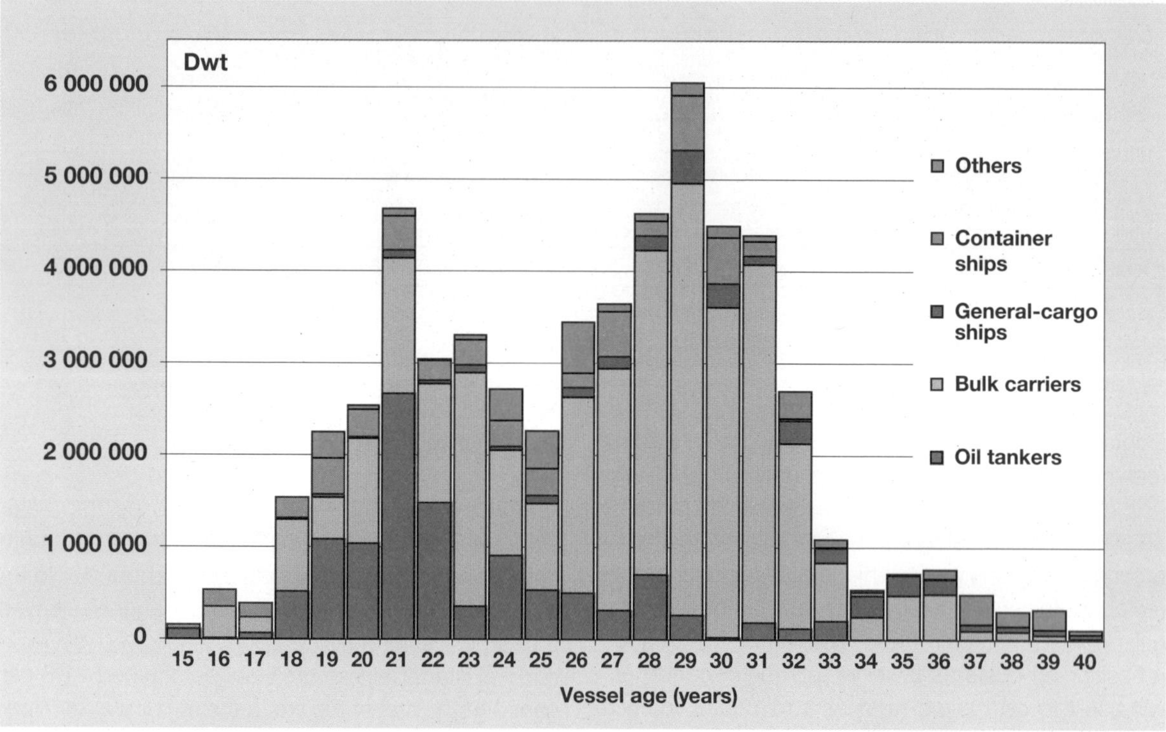

Source: UNCTAD secretariat, on the basis of data from Clarkson Research Services.

3.   Tonnage on order

Following the peaks in 2008 and 2009, the tonnage on order for all major vessel types has drastically declined over the last few years. As far fewer new orders were placed since the economic crisis of 2008, and shipyards continued to deliver pre-ordered tonnage, the order books went down by 50 per cent for container ships, 58 per cent for dry-bulk carriers, 65 per cent for tankers and by 67 per cent for general-cargo ships, as compared to the previous peaks (figure 2.10 and table 2.10).

The reduction in the order book is even more impressive if compared to the existing fleet. At the end of 2008, the dry-bulk order book was equivalent to almost 80 per cent of the fleet at that time, while the tonnage on order as of January 2013 is the equivalent of just 20 per cent of the fleet in service. For tankers, the order book went down from 50 per cent of the fleet at its peak to around 10 per cent in January 2013.

For all main vessel types, new orders are at historical lows, and the order book is declining rapidly. Unless large numbers of countercyclical investors place new orders in 2013 and 2014, by 2014 numerous shipyards will need to reduce employment. Reports from ship brokers suggest that in fact more such countercyclical investors are emerging, expecting to benefit from the current low newbuilding prices, and hoping for a revival of the shipping markets in coming years (Clarkson Research Services, 2013a). Nevertheless, from the shipyards' perspective, the current capacity is almost certainly too high for even the most optimistic scenario. According to some estimates "shipyard capacity could be slashed by as much as 40 per cent across the world and the industry would still be able to meet the demand for new ships for 2015" (*China Trade Today - Online Magazine, 2013*).

Figure 2.10. World tonnage on order, 2000–2013 (Thousands of dwt)

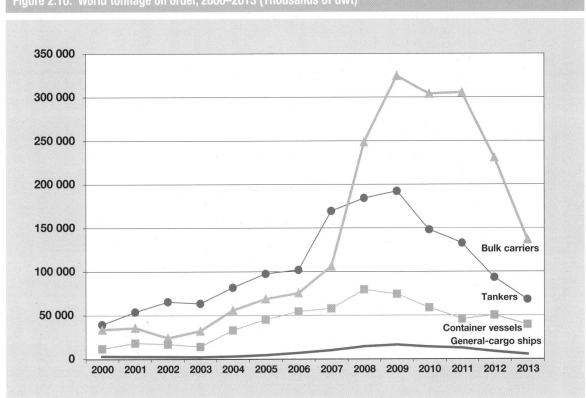

Source: Compiled by the UNCTAD secretariat, on the basis of data supplied by Clarkson Research Services.
Note: Propelled seagoing merchant vessels of 100 GT and above; beginning of year figures.

4. Tonnage utilization

Ships are capital investments with high fixed costs and relatively low running costs – only exceptionally are they kept laid off. In early 2013, almost 99 per cent of the tonnage was in service, the remainder being laid off (0.73 per cent), used for long term storage (0.16 per cent) or not in service for other reasons (0.15 per cent). Among the different vessel types, container ships had the highest utilization rate (99.85 per cent), while offshore supply vessels had the lowest (84.52 per cent) (table 2.11).

Table 2.10. World tonnage on order, 2000–2013

Beginning of month	Tankers			Bulk carriers			General cargo ships			Container vessels			Other ships			Total		
	Thousands dwt	Number of ships	Average vessel size (dwt)	Thousands dwt	Number of ships	Average vessel size (dwt)	Thousands dwt	Number of ships	Average vessel size (dwt)	Thousands dwt	Number of ships	Average vessel size (dwt)	Thousands dwt	Number of ships	Average vessel size (dwt)	Thousands dwt	Number of ships	Average vessel size (dwt)
January 2000	39 444	427	92 375	33 729	467	72 226	3 125	341	9 164	11 922	278	42 884	2 963	363	8 791	91 183	1 876	49 288
January 2001	53 832	533	100 998	35 608	535	66 557	2 797	269	10 398	18 348	413	44 426	3 274	413	8 570	113 859	2 163	53 405
January 2002	65 546	752	87 162	24 107	360	66 965	2 541	233	10 906	17 132	403	42 511	4 264	474	9 454	113 589	2 222	51 655
January 2003	63 545	862	73 719	32 127	440	73 015	2 265	226	10 023	14 230	324	43 921	4 933	481	11 035	117 100	2 333	50 935
January 2004	82 094	1 146	72 076	55 829	735	75 958	3 012	563	6 072	33 004	622	53 061	5 361	971	7 529	179 300	4 037	48 407
January 2005	97 757	1 558	63 479	68 710	851	80 741	4 405	963	5 359	45 246	898	50 385	6 110	1 707	5 290	222 229	5 977	42 201
January 2006	102 202	1 882	54 741	75 623	950	79 604	6 904	1 221	6 299	54 385	1 210	44 946	6 637	1 875	4 884	245 750	7 138	37 913
January 2007	169 798	2 703	63 075	106 149	1 363	77 879	9 919	1 448	7 293	57 937	1 286	45 052	8 353	2 231	4 643	352 155	9 031	41 430
January 2008	184 548	3 174	58 401	248 698	2 984	83 344	14 266	1 889	7 925	79 702	1 429	55 775	11 477	2 938	4 778	538 691	12 414	45 749
April 2008	187 420	3 274	57 438	278 423	3 335	83 485	16 334	2 184	7 944	78 855	1 382	57 058	12 883	3 813	4 484	573 914	13 988	44 458
July 2008	199 397	3 296	60 699	302 678	3 602	84 031	16 650	2 148	8 218	81 921	1 370	59 797	13 026	3 743	4 571	613 673	14 159	46 728
October 2008	206 413	3 205	64 605	329 557	3 863	85 311	17 242	2 149	8 452	77 875	1 280	60 840	13 199	3 561	4 842	644 286	14 058	49 167
January 2009	192 532	2 957	65 331	324 772	3 824	84 930	16 169	1 965	8 674	74 445	1 200	62 037	12 582	3 280	4 961	620 499	13 226	50 158
April 2009	175 063	2 819	62 344	323 234	3 797	85 129	16 186	2 064	8 317	70 017	1 098	63 767	13 120	3 892	4 417	597 619	13 670	47 359
July 2009	159 975	2 573	62 441	313 865	3 677	85 359	15 414	1 921	8 488	65 998	1 013	65 151	13 052	3 571	4 726	568 305	12 755	48 039
October 2009	152 156	2 390	63 904	309 077	3 629	85 169	14 614	1 783	8 678	63 004	947	66 530	12 382	3 242	4 902	551 233	11 991	49 363

Table 2.10. World tonnage on order, 2000–2013 (continued)

Beginning of month	Tankers			Bulk carriers			General cargo ships			Container vessels			Other ships			Total		
	Thousands dwt	Number of ships	Average vessel size (dwt)	Thousands dwt	Number of ships	Average vessel size (dwt)	Thousands dwt	Number of ships	Average vessel size (dwt)	Thousands dwt	Number of ships	Average vessel size (dwt)	Thousands dwt	Number of ships	Average vessel size (dwt)	Thousands dwt	Number of ships	Average vessel size (dwt)
January 2010	148 328	2 276	65 429	304 114	3 539	85 932	13 894	1 627	8 964	58 823	842	69 861	11 568	2 857	5 157	536 727	11 141	51 406
April 2010	136 373	2 186	62 614	309 728	3 648	84 903	14 017	1 637	8 957	54 530	775	70 361	11 819	3 191	4 655	526 466	11 437	49 179
July 2010	135 006	2 072	65 378	323 404	3 812	84 839	13 280	1 530	9 052	48 427	677	71 532	11 618	2 956	4 890	531 736	11 047	51 143
October 2010	135 114	1 938	69 862	307 605	3 674	83 725	12 966	1 422	9 471	46 458	637	72 932	11 522	2 658	5 317	513 665	10 329	52 517
January 2011	132 914	1 857	71 729	305 831	3 705	82 546	12 553	1 305	9 915	45 878	622	73 759	10 830	2 408	5 426	508 006	9 897	53 803
April 2011	122 327	1 737	70 465	291 326	3 535	82 412	11 728	1 189	10 102	48 405	648	74 699	11 388	2 414	5 657	485 174	9 523	53 357
July 2011	114 179	1 630	70 091	275 879	3 364	82 009	10 647	1 056	10 267	52 469	688	76 263	11 272	2 217	5 989	464 446	8 955	54 005
October 2011	103 107	1 517	67 968	253 615	3 103	81 732	9 839	949	10 511	51 462	669	76 924	10 931	1 961	6 480	428 954	8 199	54 216
January 2012	93 559	1 334	70 134	230 964	2 813	82 106	8 553	799	10 813	50 275	646	77 825	10 604	1 785	6 846	393 955	7 377	55 230
April 2012	87 083	1 282	67 928	203 541	2 507	81 189	7 697	696	11 123	45 141	579	77 964	10 007	1 598	7 189	353 470	6 662	54 785
July 2012	76 128	1 085	70 164	170 949	2 140	79 883	5 921	501	11 914	40 806	526	77 579	9 941	1 416	8 024	303 746	5 668	55 357
October 2012	70 657	1 020	69 271	152 970	1 940	78 850	5 981	462	12 975	40 881	515	79 380	10 603	1 291	9 501	281 091	5 228	55 640
January 2013	68 291	964	70 841	136 720	1 736	78 756	5 362	383	14 001	39 470	485	81 382	10 569	1 179	10 559	260 414	4 747	56 996

Source: Compiled by the UNCTAD secretariat, on the basis of data supplied by Clarkson Research Services.

Notes: Seagoing propelled merchant ships of 100 GT and above. Average vessel size calculation excludes those vessels for which no deadweight figure is available.

Table 2.11.	Tonnage utilization by type of vessel, January 2013 (Percentage of dwt or cubic metres)				
	In service	Idle and laid up	Long-term storage	Repairs and not in service for other reasons	Total
Bulk carriers	99.75	0.14	0.02	0.10	100.00
Chemical tankers	99.57	0.36	–	0.08	100.00
Container ships	99.85	0.12	–	0.03	100.00
Ferries and passenger ships	98.23	1.49	–	0.28	100.00
General-cargo ships	98.78	0.87	0.04	0.31	100.00
Liquefied-gas carriers	98.62	1.19	0.19	–	100.00
Offshore supply	94.52	4.40	–	1.08	100.00
Oil tankers	98.16	1.25	0.48	0.12	100.00
Other/n.a.	99.31	0.53	–	0.16	100.00
Total	**98.96**	**0.73**	**0.16**	**0.15**	**100.00**

Source: Compiled by the UNCTAD secretariat, on the basis of data from Clarkson Research Services.

These apparently high utilization rates hide the oversupply of vessel capacity, especially in container shipping. The data captured in table 2.11 does not include "warm" lay ups, that is, short-term withdrawals from regular container services, when ships are considered "idle". If idle capacity is excluded, only about 95 to 96 per cent of the container ship fleet was in service in January 2013. In addition, slow steaming, that is, providing services at speeds below the optimum for which the ships had been built, has helped to absorb an additional capacity of about 1.7 million TEU, as more ships are deployed to ensure the same frequency of service (Clarkson Research Services, 2013c). This is equivalent to more than 10 per cent of the existing fleet.

REFERENCES

Arvis J-F, Shepherd B, Reis JG, Duval Y and Utoktham C (2013). Trade costs and development: a new data set. *World Bank - Economic Premise*. 104:1–4.

Bernhofen DM, El-Sahli Z and Kneller R (2013). *Estimating the Effects of the Container Revolution on World Trade*. CESifo, Center for Economic Studies and Ifo Institute for Economic Research. Munich.

China Trade Today – Online Magazine (2013). Shipyard capacity could be slashed by 40pc and still meet demand. March. See http://om.shippinggazette.com/OM/OM4/index.asp (accessed 28 August 2013).

Clarkson Research Services (2013a). *The Clarkson Shipping Review and Outlook*. Spring 2013.

Clarkson Research Services (2013b). *World Fleet Monitor*. January.

Clarkson Research Services (2013c). *Container Intelligence Quarterly, Spring 2013*. May.

Cullinane KPB, ed. (2005). *Shipping Economics: Research in Transportation Economics*. Elsevier, Amsterdam.

Dynamar B.V. (2013). *Breakbulk III – Operators, fleets, markets*. Alkmaar. 244.

Fairplay (2013). Chemical tankers on cusp of rates recovery. 11 April.

International Transport Journal (2013). Maersk, MSC and CMA to establish alliance. 18 June.

Journal of Commerce (2013). Drewry: Demise of small carriers cuts competition. See http://www.joc.com/maritime-news/container-lines/drewry-demise-small-carriers-cuts-competition_20130429.html (accessed 26 August 2013).

Lloyd's List Intelligence – Containers (2013). See http://www.lloydslistintelligence.com/llint/containers/index.htm (accessed 27 August 2013).

MCI San Antonio (2013). See http://www.mcicontainers.com/aboutus/mciworldwide/pages/mcisanantonio.aspx (accessed 15 June 2013).

Shipping Intelligence Weekly (2013). Single hull VLCCs – The long goodbye. 14 June.

The Economist (2013). The humble hero. 18 May.

UNCTADStat – Statistical Database (2013). See http://unctadstat.unctad.org/ReportFolders/reportFolders.aspx (accessed 27 August 2013).

World Cargo News (2013). MCI to build reefer factory in Chile. See http://www.worldcargonews.com/htm/w20111111.049104.htm (accessed 28 August 2013).

World Shipping Council (2013). See http://www.worldshipping.org/ (accessed 29 August 2013).

ENDNOTES

1. The underlying data on the world fleet for chapter 2 has been provided by Clarkson Research Services, London. With a view to focusing solely on commercial shipping, the vessels covered in UNCTAD's analysis include all propelled sea-going merchant vessels of 100 GT and above, including offshore drillships and FPSOs, and also including the Great Lakes fleets of the United States and Canada, which for historical reasons had been excluded in earlier issues of the *Review of Maritime Transport*. We exclude military vessels, yachts, waterway vessels, fishing vessels, and offshore fixed and mobile platforms and barges. As regards the main vessel types (oil tankers, dry-bulk, container, and general-cargo) there is no change compared to previous issues of the *Review of Maritime Transport*. As regards "other" vessels, the new data includes a smaller number of ships (previously, fishing vessels with little cargo-carrying capacity had been included) and a slightly higher tonnage due to the inclusion of ships used in the offshore transport and storage. To ensure full comparability of the 2013 data with the two previous years, UNCTAD has updated the fleet data available online for the years 2011, 2012 and 2013, applying the same criteria (http://stats.unctad.org/fleet). As in previous years, the data on fleet ownership covers only ships of 1,000 GT and above, as information on the true ownership is often not available for smaller ships.

3

FREIGHT RATES AND MARITIME TRANSPORT COSTS

This chapter covers the development of freight rates and maritime transport costs. Section A encompasses some relevant developments in maritime freight rates in various market segments, namely containerized trade, liquid bulk and dry bulk shipping in 2012 and in early 2013. It highlights significant events leading to major price fluctuations, discusses recent industry trends and gives a selective outlook on future developments of freight markets. Section B provides a brief overview of recent developments in ship finance and the growing role of private equity as a new source of finance in the sector.

A. FREIGHT RATES

In general terms, the demand and the supply of maritime transport services interact with each other to determine freight rates. While there are countless factors affecting supply and demand, the exposure of freights rates to market forces is inevitable.

Cargo volumes and demand for maritime transport services are usually the first to be hit by political, environmental and economic turmoil. Factors such as a slowdown in international trade, sanctions, natural disasters and weather events, regulatory measures and changes in fuel prices have an impact on the world economy and global demand for seaborne transport. These changes may occur quickly and have an immediate impact on demand for maritime transport services. As to the supply of maritime transport services, there is generally a tendency of overcapacity in the market, given that there are no inherent restrictions on the number of vessels that can be built and that it takes a long time from the moment a vessel order is placed to the time it is delivered, and is ready to be put in service.

Therefore, maritime transport is very cyclical and goes through periods of continuous busts and booms, with operators enjoying healthy earnings or struggling to meet their minimum operating costs.

In 2012, the maritime sector continued to experience low and volatile freight rates in its various segments because of surplus capacity in the global fleet generated by the severe downturn in trade in the wake of the 2008 economic and financial crisis. The steady delivery of newbuild vessels into an already oversupplied market, coupled with a weak economy, has kept rates under heavy pressure, as described below.

1. Container freight rates

In 2012, shrinking cargo volumes, mainly on the main East–West containerized trade routes, combined with an oversupply of tonnage, in particular of large container ships, inevitably led to volatile container freight rates and a weaker market in general, while charter rates remained on the decline.

Figure 3.1. Growth of demand and supply in container shipping, 2000–2013 (Annual growth rates)

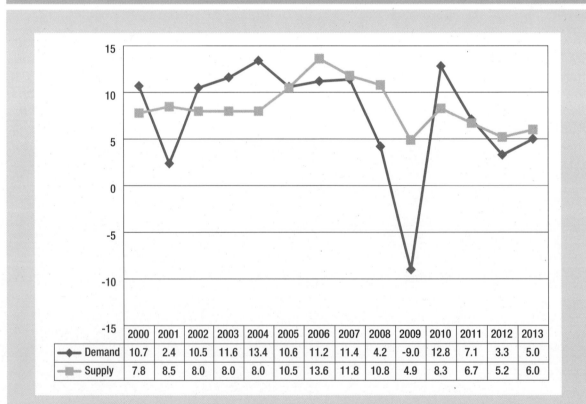

	2000	2001	2002	2003	2004	2005	2006	2007	2008	2009	2010	2011	2012	2013
Demand	10.7	2.4	10.5	11.6	13.4	10.6	11.2	11.4	4.2	-9.0	12.8	7.1	3.3	5.0
Supply	7.8	8.5	8.0	8.0	8.0	10.5	13.6	11.8	10.8	4.9	8.3	6.7	5.2	6.0

Source: Compiled by the UNCTAD secretariat on the basis of data from *Clarkson Container Intelligence Monthly*, various issues.
Note: Supply data refer to total container-carrying fleet capacity, including multi-purpose and other vessels with some container-carrying capacity. Demand growth is based on million TEU lifts. The data for 2013 are projected figures.

As seen in chapters 1 and 2, there has been an imbalance between the growth rates of demand and supply in the container market. As illustrated in figure 3.1, global container trade witnessed continuous downturn trends, with a growth in volume of 3.3 per cent in 2012, compared with 7 per cent in 2011. At the same time, the large influx of new vessels continued to affect the container shipping markets throughout 2012, with global container supply growing 5.2 per cent, outpacing global demand.

In an attempt to handle the imbalance between excessive supply and low demand, carriers deployed less capacity on routes where trade was declining, such as the main headhaul East–West routes, where trade was 5 per cent less compared with 2011. They deployed more capacity on the growing North–South routes, where trade grew by 4 per cent, and on interregional trade, which grew by

7 per cent, stimulated by increased consumer demand in emerging economies in 2012. (See chapter 1.)

Given the widening gap between the supply of vessel capacity and the demand for transport services, freight rates in the different container markets remained low, but improved in relative terms compared with 2011 (table 3.1). This can be attributed mainly to a change in shipping lines' strategy and the imposition of market discipline, that is, they were not seeking to gain market share and volume as in 2011 but rather to improve earnings. In 2011, rates remained low because the shipping lines were undercutting each other, seeking market share and volume. In an effort to control the slide of freight rates, carriers exercised in the first half of 2012 some degree of market power by applying a common pricing discipline known as general rate increases (GRIs).

Table 3.1.	Container freight markets and rates			
Freight markets	2009	2010	2011	2012
Trans-Pacific		(Dollars per FEU)		
Shanghai–United States West Coast	1 372	2 308	1 667	2 287
Percentage change		68.21	-27.77	37.19
Shanghai–United States East Coast	2 367	3 499	3 008	3 416
Percentage change		47.84	-14.03	13.56
Far East–Europe		(Dollars per TEU)		
Shanghai–Northern Europe	1 395	1 789	881	1 353
Percentage change		28.24	-50.75	53.58
Shanghai–Mediterranean	1 397	1 739	973	1 336
Percentage change		24.49	-44.05	37.31
North–South		(Dollars per TEU)		
Shanghai–South America (Santos)	2 429	2 236	1 483	1 771
Percentage change		-7.95	-33.68	19.42
Shanghai–Australia/New Zealand (Melbourne)	1 500	1 189	772	925
Percentage change		-20.73	-35.07	19.82
Shanghai–West Africa (Lagos)	2 247	2 305	1 908	2 092
Percentage change		2.56	-17.22	9.64
Shanghai–South Africa (Durban)	1 495	1 481	991	1 047
Percentage change		-0.96	-33.09	5.65
Intra-Asian		(Dollars per TEU)		
Shanghai–South-East Asia (Singapore)		318	210	256
Percentage change			-33.96	21.84
Shanghai–East Japan		316	337	345
Percentage change			6.65	2.37
Shanghai–Republic of Korea		193	198	183
Percentage change			2.59	-7.58
Shanghai–Hong Kong (China)		116	155	131
Percentage change			33.62	-15.48
Shanghai–Persian Gulf (Dubai)	639	922	838	981
Percentage change		44.33	-9.11	17.06

Source: Various issues of Container Intelligence Monthly, Clarkson Research Services.
Note: Data based on yearly averages.

As a result, average freight rates rose 51 per cent for the Far East–Europe and trans-Pacific trades in several successful rounds of GRIs, despite weak demand on the whole. Thus, rates from the Far East to the United States West Coast reached $2,600 per FEU in June 2012, up from $1,800 per FEU in January 2012. Comparably, rates on routes from the Far East to Northern Europe climbed from $750 per TEU in January 2012 to a peak of $1,900 per TEU in June 2012 (BIMCO, 2013). Nevertheless, the industry's collective resolution ceased in the second half of the year as positive operating incomes encouraged some carriers to revert to price competition and rate cutting with the aim of grabbing market share (Alphaliner, 2013). Consequently, rates to Northern Europe fell to as low as $1,000 per TEU in November 2012 as demand continued dropping (BIMCO, 2013).

The overall low freight rates observed in 2012 reduced carriers' earnings close to, and even below operating costs, especially when bunker oil prices remained both high and volatile. Accompanied by considerable price fluctuations, fuel costs stood at an average of $640 per ton in 2012, representing a 4 per cent increase over the previous year.[1] This could partially be passed on to customers by way of bunker surcharges and only adds pressure to overall increasing operating costs and low revenues.

As a result, carriers tried to apply various strategies to remedy the situation: laying up vessels,[2] going for slow or super-slow steaming,[3] postponing newbuild deliveries, raising surcharges and cutting services, suppressing running capacity on the main lanes and scrapping.[4]

Nonetheless, container carriers continued to suffer another year of negative operating earnings in 2012, although less so than in 2011. A recent survey[5] revealed that 21 carriers of the top 30 that publish financial results reported an overall operating loss of $239 million in 2012, with only seven carriers turning in positive results. Although only one third of the 21 carriers reported a profit, the overall result is seen as an improvement on the combined operating losses of almost $6 billion that these same 21 companies reported in 2011.[6]

Figure 3.2.   New ConTex Index, 2008–2013

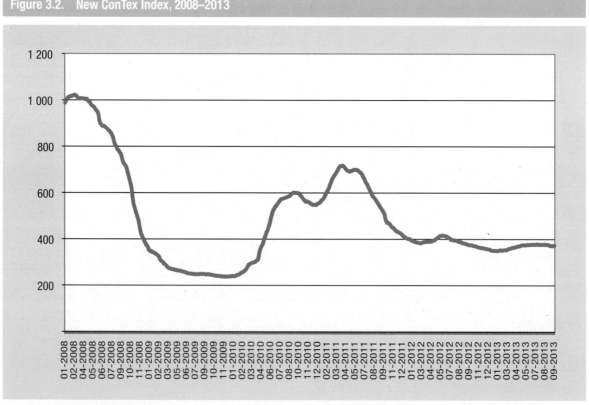

Source: Compiled by the UNCTAD secretariat, using the New ConTex index produced by the Hamburg Shipbrokers' Association. See http://www.vhss.de.

Notes: Index base: October 2007 – 1,000 points.

New ConTex is a container ship time charter assessment index calculated as an equivalent weight of percentage change from six ConTex assessments, including the following ship sizes: 1,100, 1,700, 2,500, 2,700, 3,500 and 4,250 TEUs.

On the other hand, tonnage providers, outsourcing the operation of their vessels, were direct victims of low demand and overcapacity, as clearly illustrated by low time charter rates (see table 3.2). As measured by the New ConTex[7] index (figure 3.2), the containership charter rates failed to pick up. Average charter rates remained low, with 2012 disappointing charter owners for the second year in a row. As two thirds of the laid-up tonnage average was charter-owned capacity – carriers utilized their own tonnage – there is clear evidence that the charter market suffered most in the process.[8] The largest decline in 2012 rates was observed in the larger-size vessels, which dropped 34–48 per cent com pared with the previous year (table 3.2).

Overall, surplus capacity generated by the severe downturn in trade since the 2008 economic and financial crisis has been and will remain a major threat to container shipping freight rates. The surplus of large ships (8,000+ TEUs) is leading to the cascading of capacity (redeployment over different routes) and is generating pressure on charter tonnage and freight rate volatility. Reassignment of smaller container vessels from main lanes facing declining demand to the fast growing non-main lanes has been crucial in managing the substantial delivery order of new larger ships.[9] This has also helped prevent the accumulation of vessel surplus capacity on the main lane routes where trade is low. (See chapter 2)

In 2013, global container trade is projected to grow by 5 per cent, and global container supply, by 6 per cent, according to June figures (Clarkson Research Services, 2013c). During the first half of 2013, several attempts by carriers to increase rates were again applied to several trade lines as a result of GRIs. Spot container shipping rates in Asia–Europe trade thus increased 165 per cent in the week of 4 July 2013 as GRIs implemented by carriers on 1 July took hold. The benchmark Shanghai–Rotterdam route was $2,622 per FEU, up from $990 a week earlier. On services from Asia to the West Coast of the United States, prices increased by $269 to reach $2,114 per FEU. From Asia to the East Coast of the United States, they increased by $377 to $3,361 per FEU (Lloyd's List Containerisation International, 2013). While GRIs are only temporary solutions to support comparative returns, achieving long-term market stability would enable shipping lines to deal with core market fundamentals and adjust capacity to demand.

Another important action launched by the carriers in 2013 in the face of difficult circumstances is the operational alliance called the P3 Network, agreed by the world's three largest container shipping lines: Maersk Line, Mediterranean Shipping Company (MSC), and CMA CGM. The agreement, which will go into effect in the second quarter of 2014, would allow liners to control overcapacity and reduce rates volatility. It would call for the three liners to pool vessels equivalent to 15 per cent of global capacity on three main lane trade routes (Asia–Europe, trans-Pacific and transatlantic), with an initial capacity of 255 vessels (or 2.6 million TEUs). Maersk Line will provide about 42 per cent of the alliance's capacity – including its new Triple E ships, among the world's largest carriers – while MSC will contribute 34 per cent and CMA CGM, 24 per cent (*Financial Times*, 2013a). The P3 East–West service network initiative is considered by some analysts as a positive development for the liner industry as a whole in the drive to reduce costs and stabilize the market. The same observers see no damage to the competition, where more than 15 carriers will continue operating independently and competing on most trade routes, including those sailed by the P3 partners (Drewry Container Insight, 2013).

Conclusion

In the near future, with world economies still under pressure, the sector is expected to continue facing the same weak demand volumes, especially in Europe, which would continue to have an impact on container freight rates, at least in 2013. This is compounded by surplus capacity, especially with regard to sailing larger ships on routes that have less cargo, while most of the growth is coming from non-main lane routes that require smaller ships. A major concern remains: how to reconcile the surge in supply of very large ships with trade growth generating demand for small and medium-sized units.

In the medium term, however, supply growth is likely to slow down, owing to the fewer vessel orders placed and the difficulty associated with financing new vessel builds. These variations may reduce the gap of new surplus and low demand, which would lead to improved container freight rates (Clarkson Research Services, 2013d). Likewise, changes in the world economy and in trade and seaborne shipments will influence the evolution of container freight rates.

2. Tanker freight rates

The tanker market, which encompasses the transportation of crude oil, refined petroleum products (clean and dirty products)[10] and chemicals, witnessed an equally difficult market environment in 2012. The year saw ups and downs for the tanker industry; this

Table 3.2. Container ship time charter rates (Dollars per 14-ton slot per day)

Ship type and sailing speed

Yearly averages

(TEUs)	2002	2003	2004	2005	2006	2007	2008	2009	2010	2011	2012	Percentage change 2012/2011
Gearless												
200–299 (min 14 knots)	16.9	19.6	25.0	31.7	26.7	27.2	26.0	12.5	12.4	12.4	12.6	1.4
300–500 (min 15 knots)	15.1	17.5	21.7	28.3	21.7	22.3	20.0	8.8	9.9	12.8	10.0	-21.9
Geared/gearless												
2 000–2 299 (min 22 knots)	4.9	9.8	13.8	16.4	10.5	11.7	10.0	2.7	4.8	6.3	3.3	-47.5
2 300–3 400 (min 22.5 knots)	6.0	9.3	13.2	13.0	10.2	10.7	10.7	4.9	4.7	6.2		
Geared												
200–299 (min 14 knots)	17.0	18.9	27.0	35.4	28.0	29.8	32.1	16.7	18.3	22.1	18.1	-18.1
300–500 (min 15 knots)	13.4	15.6	22.2	28.8	22.0	21.3	21.4	9.8	11.7	15.4	13.5	-12.3
600–799 (min 17-17.9 knots)	9.3	12.3	19.6	23.7	16.6	16.1	15.6	6.6	8.4	11.2	7.7	-31.3
700–999 (min 18 knots)	9.1	12.1	18.4	22.0	16.7	16.9	15.4	6.0	8.5	11.5	7.6	-34.0
1 000–1 299 (min 19 knots)	6.9	11.6	19.1	22.6	14.3	13.7	12.2	4.0	5.9	8.7	5.7	-34.8
1 600–1 999 (min 20 knots)	5.7	10.0	16.1	15.8	11.8	12.8	10.8	3.5	5.0	6.8	3.9	-42.2

Ship type and sailing speed

	Monthly averages for 2012												Monthly averages for 2013					
(TEUs)	Jan.	Feb.	Mar.	Apr.	May	Jun.	Jul.	Aug.	Sep.	Oct.	Nov.	Dec.	Jan.	Feb.	Mar.	Apr.	May	Jun.
Gearless																		
200–299 (min 14 knots)	13.1	11.7	11.7	12.4	13.6	12.4	12.3	12.6	14.6	11.9	12.6	12.9	12.1	13.4	10.0	12.6	13.3	13.1
300–500 (min 15 knots)	9.8	10.0	9.6	10.6	9.8	9.7	9.8	9.8	9.6	10.4	9.4	10.0	10.2	10.5	10.7	10.5	11.3	11.3
Geared/gearless																		
2 000–2 299 (min 22 knots)	3.4	3.3	3.4	3.4	3.4	3.5	3.3	3.2	3.2	3.1	3.2	3.1	3.2	3.0	3.1	3.3	3.3	3.4
Geared																		
200–299 (min 14 knots)	15.3	19.0	13.8	13.8	20.2	19.3	18.6	19.0	19.0	19.3	20.2	20.2	20.2	20.6	19.7	19.7	23.4	23.4
300–500 (min 15 knots)	12.3	15.2	13.1	13.0	12.7	14.5	12.6	11.4	13.3	13.1	15.8	15.4	13.8	13.8	14.0	14.2	14.1	16.5
600–799 (min 17-17.9 knots)	7.4	7.4	7.2	7.9	7.9	8.1	7.4	7.6	7.8	7.7	7.7	7.8	8.0	7.4	7.4	9.0	9.0	10.0
700–999 (min 18 knots)	7.7	7.8	7.1	7.6	7.6	7.0	7.0	7.2	7.6	8.3	7.7	8.8	8.1	8.6	8.4	9.1	9.0	8.5
1 000–1 299 (min19 knots)	6.3	5.5	5.6	5.6	5.7	6.1	5.8	5.6	5.7	5.7	5.6	5.0	5.3	5.7	5.8	6.0	6.2	6.4
1 600–1 999 (min 20 knots)	4.1	3.9	3.9	3.8	4.0	4.1	3.9	4.1	3.6	3.7	3.6	3.6	3.7	3.8	3.9	4.0	4.1	4.2

Source: Compiled by the UNCTAD secretariat based on data from *Shipping Statistics and Market Review*, various issues from 2002–2013, produced by the Institute of Shipping Economics and Logistics, Bremen, Germany. See also www.isl.org.

Abbreviation: min – minimum

Table 3.3.	Baltic Exchange Index						
	2008	*2009*	*2010*	*2011*	*2012*	*Percentage change (2012/2011)*	*2013 (Estimate)*
Dirty Tanker Index	1 510	581	896	782	719	*-8*	638
Clean Tanker Index	1 155	485	732	721	641	*-11*	649

Source: Clarkson Research Services, Shipping Intelligence Network – Timeseries, 2013.

volatility was felt across the board in many ship sizes and as a whole but perhaps slightly less so than in 2011. The average Baltic Exchange Dirty Tanker Index for the full year 2012 dropped to 719 (8 per cent less than the annual average of 2011), whereas the average Baltic Exchange Clean Tanker Index was below 700 (11 per cent less than the annual average of 2011).[11] These trends reflect the successive bad years recorded in the oil chartering market, as shown in table 3.3.

The sector was affected by a combination of factors leading to overall low freight rates: weak demand, slow imports growth, a change in the structure of tanker demand, new discoveries (e.g. the shale revolution in the United States), high oil prices, and high idle and tonnage capacity.

Freight rates and earnings for different tanker markets

Table 3.4 provides average spot freight rates quantified in Worldscale (WS), a standard measure for establishing spot rates on major tanker routes for various vessel sizes. It shows the general fall in dirty tanker rates for most routes and for most of the year, with the exception of a short peak in the last three months of 2012, which benefited from some positive rates. Large tonnage supply and lower tonnage demand pressured freight rates downwards. Despite the decline in the number of deliveries in 2012, fleet capacity remained abundant, and the new influx of dirty tankers only added to the problem, with a capacity increase of 5 per cent (OPEC, 2013).

On the demand side, most of the tanker markets bore the brunt of the weak global economic situation and the performance of large oil consumers, namely the OECD countries. Other contributing factors included a less vigorous Chinese economy and a change in the energy strategy of the United States, the world's largest consumer of petroleum. The United States started increasing its oil production and decreasing its imports accordingly (Barry Rogliano Salles, 2013).

VLCCs and the Suezmax markets were boosted somewhat in the beginning of the year, mainly when Saudi Arabia increased its production, and importers started building inventories in anticipation of the expected embargo on Iranian oil. However, once the demand for tonnage started declining and the market began slowing down, freight rates plummeted once again (Danish Ship Finance, 2013).

Despite the downward trend, crude tanker earnings rose on average by 12 per cent from $17,600 per day to $19,700 per day in 2012. This increase in earnings was spread across all segments, except Suezmax, which suffered from the decline of United States imports. VLCCs experienced the largest improvement, going from $17,000 per day to $20,500 per day in 2012 (Danish Ship Finance, 2013). However, this could barely cover operating costs estimated at $11,000–$12,000, but not the return on investment for new ships. Some vessel orders exceeded $150 million in 2008 (Barry Rogliano Salles, 2013).

For the Aframax market, 2012 has generally been a dull year. The market as a whole had come under pressure from a number of structural and unexpected challenges. The trend towards vessel upsizing, which brings vessels with capacities relatively higher than those currently deployed in respective routes, has been growing in different markets, as operators seek greater economies of scale. This has been the case of Suezmaxes taking some market share from Aframaxes, particularly in the Caribbean and the Mediterranean (Clarkson Research Services, 2013e). Moreover, the Mediterranean–Mediterranean route has proved to be particularly difficult, with rates changing from WS 130 in December 2011 to WS 85 in December 2012. A major contributing factor was the growing competition among ships for cargoes as vessels crowded into the region to take advantage of the increase in Libyan oil production and the spike in rates towards the end of 2011 (see chapter 1). Average spot earnings for Aframax across all routes were estimated to be $14,885 per day in 2012, compared with $13,528 in 2011 (Clarkson Research Services, 2013f). The operating costs of Aframax modern vessels run around $8,000–$9,000 per day.

Table 3.4.   Tanker market summary – clean and dirty spot rates, 2012–2013 (Worldscale)

Vessel type	Routes	2010 Dec	2011 Dec	Jan.	Feb.	Mar.	Apr.	May	Jun.	Jul.	Aug.	Sept.	Oct.	Nov.	Dec.	Percentage change Dec. 2012/ Dec. 2011	Jan.	Feb.	Mar.	Apr.	May
VLCC/ULCC (200 000 dwt+)																					
	Persian Gulf–Japan	61	59	67	52	59	63	63	44	36	35	38	37	41	48	-18.6	43	33	34	33	38
	Persian Gulf–Republic of Korea	56	56	61	51	58	58	55	41	33	34	38	35	40	46	-17.9	41	31	33	31	36
	Persian Gulf–Caribbean/East Coast of North America	36	37	40	34	35	42	39	30	24	23	25	23	27	28	-24.3	26	17	18	17	22
	Persian Gulf–Europe	57	59	..	52	40	44	39	29	25	24	..	22	30	26	-55.9	41	20	17	18	19
	West Africa–China	..	58	61	55	59	62	60	44	37	36	40	41	49	47	-19.0	43	34	36	37	37
Suezmax (100 000–160 000 dwt)																					
	West Africa–North-West Europe	118	86	91	77	87	68	81	70	65	57	56	59	58	70	-18.6	62	57	59	62	53
	West Africa–Caribbean/East Coast of North America	103	83	85	75	84	65	81	66	63	56	55	57	56	65	-21.7	59	52	57	57	53
	Mediterranean–Mediterranean	113	86	98	86	84	73	93	85	69	64	56	62	66	67	-22.1	70	66	73	67	62
Aframax (70 000–100 000 dwt)																					
	North-West Europe–North-West Europe	162	122	111	93	95	99	98	94	89	87	84	89	82	93	-23.8	88	87	94	94	80
	North-West Europe–Caribbean/East Coast of North America	120	..	119	99	..	..	99	..	..	..	..	..	75	80		..	..	85	..	..
	Caribbean–Caribbean/East Coast of North America	146	112	118	129	112	131	115	105	94	94	89	91	110	91	-18.8	84	96	102	87	110
	Mediterranean–Mediterranean	138	130	105	82	104	94	87	100	95	82	76	78	79	85	-34.6	82	85	86	84	71
	Mediterranean–North-West Europe	133	118	97	82	105	91	85	92	100	81	75	77	77	80	-32.2	84	86	90	79	68
	Indonesia–Far East	111	104	100	90	60	85	82	86	43	90	98	94	92	90	-13.5	83	74	68	72	68
Panamax (40 000 - 70 000 dwt)																					
	Mediterranean–Mediterranean	168	153	147	157	147	140	125	120	120	..	116	..	154	168	9.8	135	145	115	12	125
	Mediterranean–Caribbean/East Coast of North America	146	121	124	121	118	127	137	127	105	111	114	134	126	160	32.2	98	100	104	111	100
	Caribbean–East Coast of North America/Gulf of Mexico	200	133	113	148	145	131	151	141	102	..	118	105	130	156	17.3	115	133	138	113	118
All clean tankers																					
70 000–80 000 dwt Persian Gulf–Japan		125	105	100	86	84	91	88	91	99	104	96	107	122	116	10.5	88	81	93	96	80
50 000–60 000 dwt Persian Gulf–Japan		128	119	107	101	100	117	114	105	125	120	116	114	133	144	21.0	109	97	124	120	97
35 000–50 000 dwt Caribbean–East Coast of North America/Gulf of Mexico		158	155	150	165	152	155	123	..	100	108	105	117	164	162	4.5	120	126	60	120	132
25 000–35 000 dwt Singapore–East Asia		193	..	..	150	155	183	223	..	170	..	190	205	215	220		199	185	199	191	175

Source: UNCTAD secretariat, based on Drewry Shipping Insight, various issues.

Note: The figures are indexed per ton voyage charter rates for a tanker of 75,000 dwt. The basis is the value WS 100.

The freight levels of Panamax crude tankers were healthier than expected but still relatively low. This could be attributed to declining overall volumes of United States crude import levels, and upsizing, with charterers fixing larger vessels at the expense of the smaller Panamax tankers. Average Panamax dirty products spot earnings increased from $10,535 in 2011 to $14,769 in 2012 (Clarkson Research Services, 2013f). Ultimately, the dependence of the Panamax crude fleet on trade towards the United States, coupled with the shift in the crude tanker market towards larger vessels, is likely to make Panamax crude trading largely obsolete in the medium term (Clarkson Research Services, 2013f).

The product tanker market also witnessed an unstable year. The average Baltic Clean Tanker Index for 2012 was down 11 per cent from the previous year average. Weak economic growth led to low demand for oil products, thereby compounding the large oversupply of vessels. High bunker prices exacerbated the situation further. With clean capacity rising by 2 per cent (OPEC, 2013) and distance-adjusted demand growing by 0.7 per cent,[13] the imbalance between supply and demand persisted in 2012. However, some peak periods occurred, mainly due to demand stemming from the chartering activity of Asian countries in the Persian Gulf.

The overall decline in tanker freight rates has encouraged shipowners to reduce their operating costs considerably and in particular, bunker consumption. The trend of maximizing fleet efficiency, slow steaming, scrapping and idling some ships observed in 2011 also increased in 2012.

The overall picture of the tanker market and tanker freight rates has evolved since the 2008 global economic and financial crisis. During the boom, the tanker market was a robust one influenced by strong import growth from the North Atlantic and Asia, with supply capacities under control and freight rates relatively high. Since then, the tanker market has slipped into recession; average freight rates for most vessel sizes and routes have decreased, including eastern and western destinations. This has been compounded by high oil prices that also modified consumer behaviour, while environmental pressure and technical innovation helped improve energy efficiency and reduce demand for oil products (Clarkson Research Services, 2013e).

As a result, owners suffered from poor earnings and some have been facing default or bankruptcy. For example, the United States crude oil transportation firms, General Maritime Corporation[12] (Bloomberg, 2013a) and Overseas Shipholding (Bloomberg, 2013b), filed for bankruptcy protection in 2011, as they suffered from slumping freight rates and global tonnage overcapacity after having taken out big loans to fund fleet expansion.

More tanker companies may continue facing trouble and new bankruptcies may emerge, as a significant number of time charter contracts signed during the boom years in early 2008 were to end in 2013. The forecast of new bankruptcies comes after a recent poll by Lloyd's List found that 33 per cent of voters expected more than four publicly listed tanker companies to be in trouble in 2013 (Lloyd's List, 2013a). Owners who signed longer-term charters in early 2008 had been enjoying high five-year time charter values – but that is going to change. Modern 310,000 dwt VLCC contract prices halved from $62,500 per day in August 2008 to $31,000 in December 2012. Suezmax and Aframax rates experienced a 40 per cent drop during that period, while five-year contract prices for medium-range product tankers fell by one third (Lloyd's List, 2013b).

Conclusion

In 2014 and 2015, tanker freight rates should see some improvement as cargo demand and fleet supply become more balanced. However, in the long run, several factors, mainly relating to oil demand,

production and industry developments, may influence the tanker market. These are:

- Changes in consumption patterns are taking place in the global oil market as energy efficiency and clean transport programmes are being adopted in most OECD countries and many developing countries;
- The United States, a major oil consumer, is predicted to become the world's largest oil producer by 2020;
- Refineries are moving from the West to the East, with the closure of refineries in the United States and Europe and the growth of Indian, Chinese and Middle Eastern refineries;
- Arctic routes are being opened up (North West and North East passages) and the Panama Canal is being widened and is expected to be opened to Suezmaxes in 2015 (Barry Rogliano Salles, 2013); [14]
- New energy efficiency measures, introduced by IMO and which came into force at the start of 2013, aim to reduce vessel energy consumption and to increase the use of environmentally less damaging fuels.[15]

These changes, combined with fleet development, will have an impact on the development of the tanker market, freight rates and volatility mix movement.[16]

3. Dry bulk freight rates

Like other shipping markets, the dry bulk market, generally categorized either as major bulk (iron ore, coal, grain, bauxite/alumina and phosphate rock) or minor bulk (agricultural products, mineral cargoes, cement, forest products and steel products), has also suffered from the severe overcapacity and slow economy growth that have sustained low freight and charter rates (Clarkson Research Services, 2013e; Barry Rogliano Salles, 2013; Danish Ship Finance, 2013). As a result, earnings in all fleet segments continued to fall. Overall, bulk carrier average earnings went down to $6,579 per day in 2012, 41 per cent lower than in 2011 (Clarkson Research Services, 2013e).

As shown in figure 3.3, the Baltic Exchange Dry Index started 2012 with a sudden plunge from a temporal average spike of 1,928 points in the last quarter of 2011 to 867 in the first quarter of 2012. By the third quarter of 2012, the index averaged the lowest since 1998, approaching the record lows of 1986. The average Baltic Exchange Dry Index for 2012 was 923, down by some 40 per cent from the annual average of 2011.

Given these low rates, most vessels, especially in the larger segments, were running below operating costs.

Figure 3.3. Baltic Exchange Dry Index, 2007–2013 (Index base year 1985 – 1,000 points)

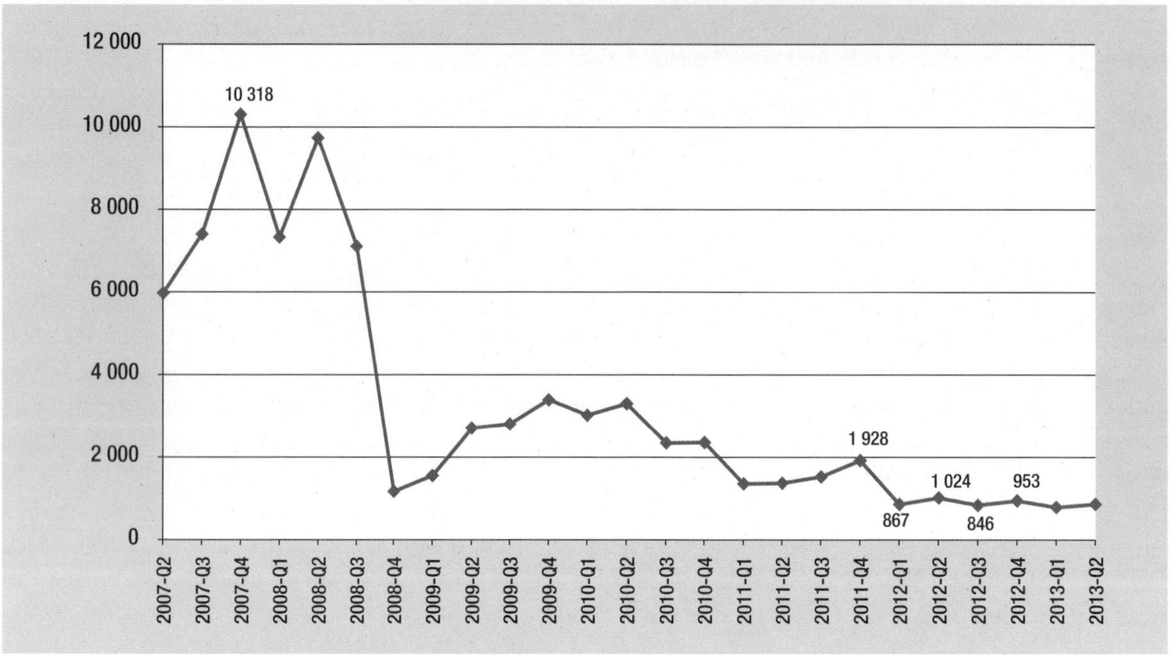

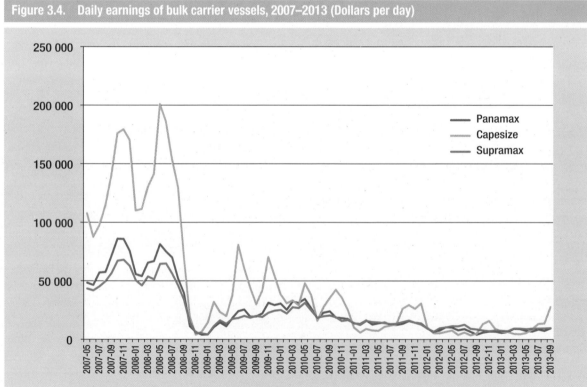

Source: UNCTAD, based on London Baltic Exchange data.

Abbreviation: Q – quarter

Note: The index is made up of 20 key dry bulk routes measured on a time charter basis. The index covers Handysize, Supramax, Panamax and Capesize dry bulk carriers, carrying commodities such as coal, iron ore and grain.

Figure 3.4. Daily earnings of bulk carrier vessels, 2007–2013 (Dollars per day)

Source: UNCTAD, based on data from Clarkson Shipping Intelligence Network, figures published by the London Baltic Exchange.

Note: Supramax – average of the six time charter routes; Panamax – average of the four time charter routes; Capesize – average of the four time charter routes.

Figure 3.4 illustrates daily earnings of three different vessels sizes: Capesize, Supramax and Panamax. It clearly shows that Capesize vessels was the segment that was hardest hit during a troubled and volatile year.

Capesize market

The biggest surge in newbuild vessels delivery took place in the Capesize market, where more than 280 Capesizes (Barry Rogliano Salles, 2013) were delivered in 2012, exerting supply-side pressure on the market and resulting in weak earnings. With 12 per cent Capesize fleet growth in 2012, which was lower than the 19 per cent expansion recorded in 2011 (Clarkson Research Services, 2013e), it still represented more than twice the growth in iron ore trade, largely serviced by Capesize vessels. This market imbalance led to a fall in average Capesize earnings to $8,356 per day in 2012, down 54 per cent year over year. Only the last quarter of 2012 witnessed a short peak in rates, where average earnings surpassed $10,000 a day during the same period, with a peak of $22,000 per day in October, sustained by a greater increase in Chinese iron ore import demand (Clarkson Research Services, 2013e).

On average, Capesize time charter rates were also lower in 2012 with a general decline over the year. At the start of 2012, the one-year time charter rate for a 170,000 dwt vessel stood at $17,562 per day, but had fallen to $11,750 per day by the end of December 2012, a disastrous development compared with the all-time high average of $161,600 per day in October 2007 (Clarkson Research Services, 2013a).

Panamax market

With an expansion of 13 per cent in the deployed capacity of Panamax fleets, oversupply had yet again a considerable effect on the Panamax market, despite the growth in steam coal trade, which increased 12 per cent in 2012.

With average earnings decreasing to just $5,838 a day in 2012, down 49 per cent, shipowners were operating below the average levels required to cover benchmark expenses.

Panamax time charter rates were also exposed to significant downward pressure, with the one-year time charter rate for a 75,000 dwt bulk carrier falling from a low average of $11,100 per day at the start of 2012, to $7,750 per day by the end of December 2012,

compared with an average of $79,375 per day in October 2007 (Clarkson Research Services, 2013a).

Handy markets

Supramax

The Supramax markets in 2012 were affected by a combination of additional supply-side pressure and a slower growth of minor bulk trade. The average Supramax trip earnings reached $8,857 per day, down 36 per cent year over year. Although Supramax earnings in 2012 remained above the benchmark levels required to cover operating expenses, profit margins of owners remained under substantial pressure. Earnings in the first half of 2012 were on average 20 per cent higher than in the second half, as further rapid supply growth took its toll, while trade volumes of some commodities weakened.

The average one-year time charter rate remained low, around $8,750 per day in December 2012, compared with $11,250 in January 2012.

Handysize

Despite slower expansion in the Handysize fleet, which stood at a mere 1 per cent in 2012, compared with previous years of strong deliveries, weaker growth in minor bulk trade contributed to a further decrease in Handysize rates in 2012.

The one-year time charter rate for a 30,000 dwt vessel began the year at an already relatively low level of $9,750 per day. It declined slowly, but steadily, throughout 2012 to reach $7,250 per day by the end of December. However, rates in the Atlantic Basin were significantly higher than those in the Pacific. Supramax rates in the Atlantic were about $9,900 ($16,500 in 2011) compared with $7,900 in the Pacific ($11,300 in 2011). Handysize rates were about $8,600 in the Atlantic, compared with $7,000 in the Pacific. These fluctuations can be explained by demand volatility induced namely by a drop in Indian iron ore trade, largely serviced by Supramaxes and Handysizes, and a large number of deliveries of new ships out of the Asian shipyards, which continued to put a heavy burden on supply.

Overall and similarly to the other segments of shipping markets, the continued deterioration of the dry bulk market pressed owners to take radical measures such as scrapping plans, deferring the delivery of new vessels, slow steaming, idling ships and implementing fuel efficiency programmes to cut costs and keep debt levels low.

Nevertheless, given the huge losses faced by the market, several owners were not able to subsist and had to file for bankruptcy. A recent example is Excel Maritime Carriers Ltd, as it could no longer service its debts. Other casualties include the United Kingdom's oldest shipping firm, Stephenson Clarke Shipping, and Italy's Deiulemar Shipping (*Reuters*, 2013).

Conclusion

In the short term, market conditions are likely to remain challenging for dry bulk shipping. Thus, the strength of Chinese demand growth for dry bulk imports will remain a key influence in offsetting the supply side of the oversupplied bulk market. However, a slower pace of newbuilding deliveries and a sustained rhythm of demolition should contribute to a more balanced dry bulk market in the future.

B. RECENT DEVELOPMENTS IN SHIPPING FINANCE: GREATER INVOLVEMENT OF PRIVATE EQUITY

This section provides a brief overview of recent developments in the shipping finance sector, with a special focus on private equity and its growing role in the wake of the 2008 global economic and financial meltdown.

Over the past few years, private equity funds, new players to this industry, have been showing growing interest and gaining momentum in filling the gap of traditional bank finance. Between 2011 and 2012, private equity funds financed no less than 22 shipping transactions with an aggregate magnitude of more than $6.4 billion (Maritime Briefing, 2013). This new source of capital is much welcomed by the sector, which has been facing tighter credit markets, low charter rates and heavy losses since the economic and financial crisis.

1. The shipping finance market before and after 2008

Prior to 2008, shipping finance was widely available as the industry was experiencing a period of sound growth and historically high shipping rates. Many shipping companies expanded and placed long-term orders for large numbers of newbuild vessels. From 2003 to 2008, the newbuild market was booming – new ships worth $800 billion were ordered, with half of the orders placed in 2007–2008, when vessel prices

were at their peak (Stopford, 2010). Banks loans were easily accessible, up to 80 per cent of loan to value for new vessels, leaving little margin for error in vessel values. Most of the new vessels were scheduled for delivery in the years immediately following the financial crisis of 2008 (PIMCO, 2012).

However, the global recession brought about by the economic and financial crisis produced a completely new scenario. After 2008, the slow growth of global demand for goods on one hand, and a new supply of vessels entering the market on the other, sent charter rates plummeting in most markets. As a result, ship values also collapsed, causing the shipping industry to struggle with losses, loans defaults and bankruptcies. Added to this was the need to find financing for newbuild vessels under yard contracts that could not be assigned or cancelled (Maritime Briefing, 2013).

In turn, the banking sector struggled, dealing with default payments and decreased value for the collateral that secured their loans. However, with the price of vessels plunging to levels below outstanding debt, banks preferred to defer repayments and to restructure the terms of loans in order to avoid writing off defaulting loans and forcing vessel foreclosures. Currently, there are about $500 billion in shipping debts. Of this, 40 top banks hold more than 90 per cent; the top 12 banks account for over half, and more than 80 per cent of shipping debt is financed by European banks (PIMCO, 2012). Losses were more pronounced for German banks, major financiers of the sector. For example, Nordbank announced that it had increased loan impairment charges by almost threefold for its ship portfolio in 2012. This situation prompted the German regulator BaFin to take action and place greater scrutiny on banks' shipping exposures in 2012 (Maritime Briefing, 2013).

In an effort to protect their existing assets, traditional banks have started restricting their financing or pulling out from financing the industry over the past few years. In fact, the top 10 banks in shipping have reduced their shipping loan books by over $50 billion since 2008 (PIMCO, 2012). This has made the shipping market more difficult and influenced further price downturns for second-hand ships. Yet, at a time when many traditional European bankers such as Nordbank, Commerzbank, Société Générale, BNP Paribas, Royal Bank of Scotland and Lloyds Banking Group are downsizing their shipping exposure, other mainly non-European banks are entering the market. United States banks such as Citigroup and Bank of America Corporation have become more active.[17] This may be explained by the fact that banks in the United States are less constrained than European lenders by the cost of funding in dollars and the impact of the new Basel III regulations, which are explained further below. The Commonwealth Bank of Australia and Chinese banks have also increased their focus on the shipping industry.

In the future and given the constraints encountered, banks may not intervene in financing the sector to the same extent as in the past. As the market slowed, the perceived safety of vessels as assets weakened, and lenders have grown cautious. Traditional finance may be available but subject to more stringent requirements (today banks finance up to 60 per cent loan–to–value ratio for new vessels) and regulations, including the implementation of the Basel III frameworks, which create new regulatory millstones. The Basel III agreement will require new capital ratios for banks and is expected to be implemented gradually between 2013 and 2019. One of the main outcomes of Basel III will be a significant rise in the banking industry's capital requirements, potentially requiring more core equity capital by shipowners and raising the cost of credit of traditional financing sources (KPMG, 2012).

The increasing role of export-import banks and export credit agencies

The retreat of traditional bank lending reinforced the role of export credit agencies and export-import (Exim) banks in the sector. To stimulate sector development and deals, export credit agencies have strengthened their programmes to support the financing of vessels. Key credit and guarantee agencies include Japan, the Republic of Korea, Brazil, Germany and Norway, which financed deals totaling $19.8 billion between January 2012 and April 2013 (Lloyd's List, 2013c).

On the other hand, the Export-Import Bank of China has allocated a bigger share to ship finance to help shipowners weather the current crisis. With a $12 billion shipping portfolio in 2012, it is expected to increase its investment by 20 per cent in 2013 (Barry Rogliano Salles, 2013). Moreover, it has been actively seeking new partnerships with other ship financing banks to increase its exposure to syndicated shipping loans. The Bank has also established a policy to encourage funding orders by foreign owners in the Chinese shipyards to support shipbuilding. This is illustrated in agreements signed in May 2013 with three Greek shipping companies, Diana Shipping, Angelicoussis and Dynagas, to provide them with loans to order high-end vessels in Chinese yards (Chinadaily.com, 2013).

The declining role of the German limited partnership system

An important form of shipping finance directly related to a specific country is the German limited partnership, commonly known by its acronym KG (*Kommanditgesellschaft*). In the 1970's, the KG model was established in Germany to raise private equity as a form of financing for projects. KG funds are tax-driven structures in the form of a German limited partnership that acquires funds from private investors participating in single-purpose companies and leveraged by bank loans. The KG structure is exempted from corporate tax and thus considered to be a cheaper source of financing than banks.

KG financing covers several types of assets: ships, real estate, aviation, renewable energy, natural resources, infrastructure, containers, life insurance policies, films and other media rights.

In the case of shipping, finance is used to buy a specific vessel (mainly containers) with a charter to a German owner and debt sourced from a German bank. In a typical case of KG financial structure, most often a shipowner will assign or sell and charter back the vessel to a the KG fund or special-purpose company, which is set up to primarily own the vessel during the charter hire period. The arranger (the fund) of the structure will negotiate with banks and sell the equity to a group of private German individuals, who will use the investment to reduce their income taxes. The arranger will then run the transaction and pay dividends to private investors. The fund or single-purpose company will be liquidated after the ship is sold. (See figure 3.5.).

At first, the generous tax breaks offered to investors made the scheme very popular. It has been estimated that around one third of the world's container ships was financed by such partnerships (*Journal of Commerce*, 2013).

However, following the ongoing and prolonged shipping downturn, the KG system has faced a major crisis. More than 150 single-ship funds have filed for bankruptcy in 2012, and a further 500 to 1,000 risk insolvency, according to some estimates (*Journal of Commerce*, 2013). Investors have therefore lost faith in the current KG financing model for shipping investments, and shipping companies are seeking complementary or alternative modes and sources of ship financing (KPMG, 2012).

2. Private equity in the shipping market

In this difficult shipping context, many private equity funds have seized the opportunity created by tight credit markets and historically low vessel values to invest in ships and shipping companies.

Private equity interest in shipping had started rather slowly, with many funds sensing an opportunity but waiting to make their investments at the bottom of the market cycle. The sector, with its cyclical and volatile charter rates markets, is not a typical private equity target. Private equity investors consider that the volatility and downside risks of the sector have made it unattractive. However, recent developments, such as the drop in asset prices, the range of investment opportunities and portfolio sales, the scarcity of available finance and the belief that the market has hit bottom, have enticed many private equity firms to enter the market. According to estimates, private equity investments in the industry accounted for about 2 per cent of the shipping companies' enterprise value in 2013. This amount could double by the end of 2014 if alternative funding markets remain unavailable (*Financial Times*, 2013b).

Private equity investment in the shipping industry

Private equity funds vary greatly in size and investment objectives. Some private equity funds look for long-term returns; others seek to make high returns on short-or medium-term investments (three to seven years). The latter have been the main force attracting private equity funds to the shipping sector, which is cyclical and has expectations for recovery and long-term growth.

Private equity generally consists of making investments in equities of non-listed companies. Besides capital, the investors become active owners and would usually provide the companies with strategic and managerial support to create value and resell at a higher price. Value creation in private equity is primarily based on achieving increased growth and operational efficiency in acquired companies. The type of investments can include a number of different structures, as follows:

- Direct equity or investment in companies;
- Bridge financing and mezzanine financing for shipping companies needing short-term liquidity;
- Debtor in possession, which entails buying the debt of operators or buying portfolios of vessels;
- Sale-leaseback transactions, which entail vessel sales of shipping companies to leasing companies, a large cash inflow and leasing the vessel back from the leasing company in order to maintain operations;
- Joint ventures formed to acquire, manage and sell shipping businesses.

The overall objective is to sell these investments and generate above-market returns once the market rebounds. In the context of shipping, private equity

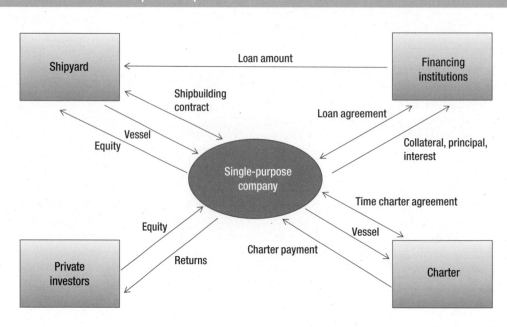

Figure 3.5. The German limited partnership model

Table 3.5.	Selected recent private equity investments in shipping				
Investor	Value estimate (millions of dollars)	Asset type	Company	Type of investment	Year
Riverstone Holdings LLC Zhejiang Marine Leasing Co.	18	Clean product carriers Vessel (Zhong Chang 118)	Ridgebury Tankers LLC Yangxi Zhong Chang Marine	Direct equity/investment Sale and leaseback agreement	2013
Oaktree Capital	135	Product tanker	Newco	5 medium-range product tankers from Torm	2013
Oaktree & Goldman Sachs	150		Excel Maritime Debt (from Nordea Bank)	Bank debt	2013
Kelso & Company LP	126	Containers (2 x 6 900 TEU ships)	Technomar Shipping	Joint venture	2013
Ontario Teachers Pension Plan	470	507 000 containers (795 000 TEUs)	SeaCube Container Leasing Ltd.	Direct investment	2013
Seaborne Intermodal (Lindsay Goldberg LLC)	420	Container	Buss Capital	Container acquisition (275 000 containers)	2013
Roullier, Group BPCE	147	Dry bulkers (4 x fuel-efficient Handysize bulk)	Louis Dreyfus Armateurs	Joint venture	2013
Perella Weinberg Southern Cross Latin America Private Equity Funds	220	Product tankers	Prime Marine Ultrapetrol	Joint venture Direct equity/investment	2012
Leasing company formed by Regions Bank and the Royal Bank of Scotland	59	Pure car truck carrier	International Shipholding Corporation	Sale and leaseback agreement	2012
Global Hunter Securities Trailer Bridge	15		Trailer Bridge, Inc	Debtor in possession	2011
JP Morgan		Project cargo/modern and young heavy lift vessels	Harren (SUMO Shipping)	Joint venture	2011
Consortium led by WL Ross & Co. (First Reserve Corporation, China Investment Corporation)	1 000	Medium-range product tankers	Diamond S Shipping	Direct equity investment	2011
Alterna Capital Partners	100	Product Tankers/ Supramax	Solo/Western Bulk		2010–2012
Apollo Management	200	Suezmax tankers	Principal Maritime First Ship Lease Ltd		2010
Kelso & Company	200	Supramax bulkers	Delphin Shipping LLC		2010
Littlejohn/Northern	100	Container ships	Soundview Maritime LLC		2010
Kelso & Company		Container ships	Poseidon Container Holdings LLC		2010
Carlyle	1 000	Container ships	CGI (with Seaspan)		2010
Eton Park/ Rhone Capital	175	Container ships	Euromar		2010
Greenbriar Equity Group	100	Product tankers	Seacove Shipping Partners		2009
Sterling Partners	170	Tankers and barges flying United States flag	United States Shipping		2009
Fortress Investments	100	Handysize bulkers	Clipper Bulk		2009
Blackstone/Cerberus	500	Tankers flying United States flag	American Petroleum Tankers		2008
New Mountain Capital		Project cargo flying United States flag	Intermarine	Andre Grikitis	2008

Source: Marine Money, Watson, Farley & Williams, Lloyds, McQuilling Services and other sources.

investors are capitalizing not only on the companies, but also on the projected growth of the market where companies are operating. This would require strong cooperation between shipping and private equity partners, and a good understanding of industry fundamentals and maritime dynamics and regulations, in particular of the following (Maritime Briefing, 2013):

- The shipping market is characterized largely by cyclical movements. These movements can expose investors to high volatility, which leads to high profits, but to considerable losses as well;

- Investments in shipping companies and shipping assets can expose private equity funds to liability under laws and regulations relating to competition and foreign sanctions, for example;

- The choice of a vessel entails various considerations that should be carefully weighed when buying ships (e.g. ship classifications, newbuilding ships versus ships in operation);

- The choice of flag can have a significant impact on the cost of operations, chartering modalities, financing and taxation issues;

- Expertise is required in the negotiation of yard contracts, charters, commercial and technical ship management agreements, and loan documents. Shipping is also subject to special environmental laws and regulations that can be a source of significant liability.

Impacts of private equity on the shipping industry

The growth of private equity can influence the shipping industry in several ways:

- In 2012, it was estimated that about $65 billion in new debt and equity alone were needed to cover orders of new ships, as well as sales and purchases of existing vessels. In 2013 and 2014, the gap will be $101 billion and $83 billion, respectively

(Bloomberg, 2012). Untapped private equity funds, estimated to be around $1 trillion (CNN Money, 2012) can fill this gap and help the industry generate economic growth and create new jobs;

- The emergence of private equity investment would likely lead to further consolidation in the industry. Under ongoing difficult circumstances, carriers have been struggling to make profits because of an overcapacity of vessels, slumping demand and high operating costs. This may prompt private equity investors to seek market consolidation with the aim of controlling supply of tonnage and costs, hence achieving price discipline and economies of scale;

- Vertical integration is another possibility for private equity funds. As private equity makes inroads into the sector, vertically integrated investment may be associated with its strategy for increased control and competitive advantage gain. Because of the high level of specialization in the maritime transport sector, there are significant opportunities for the vertical integration of companies into one or all parts of the transport value chain and logistics. Private equity funds that already have investments in several related activities might consider merging them into more a capital-intensive industry.

In conclusion, the role of private equity funds appears fundamental for the growth of the sector and could affect its development in several ways, including through the consolidation and vertical integration of transport services. This would call for improving the efficiency of the sector and building more financially sound companies. However, it must also be kept in mind that private equity funds are temporary investors whose overall objective is to sell or float their investments once the market rebounds. While their investment horizon is typically between three and seven years, they would wish to be able to make their own decision at any time as to the exit period in order to maximize profits.

REFERENCES

Alphaliner (2013). Alphaliner Weekly Newsletter. 4 February.

Barry Rogliano Salles (2013). 2013 Annual Review: Shipping and Shipbuilding Markets. Barry Rogliano Salles.

BIMCO (2013). The shipping market in 2012 and looking forward. Available at https://www.bimco.org/Reports/Market_ Analysis/2013/0104_Reflections.aspx (accessed 5 August 2013).

Bloomberg (2011). Bank retreat on shipping seen filled by private equity: Freight. 23 May. Available at http://www.bloomberg. com/news/2012-05-22/bank-retreat-on-shipping-seen-filled-by-private-equity-freight.html (accessed 2 September 2013).

Bloomberg (2012).General Maritime files for bankruptcy protection with $1.4 billion in debt. Available at http://www.bloomberg.com/ news/2011-11-17/general-maritime-files-for-bankruptcy-protection-with-1-4-billion-in-debt.html (accessed 31 July 2013).

Bloomberg (2013b). Overseas shipholding group files for bankruptcy. Available at http://www.bloomberg.com/news/2012-11- 14/overseas-shipholding-group-files-for-bankruptcy.html (accessed 31 July 2013).

Chinadaily.com (2013). EXIM bank to finance Greek ship owners. 21 May. Available at //www.chinadaily.com. cn/business/2013-05/21/content_16516813.htm (accessed 1 September 2013).

Clarkson Research Services (2013a). Shipping Intelligence Network – Timeseries. Available at http://clarksons.net/sin2010/ ts/Default.aspx (accessed 31 July 2013).

Clarkson Research Services (2013b). Container Intelligence Quarterly, First Quarter 2013.

Clarkson Research Services (2013c). *Container Intelligence Monthly*. June.

Clarkson Research Services (2013d). *Container Intelligence Monthly*. May.

Clarkson Research Services (2013e). Shipping Review & Outlook. A Half Yearly Review of the Shipping Market.

Clarkson Research Services (2013f). *Oil & Tanker Trade Outlook*. January.

CNN Money (2012). Private equity has $1 trillion to invest. 31 July. Available at http://finance.fortune.cnn.com/2012/07/31/ private-equity-has-1-trillion-to-invest/ (accessed 29 July 2013).

Danish Ship Finance (2013). Shipping Market Review. Available at http://www.shipfinance.dk/~/~/media/Shipping-Market- Review/Shipping-Market-Review---April-2013.ashx (accessed 1 September 2013).

Drewry Container Insight (2013). Maersk, MSC and CMA CGM to join forces. 23 June.

Financial Times (2013a). "Big three" container shipping groups plan alliance. 18 June.

Financial Times (2013b). Private equity investment in shipping predicted to double. 20 June.

Journal of Commerce (2013). Container ship financing remains available despite collapse of Germany's KG system. 12 March. Available at http://www.joc.com/maritime-news/ships-shipbuilding/container-ship-financing-remains-available-despite- collapse-germany%E2%80%99s-kg-system_20130312.html (accessed 29 July 2013).

KPMG (2012). Ship Financing in Flux: Searching for a New Course. Available at http://www.kpmg.com/UK/en/IssuesAndInsights/ ArticlesPublications/Documents/PDF/Market%20Sector/Transport/ship-financing-in-flux.pdf (accessed 1 September 2013).

Lloyd's List (2013a). Opinion poll predicts tanker bankruptcies. 10 January. Available at http://www.lloydslist.com/ll/sector/ tankers/article414768.ece (accessed 31 July 2013).

Lloyd's List (2013b). Clock is ticking on tanker company bankruptcies. 18 January. Available at http://www.lloydslist.com/ll/ sector/tankers/article415255.ece (accessed 31 July 2013).

Lloyd's List (2013c). Nor-Shipping: Norway's export credit agency favours safety and crew competence. Available at http://www.lloydslist.com/ll/sector/finance/article423950.ece (accessed 31 July 2013).

Lloyd's List Containerisation International (2013). Asia–Europe rates double. 28 June. Available at http://www.lloydslist.com/ ll/sector/containers/article425313.ece.

Lloyd's Loading List.com (2013a). Slow steaming: Everyone's a winner now? 7 January. Available at http://www.lloydsloadinglist. com/freight-directory/news/slow-steaming-everyones-a-winner-now/20018015270.htm#.Udl464j8LIU).

Lloyd's Loading List.com (2013b). Top box lines lost $239m last year. 10 April. Available at http://www.lloydsloadinglist.com/ freight-directory/sea/top-box-lines-lost-239m-last-year/20018037395.htm

Maritime Briefing (2013). Private equity investments in ships and shipping companies. Watson, Farley & Williams. February. Available at http://www.wfw.com/Publications/Publication1209/$File/WFW-Maritime-PrivateEquityGetsInterested.pdf (accessed 1 September 2013).

OPEC (2013). Monthly oil market report. February 2013. OPEC.

PIMCO (2012). Viewpoints. Global shipping: Any port in a storm? Available at http://www.pimco.com/EN/Insights/Pages/Devabhaktuni-and-Kennedy-on-Global-Shipping.aspx (accessed 31 July 2013).

Reuters (2013). Outlook brightens for drybulk shippers, but fewer left afloat. 28 June (accessed 1 September 2013).

SeeNews Shipping (2012). US Genmar emerges from bankruptcy. 18 May. Available at http://shipping.seenews.com/news/us-genmar-emerges-from-bankruptcy-276664 (accessed 9 September 2013).

Stopford M (2010). "A Year of Decisions for Shipping: How Will the Markets Develop?" Presentation made at the Financial Times Deutschland Ship Finance Conference. SMM International Trade Fair, Hamburg, Germany. 6 September. Available at http://www.clarksons.net/archive/research/freestuff/Martin%20Stopford%20How%20Will%20the%20Market%20Develop%20%20Sept%2010%202010%20%28paper%29.pdf (accessed 1 September 2013).

ENDNOTES

1   The benchmark Rotterdam bunker price (380 centistokes) peaked at $712 per ton in March 2012 (Clarkson Research Services, 2013a).

2   Total idle containership capacity expanded from 3.6 per cent of the fleet at the end of 2011 to 5 per cent of the fleet at the end of 2012 (Clarkson Research Services, 2013b). The most affected tonnage stands in the 3,000–5,000 TEU range, comprising 40 per cent of total unemployed capacity at the end of 2012 (Barry Rogliano Salles, 2013).

3   It has been estimated that running a 10,000 TEU containership at 18–20 knots instead of the optimal cruising speed of 20–25 knots can deliver daily savings of 175 tons of bunkers. Moreover, super-slow steaming at 15–18 knots can save an additional 100 tons per day (Lloyds Loading List.com, 2013a).

4   Scrapping activity approached the record-high level of 2009, as more than 300,000 TEUs were scrapped (Danish Ship Finance, 2013).

5   Based on Alphaliner's survey of the operating results for 21 of the top 30 carriers that have published their financial results for 2012. The survey shows that cumulative net losses of their parent companies, including the results of non-liner shipping operations and various write-offs, reached $4.7 billion. See http://www.alphaliner.com/liner2/research_files/newsletters/2013/no15/Alphaliner%20Newsletter%20no%2015%20-%202013.pdf.

6   CMA CGM registered the largest operating profit of $989 million, although this result includes its terminal business, which contributed $200 million. Maersk Line came second, with a profit of $483 million. OOCL ranked third, with $230 million. APL was the worst performer in terms of operating profit, reporting a loss of $279 million. In terms of margin, SITC was the best performer, with a margin of 6.6 per cent. CMA CGM was second, with 6.2 per cent, and Wan Hai third, with 4.5 per cent. CSAV was at the bottom of the list, with a margin of -5.6 per cent (Lloyds Loading List.com, 2013b).

7   ConTex stands for "container ship time charter assessment".

8   The proportion of the idle capacity owned by charter owners expanded from 45 per cent at the end of 2011 to 67 per cent at the end of 2012. (Clarkson Research Services, 2013b).

9   Vessels larger than 8,000 TEUs have constituted 68 per cent of the capacity delivered to the sector over the last two years. In recent years, smaller (2,000–3,000 TEUs) and mid-sized ships (3,000–5,100 TEUs) have been predominantly deployed on the non-main lanes that have been enjoying higher growth rates.

10   Clean products refer to light, refined oil products such as jet fuel, gasoline and naphtha. These products are usually carried in clean, coated tanks. Dirty products include refined oil products such as fuel oil, diesel oil or bunker oil. (Clarkson Research Services, 2013e:37).

11   In general, clean tankers carry refined petroleum products such as gasoline, kerosene or jet fuels, or chemicals. Dirty tankers carry heavier oils such as heavy fuel oils or crude oil. See http://www.shipfinance.dk/en/SHIPPING-RESEARCH/Tankskibe/Produkttankskibe.

12   As a result of its financial restructuring, General Maritime reduced its outstanding debt by some $600 million and its annual cash interest costs by some $42 million. In addition, the company received fresh capital of $175 million from Oaktree Capital Management, which will now control 98 per cent of the company. It had had debts of more than $1.3 billion before the restructuring (SeeNews Shipping, 2012).

13   Total product tanker trade grew by 1.4 per cent but fell to 0.7 per cent growth in travel distances because average trading distances to Asia, Europe and North America shortened as supply shifted from long-haul trades to short-haul trades (Danish Ship Finance, 2013).

14   However, there is still very much of a debate on whether the Arctic routes will be economically viable in the coming decades, as substantial investments have to be made in the developing and maintaining of the required infrastructure by the Russian Federation, which will lead to high costs of using this route.

15   MARPOL Annex VI stipulates that from 2015, ships steaming in emission control areas will be limited to the use of fuels with no greater than 0.1 per cent sulphur content, which is anticipated to greatly increase demand for marine gas oil. Another possible avenue for future bunker demand is the use of liquefied natural gas as fuel.

16   Some of these issues are also being covered in more detail in chapters 1 and 2 of the *Review*.

17   One example is the seven-year $140 million loan agreement to finance the construction of two VLCC tankers. It was signed in 2012 between Sovcomflot (SCF Group) and Citigroup and Bank of America–Merrill Lynch.

4

PORT DEVELOPMENTS

This chapter covers container port throughput, port finance, selected global port development projects and efforts aimed at assessing port performance. World container port throughput increased by an estimated 3.8 per cent to 601.8 million TEUs in 2012. This increase was lower than the estimated 7.3 per cent increase of 2011. The share of Chinese mainland ports in total world container port throughput remains at an estimated 25 per cent. The financing of port infrastructure remains strong as investors continue to seek long-term stable returns. Recent efforts by port customers to assess port performance are leading towards an era of increased transparency in port operations that could spur greater interport competition, increased port performance and reduced transport costs.

A. PORT THROUGHPUT

Port throughput is the amount of cargo that passes through a port and is measured in volume or units and categorized by cargo type. Ports are broadly categorized into dedicated terminals (that is, usually reserved for a single or small number of private cargo owners) or common user terminals (open to any cargo owner to use). This chapter deals with containerized cargo, which accounts for 15.6 per cent by volume, but also more than half in value, of international seaborne trade.

1. Container ports

Container port throughput is usually measured in the number of TEUs moved. The latest figures available for world container port traffic are given in table 4.1. Seventy-six developing countries and economies in transition with an annual national throughput of over 100,000 TEUs are listed. (Annex IV shows port throughput figures for 127 countries/territories). In 2011, the container throughput for developing economies grew by an estimated 8 per cent to 406.9 million TEUs. This growth is lower than the 15.8 per cent seen in the previous year, when businesses restocked inventories depleted because of uncertainties surrounding the global economic crisis. The growth rate for container throughput in developing economies for 2012 is still weak, estimated at 4.8 per cent.

Developing economies' share of world throughput continues to remain virtually unchanged at approximately 70 per cent. Out of the developing economies and countries with economies in transition listed in table 4.1, only four experienced negative growth in port throughput in 2011, whereas in the previous year 10 countries experienced negative growth. Of the top 10 developing countries and countries with economies in transition, only one, Brazil, is not located in Asia. Fifteen of the top 20 developing countries and countries with economies in transition are also in Asia, while three are in Central and South America (Brazil, Mexico and Panama) and two are in Africa (Egypt and South Africa). The dominance of Asia in container port throughput signifies the importance of the region in international trade. The countries registering the highest growth in 2012 were the Congo (44.6 per cent), Ghana (30.0 per cent), Kenya (22.7 per cent), Mauritus (19.1 per cent) Saudi Arabia (15.2 per cent), the Russian Federation (14.3 per cent), South Africa (10.9 per cent), the Philippines (8.7 per cent) and China (7.7 per cent) . The country with the largest share of container throughput continues to be China, with nine of its ports, including Hong Kong (China) among the top 20. Chinese ports, excluding Hong Kong (China),

experienced a positive growth of 9.2 per cent in 2011 to reach 143.8 million TEUs. Preliminary figures for 2011 show a reduced growth for Chinese port throughput to around 6.9 per cent, at 155 million TEUs. Chinese ports, with the exception of Hong Kong (China) and those of Taiwan Province of China, accounted for around 25.3 per cent of world container throughput in 2012, down slightly from 25.8 per cent in the previous year (a more detailed account of international trade demand and supply is given in chapter 1).

Table 4.2 shows the world's 20 leading container ports for the period 2010–2012. The top 20 container ports accounted for approximately 47 per cent of world container port throughput in 2012. Combined, these ports showed a 3.2 per cent increase in throughput in 2012, down from an 8.2 per cent increase in 2011. The list includes 16 ports from developing economies, all of which are in Asia; the remaining four ports are from developed countries, three of which are located in Europe and one in North America.

The overall picture that emerges is that while Asia continues to lead the global demand for container port services, growth is slowing. However, compared with shipping, which is affected by an oversupply of vessels and declining freight rates, the container port business is growing.

B. FINANCING PORT INVESTMENTS

Financing new port development projects is capital intensive. A recent study of the scale of future infrastructure demand examined nine economies (Brazil, China, France, Germany, India, Japan, Mexico, the United Kingdom, and the United States), collectively accounting for 60 per cent of world GDP, and found that their annual spending on long-term investment totalled $11.7 trillion for the year 2010. Extrapolating a range of growth forecasts and investment projections from external sources, the study estimated that developing countries will need annual investment of $18.8 trillion in real terms by 2020 to achieve even moderate levels of economic growth (Group of 30, 2013).

While financing infrastructure from the public purse may provide control of what infrastructure is created, in reality money could be saved by transferring the majority of projects to the private sector as sustainable businesses. This is not always the case where the infrastructure project may be more social than economic, for example, building roads or bridges to remote communities with small populations. However, on the whole, private funding sources for infrastructure development seem

Country/territory	2010	2011	Preliminary figures for 2012	Percentage change 2011–2010	Percentage change 2012–2011
China	130 290 443	143 896 697	155 017 351	10.44	7.73
Singapore [a]	29 178 500	30 727 702	32 421 602	5.31	5.51
Hong Kong, China	23 699 242	24 384 000	23 100 000	2.89	-5.27
Republic of Korea	18 542 804	20 833 508	21 453 964	12.35	2.98
Malaysia	18 267 475	20 139 382	20 866 875	10.25	3.61
United Arab Emirates	15 176 524	16 780 386	17 211 602	10.57	2.57
Taiwan Province of China	12 736 855	13 473 418	13 977 453	5.78	3.74
India	9 752 908	9 979 224	9 826 249	2.32	-1.53
Indonesia	8 482 636	8 966 146	9 324 792	*5.70*	*4.00*
Brazil	8 138 608	8 536 262	8 864 368	4.89	3.84
Egypt	6 709 053	7 737 183	8 046 670	15.32	*4.00*
Thailand	6 648 532	7 171 394	7 372 298	7.86	2.80
Panama	6 003 298	6 911 325	7 187 778	15.13	*4.00*
Viet Nam	5 983 583	6 335 437	6 588 855	5.88	*4.00*
Saudi Arabia	5 313 141	5 694 538	6 557 448	7.18	15.15
Turkey	5 574 018	5 990 103	6 229 707	7.46	*4.00*
Philippines	4 947 039	5 264 086	5 720 749	6.41	8.68
Sri Lanka	4 000 000	4 262 887	4 433 402	6.57	*4.00*
South Africa	3 806 427	3 990 193	4 424 254	4.83	10.88
Mexico	3 693 956	4 080 434	4 243 651	10.46	*4.00*
Russian Federation	3 199 980	3 448 947	3 942 628	7.78	14.31
Chile	3 171 959	3 450 401	3 588 417	8.78	*4.00*
Oman	3 893 198	3 632 940	3 292 707	-6.68	-9.37
Islamic Republic of Iran	2 592 522	2 740 296	2 849 908	*5.70*	*4.00*
Colombia	2 443 786	2 402 742	2 498 852	-1.68	*4.00*
Pakistan	2 149 000	2 193 403	2 281 139	2.07	*4.00*
Argentina	2 021 676	2 159 110	2 245 474	6.80	*4.00*
Jamaica	1 891 770	1 999 601	2 079 585	*5.70*	*4.00*
Peru	1 534 056	1 814 743	1 887 332	18.30	*4.00*
Morocco	2 058 430	2 083 000	1 800 000	1.19	-13.59
Dominican Republic	1 382 680	1 461 492	1 519 952	*5.70*	*4.00*
Bangladesh	1 356 099	1 431 851	1 489 125	5.59	*4.00*
Bahamas	1 125 000	1 189 125	1 236 690	*5.70*	*4.00*
Bolivarian Republic of Venezuela	1 226 508	1 162 326	1 208 819	-5.23	*4.00*
Ecuador	1 221 849	1 081 169	1 124 415	-11.51	*4.00*
Guatemala	1 012 360	1 070 065	1 112 867	*5.70*	*4.00*
Costa Rica	1 013 483	1 065 468	1 108 087	5.13	*4.00*
Kuwait	991 545	1 048 063	1 089 986	*5.70*	*4.00*
Kenya	696 000	735 672	903 000	*5.70*	22.74
Uruguay	671 952	861 164	895 611	28.16	*4.00*
Ghana	647 052	683 934	889 129	*5.70*	30.00
Lebanon	949 155	1 034 249	882 922	8.97	-14.63
Yemen	669 021	707 155	735 441	*5.70*	*4.00*
Ukraine	659 541	696 641	724 506	5.63	*4.00*

Table 4.1. Container port throughput for 76 developing countries/territories and economies in transition for years 2010, 2011 and 2012 (Twenty-foot equivalent units)

Table 4.1.   Container port throughput for 76 developing countries/territories and economies in transition for years 2010, 2011 and 2012 (Twenty-foot equivalent units) *(continued)*

Country/territory	2010	2011	Preliminary figures for 2012	Percentage change 2011–2010	Percentage change 2012–2011
Syrian Arab Republic	649 005	685 998	713 438	*5.70*	*4.00*
Honduras	619 867	655 199	681 407	*5.70*	*4.00*
Jordan	619 000	654 283	680 454	*5.70*	*4.00*
Côte d'Ivoire	607 730	642 371	668 065	*5.70*	*4.00*
Djibouti	600 000	634 200	659 568	*5.70*	*4.00*
Trinidad and Tobago	573 217	605 890	630 126	*5.70*	*4.00*
Congo	338 916	358 234	518 000	*5.70*	44.60
Tunisia	466 398	492 983	512 702	*5.70*	*4.00*
Sudan	439 100	464 129	482 694	*5.70*	*4.00*
United Republic of Tanzania	429 285	453 754	471 904	*5.70*	*4.00*
Mauritius	332 662	350 624	417 467	5.40	19.06
Senegal	349 231	369 137	383 903	*5.70*	*4.00*
Qatar	346 000	365 722	380 351	*5.70*	*4.00*
Benin	316 744	334 798	348 190	*5.70*	*4.00*
Papua New Guinea	295 286	313 598	326 142	6.20	*4.00*
Bahrain	289 956	306 483	318 743	*5.70*	*4.00*
Cameroon	285 070	301 319	313 371	*5.70*	*4.00*
Algeria	279 785	295 733	307 562	*5.70*	*4.00*
Mozambique	254 701	269 219	279 988	*5.70*	*4.00*
Cuba	228 346	246 773	256 644	8.07	*4.00*
Georgia	226 115	239 004	248 564	*5.70*	*4.00*
Cambodia	224 206	236 986	246 465	*5.70*	*4.00*
Myanmar	190 046	200 879	208 914	*5.70*	*4.00*
Libya	184 585	195 106	202 910	*5.70*	*4.00*
Guam	183 214	193 657	201 403	*5.70*	*4.00*
Gabon	153 657	162 415	168 912	*5.70*	*4.00*
El Salvador	145 774	154 083	160 246	*5.70*	*4.00*
Madagascar	141 093	149 135	155 101	*5.70*	*4.00*
Croatia	137 048	144 860	150 654	*5.70*	*4.00*
Aruba	130 000	137 410	142 906	*5.70*	*4.00*
Nigeria	101 007	106 764	111 035	*5.70*	*4.00*
Brunei Darussalam	99 355	105 018	109 219	*5.70*	*4.00*
Sub total	375 760 063	406 133 627	425 712 710	8.08	4.82
Other reported [b]	796 607	746 145	772 903	-6.33	3.59
Total reported	376 556 670	406 879 772	426 485 613	8.05	4.82
World total	**540 816 751**	**580 022 280**	**601 772 123**	**7.25**	**3.75**

Sources: UNCTAD secretariat, derived from information contained in *Lloyd's List Intelligence* (July 2013), from various Dynamar B.V. publications, and information obtained by the UNCTAD secretariat directly from terminal and port authorities.

[a]   In this list, Singapore includes the port of Jurong.

[b]   The term "other reported" refers to countries for which fewer than 100,000 TEUs per year were reported.

Note: Many figures, especially for 2012, are estimates (*these figures are indicated in italics*). Port throughput figures tend not to be disclosed by ports until a considerable time after the end of the calendar year. Country totals may conceal the fact that minor ports may not be included; therefore, in some cases, the actual figures may be higher than those given.

Table 4.2.	Top 20 container terminals and their throughput for 2010, 2011 and 2012 (Twenty-foot equivalent units and percentage change)				
Port name	2010	2011	Preliminary figures for 2012	Percentage change 2011–2010	Percentage change 2012–2011
Shanghai	29 069 000	31 700 000	32 500 000	9.05	2.52
Singapore	28 431 100	29 937 700	31 600 000	5.30	5.55
Hong Kong (China)	23 699 242	24 384 000	23 100 000	2.89	-5.27
Shenzhen	22 509 700	22 569 800	22 940 000	0.27	1.64
Busan	14 194 334	16 184 706	17 030 000	14.02	5.22
Ningbo	13 144 000	14 686 200	14 973 400	11.73	1.96
Guangzhou	12 550 000	14 400 000	14 520 000	14.74	0.83
Qingdao	12 012 000	13 020 000	14 500 000	8.39	11.37
Dubai	11 600 000	13 000 000	13 280 000	12.07	2.15
Tianjin	10 080 000	11 500 000	12 300 000	14.09	6.96
Rotterdam	11145804	11876921	11900000	6.56	0.19
Port Klang	8 871 745	9 603 926	9 990 000	8.25	4.02
Kaohsiung	9 181 211	9 636 289	9 781 000	4.96	1.50
Hamburg	7 900 000	9 014 165	8 930 000	14.10	-0.93
Antwerp	8 468 475	8 664 243	8 629 992	2.31	-0.40
Los Angeles	7 831 902	7 940 511	8 080 000	1.39	1.76
Dalian	5 242 000	6 400 000	8 060 000	22.09	25.94
Tanjung Pelepas	6 530 000	7 500 000	7 720 000	14.85	2.93
Xiamen	5 820 000	6 460 700	7 200 000	11.01	11.44
Laem Chabang	5 068 076	5 731 063	5 927 000	13.08	3.42
Total top 20	**253 348 589**	**274 210 224**	**282 96 392**	**8.23**	**3.19**

Source: UNCTAD secretariat and *Lloyd's List Intelligence*, July 2013.
Note: In this list Singapore does not include the port of Jurong.

to be readily available. One industry research firm has identified 662 institutions that are open to making new infrastructure investments, 56 per cent of which are actively seeking new opportunities in 2013, while the remaining have an opportunistic investment strategy (Preqin, 2013). Pensions are attracted to infrastructure investments as they expect them to produce predictable and stable cash flows over the long term. Infrastructure assets can operate in an environment of limited competition as a result of natural monopolies, government regulation or concessions. Investments can be capital intensive and include a tangible asset that must be operated and maintained over the long term (OECD, 2011). In some countries, pension funds do not directly invest into infrastructure projects because of a lack of in-house expertise. However, this is not the case for many pension funds in Australia, Canada and the Netherlands, which have been investing directly in infrastructure

over the past 20 years (*Financial Times*, 2013a). Global institutional investors put almost $214 billion into unlisted infrastructure funds between 2004 and January 2013, with nearly $111 billion heading into North America, just over $62 billion into Europe and $21 billion into Asia (Preqin, 2013).

The port is not an isolated entity and must be linked to its hinterland. A distinction needs to be made regarding which part of the port infrastructure and equipment will be paid for by the port as service-production centre or business unit, and which part the community as a whole will finance, according to development objectives and priorities. There may be certain large capital expenditure items that would place too heavy a strain on port finances. Some would argue that the connecting road and rail systems should be financed by the port while others argue that major long-term structures such as breakwaters or channel dredging should be partly or wholly charged to the central or regional government. It is for each government to decide this policy according to the financial capacity of existing ports and the expected profitability of planned new ports (UNCTAD, 1985).

In Mozambique, the dredging operations to the port of Maputo were financed by the port authority. Port customers, however, complain that the high cost of dredging is being passed onto them, whereas the cost should be borne by the government, since the benefits are for the wider population. Other ports within the same country that do not need to dredge because they are natural deepwater ports (for example, Nacala) can offer more competitive prices to its customers. This can lead to a bias towards one national port or a regional port in a neighbouring country and create extended use of land transport, which is costly both to the consumer and the environment. In addition, deciding to invest in new port facilities is not necessarily a clear-cut case. Related issues that should be explored include how much to expand or how deep to go, how to best cater for present and future demand, and how to attract customers prior to and following the modifications.

The funding of infrastructure can come from a number of primary sources such as the public sector budget, official development assistance (ODA) and the private sector (Bond et al., 2012). Table 4.3 lists some of the major international banks that are providing infrastructure lending and the share apportioned to the transportation sector.

Public–private partnerships (PPPs) in port development projects have become common place in the last 25 years. The most common form of PPP is the operation of a concession agreement. This usually involves investment by the private company to develop or rehabilitate the port followed by a defined period of operation, during which the investors recuperate their initial layout and make a profit. The concession may adopt different forms of PPP including build-operate-transfer, build-operate-own-transfer and build-transfer-operate schemes. In the period 2000–2009, 29 per cent of public–private investment in ports took place in East and South East Asia (Holman Fenwick Willan LLP, 2013). To the partnership the private sector brings much needed capital and know-how, as well as expected increased efficiency gains associated with combining construction, maintenance and operations arrangements.

Furthermore, most PPPs are attractive to governments because they are kept off government spending books. However, this could prove costly in the long run as the project may not be able to take advantage of lower

Table 4.3.	A comparison of international finance to the transport sector (2012)			
	Total lending* (Billions of US dollars)	Infrastructure lending (Billions of US dollars)	Transport Sector lending*** (Billions of US dollars)	Transportation sector share (Percentage)
European Investment Bank	57.6 (€44.8 billion)		13 (€10.1 billion)	23
Asian Development Bank	21.6		5	25
International Bank for Reconstruction and Development /International Development Association	35.3		4.4	13
International Finance Corporation	15.5	1.5		
Inter-American Development Bank	11.4		1.7	15
European Bank for Reconstruction and Development	7.7 (€6 billion)		1.6 (€1.3 billion)	21
African Development Bank	8.8 (UA 5.7 billion)	2.4** (UA 1.57 billion)	1.5 (UA 1 billion)	17

Source: Complied by UNCTAD from various annual reports 2011–2012.

Notes: 1 Unit of Aid (UA; official currency of African Development Bank projects) = $1.53527.

* For 2012 except, where indicated, may also include third-party lending, guarantees and/or credit lines.

** For 2011.

*** May include other sectors, for example, communication or environment.

government lending to reduce the cost of the venture (Engel et al., 2010). If this is the case, then the design of PPP should be streamlined by adjusting the transfer point from the public to the private sector, given that the highest risk and the most costly part usually comes at the initial construction phase. Investors often worry that projects will be delayed before coming online, so incurring higher interest rates. The removal of this risk by transferring the asset after this point will lower costs.

The leading investors into infrastructure projects are government agencies, asset managers, public pension funds, funds of fund managers, corporate investors, banks, investment companies, endowment plans, insurance companies, private-sector pension funds and foundations. Table 4.4 gives a brief overview of some of the leading infrastructure investors. According to one report more than half of current active investors in infrastructure are looking to commit between $50 million and $349 million in infrastructure in 2013, and 16 per cent of investors are looking to invest $500 million or more. For example, the $9.6 billion Kuwait Fund for Arab Economic Development is seeking to make a minimum of three new infrastructure fund commitments over the next 12 months. This government agency has a 5 per cent ($470 million) target allocation for infrastructure projects, with currently just 1 per cent ($96 million) invested (Preqin, 2013). Aviva Investors are to launch funds aimed at infrastructure investment, and the world's largest asset manager, BlackRock, launched a European infrastructure

debt division that will lend to companies in the transport sector (*Reuters*, 2012). Sovereign wealth funds have over $4 trillion in assets suitable for long-term investments such as infrastructure (Group of 30, 2013).

One study estimated that between 2013 and 2030, some $57 trillion in infrastructure investment (including transport, power, water and telecommunications) will be required to keep up with projected GDP growth and yet still be insufficient to meet maintenance deficiencies or the broader development goals of emerging economies, let alone the cost of adapting to climate change (McKinsey Global Institute, 2013). This report goes on to say that institutional investors are frustrated about not being able to find enough suitable vehicles to reach their target allocations for infrastructure and that even if pension funds and asset managers achieved their infrastructure target allocations of around 6 per cent, from 3 per cent today, it would only represent an additional $2.5 trillion in capital between now and 2030, far short of the $57 trillion (or more) needed. While the $57 trillion total includes roads, rail, ports, airports, power, water and telecommunications, transport represents around $23 trillion, with the share for ports around $1.5 trillion. In Africa, another study estimates that transport volumes will increase between six to eight times, and as much as 14 times for some landlocked countries, and port throughput will rise from 265 million tons in 2009, to more than 2 billion tons in 2040 (Commonwealth Business Council, 2013).

Table 4.4.	A brief comparison of potential investors in infrastructure				
	Global Infrastructure Partners	**The Canada Pension Plan Investment Board**	**Ontario Municipal Employees Retirement System**	**Prudential Plc.**	**Macquarie Infrastructure and Real Assets**
Description	A private equity firm that invests worldwide in infrastructure assets in the energy, transport, and water and waste industry sectors	An investment management organization that invests the assets of 18 million Canadians	Established in 1962, it manages over 930 employers' pension funds for 429,000 members, retirees and survivors	An international financial services group serving more than 24 million insurance customers	The managers of specialist funds which focus on infrastructure, real estate and adjacent sectors
Total investments	$13.9 billion (GIP II $8.25 billion)	$10.3 billion	$60 billion	$600 billion	$101 billion
Transport arm			Allianz and Borealis Infrastructure	Infracapital (M&G Investments)	
Transport-related investments	$2.8 billion	$4.6 billion		$2.3 billion	$31 billion
Significant transport investments	Gatwick Airport (United Kingdom)	Toll roads (Chile), Formula One (United Kingdom)	Associated British Ports, Channel Tunnel Rail Link (United Kingdom)	Associated British Ports, Red Funnel (United Kingdom)	M6 (United Kingdom), Autoroutes Paris–Rhin–Rhône (France), Warnow Tunnel (Germany), Incheon Grand Bridge (Republic of Korea) Busan New Port Phase 2V3 (Republic of Korea)

Source: Complied by UNCTAD from various company websites including M&G Investments, 2013 data.

During the period 2000–2009, there were some 195 private investment projects in container, dry and liquid bulk and multi-purpose cargo terminals worth $38 billion. Seventy-eight greenfield projects in Asia, the Pacific, Latin America and the Caribbean during the period equalled around $20 billion. In the same period there were 97 concession projects worth $15.5 billion while there were 11 management and lease projects totalling $305 million. China, India and Brazil have attracted the highest number of private investments in recent years. China drew almost $4 billion of private funds in 2006–2009, India $2.5 billion and Brazil $1.5 billion. During the same period Singapore's PSA International invested $2.92 billion, APM Terminals $2.46 billion and DP World $1.91 billion (Holman Fenwick Willan LLP, 2013). One Chinese firm, China Harbour Engineering Company, a subsidiary of China Communications Construction Company, has a global portfolio of projects valued in excess of $10 billion in more than 70 countries (*Cayman Net News*, 2012). The international marine engineering and infrastructure construction firm continues to win major port development contracts around the world in collaboration with the Chinese investment bank CITIC Securities, which has its headquarters in Shenzhen and is listed on the Hong Kong Stock Exchange.

In the United States some ports have secured finance for infrastructure through the issuing of bonds to the value of $12 billion to be repaid by existing and future user fees. This process helps ports to shore up cash flow and address liquidity constraints without relying on public funds. Port revenue bonds are retired through revenues, user fees and tariff charges paid principally by port customers (*PMSA*, 2013). The issuing of bonds is seen as a favourable means to raise revenue for new

infrastructure projects. In Cleveland the port authority issued a $90 million bond to construct a new building on its land which will then be tenanted to produce rental income (The Plain Dealer - cleveland.com, 2013). In India, tax-free bonds are also seen as a way to raise $769 million for port projects (*Livemint*, 2013a). In Peru, $110 million of bonds were used to finance new infrastructure at the Paita Terminal Port in the region of Piura. In this case the site was a brownfield location already generating income, and this avoided the usual problem of construction risk increasing the price of the bonds (Bacchiocchi, 2012). Table 4.5 lists the ten largest infrastructure funds for the period 2008 to September 2012.

C. RECENT PORT DEVELOPMENTS

Port development is seen as a catalyst to stimulate economic activity and create employment. In the United Kingdom, despite no longer being a major trading centre for merchandised goods, it is estimated that 262,700 jobs and £13.8 billion ($21.5 billion) were generated in 2011 through the provision of maritime services (Oxford Economics, 2013). The United Kingdom distribution industry as a whole employed an estimated 2.67 million people, 10 per cent of workplace employees in 2007 (Haven Gateway Partnership, 2010). Similarly, the six-berth London Gateway terminal development nearing completion is expected to create 12,000 new jobs and another 20,000 jobs indirectly (Holman Fenwick Willan LLP, 2013). Virtually every government, national, regional or local authority, as well as the ports themselves, have a port development plan with the aim of increasing the wealth of its citizens through the provision of some service. These plans may be driven in response to

Table 4.5.	Ten largest infrastructure funds, 2008–2012		
Fund	**Firm**	**Size (Millions of US dollars)**	**Region**
Global Infrastructure Partners II	Global Infrastructure Partners	8 250	Global
Global Infrastructure Partners	Global Infrastructure Partners	5 640	Global
Energy Capital Partners II	Energy Capital Partners	4 335	North America
EIG Energy Fund XV	EIG Global Energy Partners	4 121	Global
Alinda Infrastructure Fund II	Alinda Capital Partners	4 097	North America, Europe
Morgan Stanley Infrastructure Partners	Morgan Stanley Infrastructure	4 000	Global
Citi Infrastructure Partners	Citi Infrastructure Investors	3 400	OECD
ArcLight Energy Partners Fund V	ArcLight Capital Partners	3 310	North America, Europe
GS Infrastructure Partners II	GS Infrastructure Investment Group	3 100	North America, Europe
Brookfield Americas Infrastructure Fund	Brookfield Asset Management	2 655	North America, South America

Source: (Preqin, 2012).

customer needs, as part of a regional integration plan, or simply national aspirations aimed at capturing passing trade. The following sections provide a brief overview of some of these developments organized alphabetically. The list is not exhaustive and the ports mentioned are merely meant to give a regional perspective as well as illustrate the variety and type of developments. Other developments mentioned in previous issues of the *Review of Maritime Transport* continue at their pace.

Africa

Container traffic in Africa is growing across the continent. In West Africa a recent study highlighted that 3 million TEU passed through the region in 2011 (CATRAM, 2013). The French carrier CMA CGM, which has a strong presence in Africa, sold a 49 per cent stake in its terminal operating business, Terminal Link, to China Merchants for €400 million ($538 million) (Dynamar B.V., 2013a). The deal gives the French company a capital injection to be used in its main business, liner shipping, at a time of when shipyards are offering to build cheap ships and when banks are reluctant to lend. For the buyer it provides quick means to expand its global presence in a growing market. Another large liner shipping company, MSC, is focusing its attention upon the port of Lomé as a regional hub. While in Central Africa, the port of Pointe-Noire (the Congo) is also being considered by various parties to be in a good location to become an important trans-shipment hub for North–South shipments and shipments East–West to Latin America. Some recent infrastructure improvements made by foreign investors include a third berth in Dakar built by DP World, a third quay in Lomé for both Bolloré and TIL/MSC (part of which is now owned by China Merchants), and facilities in Cotonou (Benin) and Pointe-Noire for Bolloré (CATRAM, 2013). Some other African port-development projects currently underway are detailed in the following paragraphs.

In Abidjan, Côte d'Ivoire, port expansion plans include increasing TEU capacity to 1 million–1.5 million. In early 2013, a $933-million contract was signed between the Abidjan Port Authority and China Harbour Engineering Company Limited. The project involves waterway and basin dredging, construction of a container terminal and a ro-ro terminal, and waterway breakwater reconstruction (*Dredging Today*, 2013). APMT is investing $40 million into the container terminal so that vessels of 8,000 TEU may be catered for in Abidjan (Sea-web, 2013).

In Cameroon, the Mbalam iron-ore project progressed with the signing of a convention between the Minister of Mines, Industries and Technological Development and the Australian firm Sundance Resources through its

local partner Cam Iron. This will allow the developers to start securing the $8.7 billion needed for construction work which will include a 510-kilometre rail line for the transportation of iron ore from the Mbarga Mine to the Cameroon coast, with a 70-kilometre rail spur line connecting to the Congo. A deepwater iron-ore export terminal will be built at Lolabe, in Kribi, with the capacity to handle Chinamax iron-ore bulk carriers (Cameroon Tribune, 2012). The Cameroon–Congo–Gabon region has been likened to the Pilbara, the region in Western Australia that has some of the world's biggest iron deposits (*Financial Times*, 2013b).

In Ghana, an agreement between the Ghana Ports and Harbours Authority and China Harbour Engineering Company was signed for work to begin on the first phase of the $150-million Takoradi Port Infrastructure Development Project. The three year project includes the demolition and reconstruction of port office buildings, the expansion and reconstruction of access roads, land reclamation and the development of water and electricity facilities (*Cayman Net News*, 2012).

In Kenya, the Government has set aside $12 million (1 billion Kenya shillings) to buy land to develop Mombasa into a free port where manufacturers may undertake works at reduced tax (*Daily Nation*, 2013). The port of Mombasa handled some 19.6 million tons of cargo, of which about 4 million tons were imports and 5 million tons were transit cargo to neighbouring countries. Uganda is the largest destination of transit cargo accounting for nearly 85 per cent (4.2 million tons), of which 90 per cent comprises imports. The Democratic Republic of the Congo is the second largest transit market, taking up to 8 per cent of the total at 430,000 tons. Seventy-two per cent of cargo going through Mombasa is for Kenya's domestic market, 22 per cent is for Uganda, 2.3 per cent for the Democratic Republic of the Congo, 1.5 per cent for Rwanda and less than 1 per cent is destined for the United Republic of Tanzania, Burundi, South Sudan and Somalia (*The East African*, 2012).

In Sierra Leone, a memorandum of understanding (MOU) between the Ministry of Mines and Mineral Resources and China Kingho Energy Group Co. Ltd. was signed in May 2013. The MOU includes $6 billion of investments for the construction of a railway from Tonkolili to Sulima and a deepwater quay port for transportation of products, among others (*Awareness Times*, 2013).

In the United Republic of Tanzania, an agreement with the Government of China to build a $10 billion–$11 billion new port at the historical port city of Bagamoyo was announced in 2013. The new port will be the biggest in the whole of Africa and handle some 20 million TEUs a year when complete, compared with the 800,000 TEUs current throughput at Dar es Salaam. The project will include the building of a 34-kilometre road joining Bagamoyo to Mlandizi and 65 kilometres of railway connecting Bagamoyo to the Tanzania–Zambia Railway and the Central Railway. The bilateral deal calls for China to commit $500 million in 2013 to start the port construction with the rest of the Chinese financial aid package to follow in 2014 and 2015 (*Sabahionline.com*, 2013; *The East African*, 2013). The port is also expected to be run by Chinese operators and offer facilities to naval vessels, albeit not necessarily China's (*Africainvestor*, 2013). The new port will ease congestion at Dar es Salaam, which may find other business in niche areas. China is already financing the $1.2 billion construction of a 532-kilometre gas pipeline linking recently discovered gas reserves in the south of the United Republic of Tanzania and northern Mozambique to the port of Dar es Salaam (World Socialist Web Site, 2013). The new port is good news for the landlocked neighbouring countries of Rwanda, Burundi and Uganda, which will have a choice of importing and exporting either through Mombasa, Kenya, or Dar es Salaam. The development may negatively affect Mombasa, as shipping lines may prefer to call directly at Bagamoyo new port. Inefficiencies at Mombasa can add 50–80 per cent to the time required to move imports to landlocked countries (*The East African*, 2013).

The Americas

In the Americas the anticipated opening of the newly expanded Panama Canal and the implications this will have for ports on the eastern seaboard is driving port development. Ports on the eastern seaboard and in the Caribbean have tended to remain smaller than their peers on the Pacific coast because of the limitation on vessel size governed by the historical width of the Panama Canal. The Panama Canal expansion is set to be complete by early 2015 and will increase the size of the container ships able to transit from the present maximum of around 4,800 TEU to 13,000 TEU.

In Jamaica, China Harbour Engineering Company is set to invest between $1.2 billion and $1.5 billion in the development of a trans-shipment port. The Port Authority of Jamaica and China Harbour Engineering Company Limited had signed an MOU for the establishment a new trans-shipment port at Fort Augusta. However, the project has since been expanded and it is now necessary to find a new location with more space, which has yet to be determined (*Port Finance International*, 2013). The plans are part of a major infrastructure investment programme to meet

Jamaica's desire to be a global logistics hub by 2015, and which also include improvements to the north–south link of Highway 2000 and the dredging of Kingston harbour to accommodate larger cargo ships (*RJR News*, 2013).

In Nicaragua, plans to build a canal to rival the Panama Canal passed through congress in June 2013. The cost of the canal is estimated to be $40 billion and it will be built and operated by a Chinese company – the Hong Kong Nicaragua Canal Development Investment Co. Ltd.. The company has been granted a 50–year concession to build and operate the waterway with the option to extend the concession for another 50 years. The canal is likely to be three times longer, about 250 kilometres, than the Panama Canal and include provision for two free trade zones, an airport, a freight railway and an oil pipeline (*The Guardian*, 2013). Crucially, the Nicaragua canal will be wider than the Panama Canal and be able to cater for the world's largest cargo ships, including the Maersk Triple E vessels of 18,000 TEU (*CNNMoney*, 2012). The Nicaraguan government is expected to receive $10 million a year for 10 years from the canal (*The Guardian*, 2013).

In Peru, the Ministry of Transport and Communications and the Ministry of Land, Transport and Maritime Affairs of the Republic of Korea have signed an MOU to update the development plans for four Peruvian ports (those of Iquitos, Ilo, Salaverry and San Juan de Marcona) (*Shipping Seenews*, 2013). The port sector in Peru will benefit from more than $2 billion of investment by 2015, according to the National Port Authority. The planned investments in public ports include the first phase of DP World's $617-million investment programme in the Muelle Sur terminal at the Port of Callao in Lima, $228 million at Terminales Portuarios Euroandinos Paita port terminal, and Peru LNG's $332-million LNG export terminal at Pampa Melchorita (*Fruitnet*, 2011). Since a bilateral trade agreement came into force on 1 August, 2011, Korean exports to Peru have increased by 29 per cent – among others, exports of iron ore have increased by 263 per cent, colour televisions by 268 per cent, petrochemicals by 57 per cent and passenger cars by 42.5 per cent (around one third of all new cars sold in Peru are made in the Republic of Korea). Other sectors receiving investment from the Republic of Korea include oil, hydrocarbons and mining (*Financial Times*, 2013c).

In the United States, Virginia Ports Authority received an unsolicited $3.9 billion offer from APM Terminals to operate its marine terminals for 48 years, as well as a bid of $4.66 billion from JP Morgan for a 50-year concession. The rival JP Morgan bid was originally presented by RREEF America, part of the Deutsche Bank Group. A third offer from Carlyle Infrastructure Partners, an infrastructure investment unit of the Carlyle Group, was withdrawn (*Suffolk News-Herald*, 2013). In the end all bids were refused and the port authority instead opted to rationalize both its management and financial positions. It is thought that foreign interest in Virginia and other United States East Coast ports comes as the Panama Canal expansion means larger ships requiring better port infrastructure are likely to serve this region. In New York the Bayonne Bridge is being raised to allow bigger vessels to access the Port Newark–Elizabeth Marine Terminal, the largest container port on the East Coast.

Asia

In Asia, port development projects are largely spurred by the importation of raw materials and increased industrial output. China continues to lead the world in terms of port throughput and efficiency and increasingly as a provider of expertise in port construction and management. As Chinese labour costs increase, some of the production processes are moving to neighbouring countries and Chinese companies are able to take advantage of this movement of trade through the provision of other higher value services such as expertise in port construction.

In Cambodia a new cargo terminal officially opened in the capital in 2013, in response to a sharp increase in shipments moving through the country's existing ports. The new terminal is located in the Kien Svay district of Kandal province, about 30 kilometres from the existing port in Phnom Penh, and cost over $28 million. It was financed by the Chinese government and will be capable of handling 300,000 TEUs when the second phase is complete (*PortCalls Asia*, 2013).

In India plans to enable trust ports to lease land to private companies are being considered for the purpose of establishing industrial or special economic zones to generate more trade. This proposal will affect 12 major ports (Chennai, Kochi, Ennore, Jawaharlal Nehru, Kolkata (including Haldia), Kandla, Mormugao, Mumbai, New Mangalore, Paradip, Tuticorin and Visakhapatnam), which have a capacity to handle over 740 million tons of cargo each year and account for about 58 per cent of India's external trade shipped by sea. The proposed port land policy will allow land to be leased up to a maximum period of 30 years by a port with the approval of its board of trustees. Leases of above 30 years and for a maximum of up to 99 years will have to be recommended by the port trust board to the shipping ministry for committee approval (*Livemint*, 2013b). Elsewhere in India two new port development projects are being considered by the Cabinet Committee on Economic Affairs. One port called Dugarajapatnam is located 45 kilometres from Gudur and

about 140 kilometres north of Chennai port. The proposed port, which will occupy 5,000 acres and have an expected throughput of 50 million tons per annum, will be the second major port in Andhra Pradesh controlled by the central government after Visakhapatnam. The other slightly larger port project with an anticipated throughput of 54 million tons per annum is located at Sagar in West Bengal. The ports are part of the government's "look east policy" which aims to triple the country's cargo-loading ability to 3.13 billion tons by 2020 through PPPs (*The Hindu*, 2013). Just over one fifth of Indian cargo is containerized, which is about half the world average (*The Economist*, 2013a). The Government is set to increase this with the development of container facilities along its east coast at the ports of Ennore, Kakinada, Karaikal, Kattupalli and Krishnapatnam (*Drewry Container Insight*, 2013).

Also in India, draft guidelines to allow major ports to fix their own tariffs based on the market conditions are currently being considered. Presently tariffs are regulated by the Tariff Authority of Major Ports. It is thought that the private sector is waiting upon the final decision as to how tariffs are calculated before making investments. Indeed, it has been cited as one of the chief reasons why there have not been any private bidders at three recent port projects proposals in Chennai, Tuticorin and Visakhapatnam (*Business Standard India*, 2013). It is proposed that the new tariff structure will be adjusted once a year and partly index linked to inflation. Interestingly, statistics on cargo traffic, berth day output, average turnaround time of ships, average pre-berthing waiting time, percentage idle time of total time of vessels at berth, as well as the actual tariff levied for each major port-trust owned berth/terminal should be provided within 15 days following the end of each month (*The Economic Times*, 2013). However, some argue that Indian ports are too regulated and that the country's private ports are more profitable than the state-owned ports, suggesting that greater liberalization may be the way forward (*Lloyd's List*, 2013a).

In Myanmar, the existing port of Yangon has outdated facilities and there is a need to build new port facilities to help the country better integrate into the world trade arena. However, there is still much uncertainty as to where such new port facilities will be located. Two possible sites have been identified, one at Kyaukphyu to the north of Yangon, where oil and gas pipelines running across Myanmar to China's Yunnan province are being completed, and the other is Dawei to the south, which is only 250 kilometres from Bangkok and could be a valuable source of transit cargo. Further assessment on demand, revenue, investment, timeframes and technical aspects need to be undertaken (*The Vancouver Sun*,

2013). To directly service Yangon a new $200-million riverine port called Thilawa will be constructed just to the south of the city (*The Economist*, 2013b).

In Sri Lanka, the first stage of the Port of Colombo's third container-terminal expansion plans came online in 2013, with the final stage expected to be completed by 2016. The port has a draft of 18 metres and a gantry crane outreach of 24 containers wide, which enables it to cater for the largest container ships, including the Maersk Triple E class container vessels. The new terminal will be in a better position to serve cargo from and to Indian ports, although competition between ports in the region will grow (*Drewry Container Insight*, 2013).

In Thailand, a new PPP act is set to quicken the pace to bring projects to fruition. The act will set a limit of 180 days to the period between the winning of a government tender and the signing of the contract, as well as establish a committee for five-year strategic development plans. This examining committee will consist of 17 members led by the prime minister. The new act also states that a member of the committee cannot become a board director of the company winning the bid for three years after his or her resignation from the committee. The previous 1992 PPP act dealt with only 40 projects in its lifetime, 33 between the private sector and national state agencies and seven with provincial authorities (*The Nation*, 2013).

Reforms to the country's infrastructure include the building of high-speed rail lines, four more ports and other transport infrastructure over the next seven years, amounting to investments of $67.6 billion. The ports are to be located on the banks of Bangkok's main river, the Gulf of Thailand and on the Andaman Sea coasts. The government has said the projects will bolster Thailand's economic growth rate by 1 per cent a year and create 500,000 jobs. By borrowing the funds overseas, delays provoked by the annual government budget process can be avoided, thus alleviating investors' concerns that the project could be delayed. Funding projects through the regular annual budget can be problematic if there's a change of government or in politics, as the schemes could be discontinued. The borrowing bill will enable private investors to plan their investment to develop infrastructure more confidently (*Sea News Turkey*, 2013).

Europe

In Europe, port developments relate mainly to building new terminals within existing ports rather than developing new greenfield sites. As such, much of the reform process is more to do with the organization and operational aspects of ports.

In Belgium, organizational practices designed to spur improvements in performance had to be reviewed. DP World and its partners that operate the Antwerp Gateway, as well as PSA's Deurganck Terminal, owed the Port of Antwerp Authority some €70 million ($93 million) in underperformance penalties, principally because of a decrease in cargo volumes as a result of the global downturn (Dynamar B.V., 2012).[1]

Concession agreements to operate container terminals can contain clauses which specify minimum throughput volumes. If throughput falls below the minimum, the tenant, the terminal operator, must compensate the landlord, usually the port authority. The Port of Antwerp Authority, however, announced that it will reduce the underperformance penalties for not reaching the contractually stipulated volumes for DP World's Antwerp Gateway and PSA's Duerganck Terminal to €4.0 million ($5.1 million) and €9.47 million ($12.1 million), respectively (Dynamar B.V., 2013b).

The European Commission launched a new initiative to improve port operations at 319 key seaports. The guidelines are aimed at proposing legal changes that will help port operators upgrade their services and facilities as well as giving them more financial autonomy. Currently, 74 per cent of the goods entering or leaving Europe are transported via sea, with one fifth of this volume passing through just three ports: Rotterdam, Hamburg and Antwerp. This concentration results in congestion and extra costs for shippers, transport operators and consumers. The new proposals could save the European economy up to €10 billion ($12.8 billion) by 2030 and help develop new short sea links (*Europa*, 2013). The proposal excludes cargo handling and passenger services from market-access rules. Included is a new Social Dialogue Committee, which will handle labour reform issues. More stringent measures are planned to deal with concession and public contract awards and financial procedures, which reinforce transparency in the way that charges are set. The proposal extends the freedom of ports to levy infrastructure charges and to reduce charges for vessels with better environmental performance (*Lloyd's List*, 2013b).

In the Netherlands, the Port of Rotterdam Maasvlakte 2 port expansion area has opened to shipping, making the site accessible by road, rail and water. By the end of 2013, ship-to-ship transfer will commence. Construction of the two container terminals at Maasvlakte 2, one operated by DP World-led Rotterdam World Gateway and the other by Netherlands-based APMT, is on schedule to be operational at the end of 2014 (*Lloyd's List*, 2013a).

D. ASSESSING PORT PERFORMANCE

Efficient ports could help to lower transport costs by enabling goods to get to and from markets in a more timely and cost-effective fashion. UNCTAD has a number of mandates from its member countries which state for the need to help developing countries reduce their transport costs (Accra Accord paragraphs 57, 121, 165, 166 and Doha Mandate paragraphs 45, 47 and 48) as well as a long history of working on port reform. Previously, much focus was given to helping ports identify efficiency indicators to measure and record. The next logical step is for countries to share their data to identify lessons learn and best practices. By showing what similar-sized ports have achieved, greater operational advances and lower transport costs may result.

The considerable amount of data collected by ports includes not just information on the cargo but also upon the assets, equipment usage/performance and maintenance. This data is used by the port managers to monitor performance and plan for future needs.

However, ports tend to assess their performance on an inward-looking and historical perspective, that is, they judge themselves today on how well they did yesterday, not against how their competitors are performing today. In some countries it is mandatory for port data to be submitted to the national Government for analysis. In the previous section C (Recent port developments) an example of the Indian Government's collection of port statistics was given. However, many developing countries only have one main port and comparisons with other ports are impossible. Despite all the activity on record keeping, it is rare that the information is published at a port or national level, let alone on a global basis. Ports may be reluctant to publish data since there is no pressure to do so, nor any direct benefit without reciprocation. This is an important point, for unless there is a clear benefit to the port the situation is unlikely to change without some external intervention.

This external intervention came in early 2013 when the *Journal of Commerce* in association with Ocean Shipping Consultants obtained data from 17 liner shipping companies visiting 650 ports to produce a

Figure 4.1. A comparison of port productivity by region (2013)

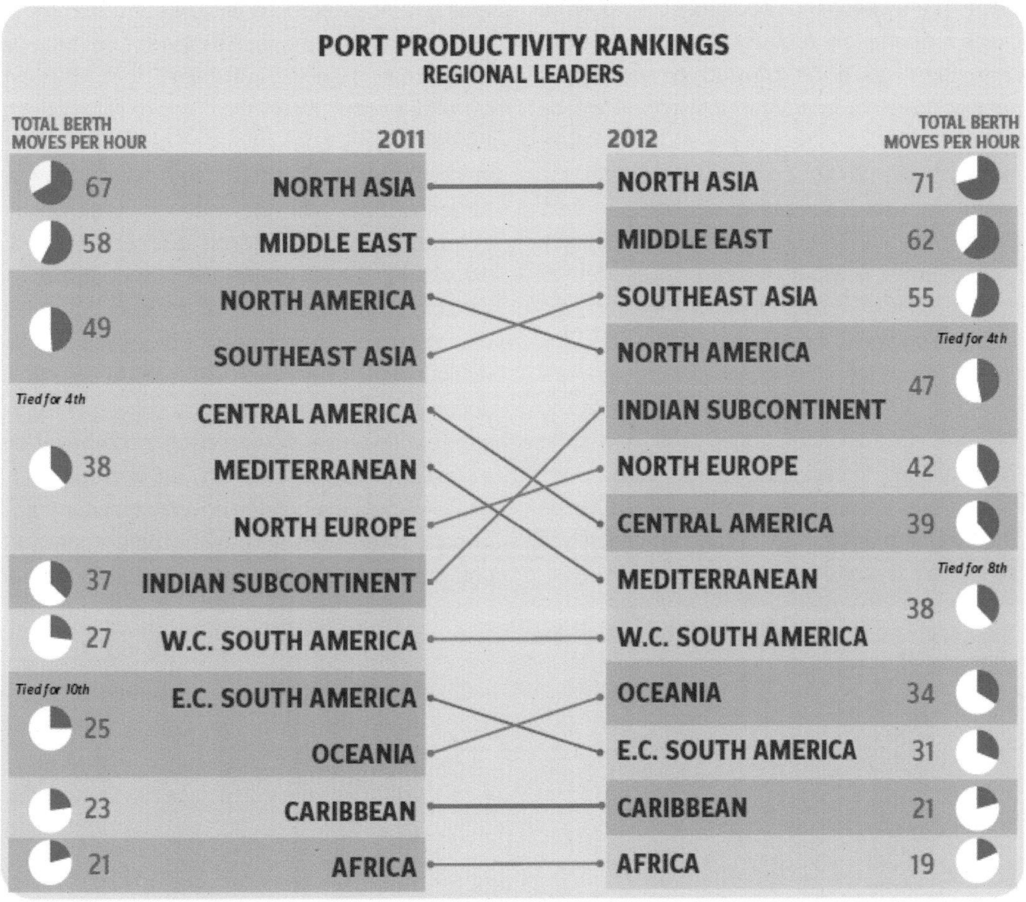

Source: *Journal of Commerce* and Ocean Shipping Consultants.

Port Productivity Ranking list (*Journal of Commerce*, 2013). The analysis of this data enables a comparison of container-port productivity by region as depicted in Figure 4.1. The results show that port performance has been assessed by the number of crane moves per hour in various broad geographical regions. The raw data and how the calculations have been made are not yet freely available. The research shows wide variations in the average cargo-handling times, from 19 moves per hour in African ports to 71 per hour in ports in North Asian. One important limitation is that ports cannot see how they rank compared against other ports, although selective port comparisons have been made in separate lists; another is that it is limited to container activities which represent about 15 per cent of global port throughput. The most significant factor is that ports are not the only holders of data on their activities. Port customers are also collecting data on port performance and if the ports do not reveal their own statistics then it will be hard for them to dispute any suggestions of inefficiency.

A way forward for ports would be to publish their own data and not rely on customer assessment of their performance. The challenge for policymakers would be to convince their ports to voluntarily share data. Official reporting systems could be devised on a national basis, but this does not guarantee that efforts will be reciprocated by other countries. A common repository of the data would still be needed to facilitate the publication of data for independent analysis. Analysis could be undertaken by the Port Performance Research Network, an informal network made up of academics from various institutions located around the world who meet annually along with the International Association of Maritime Economists. The publication of the raw data would also provide ports with an opportunity to undertake their own analysis rather than having to accept comparisons forced upon them. Thus, ports who rank low in any overall assessment could obtain a more meaningful measure by comparing themselves against their peers or ports in other regions.

What data to collect

Volume and time are the two crucial aspects of measuring performance. Volume, which is a measurement of throughput or a port's output, is expressed in either units (TEUs) or weight (tons). The time goods spend in a port is also a useful figure that is easy to compare. Examples of time measurements within a port include ship turnaround time, ship waiting time, berth occupancy rate, working time at berth, cargo dwell time and number of cargo-crane moves per hour. The primary focus when comparing global port performance, on an initial basis, should therefore be time and volume. Measuring how long a vessel spends in port and how much cargo is transferred seems an achievable first step towards creating any global assessment of port performance. The data should also cover all cargo types and not just containers.

E.   CONCLUSIONS

Global port developments are continuing despite, or perhaps because of, recent uncertainties in world trade. Ports are generally considered to be a long-term investment offering steady returns and hence their appeal to long term asset managers. At the same time ports are also becoming more capital intensive with the growth of cities creating spatial constraints that force expansion plans further out to sea, the complexity of cargo handling superstructures and operations also adding to the price of development. Developing countries, however, stand to benefit from both the need of investment portfolios to invest in long-term stable businesses and from the experience of international terminal operators that have perfected their techniques at some of the world's most voluminous ports and need new markets to invest in. Without port reform countries will struggle to get their goods to markets at competitive price levels as well as to secure their needs at reasonable prices. Port efficiency, a subject of concern to many developing countries and UNCTAD, will, through the advent of modern proliferation of data collection practices, become a reality either by port managers' own actions or that of port users.

REFERENCES

Africainvestor (2013). China builds the biggest port in Africa. 8 April.

Awareness Times (2013). $6Billion Chinese investment for Sierra Leone. 13 May.

Bacchiocchi GG (2012). The project bond evolution: Port of Paita case study. *Latin Infrastructure Quarterly*. Issue 4. June.

Bond DL, Platz D and Magnusson M (2012). Financing small-scale infrastructure investments in developing countries. DESA Working Paper No. 114. ST/ESA/2012/DWP/114. May.

Business Standard India (2013). Private bidders give port sector a miss. 11 May.

Cameroon Tribune (2012). Cameroon: Cam Iron gets mining convention for Mbalam iron project. 30 November.

CATRAM (2013). Market study on container terminals in West and Central Africa. Final report – MLTC/CATRAM. 23 January. 1–133.

Cayman Net News (2012). China Harbour wins major Ghana port project. 27 September.

CNNMoney (2012). Nicaragua OKs canal to be built by Chinese company. 27 September.

Commonwealth Business Council (2013). *Africa Infrastructure Investment Report*. ISBN 978-0-9570432-6-8. London. March.

Daily Nation (2012). Sh1bn set aside for free port project. 5 December.

Dredging Today (2013). Dredging Today – Côte d'Ivoire: CHEC Signs EPC Contract for Abidjan Port Dredging. 24 January.

Drewry Container Insight (2013). Competition heating up on India's East Coast. 17 March.

Dynamar B.V. (2012). DynaLiners Weekly. 21 December.

Dynamar B.V. (2013a). DynaLiners Weekly. 5 April.

Dynamar B.V. (2013b). DynaLiners Weekly. 29 March.

Engel EM, Fischer RD and Galetovic A (2010). The economics of infrastructure finance: Public-private partnerships versus public provision. *EIB Papers*. 15(1): 40–69.

Europa (2013). Press release – Commission proposes upgrade for 300 key seaports. 23 May.

Financial Times (2013a). Pension funds wary of UK infrastructure. 7 February.

Financial Times (2013b). Sundance calls off takeover by Hanlong. 9 April.

Financial Times (2013c). Peru: the South Koreans are coming. Beyondbrics blog. 4 May.

Fruitnet (2011). Peru to boost port investment. 16 March.

Group of 30 Working Group (2013). *Long-term Finance and Economic Growth*. ISBN 1-56708-160-6. Group of Thirty. Washington D.C.

Haven Gateway Partnership (2010). The economic impact of the ports, transport and logistics industry on the Haven Gateway area. Colechester, United Kingdom.

Holman Fenwick Willan LLP (2013). Global investment in ports and terminals. Ports and Terminals. Holman Fenwick Willan LLP. London.

Journal of Commerce (2013). Introducing JOC port productivity. *Journal of Commerce*. 14(3).

Livemint (2013a). Tax-free bonds issued by ports get poor response. 19 March.

Livemint (2013b). Policy aims to attract port infrastructure investments. 21 April.

Lloyd's List (2013a). Power ports. Lloyd's List – Ship Operations. 19 June.

Lloyd's List (2013b). Brussels moves to prevent price abuse at European ports. Lloyd's List – Ports and Logistics. 23 May.

McKinsey Global Institute (2013). Infrastructure productivity: How to save $1 trillion a year. McKinsey and Company. New York. January.

OECD (2011). Pension funds investment in infrastructure – a survey. September. Available at http://www.oecd.org/sti/futures/infrastructureto2030/48634596.pdf.

Oxford Economics (2013). The economic impact of the UK maritime services sector. Oxford Economics. February. Available at http://www.oxfordeconomics.com/publication/open/239345 (accessed 26 September 2013).

PMSA (2013). Port investment. Pacific Merchant Shipping Association. Available at http://www.pmsaship.com/port-investment.aspx (accessed 25 September 2013).

Port Finance International (2013). Chinese company to invest more than $1.2bn in new Jamaican transshipment port - Port Finance International. 5 February.

PortCalls Asia (2013). Cambodia opens new container terminal. 28 January.

Preqin (2012). 2012 Preqin Infrastructure Review. Preqin.

Preqin (2013). Infrastructure spotlight. April.

Reuters (2012). BlackRock to tap infrastructure debt demand. 26 November.

RJR News (2013). Plan for trans-shipment port at Fort Augusta abandoned, larger site being sought. 30 April.

Sabahionline.com (2013). Tanzania and China sign port development package. 27 March.

Sea News Turkey (2013). Bangkok seeks US$67m loan to build infrastructure, ports and railways. 31 March.

Sea-web (2013). News and analysis. APMT explains plans at African ports. 13 June.

Shipping Seenews (2013). Peru to update plans for 4 ports with support from South Korea. 7 March.

Suffolk News-Herald (2013). VPA punts port bids. 26 March.

The East African (2012). Congestion at Mombasa port slows down trade in EAC bloc. 13 December.

The East African (2013). With $11bn Bagamoyo port, Tanzania prepares to take on EA hub Mombasa. 11 May.

The Economic Times (2013). Major ports will soon be allowed to fix market-linked tariff. 19 March.

The Economist (2013a). China's foreign ports – the new masters and commanders – China's growing empire of ports abroad is mainly about trade, not aggression. 8 June.

The Economist (2013b). New bay dawning. 27 April.

The Guardian (2013). Nicaragua waterway to dwarf Panama canal. 12 June.

The Hindu (2013). Cabinet nod for two new major ports in West Bengal, Andhra Pradesh. 9 May.

The Nation (2013). New act tipped to speed up projects. 27 May.

The Plain Dealer - cleveland.com (2013). Port Authority board approves $90 million bond deal for new Cuyahoga County headquarters. 14 March. Available at http://www.cleveland.com/business/index.ssf/2013/03/port_authority_board_approves.html (accessed 25 September 2013).

The Vancouver Sun (2013). Thai–Burma port project stalled. 24 February.

World Socialist Web Site (2013). New Chinese president courts Africa. 28 March.

UNCTAD (1985). Port Development: A Handbook for Planners in Developing Countries. TD/B/C.4/175/Rev. 1. United Nations publication. New York.

ENDNOTES

[1]   The ownership share of all partners is as follows: DP World (42.5 per cent), Zim Ports (20 per cent), Cosco Pacific (20 per cent), Terminal Link/CMA CGM (10 per cent) and Duisport (7.5 per cent).

5 LEGAL ISSUES AND REGULATORY DEVELOPMENTS

This chapter provides information on some important legal issues and recent regulatory developments in the fields of transport and trade facilitation, together with information on the status of the main maritime conventions. Important issues include the entry into force of the 2006 Maritime Labour Convention (MLC 2006) (effective 20 August 2013), and of the 2002 Athens Convention relating to the Carriage of Passengers and their Luggage by Sea (PAL 2002) (effective 23 April 2014), as well as a range of regulatory developments relating to maritime and supply-chain security and environmental issues.

To assist in the implementation of a set of technical and operational measures to increase energy efficiency and reduce greenhouse gas (GHG) emissions from international shipping, which entered into force on 1 January 2013, additional guidelines and unified interpretations were adopted at the International Maritime Organization in October 2012 and May 2013. In addition, a Resolution on Promotion of Technical Cooperation and Transfer of Technology relating to the Improvement of Energy Efficiency of Ships was adopted in May 2013, and an agreement was reached that a new study will be initiated to carry out an update to the GHG emissions estimate for international shipping. The issue of possible market-based measures (MBMs) for the reduction of GHG emissions from international shipping remained controversial, and discussion was postponed.

Results from UNCTAD's research on national trade-facilitation implementation plans illustrate that trade facilitation remains a challenge but is also seen as a priority area for national development by the developing countries themselves. By identifying the major areas of non-compliance with a future WTO trade-facilitation agreement, the report offers insights into the range of time and resource requirements and the needs for technical assistance and capacity-building for the developing countries.

A. IMPORTANT DEVELOPMENTS IN TRANSPORT LAW

1. Entry into force of the 2006 Maritime Labour Convention

Following ratification by the Russian Federation and the Philippines on 20 August 2012, the MLC 2006 enters into force on 20 August 2013.[1] The Convention, which had been adopted in 2006 under the joint auspices of the International Labour Organization (ILO) and the IMO, consolidates and updates more than 68 international labour standards relating to seafarers, setting out their responsibilities and rights with regard to labour and social matters in the maritime sector. It is considered an important fourth pillar, complementing three major IMO conventions, namely the International Convention for the Safety of Life at Sea (SOLAS), 1974, the International Convention on Standards of Training, Certification and Watchkeeping for Seafarers (STCW), 1978, and the International Convention for the Prevention of Pollution from Ships (MARPOL).

The MLC 2006 aims to achieve both decent conditions of work for the world's more than 1.2 million seafarers and to create conditions of fair competition for shipowners. Following its entry into force, seafarers working on around 70 per cent of the world's international shipping tonnage will be covered by the new Convention. The Convention establishes minimum requirements for almost all aspects of working conditions for seafarers, and a strong compliance and enforcement mechanism based on flag State inspection and certification of seafarers' working and living conditions.

The Convention comprises three different but related parts: the Articles, the Regulations and the Code. The Articles and Regulations set out the core rights and principles and the basic obligations of Member States ratifying the Convention.[2] The Code contains detailed information on the implementation of the Regulations. It consists of part A (mandatory standards) and part B (non-mandatory guidelines).[3] The Regulations and the Code are organized into general areas under five titles containing groups of provisions relating to a particular right or principle, including (a) minimum requirements for seafarers to work on a ship; (b) conditions of employment; (c) accommodation, recreational facilities, food and catering; (d) health protection, medical care, welfare and social security protection; and (e) compliance and enforcement.[4]

The MLC 2006 also imposes certain documentary obligations on Member States. Thus, each Member State shall require its ships of over 500 GT that are involved in international voyages to carry and maintain a maritime labour certificate, as well as a declaration of maritime labour compliance, conforming to a model prescribed by the Code.[5] The working and living conditions of seafarers that must be inspected and approved by the flag State before certifying a ship are as follows:

- Minimum age;
- Medical certification;
- Qualifications of seafarers;
- Seafarers' employment agreements;
- Use of any licensed or certified or regulated private recruitment and placement service;
- Hours of work or rest;
- Manning levels for the ship;
- Accommodation;
- On-board recreational facilities;
- Food and catering;
- Health and safety, and accident prevention;
- On-board medical care;
- On-board complaint procedures;
- Payment of wages.

Two handbooks have recently been issued by ILO to assist Member States in implementing their responsibilities under the MLC 2006 (ILO, 2012a; ILO, 2012b). The first contains a model for legal provisions that implement MLC 2006, and is intended as an aid for national legislators. The second covers issues of social security for seafarers by providing both the necessary background on the subject and practical information related to the implementation of the Convention. Also worth highlighting is guidance for ship operators on Port State Control that has been issued by the global shipowners' organization, the International Chamber of Shipping (ICS) (ICS, 2013).

It should also be noted that a Special Tripartite Committee, mandated to keep the Convention under continuous review, is set to meet in early 2014 to discuss, inter alia, proposed amendments to the Code of the Convention to address the issue of financial security for crew members/seafarers and their dependents with regard to compensation in cases of personal injury, death and abandonment.[6]

2. Entry into force of the Athens Convention relating to the Carriage of Passengers and their Luggage by Sea, 2002

The 2002 Protocol to the Athens Convention relating to the Carriage of Passengers and their Luggage by Sea (PAL PROT 2002) achieved the required 10 ratifications[7] on 23 April 2013 and is set to enter into force one year later, on 23 April 2014.[8] The 2002 Protocol revises and updates the 1974 Athens Convention relating to the Carriage of Passengers and their Luggage by Sea (PAL 1974),[9] which established a liability regime in respect of passenger carriage, including personal injury or death at sea. The PAL 1974 as amended by the PAL PROT 2002 is referred to as the Athens Convention relating to the Carriage of Passengers and their Luggage by Sea, 2002 (PAL 2002).[10]

The PAL 2002 introduces some important changes to the liability regime. Key elements[11] include the following:

(a) PAL 2002 replaces the fault-based liability system of the 1974 Convention with a strict liability system for shipping-related incidents (that is, collision, stranding, explosion, fire, and defects in the ship), subject to very limited exceptions for force majeure-type incidents.

Thus, the carrier will be held liable in cases of personal injury or death of a passenger, irrespective of fault, up to a limit amounting to 250,000 Special Drawing Rights (SDR) per passenger on each occasion; if loss or damage exceeds this limit, the carrier is liable for an overall amount of up to 400,000 SDR per passenger, on each occasion, unless the carrier can prove that the incident was not due to fault or neglect on the part of the carrier, or his servants.[12] By way of comparison, under PAL 1974 the carrier's limit of liability for death or personal injury was set at 46,666 SDR per passenger. An "opt-out" clause enables States Parties to retain or introduce higher limits of liability (or unlimited liability) in the case of carriers that are subject to the jurisdiction of their courts.

(b) To ensure that claims are not frustrated, carriers are required to maintain insurance or other financial security to cover the limits for strict liability under the Convention in respect of death of and personal injury to passengers. The limit of the compulsory insurance or other financial security shall not be less than 250,000 SDR per passenger on each distinct occasion. Any passenger ship trading within an area where the PAL 2002 applies will have to be issued with a certificate attesting that insurance or other financial security is in force; where a vessel is either uninsured or a certificate is not obtained, fines will apply.[13]

(c) Regarding loss or damage to luggage, the carrier's limit of liability varies under the PAL 2002, depending on the type of luggage (cabin luggage, vehicle and luggage carried in or on such vehicles, and other luggage).[14]

(d) PAL 2002 introduces the tacit acceptance procedure for amending the limits of liability, so that any future increase in limits can enter into force more easily.[15]

The entry into force of the PAL 2002 significantly strengthens the international passenger liability regime, in particular in respect of personal injury and death. However, pending more widespread adoption of PAL 2002, the international legal framework remains complex. In this context it should be noted that PAL 1974 will remain in force for Contracting States to that Convention that have not yet acceded to the PAL PROT 2002;[16] some of these States had reserved their right to exclude the application of the 1974 Convention, and apply their own limits of liability, when both the passenger and the carrier were nationals of that State.[17] Moreover, it should be noted that a number of States have not ratified or acceded to PAL 1974, but have adopted a similar limitation regime, as a matter of domestic legislation, albeit with higher liability limits.[18]

B. REGULATORY DEVELOPMENTS RELATING TO THE REDUCTION OF GREENHOUSE GAS EMISSIONS FROM INTERNATIONAL SHIPPING AND OTHER ENVIRONMENTAL ISSUES

1. Reduction of greenhouse gas emissions from international shipping and energy efficiency

A key development, reported in the 2012 edition of the *Review of Maritime Transport* (UNCTAD, 2012a), was the adoption of a set of technical and operational measures[19] to increase energy efficiency and reduce emissions of GHGs from international shipping (IMO, 2011a, Annex 19). The new measures, introducing the Energy Efficiency Design Index (EEDI) for new ships and the Ship Energy Efficiency Management Plan (SEEMP) for all ships,[20] were adopted by way of amendments to MARPOL Annex VI, through introduction of a new Chapter 4, and entered into force on 1 January 2013. According to the Second IMO GHG Study 2009 (IMO, 2009), technical and operational measures have a significant potential for the reduction of GHG emissions from international shipping.[21] Issues related to the reduction of GHG emissions from international shipping continued to remain one of the main areas of focus of the work of the IMO's Marine Environment Protection Committee (MEPC) at its sixty-forth and sixty-fifth sessions[22] held during the current reporting period. Further information about relevant deliberations and outcomes is presented below.

Energy efficiency for ships

Complementing four sets of guidelines (IMO, 2012a, Annexes 8–11), which had been adopted earlier, the MEPC, at its sixty-fourth session, adopted additional guidelines and unified interpretations for the smooth implementation of the mandatory regulations on energy efficiency for ships, set out in Chapter 4 of MARPOL Annex VI. In particular, the MEPC adopted amendments to the "2012 Guidelines on the method of calculation of the attained EEDI for new ships", relating to the calculation of shaft-generator power and shaft-motor power (IMO, 2012b, Annex 8). The MEPC also approved the following guidance and interpretations (IMO, 2012b, Annex 7):

- Unified interpretation for the definition of "new ships" for phases 1, 2 and 3 of the EEDI framework under Regulation 2.23 of MARPOL Annex VI;

- Unified interpretation of the phrase "major conversion" under Regulation 2.24 of MARPOL Annex VI;

- Unified interpretation on the timing for existing ships to have on board a SEEMP under Regulations 5.4.4 and 22.1 of MARPOL Annex VI;

- Unified interpretation on the appropriate category to be applied for dedicated fruit-juice carriers;

- Unified interpretation for section 2.3 of the supplement to the International Air Pollution Prevention (IAPP) certificate.

- In addition, the MEPC approved:

- Subject to concurrent decision by the ninety-first session of the Maritime Safety Committee (MSC), the draft MEPC–MSC circular for the interim guidelines for determining minimum propulsion power to maintain the manoeuvrability of ships in adverse conditions (IMO, 2012c, Annex 2);

- Interim guidelines for the calculation of the coefficient "fw" for decrease of ship speed in representative sea conditions for trial use (IMO, 2012c, Annex 3);

- An amendment to the "2012 Guidelines on survey and certification of the EEDI"[23] (IMO, 2012b, Annex 9).

At its sixty-fifth session in May 2013, the MEPC:

- Approved draft amendments to MARPOL Annex VI, with a view to their adoption at the sixty-sixth session of the Committee. The amendments envisage: (a) extending the application of EEDI to ro-ro cargo ships (vehicle carriers, Liquefied Natural Gas (LNG) carriers, cruise passenger ships having non-conventional propulsion, ro-ro cargo ships and ro-ro passenger ships; (b) exempting ships not propelled by mechanical means, and platforms including Floating Production Storage and Offloading Facilities (FPSOs), Floating Storage Units (FSUs) and drilling rigs, regardless of their propulsion, as well as cargo ships having ice-breaking capability (IMO, 2013c, Annex 13);

- Adopted amendments to update the "Guidelines for calculation of reference lines for use with the Energy Efficiency Design Index (EEDI)", including the addition of ro-ro cargo ships (vehicle carriers), ro-ro cargo ships, ro-ro passenger ships, and LNG carriers (IMO, 2013c, Annex 14);

- Noted, with a view to adoption at MEPC 66, the finalized amendments to the "2012 Guidelines on the method of calculation of the Attained Energy Efficiency Design Index (EEDI) for new ships";

- Approved amendments to unified interpretation MEPC.1/Circ.795, to update the circular with regards to requirements for SEEMP, to exclude platforms (including FPSOs and FSUs), drilling rigs, regardless of their propulsion, and any other ship without means of propulsion;

- Adopted the "2013 Interim guidelines for determining minimum propulsion power to maintain the manoeuvrability of ships in adverse conditions", which are intended to assist administrations and recognized organizations in verifying that ships, complying with the EEDI requirements set out in Regulation 21.5 of MARPOL Annex VI, have sufficient installed propulsion power to maintain the manoeuvrability in adverse conditions (IMO, 2013c, Annex 16);

- Approved the "2013 Guidance on treatment of innovative energy efficiency technologies for calculation and verification of the attained EEDI", which are intended to assist manufacturers, shipbuilders, shipowners, verifiers and other interested parties related to the EEDI of ships to treat innovative energy-efficiency technologies for calculation and verification of the attained EEDI, addressing systems such as air lubrication, wind propulsion systems, high temperature waste heat recovery systems, and photovoltaic power generation systems (IMO, 2013d);

- Adopted the "2013 Guidelines for calculation of reference lines for use with the Energy Efficiency Design Index (EEDI) for cruise passenger ships having non-conventional propulsion" (IMO, 2013c, Annex 17);

- Adopted amendments to the "2012 Guidelines on survey and certification of the Energy Efficiency Design Index (EEDI)" (IMO, 2013c, Annex 18), to add references to measuring sea conditions.

The MEPC also endorsed an updated work plan to continue its work on development of the EEDI framework for ship types and sizes, and propulsion systems not covered by the current EEDI requirements, and to consider guidelines on propulsion power needed to maintain the manoeuvrability of the ship under adverse conditions (IMO, 2013e, Annex 9).

Finally, it should be noted that the MEPC decided to establish a new sub-item under its agenda item 4 ("Air pollution and energy efficiency") for the discussion of further technical and operational measures to enhance the energy efficiency of international shipping; a working group will be established under this sub-agenda item at the MEPC's sixty-sixth session (IMO, 2013c, paragraphs 4.136–4.147). The decision followed discussions related to an amended proposal for the establishment of attained energy-efficiency standards for new and existing ships through a phased approach, starting with a data-collection phase.[24]

Technical cooperation and transfer of technology

Chapter 4 of MARPOL Annex VI, adopted in July 2011, includes Regulation 23 on "Promotion of technical cooperation and transfer of technology relating to the improvement of energy efficiency of ships". Under this regulation, administrations, in cooperation with IMO and other international bodies, are required to promote and provide, as appropriate, support, directly or through IMO, to States, especially developing States that request technical assistance. The regulation also requires administrations to cooperate actively with one another, and, subject to their national laws, regulations and policies, "to promote the development and transfer of technology and exchange of information to States, which request technical assistance, particularly developing States, in respect of the implementation of measures to fulfill the requirements of Chapter 4 [of MARPOL Annex VI]".

At the time of the adoption of Chapter 4, MEPC agreed to develop a resolution linked to the implementation of Regulation 23, and of the other energy-efficiency measures. Following extensive deliberations over the course of several working sessions, the work was completed, and resolution MEPC.229(65) on "Promotion of technical cooperation and transfer of technology relating to the improvement of energy efficiency of ships" (IMO, 2013c, Annex 4), was adopted during the sixty-fifth session of the MEPC. In its preamble, the resolution makes reference both to the IMO principles of non-discrimination and no more favourable treatment,[25] and to the principle of common but differentiated responsibilities and respective capabilities under the UNFCCC and its Kyoto Protocol.[26]

The resolution requests the IMO, through its various programmes, to provide technical assistance to its Member States to enable cooperation in the transfer of energy-efficient technologies to developing countries in particular, and further assist in the sourcing of funding for capacity-building and support to States, in particular developing States, which have requested technology transfer.[27]

The resolution also urges Member States, subject to their ability, and subject to their respective national laws, regulations and policies, "to promote the provision of support especially to developing States … including, but not limited with regard to:

1. Transfer of energy-efficient technologies for ships;

2. Research and development for the improvement of energy efficiency of ships;

3. Training of personnel, for the effective implementation and enforcement of the regulations in Chapter 4 of MARPOL Annex VI; and

4. The exchange of information and technical cooperation relating to the improvement of energy efficiency for ships."

In relation to technical cooperation and capacity-building, it should also be noted that the IMO Integrated Technical Cooperation Programme (ITCP) and the Korean International Cooperation Agency (KOICA) have recently concluded an agreement for implementation of a project on "Building capacities in East Asian Countries to address GHG emissions from ships". A comprehensive portfolio of training material for capacity-building activities on energy efficiency for shipping has been produced under that agreement. In addition, a series of capacity-building workshops and training courses have been implemented in countries including Bulgaria, Indonesia, Malaysia, the Philippines, the Republic of Korea, Thailand, Uruguay, and Viet Nam, and IMO is seeking additional funding from various sources including the Global Environment Facility (GEF) to scale up these activities.[28]

Market-based measures and related matters

Despite improvements in the fuel-efficiency of ships, GHG emissions from maritime transport are projected to increase rapidly over the coming decades. To address their growth, market based measures (MBMs) for the reduction of GHG emissions from international shipping[29] have been proposed to complement technical and operational measures already adopted. While discussions on different proposals for possible MBMs have been ongoing for some years under the auspices of the IMO, the issue remains one of the most controversial on the MEPC agenda.[30]

One of the main issues in the debate on MBMs at the IMO has been their impact on developing countries and especially on remote economies. Worth mentioning in this context is a recent study (Climate Strategies et al., 2013) that quantifies the economic impacts of MBMs for 10 case-study economies as well as globally.[31] According to the study report, the case-study economies were selected in the expectation that they would be relatively highly impacted because of their remoteness or dependence on international aviation or maritime transport. The key findings of the report – reflected here for the purposes of information only – are as follows:

(1) Economic impacts of Market Based Measures (MBMs) for International Shipping and Aviation on Developing Countries considered in this study, and globally, are small. The reductions in GDP are less than 0.01 per cent on average and less than 0.2 per cent for all but a few of the case study countries. MBMs which raise more revenues have a larger impact.

2) The volume and certainty of CO_2 reductions achieved by the MBMs considered for the time frame (2015–2025) in this study are comparable to each other, although emission reductions from project-based emissions reductions (offsets) are the most significant. In the longer term, innovations in fuel-efficiency may decrease in-sector emission reductions costs and the associated in-sector CO_2 reductions could be more significant.

3) In most cases, aviation MBMs have larger economic impacts than those associated with the implementation of shipping schemes. Aviation has larger impacts on tourism, and shipping is less responsive to price increases and less carbon intensive.

4) Countries with a higher dependency on tourism and trade are likely to experience greater economic impacts. Some of these countries are small island developing states that are also vulnerable to climate change impacts.

5) Undesired economic impacts can be addressed. However, since the factors that cause these vary between countries, applicable measures vary as well. Instead, a combination of appropriate measures could be taken to address the impacts in question. Exemptions, lump-sum rebates, investments in infrastructure efficiency and into the development of more efficient ships and aircraft could be considered.

At the IMO, discussions related to market-based measures have been ongoing for several years, but are moving only slowly. A number of revised and updated proposals were submitted at the sixty-fourth session of the MEPC. However, due to time constraints, the Committee agreed to postpone relevant detailed debate to the sixty-fifth session. In addition, the co-sponsors[32] of one of the submissions (IMO, 2012d) suggested that high priority should be given to the development of an MEPC resolution to ensure that financial, technological and capacity-building support from developed countries for the implementation of regulations on energy efficiency for ships by developing countries. Hence, they considered that all further decisions on MBMs must await the adoption of this resolution, and that future consideration of MBMs must fully take into account potential impacts of those measures on developing countries. As a result, pending the adoption of the resolution, during its sixty-fifth session, the MEPC agreed to suspend discussions on market-based measures and related issues to a future session.[33]

Update of the GHG emission estimate for international shipping

The MEPC, at its sixty-third session, had noted that uncertainty existed in the estimates and projections of emissions from international shipping and agreed that further work should take place to provide reliable and up-to-date information for the Committee to base its decisions on. At the sixty-fourth session of the MEPC, an outline document regarding the need for an update of the GHG emissions estimate for international shipping prepared by the IMO Secretariat was considered (IMO, 2012e). The outline document highlights the need for an updated GHG inventory, as the current estimate contained in the *Second IMO GHG Study 2009* (IMO, 2009) does not take into account the economic downturn experienced globally since 2008.[34] In addition, analytical work undertaken since the publication of the Second IMO GHG Study 2009 and information obtained through analysis of the Automatic Identification System (AIS), as well as other sources for ship activity data, indicate that some of the assumptions used at that time may need to be reconsidered. The document proposed that the update would build on the methodology developed under the Second IMO GHG Study 2009 and would be based on available data on fleet composition and size as well as on other technical ship-specific data. The inventory would include current global emissions of GHGs and relevant substances emitted from ships of 100 GT and above engaged in international transport.

In the context of consideration of the IMO Secretariat document, the MEPC report (IMO, 2012b) expressly notes the following views from delegations:

- An update of the GHG estimate for international shipping must be undertaken in a fair, open and transparent manner and in coordination with the Subsidiary Body for Scientific and Technological Advice of the UNFCCC, whose agenda includes a specific item for the consideration of emissions from fuel used for international aviation and maritime transport, and that this work should take into consideration the methodological work developed by the Intergovernmental Panel on Climate Change (IPCC);

- Further consideration is needed to be given to ensuring the estimates related to those made by other international organizations, that the work is scientifically based, equitable and balanced, which will be tasked to undertake the work, how the data will be used and the methodology to be used;

- There is an urgent need for information on the actual fuel consumption of ships and hence highlighted the need of moving forward with a bottom-up (ship activity)

approach of the GHG emissions estimate as well as top-down analysis which has been used in the past; and

- Monitoring and reporting of data was also important.[35]

Following further discussion at an expert workshop[36] held in early 2013, the MEPC at its sixty-fifth session, approved the terms of reference[37] for an Update GHG Study, and agreed that (a) the Update Study should focus on global inventories (as set out in paragraph 1.3 of the terms of reference) and, resources permitting, should also include future scenarios of emissions (as set out in the chapeau and paragraph 1.10 of the terms of reference); (b) its primary focus should be to update the CO_2 emission estimates for international shipping, and subject to adequate resources, the same substances as those estimated by the *Second IMO GHG Study 2009* should also be estimated; (c) a steering committee should be established that should be geographically balanced, should equitably represent developing and developed countries and should be of a manageable size.[38] The final report of the Update Study is expected to be submitted to the MEPC at its sixty-sixth session, in March 2014.

WTO-related issues

Related to the issue of possible MBMs for international shipping, the MEPC during its sixty-fourth session considered a submission[39] that argued that MBMs show incompatibility with the WTO rules (IMO, 2012f). The document also considers that the conclusion of the third Intersessional Meeting of the Working Group on GHG Emissions from Ships (GHG-WG 3) – that MBMs are, in principle, compatible with the WTO rules – was premature, since most of the MBM proposals were not yet sufficiently elaborated to support that conclusion.

At the request of the IMO Council, comments were sought from WTO on the above document, and note was taken of the response by the WTO Secretariat (IMO, 2013h) during the sixty-fifth session of the MEPC. In its response, the WTO Secretariat indicated that it was not authorized to interpret WTO rules, as this was the exclusive prerogative of WTO members. However, it had prepared a neutral document which set out the WTO disciplines most relevant to the types of MBMs that the IMO was considering.[40]

Matters concerning the United Nations Framework Convention on Climate Change

With respect to matters concerning UNFCCC, during its sixty-fourth and sixty-fifth sessions the MEPC noted a number of documents.[41] The Committee also noted the latest status reports as contained in Annex 11 of IMO (2012b) and Annex 20 of IMO (2013c), by the UNFCCC Secretariat on the current state of negotiations in general and on bunker fuels in particular.

2.   Ship-source pollution and protection of the environment

(a) Developments regarding the International Convention on Liability and Compensation for Damage in Connection with the Carriage of Hazardous and Noxious Substances by Sea, 1996, as amended by its 2010 Protocol

As may be recalled, in 2012 a report with a focus on ship-source oil pollution was published by the UNCTAD secretariat. The report, entitled *Liability and Compensation for Ship-Source Oil Pollution: An Overview of the International Legal Framework for Oil Pollution Damage from Tankers* (UNCTAD, 2012b) was prepared to assist policymakers, particularly in developing countries, in their understanding of the complex international legal framework and in assessing the merits of accession to the latest of the relevant international legal instruments. [42] As noted in the report, accession could offer considerable benefits to a number of coastal developing States that may be vulnerable to oil pollution from tankers.

While the report focuses on the international liability and compensation framework for oil pollution from tankers, known as the International Oil Pollution Compensation Fund (IOPC Fund) regime,[43] it also highlights some of the key features of two important related international conventions that provide for liability and compensation in respect of other types of ship-source pollution. These are the International Convention on Civil Liability for Bunker Oil Pollution Damage 2001 (2001 BOPC),[44] which covers bunker oil spills from ships other than oil tankers, and the 1996 International Convention on Liability and Compensation for Damage in Connection with the Carriage of Hazardous and Noxious Substances by Sea (1996 HNS Convention), which deals with liability and compensation arising in connection with the carriage of a broad range of hazardous and noxious substances (HNS). An amending Protocol to the 1996 HNS Convention had been adopted in April 2010[45] to address a range of practical problems that had prevented many States from ratifying the 1996 Convention.

While the 2001 BOPC is in force internationally, the 1996 HNS Convention, as amended by its 2010 Protocol (2010 HNS Convention) has not yet attracted the required number of accessions for its entry into force. Thus, at present, no international regime is in force to provide for liability and compensation arising in connection with the carriage of HNS cargos. This is a matter of concern, given the potential for coastal pollution, as well as personal injury and death that may be associated with an incident involving the carriage of chemicals and other HNS cargos.

The 1996 HNS Convention is modelled on the IOPC Fund regime and establishes a two-tier system for compensation to be paid in the event of pollution incidents involving HNS such as chemicals. Tier one provides for shipowner liability, backed by compulsory insurance cover. Tier two provides for compensation from a fund, financed through contributions from the receivers of HNS in cases when the shipowner's insurance does not cover a given HNS incident or is insufficient to cover the claim.

One of the major obstacles to ratification of the 1996 HNS Convention had been difficulties regarding one of the key requirements under the Convention, the submission of reports on "contributing cargo", that is, on HNS cargo received in each State. Other obstacles appeared to be related to the setting up of a reporting system for packaged goods and the difficulty of enforcing payment, in non-States Parties, of contributions to the liquefied natural gas account established under the Convention. By addressing these problems, the 2010 Protocol to the 1996 HNS Convention was considered an important development towards the strengthening of the international liability framework for ship-source pollution. The 2010 HNS Protocol was open for signature from 1 November 2010 to 31 October 2011 and thereafter has been open for accession.

While so far no State has yet acceded to the Protocol, it should be noted that a set of guidelines for reporting contributing cargo under the 2010 HNS Convention (IMO, 2013j) was agreed by delegates from 29 States at a workshop on reporting of HNS organized in late 2012 by the IMO in cooperation with the IOPC Funds.[46] The guidelines are intended to assist States with the Convention's accession or ratification, and were endorsed by the Legal Committee of the IMO during its 100th session, in April 2013. In so doing, the Legal Committee expressed the following views:

- The guidelines were the result of the work of a large number of Member States and observers;

- It was of paramount importance that the Convention be applied uniformly and the guidelines could assist this process;

- The guidelines were not binding, but were merely intended to facilitate the implementation and entry into force of the 2010 HNS Protocol, particularly States' submissions of contributing cargo to the Secretary-General of IMO, on ratification, or accession to the HNS Protocol;

- The proposed solutions in the guidelines should not exclude the use by implementing States of other options which were also provided for in the HNS Protocol.[47]

It is hoped that the international community's collective efforts towards the entry into force of the 2010 HNS Convention will continue and eventually be successful, thus closing an important regulatory gap.

(b) Liability and compensation issues connected with transboundary pollution damage from offshore oil exploration and exploitation

The Legal Committee during its 100th session noted information on the outcome of the second International Conference on Liability and Compensation Regime for Transboundary Oil Damage Resulting from Offshore Exploration and Exploitation Activities, held in Bali in November 2012 (IMO, 2013k), as well as a submission containing principles for guidance on model bilateral/regional agreements or arrangements on liability and compensation issues connected with transboundary pollution damage from offshore exploration and exploitation activities (IMO, 2013l).

The Committee recalled its previous decision to analyse further the liability and compensation issues connected with transboundary pollution damage resulting from offshore oil exploration and exploitation activities, with the aim of developing guidance to assist States interested in pursuing bilateral or regional arrangements.[48] It agreed that assistance should be provided to those States which are in need of guidance for bilateral and multilateral agreements. Member States were invited to send examples of relevant legislation and, in particular, examples of existing bilateral and regional agreements to the secretariat.[49]

(c) Other developments at the International Maritime Organization

During its sixty-fourth and sixty-fifth sessions, the MEPC approved draft amendments and adopted guidelines related to MARPOL Annex VI Regulation 13 on nitrogen oxides (NOx), the NOx Technical Code, 2008 and the implementation of the revised MARPOL Annex V "Prevention of pollution by garbage from ships". It also adopted two sets of guidelines, which together with the four sets of guidelines previously adopted, complete the development of all guidelines referred to in the text of the Hong Kong International Convention for the Safe and Environmentally Sound Recycling of Ships, 2009 (Hong Kong Convention). The MEPC also granted basic and final approval to a number of ballast water management systems that make use of active substances, approved a draft resolution to facilitate the smooth implementation of the 2004 International Convention for the Control and Management of Ships' Ballast Water and Sediments (BWM Convention), and issued a number of ballast water management circulars. A more detailed overview of relevant issues is presented in the following sections.

(i) Air pollution from ships

In addition to striving to reduce its carbon footprint from international shipping, IMO is working on regulations to reduce emissions of other toxic substances from burning fuel oil, particularly sulphur oxides (SOx) and NOx. These significantly contribute to air pollution from ships and are covered by Annex VI of MARPOL,[50] which was amended in 2008 to introduce more stringent emission controls.[51]

Sulphur oxide emissions

As reported in the 2012 edition of the *Review of Maritime Transport*, with effect from 1 January 2012, MARPOL Annex VI established reduced SOx thresholds for marine bunker fuels, with the global sulphur cap reduced from 4.5 per cent (45,000 parts per million (ppm)) to 3.5 per cent (35,000 ppm). The global sulphur cap will be reduced further to 0.50 per cent (5,000 ppm) from 2020 (subject to a feasibility review in 2018).[52] Annex VI also contains provisions allowing for special SOx Emission Control Areas (ECAs) to be established where even more stringent controls on sulphur emissions apply.[53] Since 1 July 2010, these ECAs have SOx thresholds for marine fuels of 1 per cent (from the previous 1.5 per cent); from 1 January 2015, ships operating in these areas will be required to burn fuel with no more than 0.1 per cent sulphur. Alternatively, ships must fit an exhaust gas cleaning system,[54] or use any other technological method to limit SOx emissions.

The European Union has recently revised its directive on sulphur in fuels, generally including MARPOL Annex VI provisions. According to the new directive, the limits for the sulphur content of marine fuels used in designated SOx ECAs (SECAs) will be 1 per cent until 31 December 2014, and 0.1 per cent from 1 January 2015. In addition, the IMO sulphur limit of 0.5 per cent will become mandatory in waters of European Union Member States by 2020.[55] The inclusion of this fixed entry-into-force date (2020) has raised concerns about possible inconsistency with the IMO provision which makes such a date dependent on the outcome of the 2018 feasibility study (*Platts*, 2012).

As noted in the previous *Review of Maritime Transport*, the shipping industry, while supportive of the 2008 amendments, has expressed concerns about some aspects of the implementation of the requirements. This includes in particular the availability of compliant low-sulphur fuel to meet the new demand (*MarineLink.com*, 2012).

During its sixty-fourth session, the MEPC discussed proposals (IMO, 2012i;[56] IMO, 2012j[57]) related to a review on the availability of compliant fuel oil to meet the requirements set out in MARPOL Annex VI, Regulation 14 on emissions of SOx from ships.

A number of delegations recognized that a preliminary study for the assessment of the availability of compliant fuel oil in 2020 could provide further information to industries, and that it would be important in identifying sooner rather than later what action is necessary to ensure availability of compliant fuel oil. Other delegations expressed the view that the preliminary study could not provide additional certainty with respect to the availability of compliant fuel oil due to the difference in sulphur limits of the fuels to be studied and the specific geographic location in which the ECA-compliant fuel oil was to be used, and observed that the assessment methodology already developed by the correspondence group contains proven models that do not need revalidation. The MEPC agreed to revisit the matter of a review at a future session, and invited relevant submissions to its sixty-sixth session in 2014.

The MEPC also noted that, based on the monitoring of the worldwide average sulphur content of marine fuel oils supplied for use on board ship, in 2011 the average sulphur content of residual fuel worldwide

was 2.65 per cent, and that of distillate was 0.14 per cent (IMO, 2012k).

Emissions of nitrogen oxides

In addition to SOx, ship engines emit elevated levels of the harmful compounds of the general formula NOx, which have negative effects that include GHG formation in the atmosphere and damage to respiratory health. Progressive reductions in NOx emissions from ship engines have also been agreed at IMO. For specified ships that operate in ECAs,[58] the strictest controls are applicable to ships constructed on or after 1 January 2016. Such ships must produce NOx emissions below a level known as "tier III". For ships operating outside such areas, tier II controls apply.[59] Unlike SOx, where emission reductions can be achieved fairly simply, albeit at some cost, by switching to low-sulphur fuels or installing exhaust gas SOx scrubbers, major adjustments are needed to ensure compliance with NOx tier III requirements.

According to a correspondence group report (IMO, 2013m) on technology availability submitted at the sixty-fifth session of the MEPC, technologies identified that may be used to achieve the tier III NOx limits included the following:

- Selective catalytic reduction (SCR);

- Exhaust gas recirculation (EGR);

- LNG, either in a dual-fuel or alternative-fuel arrangement;

- Other technologies: direct water injection; humid air motor, scrubbers, treated water scrubber; variable valve timing and lift; dimethyl ether as an alternative fuel.

However, there was broad agreement among members of the correspondence group that SCR can meet the tier III limits as a sole emission-reduction strategy for most, if not all, marine engines and vessel applications. It is an emission reduction method that reduces NOx emissions, through after-treatment technology, by using a catalyst to chemically reduce NOx. Some marine engine manufacturers are already marketing SCR-based tier III-compliant SCR engines (IMO, 2013m).

During its sixty-fifth session, the MEPC:

- Considered and agreed to proposed draft amendments to MARPOL Annex VI Regulation 13 on NOx to amend the date for the implementation of tier III standards within ECAs to 1 January

2021, from the current effective date of 1 January 2016. The draft amendments will be circulated for consideration at the sixty-sixth session of MEPC (MEPC 66) in 2014, with a view to adoption;

- Approved, with a view to subsequent adoption, draft amendments to the NOx Technical Code, 2008, concerning use of dual-fuel engines (IMO, 2013c, Annex 7);

- Adopted guidelines in respect of non-identical replacement engines not required to meet the tier III limit (IMO, 2013c, Annex 8);

- Adopted a unified interpretation on the "time of the replacement or addition" of an engine for the applicable NOx tier standard for the supplement to the IAPP certificate (IMO, 2013c, Annex 9).

(ii) Port reception facilities and garbage management

Garbage from ships can be just as dangerous to marine life as oil or chemicals. As pointed out in the previous issue of the *Review of Maritime Transport*, amendments to MARPOL Annex V "Prevention of pollution by garbage from ships", were adopted that entered into force on 1 January 2013 (IMO, 2011a, Annex 13). The revised Annex V prohibits the discharge of all garbage into the sea, except as provided otherwise.[60] Guidelines were also adopted to assist in the implementation of the revised MARPOL Annex V.

During its sixty-fifth session, the MEPC adopted amendments to the "2012 Guidelines for the implementation of MARPOL Annex V", concerning electronic wastes, such as electronic cards, gadgets, computers, printer cartridges, and the like, generated on board during normal operation, maintenance or upgrading of vessels (IMO, 2013c, Annex 28). The MEPC also approved draft amendments to the form of the "Garbage Record Book" under MARPOL Annex V, to update the record of garbage discharges, for circulation with a view to adoption at MEPC 66 (IMO, 2013c, Annex 27), and an MEPC circular on adequate port reception facilities for cargoes declared as harmful to the marine environment under MARPOL Annex V (IMO, 2013n).[61]

(iii) Ship recycling

The MEPC, at its sixty-fourth session adopted the following:

- The "2012 Guidelines for the survey and certification of ships under the Hong Kong Convention[62]" (IMO, 2012b, Annex 2);

- The "2012 Guidelines for the inspection of ships under the Hong Kong Convention" (IMO, 2012b, Annex 3).

These two sets of guidelines, together with the four sets of guidelines adopted earlier,[63] complete the development of all guidelines referred to in the text of the Hong Kong Convention. The guidelines are intended to assist ship-recycling facilities and shipping companies to introduce voluntary improvements to meet the requirements of the Hong Kong Convention, which was adopted in May 2009 but has not yet entered into force.[64]

An intersessional correspondence group was re-established[65] during MEPC 65 and instructed to finalize the development of threshold values and exemptions applicable to the materials to be listed in Inventories of Hazardous Materials as well as to amend accordingly the "2011 Guidelines for the development of the Inventory of Hazardous Materials". It will report the outcome of its deliberations to the MEPC 66.

(iv) Ballast water management

In February 2004, the BWM Convention had been adopted, under the auspices of the IMO, to prevent, minimize and ultimately eliminate the risks to the environment, human health, property and resources arising from the transfer of harmful aquatic organisms carried by ships' ballast water from one region to another.[66] The Committee urged those States which have not yet ratified the Convention to do so at the earliest possible opportunity.

After considering the reports of the twenty-first–twenty-fifth meetings of the Joint Group of Experts on the Scientific Aspects of Marine Environment Protection Ballast Water Working Group, which took place in 2012 and the beginning of 2013, the MEPC granted basic approval to eight,[67] and final approval to six ballast water management systems[68] that make use of active substances during its sixty-fourth and sixty-fifth sessions.

The MEPC at its sixty-fifth session approved a draft Assembly resolution on the application of Regulation B-3 of the BWM Convention to ease and facilitate the smooth implementation of the Convention (IMO, 2013c, Annex 3), which will be submitted to the twenty-eighth session of the IMO Assembly[69] for approval. The draft resolution recommends that ships constructed before the entry into force of the BWM Convention will not be required to comply with Regulation D-2 (ballast water performance standard) until their first renewal survey following the date of entry into force of the Convention. The aim of the draft resolution is to clarify uncertainty in relation to the application of Regulation B-3, through the application of a realistic timeline for enforcement of Regulation D-1 (ballast water exchange standard) and Regulation D-2 (ballast water performance standard), upon entry into force of the Convention.

The MEPC also approved:

• The BWM Circular on clarification of "major conversion";

• The BWM Circular on Guidance on ballast water sampling and analysis for trial use;

• Amendments to the MEPC resolution (IMO, 2013c, Annex 1), on information reporting on type approved ballast water management systems;

• The BWM Circular on amendments to the Guidance for administrations on the type approval process for ballast water management systems;

• The BWM Circular on options for ballast water management for offshore support vessels.[70]

Key developments in summary

As the above overview of regulatory developments shows, in the year under review, several regulatory measures have been adopted to strengthen the legal framework relating to ship-source air pollution, port reception facilities and garbage management. Moreover, different sets of guidelines have been developed with a view to facilitating the widespread adoption of the 2010 HNS Convention and the 2009 Hong Kong Convention on ship recycling; progress has also been made in respect of technical matters related to the implementation of the 2004 BWM Convention. As concerns the reduction of GHG emissions from international shipping, significant progress has been made in respect of technical and operational measures. Thus, a number of guidelines and unified interpretations have been issued to ensure the smooth implementation of the new mandatory regulations on energy efficiency for ships under Chapter 4 of MARPOL Annex VI; further technical and operational measures to enhance the energy efficiency of international shipping have been scheduled for discussion as part of the MEPC deliberations on air pollution and energy efficiency. Moreover, a study has been initiated to provide an updated GHG emissions estimate for international shipping by the spring of 2014. Particularly worth highlighting is also

the adoption of an important resolution to promote technical cooperation and the transfer of technology relating to the improvement of energy efficiency of ships. This is an issue of particular practical relevancy from the perspective of developing countries and adoption of the resolution represents an important step towards ensuring all countries have access to and benefit from energy-efficient technologies for ships.

C. OTHER LEGAL AND REGULATORY DEVELOPMENTS AFFECTING TRANSPORTATION

This section highlights some key issues in the field of maritime security and safety that may be of particular interest to parties engaged in international trade and transport. These include developments relating to maritime and supply-chain security and some issues related to piracy. Matters related to piracy will, for reasons of space, not be covered extensively here, but are the subject of a separate report by the Secretariat.

1. Maritime and supply-chain security

There have been a number of developments in relation to existing maritime and supply-chain security standards that had been adopted under the auspices of various international organizations such as the World Customs Organization (WCO), IMO and the International Organization for Standardization (ISO), as well as at the European Union level and in the United States, both important trade partners for many developing countries.

(a) World Customs Organization Framework of Standards to Secure and Facilitate Global Trade

As noted in previous editions of the *Review of Maritime Transport*, in 2005 WCO had adopted the Framework of Standards to Secure and Facilitate Global Trade (the SAFE Framework),[71] with the objective of developing a global supply-chain framework. The SAFE Framework provides a set of standards and principles that must be adopted as a minimum threshold by national customs administrations. These standards are contained within two pillars – pillar 1, customs-to-customs network arrangements and pillar 2, customs–business partnerships.[72]

The SAFE Framework has been updated and has evolved over the years as a dynamic instrument, aiming to balance trade facilitation and controls while ensuring the security of the global supply chain. It is a widely accepted instrument that serves as an important reference point for customs and for economic operators alike.[73]

In June 2010, the WCO issued its SAFE Package, bringing together all WCO instruments and guidelines that support its implementation.[74] As part of yearly updates, the 2012 version of the SAFE Framework includes a new part 5 in respect of coordinated border management, and a new part 6 in respect of trade continuity and resumption. The text on mutual recognition has thus been moved to a new part 7; that concerning the authorized economic operator (AEO) conditions, requirements and benefits has been moved to a new Annex III, and the text of the Customs Cooperation Council resolution on the SAFE Framework has been moved to a new Annex IV. In addition, a new Annex I has been created, containing definitions, including the definition of "high risk cargo".[75]

As an important feature of the SAFE Framework, the AEOs[76] are private parties that have been accredited by national customs administrations as compliant with WCO or equivalent supply-chain security standards. AEOs have to meet special requirements in respect of physical security of premises, hidden camera surveillance and selective staffing and recruitment policies. In return, AEOs are typically rewarded by way of trade-facilitation benefits, such as faster clearance of goods and fewer physical inspections. Over the course of recent years, a number of mutual recognition agreements (MRAs)[77] of respective AEOs have been adopted by customs administrations, usually on a bilateral basis. However, it is hoped that these will, in due course form the basis for multilateral agreements at the sub-regional and regional level.[78] As of 30 June 2013, 26 AEO programmes had been established in 52 countries[79] and seven further countries plan to establish them in the near future.[80]

Capacity-building assistance under the WCO Columbus Programme remains a vital part of the SAFE implementation strategy. Implementation is further supported by Customs and private sector working bodies established within the WCO Secretariat and working in close collaboration to maintain the relevance of the SAFE Framework in a changing trade environment.[81]

(b) Developments at the European Union level and in the United States

For many developing countries, trade with the European Union and the United States remains of particular importance. Hence, certain relevant developments in the field of maritime and supply-chain security are also reported here.

As regards the European Union, previous editions of the *Review of Maritime Transport* have provided information on the Security Amendment to the Community Customs Code (Regulation (EC) 648/2005 and its implementing provisions), which aims to ensure an equivalent level of protection through customs controls for all goods brought into or out of the European Union's customs territory.[82] Part of these changes was the development of common rules for customs risk management, including setting out common criteria for pre-arrival/pre-departure security risk analysis based on electronically submitted cargo information. Since 1 January 2011, this advance electronic declaration of relevant security data has been an obligation for traders and is no longer optional; relevant security data have had to be sent before the arrival of the goods on the European Union customs territory. If such data is not sent in advance, then the goods need to be declared immediately on arrival at the border, which may delay the customs clearance of consignments at the border pending the results of risk analysis for safety and security purposes.[83] The Security Amendment to the Customs Code also introduced a sophisticated common Customs Risk Management Framework, encompassing detailed common risk criteria and standards. In this context, the European Commission commissioned a study to evaluate the existing strengths and weaknesses of European Union risk analysis and targeting capabilities, and assess some potential options for improvement (PricewaterhouseCoopers, 2012).[84] The study concluded that several issues required urgent action, including data quality, supply-chain modelling and certain aspects of the methodology applied.

Subsequently, in January 2013, the European Commission adopted a "Communication on Customs risk management and the security of the supply chain" (European Commission, 2013). The Communication characterizes the European Union's current cargo risk assessment strategy as "not sufficient", and states that "a new approach to EU risk management is needed".[85] It sets out a strategy to enable Customs to better tackle risks associated with goods being traded in international supply chains and suggests a number of key actions to be taken.[86] Following the adoption of the above Communication outlining the European Union's approach, concerns have been expressed by industry associations about the complexity of the current European Union advance cargo security system and about the fact that a single, unified European Union customs regime may not be a realistic option in the near term.[87] In a joint submission to the European Parliament and Council (International Air Transport Association et al., 2013), a number of major carrier and freight forwarder trade associations have drawn attention to several issues that remain to be clarified and decided through ongoing deliberations at the European Union. These include the need to define and identify what additional data elements will be required for a proper advance cargo risk assessment, who will be required to file such data, through which system and when.

Part of the changes to the European Union Customs Code was also the introduction of provisions regarding AEOs, a status which reliable traders may be granted and which entails benefits in terms of trade-facilitation measures. In this context, subsequent related developments – such as the recommendation for self-assessment of economic operators to be submitted together with their application for AEO certificates,[88] and the issuance of a revised self-assessment questionnaire,[89] to guarantee a uniform approach throughout all European Union Member States, are also worth noting.

In respect of mutual recognition of AEO programmes through agreements between the European Union and third countries including major trading partners,[90] it is worth noting that the decision between the European Union and the United States regarding mutual recognition of their "secure traders" programmes, namely the European Union AEO and the United States Customs-Trade Partnership against Terrorism (C–TPAT)[91] programmes, signed on 4 May 2012 (European Union–United States Joint Committee, 2012), was fully implemented as of 31 January 2013. The final phase of the agreement that this decision represents provides reciprocal benefits to safe traders, including lower risk score and less examination by customs when shipping cargo (United States Customs and Border Protection (CBP), 2013).

It should also be noted that the CBP has recently announced that as part of their Trusted Trader Program, they are planning to join the C-TPAT and Importer Self-Assessment processes. This is intended to enable CBP to provide additional incentives to participating low-risk partners, while benefiting from the added efficiencies of managing supply chain and trade compliance within one partnership programme. A number of participants will serve as pilots, and the implementation of the first phase of the programme is targeted to begin by the end of the fiscal year 2013.[92]

(c) International Maritime Organization

(i) Measures to enhance maritime security

The Maritime Safety Committee (MSC), the Legal Committee (LEG) and the Facilitation Committee (FAL) of IMO cover issues related to maritime security, including piracy, as part of their agenda. In this respect, certain developments at the most recent sessions of these committees over the past year – relating to the effective implementation of SOLAS chapter XI-2 and the International Ship and Port Facilities Security (ISPS) Code, combating piracy and armed robbery, requirements related to privately contracted armed security personnel on board ships, and enhancing maritime trade recovery in the event of large-scale emergencies – are worth noting.

Maritime Safety Committee

The MSC at its ninety-first session[93] noted that a number of Contracting Governments were not fulfilling their obligations under SOLAS Regulation XI-2/13 on communication of information. Therefore, it urged these Governments to review their information in the Global Integrated Shipping Information System (GISIS) and update it as necessary; in this context, the intention of the secretariat to review and enhance the module's accessibility and value as an information source was also noted. The MSC further noted the current availability of the IMO *Guide to Maritime Security and the ISPS Code* (IMO sales number: IA116E; ISBN: 978-92-801-1544-4) in English and French, and its expected availability in Spanish later in 2013, and the need to follow the procedures detailed therein (IMO, 2012l).

The MSC also reviewed the latest statistics on piracy and armed robbery against ships (IMO, 2012m) and noted the encouraging downward trend in piracy attacks in the western Indian Ocean. However, it was noted that there were still many innocent seafarers held hostage in Somalia, some for more than two years. In addition, a major concern was the increase in the number of incidents of piracy and armed robbery against ships in the Gulf of Guinea, and the increasing level of violence of those attacks (IMO, 2012n, pages 59–62).

At its ninety-second session,[94] the MSC noted that a study on the human cost of maritime piracy in 2012 had just been released (Oceans Beyond Piracy, 2013). While referring to the issue of piracy and armed robbery against ships in the Gulf of Guinea, the Committee welcomed the regional initiative by the Economic Community of Central African States (ECCAS), the Economic Community of West African States (ECOWAS) and the Gulf of Guinea Commission, pursuant to United Nations Security Council resolutions 2018 (2011) and 2039 (2012), to develop a Code of Conduct on the repression of piracy, armed robbery against ships and other illicit activities at sea. This Code of Conduct, which complemented the integrated coastguard function network project, launched by IMO and the Maritime Organization of West and Central Africa (MOWCA) in 2006, and the African Union's Integrated Maritime Strategy 2050, was adopted at a ministerial meeting in Cotonou, Benin, in March 2013. The Code was adopted formally by the meeting in Yaoundé, attended by 13 Heads of State from West and Central African countries, and was opened for signature on 25 June, 2013.[95]

Under the new Code, signatories commit to cooperate to the fullest possible extent in the prevention and repression of piracy and armed robbery against ships, transnational organized crime in the maritime domain, maritime terrorism, illegal, unreported and unregulated fishing and other illegal activities at sea with a view towards:

- Sharing and reporting relevant information;

- Interdicting ships and/or aircraft suspected of engaging in such illegal activities at sea;

- Ensuring that persons committing or attempting to commit illegal activities at sea are apprehended and prosecuted;

- Facilitating proper care, treatment and repatriation for seafarers, fishermen, other shipboard personnel and passengers subject to illegal activities at sea, particularly those who have been subjected to violence.[96]

With respect to piracy and armed robbery against ships in waters off the coast of Somalia, the Committee noted that although the numbers of piracy attacks in the Gulf of Aden and western Indian Ocean had significantly reduced, it still remained a significant threat and there was no cause to relax (IMO, 2013o, page 63).

Legal Committee

The Legal Committee at its 100th session[97] received a document (IMO, 2013p)[98] in response to its earlier request for the IMO to approach agencies in those regions directly involved in combating piracy and armed robbery (primarily the European Union Naval Force Somalia (EU NAVFOR), the North Atlantic Treaty Organization (NATO) and the United Nations Office on Drugs and Crime (UNODC)) to obtain information on the number of pirates captured and handed ashore for further investigation, as well as information on the difficulties identified in the apprehension of pirates. The following views were expressed in respect of the above document and the written comments to it:

- transparency in identifying problems related to the apprehension of pirates was beneficial to all parties involved in combating piracy or struggling with the consequences of this crime;

- as the information on the number of pirates captured and handed ashore for further investigation, as well as information on the difficulties identified in the apprehension of pirates, had only been received from UNODC, the Committee was still far from meeting its goal of obtaining the information it was seeking;

- the information related to the piracy suspects/ convicted pirates held in other States provided by UNODC in document LEG 100/6/1 needed to be updated following the reports provided by States attending the WG 2 piracy meeting which took place in April 2013;

- Member States and organizations in consultative status with IMO should share their experience in resolving problems related to apprehension of pirates and should provide related information to IMO;

- IMO is the primary forum within the United Nations system responsible for coordinating efforts of the wider international community in its fight against piracy; and

- it is important to include in the database States whose national law does not allow the use of Privately Contracted Armed Security Personnel (PCASP) in its territorial waters.[99]

With respect to the last point, a circular containing a questionnaire[100] on information on port and coastal State requirements related to PCASP on board ships (IMO, 2011b), includes information on national laws on the use of PCASP, firearms and security-related equipment.

Another document was introduced, containing information on the database on court decisions related to piracy (IMO, 2013r) established by the United Nations Interregional Crime and Justice Research Institute (UNICRI).[101] Statistics were also provided by UNICRI, drawn from its piracy analysis, including the average age of pirates, the region and clans they come from, their occupations, when attacks are most likely to occur, the number of pirates participating in individual attacks, the use of motherships, the number of casualties occurring in pirate ranks and the number and type of ships boarded. The UNICRI piracy portal also provided information on court decisions, intended to make the database more comprehensive, as well as links to other databases in different jurisdictions and regions and information on post-trial transfers. There was general support for the database and the Legal Committee agreed to collaborate closely with UNICRI with regard to piracy-related issues.[102]

The Legal Committee at its 100th session, also adopted draft Guidelines on the preservation and collection of evidence following an allegation of a serious crime having taken place on board a ship, or following a report of a missing person from a ship, and on pastoral and medical care of victims. These draft guidelines focus on what can practically be carried out on board a ship to preserve and/or collect evidence and protect persons affected by serious crimes, until such time that the relevant law enforcement authorities commence an investigation. They were submitted for consideration and adoption at the twenty-eighth session of the IMO Assembly to be held in November 2013, along with a related draft resolution.

The main purpose of the draft guidelines is to assist ship masters in the preservation of evidence and in the pastoral and medical care of persons affected and, when appropriate, in the collection of evidence during the period between the report or discovery of a possible serious crime and the time when law enforcement authorities or other professional crime scene investigators take action.[103]

Facilitation Committee

A number of maritime security-related measures were considered during the thirty-eighth session of the Facilitation Committee held from 8 to 12 April 2013. The Committee approved "Guidelines on measures towards enhancing maritime trade recovery related to the global supply-chain system and maritime conveyances" (IMO, 2013s). These are intended to be a practical tool, to be used by IMO Member States and industry for the purpose of considering relevant issues to increase the resilience of the global supply chain and minimize the impact of disruptions in the event of large-scale emergencies. The guidelines consist of three parts: (a) a listing of information requirements critical to improving supply-chain resilience and facilitating trade recovery following a severe disruption to the maritime supply chain; (b) information relating to the development of communication mechanisms between parties; (c) information relevant to the establishment of industry support groups.

The guidelines take into account work done by the Asia-Pacific Economic Cooperation Trade Recovery Programme (APEC), WCO and ISO in developing guidelines for Customs administrations and organizations to improve and facilitate trade recovery.[104]

The Committee considered a document (IMO, 2013t) that contained information related to the questionnaire (IMO, 2011b)[105] on port and coastal State requirements in relation to privately contracted armed security personnel on board ships. The circular urged Member Governments and, in particular, those of the coastal States bordering the Indian Ocean, Arabian Sea, Gulf of Aden and Red Sea, to raise awareness of their relevant national legislation, policies and procedures relating to the carriage, embarkation and disembarkation of firearms and security-related equipment through their territory and to the movement of PCASP, by completing the questionnaire and submitting it to the IMO.

A number of developments related to supply-chain security in the work of the Facilitation Committee are also worth noting. In particular, the Committee approved:

- "Interim guidelines for use of printed versions of electronic certificates" (IMO, 2013u). The purpose of the guidelines was limited to providing information to administrations using electronic certificates; the guidelines were only the first step in the transition to a paperless system and greater reliance on web-based electronic access to certificates. Inputs from other IMO committees were expected as well.

- "Revised IMO Compendium on facilitation and electronic business" (IMO, 2013v). The compendium provides updated information, guidance and recommended formats for electronic exchange of information required by public authorities for the arrival, stay, and departure of the ship, persons and cargo to facilitate clearance processes.

- "List of certificates and documents required to be carried on board ships, 2013" (IMO, 2013w). Only the certificates and documents that are required under IMO instruments are listed, but not certificates or documents required by other international organizations or governmental authorities.

- "Amendments to the International Convention for Safe Containers (CSC), 1972" (IMO, 2013o, Annex 7). These include amendments relating to the safety approval plate and to the approval of existing and new containers.

(ii) Other issues

Fair treatment of seafarers

The Legal Committee at its 100th session was provided with the findings of a survey conducted by Seafarers' Rights International (SRI), concerning respect for the rights of seafarers facing criminal prosecution (IMO, 2013x). The survey, conducted in eight languages, was carried out over a 12-month period, ending in February 2012. A total of 3,480 completed questionnaires had been submitted by seafarers from 68 different nationalities.[106] The findings of the survey strongly suggested that the rights of seafarers, as enshrined in the "Guidelines on fair treatment of seafarers in the event of a maritime accident", adopted jointly by the IMO and ILO, are often subject to violation. The views expressed during the meeting included the following:

- The statistics demonstrated the need to maintain the focus on the guidelines and to keep up the pressure for their better implementation;

- Seafarers were more exposed to criminal proceedings than many other workers and therefore needed special assistance;

- Legal assistance for seafarers should, in the first place, be provided by the shipowner;

- The findings of the survey could be taken into account by the Legal Committee during the drafting of guidelines on the collation and preservation of evidence following an allegation of a serious crime having taken place on board a ship or following a report of a missing person from a ship, and pastoral and medical care of victims.

The Legal Committee expressed general support for the continuous promotion of the guidelines, and agreed that the issue of fair treatment of seafarers in the event of a maritime accident should remain on the agenda of the Committee. Delegations were invited to submit proposals for outputs to improve compliance with the guidelines to its next session.[107]

(d) International Organization for Standardization

As pointed out in earlier editions of the *Review of Maritime Transport*, during the last decade, ISO has been actively engaged in matters of maritime transport and supply-chain security. Shortly after the release of the ISPS Code, and to facilitate its implementation by the industry, the ISO technical committee ISO/TC 8 published ISO 20858:2007, "Ships and marine technology – Maritime port facility security assessments and security plan development".

Relevant also is the development of the ISO 28000 series of standards "Security management systems for the supply chain", which are designed to help the industry successfully plan for, and recover from, any disruptive event that is ongoing (see box on the current status of the ISO 28000 series of standards). The core standard in these series is ISO 28000:2007, "Specification for security management systems for the supply chain", which serves as an umbrella management system that enhances all aspects of security: risk assessment, emergency preparedness, business continuity, sustainability, recovery, resilience and/or disaster management, whether relating to terrorism, piracy, cargo theft, fraud, or many other security disruptions. It also serves as a basis for AEO and C-TPAT certifications. Various organizations adopting such standards may tailor an approach compatible with their existing operating systems. ISO 28003:2007, also a published standard in force since 2007, provides requirements for providing audits and certification to ISO 28000:2007.

A new ISO/PAS 28007:2012 that has recently been developed by ISO/TC 8 sets out guidance for applying ISO 28000 to private maritime security companies and establishes criteria for selecting companies that provide armed guards for ships. It provides guidelines containing additional sector-specific recommendations, which companies or organizations that comply with ISO 28000 can implement before they provide PCASP on board ships.

Key developments in summary

The reporting period has been characterized by continued progress made by countries and international and regional organizations, supported by Customs and the private sector, regarding the implementation of the existing framework and programmes in the field of maritime and supply-chain security. Main areas of progress include enhancements to regulatory measures on maritime security and safety, primarily under the auspices of the IMO, as well as implementation and mutual recognition of AEO programmes. For the benefit of traders compliant with internationally required supply-chain security standards, it is hoped that the increasing number of bilateral mutual recognition agreements will, in due course, form the basis for mutual recognition of

AEOs at a multilateral level. In relation to the incidence of maritime piracy, an encouraging downward trend may be observed off the Coast of Somalia, the Gulf of Aden and the Western Indian Ocean. However at the same time, the number and violence of piracy attacks has increased in the West African Gulf of Guinea area. To address the issue, a regional Code of Conduct on the repression of piracy, armed robbery against ships and other illicit activities at sea was adopted by Heads of State from West and Central African Countries in Yaoundé in June 2013. It is hoped that this Code of Conduct will serve as an effective framework for its signatory States – 22 so far – to cooperate to the fullest possible extent in the prevention and repression of piracy and armed robbery against ships, and related crimes.

Box 5.1.   The current status of the ISO 28000 series of standards

Standards published:

- **ISO 28000:2007** – "Specification for security management systems for the supply chain." This provides the overall "umbrella" standard. It is a generic, risk-based, certifiable standard for all organizations, all disruptions, all sectors. It is widely in use and constitutes a stepping stone to the AEO and C-TPAT certifications.

- **ISO 28001:2007** – "Security management systems for the supply chain – Best practices for implementing supply-chain security, assessments and plans." This standard is designed to assist the industry meet the requirements for AEO status.

- **ISO 28002:2011** – "Security management systems for the supply chain – Development of resilience in the supply chain – Requirements with guidance for use." This standard provides additional focus on resilience, and emphasizes the need for an on-going, interactive process to prevent, respond to and assure continuation of an organization's core operations after a major disruptive event.

- **ISO 28003:2007** – "Security management systems for the supply chain – Requirements for bodies providing audit and certification of supply-chain security management systems." This standard provides guidance for accreditation and certification bodies.

- **ISO 28004-1:2007** – "Security management systems for the supply chain – Guidelines for the implementation of ISO 28000 – Part 1: General principles." This standard provides generic advice on the application of ISO 28000:2007. It explains the underlying principles of ISO 28000 and describes the intent, typical inputs, processes and typical outputs for each requirement of ISO 28000. This is to aid the understanding and implementation of ISO 28000. ISO 28004:2007 does not create additional requirements to those specified in ISO 28000, nor does it prescribe mandatory approaches to the implementation of ISO 28000.

- **ISO/PAS 28004-2:2012** – "Security management systems for the supply chain – Guidelines for the implementation of ISO 28000 – Part 2: Guidelines for adopting ISO 28000 for use in medium and small seaport operations." This provides guidance to medium and small ports that wish to adopt ISO 28000. It identifies supply-chain risk and threat scenarios, procedures for conducting risks/threat assessments, and evaluation criteria for measuring conformance and effectiveness of the documented security plans in accordance with ISO 28000 and ISO 28004 implementation guidelines.

- **ISO/PAS 28004-3:2012** – "Security management systems for the supply chain – Guidelines for the implementation of ISO 28000 – Part 3: Additional specific guidance for adopting ISO 28000 for use by medium and small businesses (other than marine ports)." This has been developed to supplement ISO 28004-1 by providing additional guidance to medium and small businesses (other than marine ports) that wish to adopt ISO 28000. The additional guidance in ISO/PAS 28004-3:2012, while amplifying the general guidance provided in the main body of ISO 28004-1, does not conflict with the general guidance, nor does it amend ISO 28000.

- **ISO/PAS 28004-4:2012** – "Security management systems for the supply chain – Guidelines for the implementation of ISO 28000 – Part 4: Additional specific guidance on implementing ISO 28000 if compliance with ISO 28001 is a management objective." This provides additional guidance for organizations adopting ISO 28000 that also wish to incorporate the best practices identified in ISO 28001 as a management objective on their international supply chains.

Box 5.1. The current status of the ISO 28000 series of standards *(continued)*

- **ISO 28005-1:2013** – "Security management systems for the supply chain – Electronic port clearance (EPC) – Part 1: Message structures." This standard provides for computer-to-computer data transmission.

- **ISO 28005-2:2011** – "Security management systems for the supply chain – Electronic port clearance (EPC) – Part 2: Core data elements." This standard contains technical specifications that facilitate efficient exchange of electronic information between ships and shore for coastal transit or port calls, as well as definitions of core data elements that cover all requirements for ship-to-shore and shore-to-ship reporting as defined in the ISPS Code, FAL Convention and relevant IMO resolutions.

- **ISO/PAS 28007:2012** – "Ships and marine technology – Guidelines for private maritime security companies (PMSC) providing privately contracted armed security personnel (PCASP) on board ships (and pro forma contract)." This gives guidelines containing additional sector-specific recommendations, which companies(organizations) that comply with ISO 28000 can implement to demonstrate that they provide PCASP on board ships.

- **ISO 20858:2007** – "Ships and marine technology – Maritime port facility security assessments and security plan development." This standard establishes a framework to assist marine port facilities in specifying the competence of personnel to conduct a marine port facility security assessment and to develop a security plan as required by the ISPS code. In addition, it establishes certain documentation requirements designed to ensure that the process used in performing the duties described above was recorded in a manner that would permit independent verification by a qualified and authorized agency. It is not an objective of ISO 20858:2007 to set requirements for a contracting Government or designated authority in designating a Recognized Security Organization (RSO), or to impose the use of an outside service provider or other third parties to perform the marine port facility security assessment or security plan if the port facility personnel possess the expertise outlined in this specification. Ship operators may be informed that marine port facilities that use this document meet an industry-determined level of compliance with the ISPS code. ISO 20858:2007 does not address the requirements of the ISPS code relative to port infrastructure that falls outside the security perimeter of a marine port facility that might affect the security of the facility/ship interface. Governments have a duty to protect their populations and infrastructures from marine incidents occurring outside their marine port facilities. These duties are outside the scope of ISO 20858:2007.

Standards under development:

- **ISO 28006** – "Security management systems for the supply chain – Security management of RO-RO passenger ferries." This includes best practices for application of security measures.

Note: For more information, including on the procedure of preparing international standards at ISO, see www.iso.org.

D. STATUS OF CONVENTIONS

A number of international conventions in the field of maritime transport were prepared or adopted under the auspices of UNCTAD. Table 5.1 provides information on the status of ratification of each of these conventions as at 30 June 2013.

Table 5.1. Contracting Parties to selected international conventions on maritime transport, as at 30 June 2013

Title of Convention	Date of entry into force or conditions for entry into force	Contracting States
United Nations Convention on a Code of Conduct for Liner Conferences, 1974	Entered into force 6 October 1983	Algeria, Bangladesh, Barbados, Belgium, Benin, Burkina Faso, Burundi, Cameroon, Cape Verde, Central African Republic, Chile, China, Congo, Costa Rica, Côte d'Ivoire, Cuba, Czech Republic, Democratic Republic of the Congo, Egypt, Ethiopia, Finland, France, Gabon, Gambia, Ghana, Guatemala, Guinea, Guyana, Honduras, India, Indonesia, Iraq, Italy, Jamaica, Jordan, Kenya, Kuwait, Lebanon, Liberia, Madagascar, Malaysia, Mali, Mauritania, Mauritius, Mexico, Montenegro, Morocco, Mozambique, Niger, Nigeria, Norway, Pakistan, Peru, Philippines, Portugal, Qatar, Republic of Korea, Romania, Russian Federation, Saudi Arabia, Senegal, Serbia, Sierra Leone, Slovakia, Somalia, Spain, Sri Lanka, Sudan, Sweden, Togo, Trinidad and Tobago, Tunisia, United Republic of Tanzania, Uruguay, Venezuela (Bolivarian Republic of), Zambia **(76)**
United Nations Convention on the Carriage of Goods by Sea, 1978 (Hamburg Rules)	Entered into force 1 November 1992	Albania, Austria, Barbados, Botswana, Burkina Faso, Burundi, Cameroon, Chile, Czech Republic, Dominican Republic, Egypt, Gambia, Georgia, Guinea, Hungary, Jordan, Kazakhstan, Kenya, Lebanon, Lesotho, Liberia, Malawi, Morocco, Nigeria, Paraguay, Romania, Saint Vincent and the Grenadines, Senegal, Sierra Leone, Syrian Arab Republic, Tunisia, Uganda, United Republic of Tanzania, Zambia **(34)**
International Convention on Maritime Liens and Mortgages, 1993	Entered into force 5 September 2004	Albania, Benin, Ecuador, Estonia, Lithuania, Monaco, Nigeria, Peru, Russian Federation, Spain, Saint Kitts and Nevis, Saint Vincent and the Grenadines, Serbia, Syrian Arab Republic, Tunisia, Ukraine, Vanuatu **(17)**
United Nations Convention on International Multimodal Transport of Goods, 1980	Not yet in force – requires 30 Contracting Parties	Burundi, Chile, Georgia, Lebanon, Liberia, Malawi, Mexico, Morocco, Rwanda, Senegal, Zambia **(11)**
United Nations Convention on Conditions for Registration of Ships, 1986	Not yet in force – requires 40 Contracting Parties with at least 25 per cent of the world's tonnage as per Annex III to the Convention	Albania, Bulgaria, Côte d'Ivoire, Egypt, Georgia, Ghana, Haiti, Hungary, Iraq, Liberia, Libya, Mexico, Morocco, Oman, Syrian Arab Republic **(15)**
International Convention on Arrest of Ships, 1999	Entered into force 14 September 2011	Albania, Algeria, Benin, Bulgaria, Ecuador, Estonia, Latvia, Liberia, Spain, Syrian Arab Republic **(10)**

Note: For official status information, see http://treaties.un.org.

E. INTERNATIONAL AGREEMENTS ON TRADE FACILITATION

1. A trade facilitation agreement at the World Trade Organization: an opportunity for the Bali Ministerial

Trade facilitation has a long history in UNCTAD, whose mandate in this area dates from the final act of its first Ministerial Conference in 1964. The work of UNCTAD in the trade-facilitation area has taken various forms, constantly adjusting to the needs and the priorities of UNCTAD member States. An example of the work of UNCTAD in this area is the Automated SYstem for CUstoms DAta (ASYCUDA), used by more than 90 countries. With regard to the transport sector, trade facilitation is an essential element to ease the burden of international transport operations, which are often hampered by excessive and repetitive procedures, in particular at border crossing along the transport chain.

The window of opportunity for WTO members to reach a trade-facilitation agreement at the ninth WTO Ministerial Conference to be held in Bali, Indonesia (3–6 December 2013) remains open. Expectations are that the Ministerial Conference will deliver on some elements of the Doha package, including trade facilitation, a package for the LDCs and some aspects of agriculture and development issues. There are diverging views amongst the WTO membership on whether a deliverable on trade facilitation is possible, and some have questioned the desirability of focusing on only a few issues while others of high importance for developing countries, such as agriculture, may not be programmed for discussion at Bali. This lack of consensus was previously noted in the 2012 edition of the *Review of Maritime Transport*, that is, the linkage of the trade facilitation to other items of the Doha round and the need to fine tune the agreement itself to provide the appropriate balance between commitments and flexibilities (UNCTAD, 2012a).

Efforts persist on many fronts to emphasize the potential benefits of having a multilateral agreement on trade facilitation for the world economy as a whole and for developing countries in particular. In the WTO, in parallel to the negotiations on the text of the trade-facilitation agreement, there have been a series of regional and global conferences to address the practical experience of implementing trade-facilitation reforms, including their costs and benefits. These events included dedicated sessions on showcasing

trade-facilitation programmes supported by bilateral and multilateral development partners and highlighted the wealth of existing technical assistance and capacity-building programmes in the trade-facilitation area. In addition, with the launch in November 2012 of the WTO Technical Assistance Programme for National Self-Assessments of Trade Facilitation Needs and Priorities 2012-2014, the focus was once again on identifying and evaluating the gaps in the implementation capacity of developing countries, especially amongst LDCs. Ensuring that the needs of the developing countries are well matched by the assistance offered by the international community of donor countries and organizations remains the major goal and challenge of all these activities.

However, there remain some WTO members that are concerned with the lack of progress in preparing the package of deliverables for the Bali Ministerial Conference (Miles, 2013; International Centre for Trade and Sustainable Development Reporting, 2013). This need to accelerate the speed and progress in the negotiations is reflected in the establishment of an ambassador-level "friends of the chair" process to intensify the negotiations around the three articles V, VII and X, as well as on section II on "Special and differential treatment". Although it is clear that this new approach has brought renewed vigour to the negotiations, some systemic issues remain to be closed, primarily around the notion of the level of ambition in section I and the extent of the flexibilities in section II.

Progress has certainly been made on improving the language in most of the provisions of the draft consolidated negotiating text and, especially, the provisions related to publication of and access to trade-related information, appeal procedures, penalty disciplines, release and clearance of goods, authorized operators, freedom of transit and customs cooperation.[108] Far from restricting the negotiations to the proposals already included in the text, in 2013 the Negotiating Group on Trade Facilitation also included a few new substantive provisions. These include a new paragraph on the electronic payment for duties, taxes, fees and charges collected by customs (article 7, paragraph 2), a new paragraph on release and clearance of perishable goods (article 7, paragraph 9) and a separate paragraph on acceptance of copies (article 10, paragraph 3).

Work is also continuing intensively on section II of the draft that contains special and differential treatment provisions for developing countries and LDCs. The last revision, revision 16, takes into account the recent proposals tabled by a number of developing countries and illustrates some progress made in the categorization of the obligations and changing (shifting) amongst the categories after notification. In particular, shifting from categories B and C, though still subject to notification and consideration by the proposed WTO Trade Facilitation Committee, is no longer reserved for the cases with "exceptional circumstances". The proposed grace period for the application of the WTO dispute settlement system to the LDCs is now taking a more precise form, with some suggestions for actual time periods being placed on the table. Progress has also been made on clarifying the proposal which calls on developed countries to make available annual information on the provided technical assistance and capacity-building, contact points and process and mechanisms for requesting assistance. Important gaps remain, however, including concerning the practicalities related to the notification of measures under section II and, in particular, measures in category C, where the developing countries' commitment to the exact implementation times and schedule is dependent on the donor's commitment to provide technical assistance and capacity-building (TACB) and the exact scope and timeframe of such aid.

It remains to be seen whether these developments alleviate the developing countries' concerns regarding the costs and other challenges of implementing an eventual trade-facilitation agreement in WTO. In this context, some lessons can be drawn from the recent UNCTAD work on helping developing countries establish national implementation plans for the trade-facilitation measures currently considered in WTO.

2. Lessons on trade-facilitation implementation from the UNCTAD project "Implementation Plans for WTO Trade Facilitation Agreement in Developing Members" (2011–2013)[109]

During the period 2011–2013, UNCTAD has worked closely with 26 developing countries on updating the current implementation status of the trade-facilitation measures addressed by WTO and on identifying the activities, time, resources and TACB required for achieving compliance with the measures yet to be fully implemented. This work was carried out with the financial support of the European Union, Norway,

the United Nations Development Account, the United Nations Development Programme and the World Bank, and in close cooperation with other Annex D organizations, including OECD and WCO. The participating countries included LDCs, middle-income developing countries, landlocked countries, transit developing countries, and small island economies in Africa, Asia, the Caribbean and Latin America.

The consolidated results of these 26 national implementation plans shed some light on the challenges that some developing countries currently have regarding implementation of some of the modalities currently envisaged in the draft text but also on the opportunities for building the capacity to implement and sustain the measures which are currently on the table.

These national assessments have been particularly useful in highlighting the existing gaps between what is being proposed at the WTO and what is being implemented on the ground, in developing countries, and in LDCs in particular. As illustrated in figure 5.1, in the majority of the participating developing countries, less than 50 per cent of the trade-facilitation measures under discussion in the WTO are currently fully implemented. In all of the participating countries, the rate of full implementation was below 76 per cent, with the lowest implementation rate being 19 per cent. The implementation rate is even lower for LDCs, with the majority of them below the 40 per cent level. At the same time, the measures that have not yet been implemented constitute a clear minority, ranging from 3 to 28 per cent, which suggests that only a small number of the proposed trade-facilitation reforms are completely new to the developing countries.

Another conclusion from the consolidated results is that the level of full implementation of the individual trade-facilitation measures suggests that measures with the strongest customs-related component, covered by articles 4, 7, 9bis, 10, 11 and 12 are characterized by high implementation rates. At the same time, most of the cross-sectoral or cross-agency measures, such as single window, enquiry points, publication of trade-related information, disciplines on fees and charges, together with some advanced customs techniques, such as advance ruling and authorized operators, have the lowest implementation rates, especially in LDCs. This suggests that many challenging trade-facilitation measures remain to be implemented by developing countries in terms of the level of inter-agency cooperation and sophistication of the institutional, legal and regulatory frameworks.

Figure 5.1.   Level of implementation of trade-facilitation measures per country

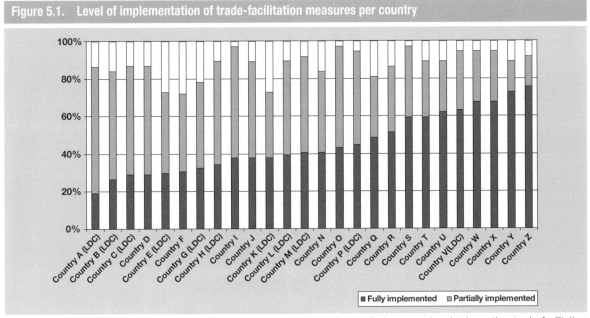

Source: Forthcoming report – *The new frontier of competitiveness in developing countries: Implementing trade facilitation*, UNCTAD, 2013.

Moreover, the national implementation plans reveal that there remain numerous obstacles to trade-facilitation reforms in developing countries (figure 5.2). The reasons offered by the trade-facilitation stakeholders in the participating countries to explain the absent or partial implementation of the trade-facilitation measures go beyond the mere lack of resources and include the gaps in the existing legal framework, lack of awareness about the benefits of the particular trade-facilitation measure both for traders and the administrations involved, information and communication technology and infrastructure issues, lack of inter-agency cooperation, and lack of organizational or institutional framework (figure 5.3). At the same time, the lack of resources remains one of the main obstacles for the implementation, especially in LDCs.

On the other hand, several encouraging developments for the trade-facilitation implementation could also be observed. One of these developments is the growing recognition in developing countries of the importance of effective trade facilitation for growth, development and investment. The trade-facilitation stakeholders in the participating countries considered most of the trade-facilitation measures as having a medium to high priority rate for the national economic development. The positive impact of trade-facilitation reforms seems to be more recognized in non-LDCs, which tend to award higher priority to the trade-facilitation measures than LDCs.

Moreover, the estimates on the time requirements for achieving the full implementation of these trade-facilitation measures show the acceptable time parameters within which this full implementation could be achieved. The estimated implementation time for the majority of the measures was, on average, about 3 years and not higher than five years for most of the remainder of the reforms. This makes it possible for most of the countries to envisage full implementation status within a five-year period. Estimating the necessary financial resources was a much more difficult task and varied greatly depending on the country. However, in general the amount remained reasonably modest, especially in the light of the substantial and continuous increase in the international aid for trade facilitation-related TACB.

Finally, for the participating countries, it seemed possible to fully reduce the trade-facilitation implementation gap, using the flexibilities proposed in section II of the draft consolidated negotiating text. The results of the national implementation plans showed that to move forward with the trade-facilitation implementation, the developing countries expected to rely significantly on these flexibilities both in terms of the additional implementation times and the TACB which would be provided. Depending on the country, the percentage of the measures that would either require additional time, or additional time and TACB, ranges from 10 per cent to 67 per cent (figure 5.4). For the majority of the countries and for most of the LDCs, these measures constitute, at least, one third of the measures currently included in the draft WTO text.

Figure 5.2. Full implementation level per area of trade-facilitation measures

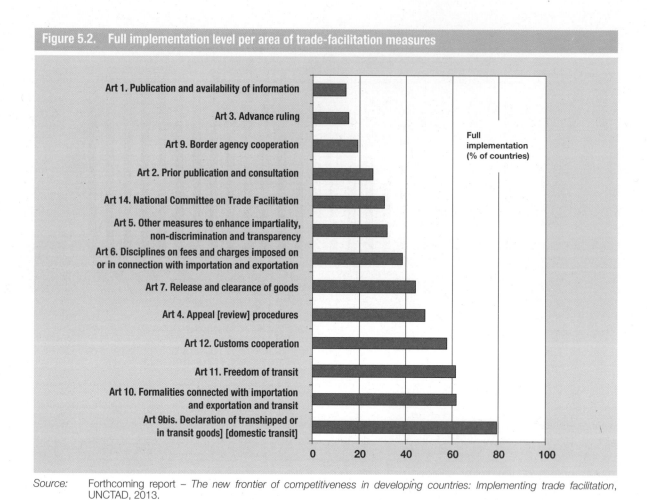

Source: Forthcoming report – *The new frontier of competitiveness in developing countries: Implementing trade facilitation*, UNCTAD, 2013.

Figure 5.3. Most-quoted reasons for non-implementation

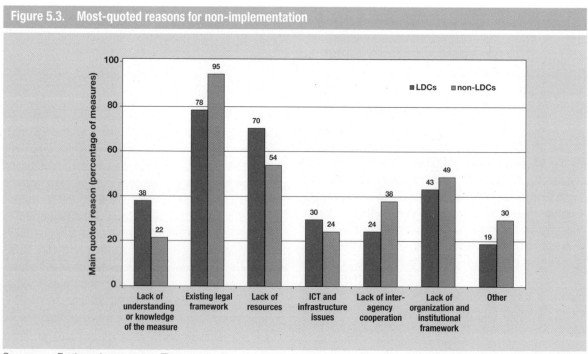

Source: Forthcoming report – *The new frontier of competitiveness in developing countries: Implementing trade facilitation*, UNCTAD, 2013.

Figure 5.4. Percentage of the measures requiring technical assistance and capacity-building

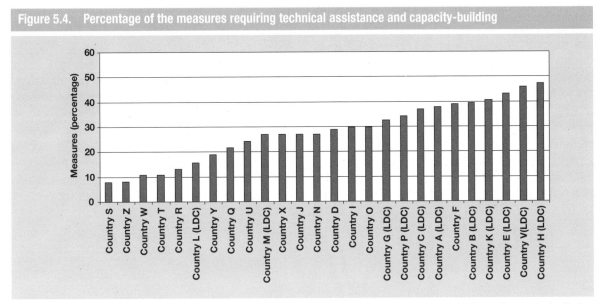

Source: Forthcoming report – *The new frontier of competitiveness in developing countries: Implementing trade facilitation*, UNCTAD, 2013.

The need for TACB was considered to be highest for the 10 measures detailed in table 5.2, which correspond to the measures with the lowest implementation levels in the developing countries and which represent a combination of measures requiring intensive domestic or cross-border cooperation, infrastructure and information and communication technology investments, and use of advanced customs techniques.

The consolidated results of the national trade-facilitation implementation plans, developed by UNCTAD, illustrate that trade facilitation remains a challenge but is also seen as a priority area for national development by the developing countries themselves. By identifying the major areas of non-compliance, the range of time and cost requirements, and the

Table 5.2.	Top 10 measures with the highest estimated need for technical assistance and capacity-building

Single window (TN/TF/165/W/Rev. 16, article 10, paragraph 5)

Test procedures (article 5, paragraph 3)

Information available through Internet (article 1, paragraph 2)

Border agency cooperation (article 9)

Advance ruling (article 3)

Enquiry points (article 1, paragraph 3)

Disciplines on fees and charges imposed on or in connection with importation and exportation (article 6, paragraph 1)

Publication (article 1, paragraph 1)

Reduction/limitation of formalities and documentation requirements (article 10, paragraph 2)

Risk management (article 7, paragraph 4)

needs for TACB, this work offers valuable insights into the priority needs of developing countries and the national and regional ambitions in implementing trade-facilitation reforms. In this respect it provides some important guidance for both developing countries and their development partners.

3. Conclusions

On 8 July 2013, on the occasion of the fourth Global Review of Aid for Trade in Geneva, high-level representatives of 27 Governments and organizations, including UNCTAD, issued a "Joint Statement – Trade Facilitation Assistance" for trade-facilitation implementation. The statement emphasized the benefits of concluding a trade-facilitation agreement in Bali and highlighted the Governments'/organizations' strong commitment to continue to provide support for its implementation.[110]

Much of the discourse of most multilateral and bilateral development partners continues to focus on the volume of the aid to trade facilitation. However, for potential beneficiary countries the challenge remains to effectively match not only the volume but also the scope and nature of this assistance to their needs and priorities. Indeed, the assistance required for many trade-facilitation reforms will likely have to go beyond a financial aid and will have to involve significant efforts in long-term sustainable capacities, technological and institutional infrastructure development, and training and reforms aimed at better governance.

Developing countries need to carefully evaluate the specific requirements and available resources so that they can accurately plan the implementation of the trade-facilitation reforms both in terms of time, possible technical assistance and capacity-building. They should also define appropriate sequencing of actions required to ensure full compliance with their trade-facilitation commitments and programme their implementation time and scope effectively taking advantage of the flexibilities offered in section II of the draft consolidated negotiating text (Rubiato and Hoffmann, 2013).

The national implementation plans approach, developed by UNCTAD, and the WTO needs assessments are important steps in this direction, but remain one part of the whole journey, which, in the end, will rely extensively on the countries' capacity to maintain an inclusive and productive national dialogue on the trade-facilitation reforms. In this context, supporting the establishment and operationalization of national trade-facilitation committees in developing countries will prove to be an important element in effectively implementing and monitoring needs and progress under an eventual WTO agreement.

REFERENCES

Asariotis R and Benamara H, eds. (2012). *Maritime Transport and the Climate Change Challenge*. United Nations and Earthscan/Routledge. Available at http://unctad.org/en/Pages/DTL/TTL/Legal.aspx (accessed 18 October 2013).

Chiew H (2013). UNFCCC principles must guide work of IMO and ICAO - say developing countries. Third World Network. *TWN Bonn News Update* 4. June 5. Available at http://www.twnside.org.sg/title2/climate/news/Bonn11/TWN_update4. pdf (accessed 18 October 2013).

Climate Strategies, Cambridge Econometrics, University of Cambridge, CE Delft, and Transport Analysis and Knowledge Systems (2013). Research to assess impacts on developing countries of measures to address emissions in the international aviation and shipping sectors. Available at http://www.cedelft.eu/publicatie/research_to_assess_ impacts_on_developing_countries_of_measures_to_address_emissions_in_the_international_aviation_and_shipping_ sectors/1389 (accessed 7 November 2013).

European Commission (2012). Roadmap: Commission communication on EU risk management and supply-chain security. Available at http://ec.europa.eu/governance/impact/planned_ia/docs/2012_taxud_10_risk_management_en.pdf (accessed 18 November 2013).

European Commission (2013). Communication from the Commission to the European Parliament, the Council and the European Economic and Social Committee on Customs Risk Management and Security of the Supply Chain. Available at http://ec.europa.eu/taxation_customs/resources/documents/customs/customs_controls/risk_management/customs_ eu/com_2012_793_en.pdf (accessed 18 November 2013).

European Union–United States Joint Committee (2012). Decision of the US–EU Joint Customs Cooperation Committee of 4 May 2012 regarding mutual recognition of the Customs–Trade Partnership Against Terrorism Program (C-TPAT) in the United States and the Authorised Economic Operators Programme of the European Union. 2012/290/EU. Available at http://eur-lex.europa.eu/LexUriServ/LexUriServ.do?uri=OJ:L:2012:144:0044:0047:EN:PDF (accessed 18 November 2013).

ICS (2013). *The ILO Maritime Labour Convention, 2006: Guidance for Ship Operators on Port State Control as from 20 August 2013*. Available at http://www.ics-shipping.org/docs/default-source/resources/safety-security-and-operations/ilo-mlc-2006-guidance-on-psc.pdf (accessed 26 November 2013).

International Air Transport Association, Association Of European Airlines, World Shipping Council, European Association for Forwarding, Transport, Logistics and Customs Services, European Community Shipowners' Associations, The International Air Cargo Association, International Road Transport Union and Federation of European Trade Facilitation Organisations (2013). Recommendation to the European Parliament and Council – Establishing a multiple filing option for security in the UCC. Available at http://www.worldshipping.org/industry-issues/security/cargo-and-the-supply-chain/2013_Joint_Industry_Statement_to_EU_on_Customs_Changes.pdf (accessed 25 November 2013).

International Centre for Trade and Sustainable Development Reporting (2013). "Rapid acceleration" needed to ensure results at the WTO Ministerial, Lamy warns. *Bridges Weekly*. 17(13):1–4. 18 April.

ILO (2012a). *Handbook: Guidance on implementing the Maritime Labour Convention 2006 – Model National Provisions*. Available at http://www.ilo.org/wcmsp5/groups/public/---ed_norm/---normes/documents/publication/wcms_170389. pdf (accessed 16 October 2013).

ILO (2012b). *Handbook: Guidance on implementing the Maritime Labour Convention 2006 and Social Security for Seafarers*. Available at http://www.ilo.org/wcmsp5/groups/public/---ed_norm/---normes/documents/publication/wcms_170388. pdf (accessed 16 October 2013).

IMO (2009). *Second IMO GHG Study 2009*. IMO. London. Available at http://www.imo.org/blast/blastDataHelper.asp?data_ id=27795&filename=GHGStudyFINAL.pdf (accessed 17 October 2013).

IMO (2011a). Report of the Marine Environment Protection Committee at its sixty-second session. MEPC 62/24. London.

IMO (2011b). Questionnaire on information on port and coastal State requirements related to privately contracted armed security personnel on board ships. MSC-FAL.1/Circ.2. London.

IMO (2012a). Report of the Marine Environment Protection Committee on its sixty-third session. MEPC 63/23. London.

IMO (2012b). Report of the Marine Environment Protection Committee on its sixty-fourth session. MEPC 64/23. London.

IMO (2012c). Report of the Working Group on Air Pollution and Energy Efficiency. MEPC 64/WP.11. London.

IMO (2012d). Further work on GHG emissions from ships. Submitted by Brazil, China, India, Peru, Saudi Arabia and South Africa. MEPC 64/5/9. London.

IMO (2012e). Draft outline for an update of the GHG emissions estimate for international shipping. Note by the Secretariat. MEPC 64/5/5. London.

IMO (2012f). Possible incompatibility between the WTO rules and market-based measures for international shipping. Submitted by India and Saudi Arabia. MEPC 64/5/3. London.

IMO (2012g). Outcome of the United Nations Climate Change Conference held in Bonn, Germany from 14 to 25 May 2012. Note by the Secretariat. MEPC 64/5/1. London.

IMO (2012h). Green Climate Fund. Note by the Secretariat. MEPC 64/INF.31. London.

IMO (2012i). Ensuring availability of fuels compliant with MARPOL Annex VI by 2020. Submitted by the International Chamber of Shipping. MEPC 64/4/17. London.

IMO (2012j). Assessment of availability of fuel oil under MARPOL Annex VI. Submitted by the United States. MEPC 64/4/41. London.

IMO (2012k). Sulphur monitoring for 2011. Note by the Secretariat. MEPC 64/4. London.

IMO (2012l). Information provided pursuant to SOLAS Regulation XI-2/13, the maritime security module of GISIS and the IMO *Guide to Maritime Security and the ISPS Code*. Note by the Secretariat. MSC 91/4. London.

IMO (2012m). Developments since MSC 90. Note by the Secretariat. MSC 91/17. London.

IMO (2012n). Report of the Maritime Safety Committee on its ninety-first session. MSC 91/22. London.

IMO (2013a). Report of the Legal Committee on the work of its one-hundredth session. LEG 100/14. London.

IMO (2013b). Status of multilateral conventions and instruments in respect of which the International Maritime Organization or its Secretary-General performs depositary or other functions. London. Available at http://www.imo.org/About/Conventions/StatusOfConventions/Documents/Status%20-%202013.pdf (accessed 17 October 2013).

IMO (2013c). Report of the Marine Environment Protection Committee on its sixty-fifth session. MEPC 65/22. London.

IMO (2013d). Guidance on treatment of innovative energy efficiency technologies for calculation and verification of the attained EEDI. MEPC.1/Circ.815. London.

IMO (2013e). Report of the Working Group on Air Pollution and Energy Efficiency. MEPC 65/WP.10. London.

IMO (2013f). Report of the Expert Workshop on the Update of GHG Emissions Estimate for International Shipping (Update-EW). Note by the Secretariat. MEPC 65/5/2. London.

IMO (2013g). Membership of the Steering Committee for the Update of the GHG Emissions Estimate for International Shipping. Circular letter No.3381/Rev.1. London.

IMO (2013h). World Trade Organization's views on document MEPC 64/5/4 submitted by India and Saudi Arabia. MEPC 65/INF.18. London.

IMO (2013i). Outcome of the United Nations Climate Change Conference held in Doha, Qatar, from 26 November to 8 December 2012. Note by the Secretariat. MEPC 65/5. London.

IMO (2013j). Workshop on HNS reporting in preparation for the entry into force of the HNS Protocol, 2010. Submitted by Canada. LEG 100/3. London.

IMO (2013k). Information on the second International Conference on Liability and Compensation Regime for Transboundary Oil Damage Resulting from Offshore Exploration and Exploitation Activities. Submitted by Indonesia. LEG 100/13. London.

IMO (2013l). Principles for guidance on model bilateral/regional agreements or arrangements on liability and compensation issues connected with transboundary pollution damage from offshore exploration and exploitation activities. Submitted by Indonesia. LEG 100/13/2. London.

IMO (2013m). Final report of the Correspondence Group on assessment of technological developments to implement the tier III NOx emission standards under MARPOL Annex VI. Submitted by the United States. MEPC 65/4/7. London.

IMO (2013n). Adequate port reception facilities for cargoes declared as harmful to the marine environment under MARPOL Annex V. MEPC.1/Circ.810. London.

IMO (2013o). Report of the Maritime Safety Committee on its ninety-second session. MSC 92/26. London.

IMO (2013p). Piracy. Note by the Secretariat. LEG 100/6/1. London.

IMO (2013q). Piracy. Submitted by Ukraine. LEG 100/6/2. London.

IMO (2013r). Update on the establishment of a database on court decisions related to piracy off the coast of Somalia and related activities: work in progress. Submitted by UNICRI. LEG 100/6/3. London.

IMO (2013s). Guidelines on measures toward enhancing maritime trade recovery related to the global supply chain system and maritime conveyances. FAL.6/Circ.16. London.

IMO (2013t). Questionnaire on information on port and coastal State requirements related to privately contracted armed security personnel on board ships. Note by the Secretariat. FAL 38/7/1. London.

IMO (2013u). Interim guidelines for use of printed versions of electronic certificates. FAL.5/Circ.39. London.

IMO (2013v). Revised IMO Compendium on facilitation and electronic business. FAL.5/Circ.40. London.

IMO (2013w). List of certificates and documents required to be carried on board ships, 2013. FAL.2/Circ.127, MEPC. 1/Circ.817, MSC.1/Circ.1462. London.

IMO (2013x). Fair treatment of seafarers in the event of a maritime accident. Submitted by the International Transport Workers' Federation and the International Federation of Shipmasters' Associations. LEG 100/5/1. London.

Koch C (2013). Potential for chaos as Europe ponders tighter supply chain security rules. *Lloyd's List*. 8 April. Available at http://www.lloydslist.com/ll/sector/containers/article420502.ece (accessed 9 July 2013).

Lloyd's List (2013). Making the Baltic a NOx emission-control area faces many challenges. March. Available at http://www.lloydslist.com/ll/sector/regulation/article418151.ece (accessed 12 November 2013).

MarineLink.com (2012). Will low-sulphur fuel be sufficiently available asks ICS. July. Available at http://www.marinelink.com/news/sufficiently-lowsulphur346458.aspx (accessed 19 November 2013).

MarineLink.com (2013). Maritime law & piracy code adopted by African nations. June. Available at http://www.marinelink.com/news/maritime-adopted-african356075.aspx (accessed 9 July 2013).

Miles T (2013). U.S. warns WTO global trade talks "hurtling towards irrelevance. Business and Financial News. Reuters. 11 April.

Oceans Beyond Piracy (2013). The human cost of maritime piracy 2012. Working paper. Available at http://oceansbeyondpiracy.org/sites/default/files/attachments/View%20Full%20Report.pdf (accessed 19 November 2013).

Platts (2012). EU Council amends directive on sulfur content in marine fuels. Available at http://www.platts.com/latest-news/shipping/london/eu-council-amends-directive-on-sulfur-content-8859750 (accessed 9 July 2013).

PricewaterhouseCoopers (2012). Study on possible ways to enhance EU-level capabilities for customs risk analysis and targeting. 31 May.

Rubiato JM and Hoffmann J (2013). Promoting African intra-regional trade through trade facilitation negotiations. *Bridges Africa*. 2(3):4–6.

UNCTAD (2004). Container security: Major initiatives and related international developments. UNCTAD/SDTE/TLB/2004/1. New York and Geneva. Available at http://unctad.org/en/Docs/sdtetlb20041_en.pdf (accessed 18 November 2013).

UNCTAD (2008). *Review of Maritime Transport 2008*. United Nations publication. UNCTAD/RMT/2008. New York and Geneva. Available at http://unctad.org/en/pages/PublicationArchive.aspx?publicationid=1686 (accessed 12 November 2013).

UNCTAD (2010). *Review of Maritime Transport 2010*. United Nations publication. UNCTAD/RMT/2010. New York and Geneva. Available at http://unctad.org/en/pages/PublicationArchive.aspx?publicationid=1708 (accessed 17 October 2013).

UNCTAD (2011a). *Review of Maritime Transport 2011*. United Nations publication. UNCTAD/RMT/2011. New York and Geneva. Available at http://unctad.org/en/pages/PublicationArchive.aspx?publicationid=1734 (accessed 17 October 2013).

UNCTAD (2011b). The 2004 Ballast Water Management Convention – with international acceptance growing the Convention may soon enter into force. UNCTAD Transport Newsletter No.50. Second Quarter 2011, page 8. Available at http://unctad.org/en/Docs/webdtltlb20113_en.pdf (accessed 12 November 2013).

UNCTAD (2012a). *Review of Maritime Transport 2012*. United Nations publication. UNCTAD/RMT/2012. New York and Geneva. Available at http://unctad.org/en/pages/PublicationWebflyer.aspx?publicationid=380 (accessed 17 October 2013).

UNCTAD (2012b). *Liability and Compensation for Ship-Source Oil Pollution: An Overview of the International Legal Framework for Oil Pollution Damage from Tankers*. United Nations publication. UNCTAD/DTL/TLB/2011/4. New York and Geneva. Available at http://unctad.org/en/PublicationsLibrary/dtltlb20114_en.pdf (accessed 11 November 2013).

United States Customs and Border Protection (CBP) (2013). EU, US fully implement mutual recognition decision. News release. 8 February. Available at http://cbp.gov/xp/cgov/newsroom/news_releases/national/02082013_6.xml (accessed 9 July 2013).

WCO (2012a). SAFE Framework of Standards to secure and facilitate global trade. June. Available at http://www.wcoomd.org/en/topics/facilitation/instrument-and-tools/tools/~/media/55F00628A9F94827B58ECA90C0F84F7F.ashx (accessed 13 November 2013).

WCO (2012b). Compendium of authorized economic operator programmes. WCO research paper No.25. Available at http://www.wcoomd.org/en/topics/research/activities-and-programmes/~/media/930340C77B3740D6B3894F747AF6A7FF.ashx (accessed 18 November 2013).

WCO (2013a). WCO Americas and Caribbean Region adopts AEO regional strategy. News. April 3. Available at http://www.wcoomd.org/en/media/newsroom/2013/april/wco-americas-and-caribbean.aspx (accessed 9 July 2013).

WCO (2013b). Importance of AEO programmes recognized at the AEO Regional Forum in Astana. News. June 3. Available at http://www.wcoomd.org/en/media/newsroom/2013/june/aeo-regional-forum-astana.aspx (accessed 9 July 2013).

WCO (2013c). Working meeting held in promoting AEO project in East African Economic Community. News (June 19). Available at http://www.wcoomd.org/en/media/newsroom/2013/june/working-meeting-in-promoting-aeo-project.aspx (accessed 18 November 2013).

WCO (2013d). Seminar on the authorized economic operator (AEO) concept. News. April 16. Available at http://www.wcoomd.org/en/media/newsroom/2013/april/aeo-seminar.aspx (accessed 9 July 2013).

NOTES

1   The MLC 2006 enters into force 12 months after the date on which it was ratified by 30 members accounting for a total share in the world ship GT of at least 33 per cent. The Convention is now in force in 38 International Labour Organization (ILO) member States representing 69 per cent of the world ship GT. The status of ratification of the MLC 2006 is based on information on the ILO website, as of 9 July 2013. For a list of international conventions that will be revised after the entry into force of MLC 2006 see http://www.ilo.org/global/standards/maritime-labour-convention/WCMS_150389/lang--en/index.htm (accessed 17 October 2013).

2   The text of MLC 2006 is available at http://www.ilo.org/global/standards/maritime-labour-convention/WCMS_090250/lang--en/index.htm (accessed 17 October 2013). See also the "Explanatory Note to the Regulations and Code of the Maritime Labour Convention", on page 12 of the International Labour Conference document above. The articles and regulations can only be changed by the Conference in the framework of article 19 of the Constitution of the International Labour Organisation (see Article XIV of the Convention).

3   The Code can be amended through the simplified procedure set out in Article XV of the Convention.

4   See MLC 2006.

5   See MLC 2006 Regulation 5.1.3.

6   See "Report of the Legal Committee on the work of its one-hundredth session" (IMO, 2013a), paragraph 4.4. The amendments to be discussed were based on the recommendations of the joint IMO/ILO Ad Hoc Expert Group on Liability and Compensation regarding Claims for Death, Personal Injury and Abandonment of Seafarers, adopted in 2009.

7   The entry into force of PAL PROT 2002 followed the submission of the instrument of ratification by Belgium on 23 April 2013. Instruments of ratification had been earlier submitted by Albania, Belize, Denmark, Latvia, the Netherlands, Palau, Saint Kitts and Nevis, Serbia, the Syrian Arab Republic, and the European Union.

8   It is worth noting that for the first time in an IMO Convention, express provision has been made for signature, approval or accession by a regional economic integration organization, conferring upon such organization "the rights and obligations of a State Party, to the extent that the Regional Economic Integration Organization has competence over matters governed by this Protocol" (see Article 19 of the Convention). The European Union acceded to the 2002 Protocol at the end of 2011. However, this does not substitute for individual ratification by its member States.

9   PAL 1974 was adopted on 13 December 1974 and entered into force on 28 April 1987. A 1976 Protocol to the Convention introduced the SDR as the applicable unit of account, replacing the "Poincaré franc", based on the "official" value of gold. A 1990 Protocol to the Convention was intended to raise the relevant limits of liability but did not enter into force and was later superseded by the 2002 Protocol. The PAL PROT 2002 was adopted on 1 November 2002 and will enter into force on 23 April 2014.

10   Article 15(3) of PAL PROT 2002 states that Articles 1 to 22 of the Convention, as revised by the Protocol, together with Articles 17 to 25 of the Protocol and the Annex thereto, shall constitute and be called the Athens Convention relating to the Carriage of Passengers and their Luggage by Sea, 2002 (PAL 2002).

11   For some further information, see also a compilation of documents on the Athens Convention, available at http://www.gard.no/ikbViewer/Content/72411/Athens%20Convention%20and%20ratifications%20April%202013.pdf (accessed 25 November 2013).

12   See Articles 3(1) and 7(1) of the Convention. However, it should be noted that the Convention envisages the possibility for Contracting States to enter certain reservations.

13   See Article 4bis of the Convention.

14   For loss or damage to cabin luggage, the carrier's liability is limited to 2,250 SDR per passenger, per carriage. Liability for loss of or damage to vehicles, including all luggage carried in or on the vehicle, is limited to 12,700 SDR per vehicle, per carriage. Liability for loss of or damage to other luggage is limited to 3,375 SDR per passenger, per carriage.

15   Under PAL 1974, limits can only be raised by adopting amendments to it, which require a specified number of States' acceptances to bring the amendments into force. For instance, an earlier Protocol to PAL 1974, adopted in 1990, which was also intended to increase the liability limits, did not enter into force and was superseded by PAL PROT 2002. Under the tacit acceptance procedure, described in Article 23 of the Convention, a proposal to amend the limits, as requested by at least one half of the Parties to the Protocol, but in no case less than six, would be circulated to all IMO member States and all States Parties and would then be discussed in the IMO Legal Committee. Amendments would be adopted by a two-thirds majority of the States Parties to the Convention as amended by the Protocol present and voting in the Legal Committee, on condition that at least one half of these States shall be present at the time of voting, and would enter into force 18 months after its deemed acceptance date. The deemed acceptance date would be 18 months after adoption, unless within that period not less than one fourth of the States that were States Parties at the time of the adoption of the amendment have communicated to the IMO Secretary-General that they do not accept the amendment.

16   See Article 17.5 of PAL PROT 2002. As a precondition for joining, Parties to the PAL PROT 2002 are required to denounce PAL 1974 and its 1976 and 1990 Protocols. As of 30 June 2013, PAL 1974 was in force in 35 Contracting States, representing 45.88 per cent of world GT. This will reduce to 31 States on 23 April 2014. As of 30 June 2013, PAL PROT 1976 was in force in 26 Contracting States; this will reduce to 23 States on 23 April 2014.

17   Relevant declarations were made by Argentina and the Russian Federation, in accordance with Article 22 of PAL 1974.

18   These are Canada, Denmark, Finland, Germany, Norway and Sweden. Relevant liability limits under domestic legislation are in line with or very similar to the amounts set out in a 1990 Protocol to the PAL 1974 which, however, never entered into force. It should be noted that Denmark has now ratified PAL PROT 2002 and will thus be a Party to PAL 2002. For further information on the status of these conventions as at 30 June 2013, see IMO (2013b).

19   The set of measures were added as an amendment to MARPOL Annex VI "Regulations on the prevention of air pollution from ships", as a new Chapter 4 entitled "Regulations on energy efficiency for ships".

20   For a summary of the content of the regulations, see UNCTAD (2012a), pages 97–98. For an overview of the discussions on the different types of measures, see UNCTAD (2010), pages 118–119 and UNCTAD (2011a), pages 114–116.

21   The study suggests that, if implemented, relevant measures could increase energy efficiency and reduce the emissions rate by 25–75 per cent below the current levels. For a detailed insight on a range of the potential implications of climate change for shipping see also an edited volume, *Maritime Transport and the Climate Change Challenge*, published in May 2012 (Asariotis and Benamara, 2012). The book, a United Nations co-publication with Earthscan/Routledge, includes contributions from experts from academia, international organizations – such as the IMO, the United Nations Framework Convention on Climate Change (UNFCCC) secretariat, OECD, the International Energy Agency and the World Bank – as well as the shipping and port industries. Issues covered include the scientific background; GHG emissions from international shipping and potential approaches to mitigation; the state of play in terms of the relevant regulatory and institutional framework; potential climate-change impacts and approaches to adaptation in maritime transport; and relevant cross-cutting issues such as financing and investment, technology and energy. For further information, see the UNCTAD website at www.unctad.org/ttl/legal.

22   The MEPC held its sixty-fourth session 1–5 October 2012 and its sixty-fifth session 13–17 May 2013.

23   This amendment updated a footnote referring to the International Towing Tank Conference recommended procedure 7.5-04-01-01.2 as the preferable standard.

24   The proposal of the United States to enhance energy efficiency in international shipping. Additional documents considered by the Committee under this item include those by: IMarEST, providing information relating to a goal-based approach to "fuel consumption measurement"; CSC, providing comments on the submissions by the United States and IMarEST, and offering additional information on the different approaches to monitoring and reporting fuel consumption and carbon dioxide (CO_2) emissions from ships; Belgium, Canada, Denmark, Germany, Japan, Norway and the United Kingdom, supporting the development of technical and operational measures to increase the energy efficiency of ships.

25   "BEING COGNIZANT of the principles enshrined in the Convention on the Organization, including the principle of non-discrimination, as well as the principle of no more favourable treatment enshrined in MARPOL and other IMO Conventions."

26   "BEING COGNIZANT ALSO of the principles enshrined in the UNFCCC and its Kyoto Protocol including the principle of common but differentiated responsibilities and respective capabilities."

27   Several delegations made statements on the resolution, which are set out in Annex 5 of IMO (2013c). As reported by the Third World Network (Chiew, 2013), during the subsequent UNFCCC Climate Change Conference in Bonn, in June 2013, a group of developing countries have taken the express reference in the IMO resolution to the principle of "common but differentiated responsibilities"(CBDR) as a clear signal that the IMO respects the principles and provisions of the UNFCCC in its work related to climate change. An opposing view was expressed by some developed-country delegations, including Japan, asserting that the adoption of the preamble paragraph in the Resolution, which refers to "being cognizant" of CBDR should not limit the activities under the principles of the IMO, pointing out that the reiteration of this point was recorded in the MEPC 65 report.

28   See a note by the IMO to the thirty-eighth session of the Subsidiary Body for Scientific and Technological Advice, Bonn, 3 to 14 June 2013, providing an update on the IMO work to address emissions from fuel used for international shipping, available at http://unfccc.int/resource/docs/2013/sbsta/eng/misc15.pdf (accessed 7 November 2013).

29   In respect of possible MBMs, see particularly UNCTAD (2011a) pages 114 and 117–119 and UNCTAD (2012a), pages 99–101.

30   It should be noted that a range of concerns on matters of principle and policy concerning reduction of GHG emissions and in respect of potential MBMs have been expressed by a number of developing countries' delegations, including in particular the delegations of Brazil, China and India. For further details, see also the statements by several delegations (IMO, 2012c, Annexes 14–17).

31   The countries studied include Chile, China, the Cook Islands, India, Kenya, the Maldives, Mexico, Samoa, Togo, and Trinidad and Tobago.

32   Brazil, China, India, Peru, Saudi Arabia and South Africa.

33   Based on a proposal by its Chair, the MEPC agreed to suspend discussions on market-based measures and related issues to a future session and consider only the following three items: (a) update of the GHG emission estimate for international shipping; (b) WTO-related matters; (c) UNFCCC matters (IMO, 2013c, paragraph 5.1).

34   As reported in previous issues of the *Review of Maritime Transport*, key figures in the latest (second) IMO GHG Study (IMO, 2009) estimated that international shipping emitted 870 million tons, or about 2.7 per cent, of the global emissions of CO2 generated by human activity in 2007.

35   See IMO (2012b), page 36.

36   The expert workshop to further consider the methodology and assumptions to be used in the update of GHG emissions estimate for international shipping was held from 26 February to 1 March 2013. Its report is contained in document IMO (2013f).

37   The terms of reference of the Update Study are set out in the Annex to the document (IMO, 2013f).

38   The steering committee was subsequently established by the IMO Secretary-General on 12 July 2013 by circular letter (IMO, 2013g).

39   By India and Saudi Arabia.

40   It should be noted that the delegation of India expressed the view that the WTO Secretariat was not in a position to provide the information requested and, therefore, the information in the Annex to the document should not have been requested nor should it be considered further (IMO, 2013c, paragraph 5.20).

41   Documents submitted by the IMO Secretariat were as follows: IMO (2012g) on the outcome of a United Nations Climate Change Conference held in Bonn from 14 to 25 May 2012; IMO (2012h) on the first board meeting of the Green Climate Fund which was held from 23 to 25 August 2012 in Geneva, Switzerland; IMO (2013i) on the outcome of the United Nations Climate Change Conference held in Doha from 26 November to 8 December 2012.

42   The report highlights central features of the international legal framework and provides an analytical overview of key provisions of the most recent of the international legal instruments in force. It also offers considerations for national policymaking.

43   This covers the International Convention on Civil Liability for Oil Pollution Damage 1969 and its 1992 Protocol as well as the International Convention on the Establishment of an International Fund for Compensation for Oil Pollution Damage (Fund Convention) 1971 and its 1992 and 2003 Protocols.

44   The convention entered into force on 21 November 2008 and as of 30 June 2013 had 70 States Parties representing 90.04 per cent of world tonnage. The convention covers oil pollution from ships other than tankers, for example, container vessels, reefers, chemical tankers, general cargo ships, cruise ships and ferries.

45   The 2010 Protocol to the International Convention on Liability and Compensation for Damage in Connection with the Carriage of Hazardous and Noxious Substances by Sea, 1996. The Protocol has not yet entered into force. See also UNCTAD (2010), pages 124–125.

46   The workshop took place in London, in November 2012. For further information see www.hnsconvention.org (accessed 11 November 2013).

47   IMO (2013a), pages 5–6.

48   Particularly following the Deepwater Horizon incident in 2010 and the 2009 incident on the Montara offshore oil platform, located in the Australian Exclusive Economic Zone, in which a well exploded, leading to a significant oil spill.

49   For a summary of views expressed by the delegations see IMO (2013a), pages 21–24. Also noted in the report is an informal consultative group to discuss issues connected with transboundary pollution damage from offshore exploration and exploitation activities and coordinated by the delegation of Indonesia. The online address for participating in this group is ind_offshorediscussion_imoleg@yahoogroups.com.

50   MARPOL Annex VI came into force on 19 May 2005, and as at 30 June 2013 it had been ratified by 72 States, representing approximately 94.30 per cent of world tonnage. Annex VI covers air pollution from ships, including SO_x and NO_x emissions and particulate matter.

51   See UNCTAD (2008), page 119.

52   In case of a negative conclusion of the review, the new global cap should be applied from 1 January 2025.

53   The first two SOx ECAs, the Baltic Sea and the North Sea areas, were established in Europe and took effect in 2006 and 2007, respectively. The third established was the North American ECA, taking effect on 1 August 2012. In addition, in July 2011, a fourth ECA, the United States Caribbean Sea, was established. This latter area covers certain waters adjacent to the coasts of Puerto Rico (United States) and the United States Virgin Islands, and will take effect on 1 January 2014.

54   Also called exhaust gas SOx scrubbers.

55   Directive 2012/33/EU of the European Parliament and of the Council of 21 November 2012, amending Council Directive 1999/32/EC as regards the sulphur content of marine fuels; OJ L 327, 27 November 2012, pages 1–13. Available at http://eur-lex.europa.eu/LexUriServ/LexUriServ.do?uri=OJ:L:2012:327:0001:0013:EN:PDF (accessed 12 November 2013).

56   This proposal by the ICS suggested that, during the period 2012–2014, the fuel-availability model proposed by the Correspondence Group on the assessment of availability of fuel oil under MARPOL Annex VI should be used to carry out a preliminary study to provide fuel availability scenarios for the period 2015–2016.

57   This proposal by the United States opposed the early initiation of the assessment of availability of fuel oil under MARPOL Annex VI, as the results of an earlier preliminary analysis would be of little value in assessing fuel availability in 2020, for several reasons.

58   So far, only the North American ECA is designated for NOx control. An application to make the Baltic Sea an ECA is being discussed by the surrounding States through the Helsinki Commission. For more information see *Lloyd's List* (2013).

59   Limits of tier III are almost 70 per cent lower than those of tier II, thus requiring additional technology.

60   For an overview of the revised MARPOL Annex V discharge provisions, see UNCTAD (2012a), table 5.1, page 104.

61   According to this circular, until 31 December 2015 cargo hold wash water from holds having previously contained solid bulk cargoes classified as harmful to the marine environment may be discharged outside special areas under specific conditions. The circular also urges Parties to MARPOL Annex V to ensure the provision of adequate facilities at ports and terminals for the reception of solid bulk cargo residues, including those contained in wash water.

62   The Hong Kong International Convention for the Safe and Environmentally Sound Recycling of Ships 2009.

63   These are the "2012 Guidelines for safe and environmentally sound ship recycling", (IMO, 2012a, Annex 4), the "2012 Guidelines for the authorization of ship recycling facilities" (IMO, 2012a, Annex 5), the "2011 Guidelines for the development of the Inventory of Hazardous Materials" (IMO, 2012a, Annex 3), and the "2011 Guidelines for the development of the Ship Recycling Plan" (IMO, 2011a, Annex 2).

64   The Hong Kong Convention has been opened for accession since 1 September 2010 and it is not yet in force. It will enter into force 24 months after the date on which 15 States, representing 40 per cent of the world's merchant fleet tonnage, have become parties to it. As of 30 June 2013, only Norway had acceded to the Convention.

65   This group was initially established during the MEPC 64 to develop threshold values and exemptions applicable to the materials to be listed in Inventories of Hazardous Materials and to consider the need to amend, accordingly, the "2011 Guidelines for the development of the Inventory of Hazardous Materials".

66   The BWM Convention has not yet entered into force. As of 30 June 2013, 37 States, with an aggregate merchant shipping tonnage of 30.32 per cent of the world total, have ratified it. The Convention will enter into force twelve months after the date on which no fewer than 30 States, the combined merchant fleets of which constitute not less than 35 per cent of the GT of the world merchant shipping, have become parties to it. Several delegations had indicated earlier that they were expecting to submit their instruments of ratification to IMO in the near future, since the process of ratifying the Convention is in the final or advanced stage in their countries. See also UNCTAD (2011b, page 8).

67   These ballast water systems were proposed by China, the Netherlands, Norway and the Republic of Korea. Details of these systems can be found in the respective documents submitted during MEPC 64 and 65, available at www.imo.org.

68   These systems were proposed by China, Denmark, Japan, the Netherlands and the Republic of Korea. Details of these systems can be found in the respective documents submitted during the MEPC 64 and 65, available at www.imo.org. Many types of ballast water treatment systems have been granted IMO approval in the last few years. Some of them have later been withdrawn from the market again for lack of compliant operation after installation on ships.

69   To be held from 25 November to 4 December 2013.

70   Copies of these BWM circulars (BWM.2/Circ.42–45) are available at www.imo.org.

71   A June 2012 updated version of the SAFE Framework can be found in document WCO (2012a).

72   Pillar 1 is based on the model of the Container Security Initiative introduced in the United States in 2002. Pillar 2 is based on the model of the Customs–Trade Partnership against Terrorism (C-TPAT) programme introduced in the United States in 2001. For more information on these as well as for an analysis of the main features of the customs supply-chain security, namely advance cargo information, risk management, cargo scanning and authorized economic operators (AEOs), see WCO research paper No.18, "The Customs supply chain security paradigm and 9/11: Ten years on and beyond September 2011", available at www.wcoomd.org. For a summary of the various United States security programmes adopted after September 11 see UNCTAD (2004).

73   As of 30 June 2013, 168 out of 179 WCO members had expressed their intention to implement the SAFE Framework.

74   See also UNCTAD (2011a), pages 121–122. The Package includes the *SAFE Framework of Standards*; *Customs Guidelines on Integrated Supply Chain Management*; *AEO Implementation Guidance*; *AEO Compendium*; *Model AEO Appeal Procedures*; *AEO Benefits: A contribution from the WCO Private Sector Consultative Group*; *Guidelines for the Purchase and Deployment of Scanning/Imaging Equipment*; *SAFE Data Element Maintenance Mechanism*; *Trade Recovery Guidelines*; *FAQ for Small and Medium Enterprises*. The SAFE Package is available at: http://www.wcoomd.org/en/topics/facilitation/instrument-and-tools/tools/safe_package.aspx (accessed 25 November 2013).

75   For more information, see the WCO website http://www.wcoomd.org/en/topics/facilitation/instrument-and-tools/tools/safe_package.aspx (accessed 18 November 2013).

76   The SAFE Framework AEO concept has its origins in the revised Kyoto Convention, which contains standards on "authorized persons", and national programmes.

77   For more information on the concept of mutual recognition in general, as well as on the guidelines for developing an MRA, included in the SAFE Package, and the WCO research paper No.18 on the issue, see UNCTAD (2012a), pages 106–107.

78   The first MRA was concluded between the United States and New Zealand in June 2007. As of 30 June 2013, 19 bilateral MRAs had been concluded and a further 10 were being negotiated between, respectively, China–European Union, China–Japan, Japan–Malaysia, China–Republic of Korea, Hong Kong (China)–Republic of Korea, India–Republic of Korea, Israel–Republic of Korea, New Zealand–Singapore, Norway–Switzerland and Singapore–United States.

79   Due to the fact that 27 European Union countries have one common uniform AEO programme.

80   This is according to information provided by the WCO Secretariat. For more information see the latest "Compendium of AEO Programmes" (WCO, 2012b).

81   For more information see WCO, 2013a, 2013b, 2013c and 2013d.

82   See in particular UNCTAD (2011a) which provided an overview of the major changes this amendment introduced to the Customs Code, at pages 122–123.

83   For more information see http://ec.europa.eu/ecip/security_amendment/index_en.htm (accessed 18 November 2013).

84   A redacted copy of the document has been made available to UNCTAD by the European Commission Taxation and Customs Union Directorate-General.

85   See European Commission (2013) page 9.

86   For background, see also European Commission (2012).

87   See article by the World Shipping Council President and Chief Executive Officer (Koch C, 2013). Members of the World Shipping Council operate approximately 90 percent of the global liner ship capacity.

88   According to information provided by the European Commission's Taxation and Customs Union Directorate General, as of 25 June 2013, a total of 15,359 applications for AEO certificates had been submitted, and a total of 13,104 certificates had been issued. The total number of applications rejected up to 15 June 2013 was 1,523 (10 per cent of the applications received) and the total number of certificates revoked was 691 (5.3 per cent of certificates issued). The breakdown reported per certificate type issued as of 31 December 2012, was: AEO-F 6023 (49 per cent); AEO-C 5969 (48 per cent); and AEO-S 354 (3 per cent).

89   For the self-assessment questionnaire, see http://ec.europa.eu/taxation_customs/resources/documents/customs/policy_issues/customs_security/aeo_self_assessment_en.pdf (accessed 18 November 2013). Explanatory notes are also available at http://ec.europa.eu/taxation_customs/resources/documents/customs/policy_issues/customs_security/aeo_self_assessment_explanatory_en.pdf (accessed 18 November 2013).

90   The European Union has already concluded MRAs with Japan, Norway, Switzerland and the United States. Negotiations are ongoing with China, and will soon start with Canada. The United States, in addition to the European Union, has MRAs with Canada, China, Taiwan Province of, Japan, Jordan, New Zealand and the Republic of Korea.

91   Membership in the C-TPAT as of May 2013 reached 10,512 companies accounting for over 50 per cent (by value) of goods imported into the United States. As of March 2013, CBP had signed MRAs with Canada, China, Taiwan Province of, the European Union, Japan, Jordan, New Zealand and the Republic of Korea. For more information, see www.cbp.gov.

92   For more information see the CBP website, available at http://www.cbp.gov/xp/cgov/trade/trade_outreach/coac/coac_13_meetings/may22_meeting_dc/ (accessed 19 November 2013).

93   Held from 26 to 30 November 2012.

94   Held from 12 to 21 June 2013.

95   The document was signed, bringing the Code into effect for 22 signatory States: Angola, Benin, Cameroon, Cape Verde, Chad, the Congo, Côte d'Ivoire, the Democratic Republic of the Congo, Equatorial Guinea, Gabon, Gambia, Ghana, Guinea, Guinea-Bissau, Liberia, Mali, Niger, Nigeria, Senegal, Sierra Leone, São Tomé and Principe, and Togo.

96   The full text of the Code is available at https://195.24.195.238/en/multimedia/documents/437-sommet-sur-la-piraterie-code-de-conduite-english (accessed 19 November 2013). See also *MarineLink.com* (2013).

97   Held from 15 to 19 April 2013.

98   The document provided information by UNODC. Written comments to it were provided in document IMO (2013q). The Committee noted with regret that NATO had informed the Secretariat that it had no relevant records or information and that no response had been received from the European Union Naval Force Somalia.

99   See IMO (2013a), page 10.

100 The answers provided by member States to this questionnaire are available at the IMO website, see http://www.imo.org/OurWork/Security/PiracyArmedRobbery/Pages/Responses-received-on-Private%20Armed%20Security.aspx (accessed 19 November 2013).

101   See http://unicri.it/topics/piracy/database/ (accessed 19 November 2013).

102   As regards the inclusion of national legislation on piracy in the database, this information may be found in the database established by the Division for Ocean Affairs and the Law of the Sea, available at http://www.un.org/depts/los/piracy/piracy_national_legislation.htm (accessed 19 November 2013).

103   For further information see IMO (2013a) pages 12–16.

104 ´ Relevant guidance from the WCO Trade Recovery Guidelines, the Asia-Pacific Economic Cooperation Trade Recovery Programme and ISO 28002:2011 has been consolidated and integrated into the Guidelines (IMO, 2013s).

105   This questionnaire was finalized by an intersessional meeting of the Maritime Security and Piracy Working Group.

106   The full text of the report is available on the Seafarers' Rights International website at www.seafarersrights.org (accessed 19 November 2013).

107   For further information, see IMO (2013a), pages 7–9.

108   The content of this and the following paragraphs is based on the comparison between revision 12 and revision 16 of the draft consolidated negotiating text (TN/TF/165).

109   This section is based on the forthcoming UNCTAD report, "The competitiveness' new frontier: Implementing trade facilitation in developing countries".

110   The full text of the statement is available at http://www.wto.org/english/news_e/news13_e/fac_08jul13_e.htm (accessed 20 November 2013).

6

SECURING RELIABLE ACCESS TO MARITIME TRANSPORT FOR LANDLOCKED COUNTRIES

The passage of trade of landlocked countries through coastal territories to access shipping services is generally governed by a standard principle: goods in transit and their carriage are granted crossing free of fiscal duties and by the most convenient routes. In practice, however, the implementation of this basic norm suffers from numerous operational difficulties, resulting in high transport costs and long travel times, which undermine trade competitiveness and ultimately the economic development of landlocked countries. Over the past decade, under the Almaty Programme of Action launched in 2003, new analytical tools and extensive field research have brought fresh knowledge about the mechanisms explaining detected inefficiencies. Among other things, it has revealed that rent-seeking stakeholders may play against improvements, making transit operations unnecessarily complex and unpredictable, to the detriment of governmental and traders' efforts. Thus, by exposing conflicting forces at play along transit chains, the analysis shows that the trade of landlocked countries primarily suffers from unreliability resulting from a lack of cooperation among stakeholders, often explaining high transport costs and long transit times.

This chapter provides an overview of these findings, and based on them, explores a new paradigm that should allow for a radical transformation of transit transport systems, providing landlocked countries reliable access to global value chains and allowing them to act in ways other than as providers of primary goods.

The proposed approach aims to make the predictability of transit logistics chains a priority of the governments of both landlocked and transit countries – in partnership with traders, port operators and shipping lines, who stand to benefit the most from such an improvement – as well as a priority of the new development agenda for landlocked and transit developing countries to be adopted in 2014.

A.   OBSTACLES TO TRANSIT CHAINS

The many obstacles faced by landlocked countries' trade transiting through other territories are commonly known. They range from long distances to inadequate transport services and infrastructure, and inefficient institutional and operational transit frameworks. Until recently, higher costs and longer times had been seen as the reasons for the lack of competitiveness of traders from landlocked countries. However, in the past decade, new research and field studies on local transit economics (Limao, 2001; Faye et al., 2004; Collier, 2007; Arvis et al., 2011, UNCTAD 2013,) show that the unreliability of the transit logistics system is the greatest impediment faced by manufacturers in landlocked developing countries as they attempt to enter value chains at both the regional and global levels. Other findings are briefly discussed here.

1.   Distances, travel times and transport costs

In many landlocked developing countries, production and consumption centres are located more than 800 kilometres (km) away from the closest seaport (table 6.1), which translates in two or more days' travel time. Although extremely long hauls ranging between 2,500 km and 6,000 km or shorter distances of less than 500 km remain the exception, in all cases the distance to the sea not only adds costs and travel time, but also has consequences at the operational level: long travel times imply fewer turnovers of a given vehicle over a given period, often facing costly and long empty returns, and, ultimately, entailing lesser return on investment for the owner. Such a sequence dissuades investing in renovating the vehicles and leads to low quality of services provided by old, less reliable and less carbon-friendly equipment. In some cases, discussed below, prevailing protectionist regulations have had their share in defending the use of aging trucking fleets. (Arvis et al., 2010; Kunaka et al., 2013).

The remoteness from the sea has long been an obvious explanation of the disadvantage of long travel times and high transport costs affecting trade to and from landlocked territories. Widely documented (Arvis et al., 2010, 2011), these extra costs and times have also been generally qualified as excessive based on the comparison with data for coastal countries crossed by the landlocked cargoes or on international benchmarks providing comparison of other countries. Both types of comparison lead one to conclude that the difference of cost and times associated with remoteness from the sea cannot be denied and constitutes a serious disadvantage.

Nevertheless, because of the way these figures are collected, these comparisons might be misleading.

Transport times and costs given for coastal countries' trade usually reflect the ocean transport to a port of entry in the coastal country. These do not include the necessary steps – and associated times and costs – required for traders in coastal countries to have their goods on their premises and that include unloading from the ship, cargo storage at ports, customs clearance procedures and inland transport. In contrast, figures for landlocked countries do include all port charges and other cargo handling and transport costs – and times – necessary for the carriage of trade to reach the final inland destination. The use of data not reflecting a similar content for times and costs in the comparison between the trade of landlocked and costal countries results in cost differences (figure 6.1) and time differences (table 6.2).

Table 6.1.	Distances to ports from selected landlocked developing countries		
Landlocked developing country	Ports	Range (km)	Mode
Afghanistan	2	1 200–1 600	road
Armenia	2	800–2 400	rail, road
Azerbaijan	2	800	rail-road
Bolivia (Plurinational State of)	8	500–2 400	rail, river, road
Botswana	4	950–1 400	rail, road
Burkina Faso	5	1 100–1 900	rail, road
Burundi	2	1 500–1 850	lake, rail, road
Bhutan	1	800	rail, road
Central African Republic	2	1 500–1 800	rail, road
Chad	2	1 800–1 900	rail, road
Ethiopia	3	900–1 250	rail, road
Kyrgyzstan	4	4 500–5 200	rail, road
Lao People's Democratic Republic	3	600–750	rail, road
Lesotho	2	500	rail, road
Malawi	3	600–2 300	rail, road
Mali	6	1 200–1 400	rail, road
Mongolia	4	1 700–6 000	rail, road
Nepal	2	1 100–1 200	rail, road
Niger	3	900–1 200	rail, road
Paraguay	4	1 200–1 400	rail, river, road
Republic of Moldova	2	800	rail, road
Rwanda	2	1 500–1 700	lake, rail, road
Swaziland	4	250–500	rail, road
Uganda	2	1 300–1 650	lake, rail, road
Uzbekistan	3	2 700	rail, road
Tajikistan	3	1 500–2 500	rail, road
The former Yugoslav Republic of Macedonia	1	600	rail, road
Turkmenistan	3	4 500	rail, road
Zambia	8	1 300–2 100	rail, road
Zimbabwe	3	850–1 550	rail, road

Source: Compiled by the UNCTAD secretariat based on data from the Economic Commission for Africa, Economic and Social Commission for Asia and the Pacific, ECLAC and the World Bank.

Figure 6.1.   Cost to import (Dollars per container)

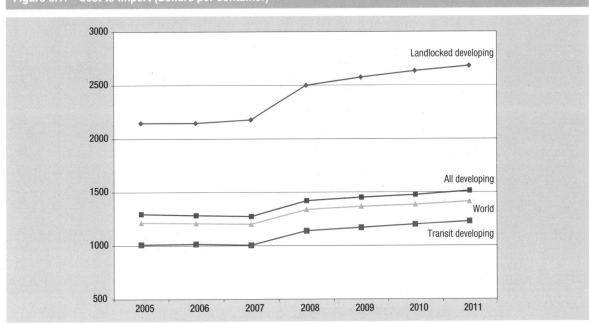

Source: Office of the High Representative for the Least Developed Countries, Landlocked Developing Countries and Small Island Developing States (OHRLLS) 2013, based on World Bank Indicators.

Table 6.2.   Number of days to export

	2005	2006	2007	2008	2009	2010	2011
Landlocked developing countries	49	49	48	48	46	44	43
Transit developing countries	30	27	26	25	24	23	23
All developing countries	32	30	29	28	27	26	26
World	28	26	25	25	24	23	23

Source: OHRLLS, based on World Bank indicators.

That these comparisons may exacerbate the actual difference and thereby exaggerate the handicap suffered by landlocked countries is important. But more importantly, because geographical distance – which cannot be shortened – is only one aspect of the problem, its relative weight should be more accurately assessed.

A close look at recently studied transit corridors shows that truck or rail operating costs (ton/km) in both transited and landlocked countries remain very close to or even lower than global standards or benchmarks in developed countries (UNCTAD, 2013). If carriers' costs are similar but freight paid by users is much higher than in comparable circumstances in other parts of the world, then distance per se cannot explain a transport cost of being landlocked showing surpluses of up to 60 per cent and an average of 45 per cent (figure 6.2). In other words, apart from the distance factor, the difference between the freight costs paid by traders in landlocked and coastal developing countries for an equivalent transport must be due to other factors not associated with the remoteness

from the sea.   This is precisely one of the relevant outcomes of the most recent field studies: there are factors other than distance and transport costs that make trade expensive for landlocked developing countries. These factors must be sought in the environment that surrounds transit operations, and regulatory frameworks are central among them.

2.   Impacts of regulatory arrangements for transit

Borders may be more than just political boundaries. They also set the limits of different business and of technological and administrative cultures. Crossing a border entails entering distinctive market spaces where diverse requirements govern practices and different rules apply. Goods in transit and their carriers must adapt to these changing rules and standards. Research has shed some light on the consequences of rules and procedures being applied to cargoes in transit.

Figure 6.2.   Transport cost of being landlocked (Ratio)

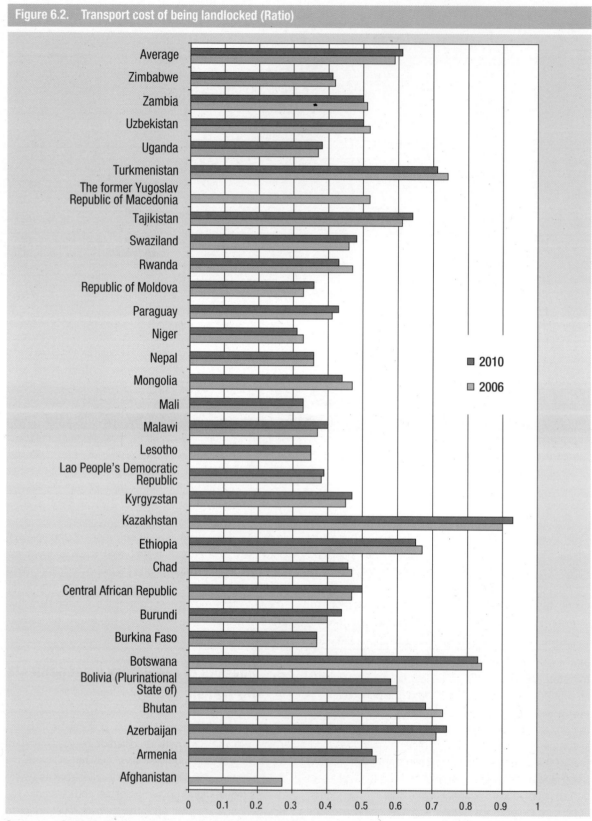

Source: OHRLLS, 2013.
Note: For example, a value of 0.5 means that the transport cost is 50 per cent higher in a landlocked country, compared with
             that of a representative coastal economy. Data for 2010 were not available for the former Yugoslav Republic of Macedonia
             and Afghanistan.

These studies also show that private sector operators, performing under the protection of restrictive regulatory schemes and obtaining rent-seeking monopolistic or oligopolistic positions, may become the strongest opponents to any type of facilitation efforts to bring transparency and simplicity to the transit system (Arvis et al., 2011). While road transport is currently a dominant mode of transport in transit systems serving landlocked countries, it is also a major factor for high freights paid for transport services by traders in these countries. Transit logistics costs, which include all the different steps of transit operations, could in fact be considerably reduced and become more environmentally efficient by either improving the efficiency of road transport operations or by designing systems leading to a modal shift to rail or river transport.

A recent study by the World Bank (Kunaka et al., 2013) shows that while great attention has been given to road infrastructures, in many cases the management of international road transport services continues being based on regulations favouring market access restrictions to protect national carriers. Thus many bilateral agreements governing road transport, including transit agreements, have turned into barriers for transit facilitation, even in integrated economic schemes. Although reciprocity and territoriality are key principles in bilateral instruments, agreements may provide for embedded operational restrictions stemming from the nationality of the operator or country of registration of the vehicles, traffic rights on certain routes, quotas governing the number of trips, cargo volumes, carrying capacity or numbers of permits for authorized carriers to undertake cross border transport. This leads to empty returns, distortions in available carrying capacities, transport supply chains interrupted or fragmented by mandatory transhipments, high freight rates unrelated to actual operating costs, long travel times, and in general, greater uncertainty in cargo flows.

B. THE COST OF TRANSIT UNRELIABILITY

As mentioned previously, distance also brings additional problems. The longer the road or the track, the higher the possibility of facing an unforeseen event resulting in transport disruptions. These likely incidents mean that there will be an increased uncertainty of transport times due to extended risks of mechanical failures, and accidents resulting from driver fatigue over long working hours or as a result of poor road or rail maintenance. Long routes are also a risk factor of theft and numerous

stops due to checkpoints along the road, including weighbridges or stops at railway stations, and border crossings. However, many of these stops may also take place along fairly short distances and remain unrelated to official controls applied to transit transport. A natural exception must, however, be made for required rest stops for drivers along the route (Fitzmaurice and Hartmann, 2013).

As a result of these long delays and uncertainties concerning deliveries, traders in landlocked countries may have to bear considerable inventory costs that may sometimes be even higher than transport costs, reaching more than 10 per cent of the value of the goods (World Bank, 2013). The main sources of transit logistics costs are found in the relationships and interests governing the interactions of participants in the corridor supply chain: traders, transport companies, customs brokers, freight forwarders, banks, insurance companies, customs and other government agencies. Because these different parties have diverse and sometimes conflicting vested interests, the transit supply chain, which operates over long distances, is relatively complex and appears frequently as a fragmented sequence of a series of disconnected steps.

Another source of costs is linked to various official and informal payments levied along the transit route (Arvis et al., 2011). For example, "In many environments the complexity of the supply chain means that traders or their forwarders need to spend more time and staff to get things done, and this adds to the costs. It has been shown that in some cases, like Western Africa, these additional costs are on a par with the cost of trucking". Transit chains are thus subject to inefficiencies and "even rent-seeking activities and corruption" (World Bank, 2013).

Supply chains, such as the transit systems connecting landlocked countries to seaports, need predictable events so that they can be organized and their sequence efficiently arranged. Global production value chains, which engage processes distributed over several geographically distant centres, also rely on strict delivery times for both dispatches and deliveries. The lack of predictability of transit delivery schedules may constitute the most important single obstacle for producers in landlocked countries to enter value chains other than at a very initial stage, as providers of the primary input.

1. Different views

Reliability may not have the same value or relevance for different parties intervening along the transit chain. For government authorities, it may mean having the certainty that all relevant rules are fully applied. For customs, this may mean that fiscal risk, resulting from diversion to national markets, is minimized or fully covered through guarantee schemes. For agencies dealing with sanitary risks, certainty may mean the country remains safe from possible hazards to animal or vegetal contamination from goods in transit. For providers of transport and trade support services operating along a transit route, predictability may mean foreseeable volumes of freight allowing for investment and business development. For transport planners, infrastructure service providers and terminal operators, predictability may mean ensuring the best use of infrastructures and equipment and correctly size their development. For traders, predictability means transit times, including carriage and pre- and post-transport stages, and the logistics chain as a whole are safe and reliable in terms of quality and time; it also means the goods are in the hands of qualified operators and will reach their destination in good condition. For traders, the low reliability of transit supply chains is more worrisome than the average transit time. For instance, retail operators such as local supermarkets must maintain several months' inventory in landlocked developing countries instead of a few weeks in developed markets (World Bank, 2013).

This way, together with cost effectiveness and speed, reliability constitutes a primary objective to be pursued for the supply chain of transit services linking seaports and landlocked countries. As mentioned before, while the multiplicity of actors in the chain and their vested and sometimes conflicting interests remain a main cause of uncertainty, there are ways of turning silo-minded players into sharing a systemic collective understanding.

2. Seeking closer cooperation

As early as 2003, UNCTAD developed a supply chain management approach applied to transit transport services (Hansen and Annovazzi-Jakab, 2008) which, emulating assembly lines in manufacturing industry sectors, allowed for cluster development and transit corridors stakeholders' cooperation to improve transit operations. The methodology, based on the observation of the sequence of interventions in transit operations, showed that actors along the chain operate on a user–provider or client–supplier relationship. Although players' actions are interrelated and dependent on each other, they often do not occur in the way and time expected by the user of the service provided. This is mainly due to a lack of exchange of information between users and

providers regarding their respective needs and goals, which in turn results from a lack of trust among the players. Such malfunctions result in two types of activities taking place in the operation of the transit chain: those adding value at a cost and those adding cost at no value. The latter translate into unnecessary delays, high costs and efficiency losses.

UNCTAD implemented this approach from 2003–2007 in the framework of a technical assistance project conducted in three pilot corridors. The project showed that clusters as cooperative platforms would allow stakeholders along transit corridors to acquire a comprehensive understanding of their respective roles along the whole transit supply chain. It also revealed the impact of the actions of their members on the performance of various stages along the transit chain as well as the benefits accruing from collectively optimizing the chain as a whole, as opposed to trying to maximize individual returns. Such collaborative schemes constitute an essential step towards building a new vision and common goals for the different players in transit systems with the common aim of ending the unreliability of transit operation.

3. Prospects for solutions

Even after 10 years of continuous efforts and detailed field research, and despite the progress achieved on many fronts, scepticism remains as to the possibility of finding effective and comprehensive solutions. Because possible solutions would probably antagonize transport sectors by breaking current protective freight allocation arrangements or by opening transport markets to foreigners (Arvis et al., 2011), some conclude that "feasible implementation strategies of corridor improvement are extremely constrained. On the one hand, a reform package should change the paradigm of corridor organization and introduce quality-based regulation of incentives. On the other hand, it should offer options to those numerous operators who are unlikely to meet the requirements of the reformed freight and transit system." They also argue that this would entail a "transition in market for services with some form of dual market structure, with a modern sector open to international competition and meeting the standards of a fast-track system, while the old procedures and control may remain available for the rest" (Arvis et al., 2011). The "rest" were sheltered by current arrangements dating from the 1970s to the early 1980s, in which many of the market transit systems favoured small independent operators, regardless of the quality of service they offered.

C. A MODEL FOR A CHANGE OF PARADIGM IN TRANSIT

In view of the possible reluctance from some sectors of stakeholders with vested interests in currently operating transit chains, chances are that the change of paradigm in transit corridor operations might need to come at least in part inspired by successful solutions in transport and logistics systems that differ from transit ones. The following proposal builds on three pillars sourcing respectively from the best practice model offered by the high performing integrated logistics of mining industry, the regular services offered by liner shipping maritime activities and an anchor inland station in the form of a freight consolidation centre also known as a dry port.

Briefly described, the proposed design framework model may be seen as a conveyor belt type system supplying continuous overland transport capacity between two locations along a transit corridor: a transit seaport and a connected inland dry port. The model could also apply between two inland dry ports if one is connected to a transit seaport. The basic rationale of this model and some general details are discussed below.

1. The concept of the conveyor belt in shipping

In 2011, a major shipping line started offering a daily call service aimed at guaranteeing a fixed time transportation service based on frequency, reliability and consistency. According to the company, these three basic, most highly sought qualities of any transport system were inspired by the proposal of one customer interested in having the flexibility of a continuous service available every day, which would make it possible to miss the ship one day, knowing that the next day it would be available again. The suggestion consisted of developing a conveyor belt type system in which goods could be delivered to the shipping line at any time, knowing that, in any case, they would depart soon after on ships calling on a regular basis. This way, and as in a conveyor belt operation, goods will reach the end of the belt at a given time. The shipping line subscribed to the idea and explained that linking "four ports in Asia (Ningbo, Shanghai, Yantian and Tanjung Pelepas) and three ports in Europe (Felixstowe, Rotterdam and Bremerhaven) amounts to a giant ocean conveyor belt for the world's busiest trade lane" (Maersk, 2011). After one year, and due to low volumes, the service had to be limited to five days per week; at the same time, it was extended to two additional other ports at each end of the belt.

The rationale of guaranteeing consistency, reliability and frequency is based on the fact that guaranteed and predictable transport times are more relevant than actual speed. This is what is actually missing in transit systems connecting landlocked countries with world seaports.

The conveyor belt concept for a regular transport service can be transposed in its essence from sea shipping to land transport transit services. It should function as a shuttle-like service, linking one transit port to one inland destination in a landlocked country or within the same coastal country as a part of a transit corridor.

2. The integrated logistics chain in mining operations

To a certain extent, the conveyor belt operation resembles that of integrated intermodal transport chains developed for minerals. These systems are developed to carry homogeneous cargo, each piece, pellet or material unit, of which is constant and identical to the other. That thinking was behind the development of the container as a standard box that would unitize cargo and make break-bulk loads appear uniform for transport operators The containerization of cargo is in its essence a method designed to ensure that different cargoes, fruits, electronics, garment or spare parts are handled with standard equipment and transport means. The container is a successful attempt to make general cargo behave like bulk cargo on a different scale, but allowing for continuous transport of loads through different means and via integrated transport logistics systems.

The conveyor belt approach developed by the shipping line mentioned above, now applied to land transit transport connecting the seaport and inland dry port, could operate based on the bulk-cargo-carrying model, making no distinction between the type and origin of boxes and assuring the shipper that the goods will be delivered at the other end of the belt, alternatively the seaport and the dry port, at a given time and on a regular basis.

Such an idea had been addressed more than 10 years ago in ECLAC studies on best practices for intermodal transport (Rubiato, 2001). The study looked at mineral extraction transport to port and shipping overseas for copper and iron ore, in Chile and Brazil respectively. While the Minera Escondida example described the use of pipelines ("slurry pipelines" or "mineroducts") to carry liquefied copper mineral, the Vale case (the company was called Vale Do Rio Doce at the time) boasted impressive performances for an intermodal system involving truck carriages, car dumpers, rail transport and ocean shipping all linked and articulated around 160-wagon 6,400-ton-unit trains. These departed every 45 minutes from the mine, reaching the port of Tubarao 700 km away and achieving a total annual transport of 50 million tons or 140,000 tons a day; 300,000 dwt ocean vessels were being fully loaded in two to three days (see figure 6.3).

In terms of the lessons that mining systems could offer for application to other types of transport systems, the following are relevant for transit transport systems:

- *Ensuring continuous regular and large flows of cargoes* – Where large volumes of transit loads are not available, terminal operators at freight consolidation centres or dry ports (see box 6.1) may play a role in gathering necessary volumes to ensure the best use of transport means and infrastructures;

- *Organizing transport to serve traders* – Securing means of transport adapted to the specific product, flat trucks or wagons in the case of containers for transit purposes, for instance, is key to the cost of transport and the final value of the product but also with regard to its rhythms and periodicity of delivery, volumes and service of trade according to traders' needs;

- *Ensuring interconnectivity and interoperability between different modes of transport* – Compatibility between different modes is a basic condition in the operation of intermodal transport systems, such as those used in transit corridors The adaptation of means and the management of the system as a whole, ideally under a central command either by a single operator or a consortium, is one of the aspects better addressed in bulk transport logistics chains;

- *Operating with long-term contracts and long-standing partnerships* – Regular guaranteed cargo flows allow contracts and long-standing cooperation with different transport and logistics companies and enable investments in transport equipment and supply chain management technologies;

- *Designing the transport system in cooperation with all stakeholders* – Large mining companies maintain a close relationship with many suppliers and base logistics systems with all partners concerned in the operation.

3. Applying the mining operation model to a sea–land logistics chain

Although specific transit corridor operations would require a business process mapped and designed in detail for a tailored implementation of the transit belt model, successful operations would include the following key features:

- *Frequency of availability of service* – This should be adapted first to known existing and potential volumes and types of cargo, origins and destinations. The design should then be validated with pre- and post-carriage players, including cargo handling and terminal operators, government agencies such as customs and other intervening public agencies, at both ends, in the transit port and the inland dry port. Depending on estimated needs, the belt service could start on the basis of several rounds per week;

- *Choice in modes of transport* – Wherever rail transport would be available, it would be used as the primary mode to develop the system. Examples already exist in other parts of the world

Figure 6.3.   Mineral ore extraction and intermodal transport chain

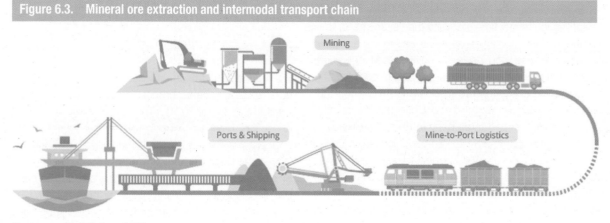

Source: Quintiq Inc., 2013.

of established regular connections between seaports and inland terminals, such as that of the Interporto in Bologna, Italy, where up to 15 trains a day, consisting of container-carrying flat wagons, link this freight village to different seaports in Italy and northern Europe. These regular services also operate as a conveyor belt. Cargoes would be dispatched from the dry port to final destinations by road or carried to the transit port in the case of outbound traffic. Wherever road transport remains the main or only choice, a system should be designed to allow free access to cargoes by qualified trucking companies eligible to function as trusted transit operators according to quality and reliability criteria;

- *Uninterrupted transit flows along the transit belt* – In order for transport of transit cargoes to be fully efficient, they should benefit from an uninterrupted transit status based on a trusted transit operator scheme (see box 6.2). This issue is discussed in recent UNCTAD research (2013) in which a three-pronged approach is proposed, including transit coordination by means of a corridor management arrangement, secure transit operators by means of risk-management and authorized operators customs schemes, and consolidation centres along the corridor.

4. Main drivers in developing a transit belt system

Three main sectors should benefit from a more predictable operation of transit system both in landlocked and transit countries:

Table 6.3.	Presence of main container shipping lines in landlocked developing countries, 2013 (Number of offices)		
Landlocked developing countries by region	Maerskline	MSC	CGM-CMA
Africa (14)	11	8	2
Asia (13)	1	4	-
Latin America (2)	2	2	2
Total (31)	14	14	4

Source: UNCTAD secretariat – Websites of the above-mentioned shipping companies. It would appear that the following landlocked developing countries do not have a local subsidiary office for any of the three largest container shipping lines: Afghanistan, Bhutan, Tajikistan, Lesotho and Swaziland (probably served by agencies based in neighbouring South Africa).

- *Government agencies and control authorities* dealing with trustable and well-controlled operations should find benefits in terms of confidence in trade sectors, which would release important highly qualified resources towards more troublesome traffic. Due to the expected higher volumes of orderly and better-monitored trade, revenues should also increase. Last but not least, a transit belt system offers an opportunity to build a smoothly operating, secured system on the basis of PPPs in both landlocked and transit countries;

- *Traders and manufacturers* in landlocked countries will be the main beneficiaries of reliable and predictable transit connections. A major factor in the possibility to integrate a global value chain resides in a performing logistics system, which in turn requires a last-mile link, in our case, the land transit one. Inventory cost would also benefit from reliable logistics, which would diminish the need for keeping large stocks. Over time, and through better returns on investment for carriers, transport costs should also decrease, resulting in lower freight rates. Predictability also permits stable arrangements, including long-term contracts between shippers and transport service providers, leading to investment in fleets and handling equipment by carriers and freight terminal operators;

- *Liner shipping companies and terminal operators, including seaports and dry ports* – Initially, in particular those operating containerized trade, would find a significant practical advantage in being able to see the containers leave and return to the port on schedule. A straightforward continuous operation would allow boxes to exit the port over shorter dwell times, thereby increasing the handling and storage capacity of sea terminals, and ultimately increasing the efficiency of vessel operations in ports. Finally, higher traffic volumes are of direct interest to sea carriers, eager to attract cargoes from and to inland markets, as shown by their current presence in landlocked countries (see table 6.3) .

5. Prerequisites to support the establishment of a transit belt system

At the conceptual design stage, which would need to be adapted to local needs and capacities in each case, a transit belt system requires three components to be in place and ready for operation:

Box 6.1.   Inland terminals

Inland terminals have become an intrinsic part of the transport system, particularly in gateway regions with a high reliance on trade. The integration of maritime and inland freight distribution systems has favoured the setting of inland ports to integrate with the maritime terminal and support efficient access to the inland market both for inbound and outbound traffic. Since the inland terminal is essentially an extension of some port activities inland, the term "dry port" has gained acceptance. However, there seems to be no consensus on the terminology, resulting in a wide range of terms such as dry ports, inland terminals, inland ports, inland hubs, inland logistics centres and inland freight villages. Regardless of the terminology used, three fundamental characteristics are related to an inland node:

- An intermodal terminal, either rail or barge that has been built or expanded;

- A connection with a port terminal through rail, barge or truck services;

- An array of logistical activities that supports and organizes the freight transited.

The functional specialization of inland terminals has been linked with the cluster formation of logistical activities. They have become excellent locations for consolidating a range of ancillary activities and logistics companies. Inland terminals are part of a port regionalization strategy supporting a more extensive hinterland. Each dry port is confronted with a local or regional economic, geographical and regulatory setting that not only defines the functions taken up by the dry port, but its relations with seaports. Best practices can only be applied successfully by taking into account the relative uniqueness of each dry port setting.

Source: http://people.hofstra.edu/geotrans/eng/ch4en/appl4en/ch4a4en.html.

Box 6.2.   Proposed trusted transit operator scheme

Authorized economic operators, an international production and distribution model set out in the World Customs Organization's SAFE Framework of Standards to Secure and Facilitate Global Trade, would provide a suitable option for developing a mechanism for customs transit procedures tailored to the needs of landlocked country traders. Some basic principles could apply to transit operators, including traders, carriers and logistics operators, in the framework of a regional trusted transit operator programme:

- Automatic inclusion in the programme: Trusted operators with established good compliance histories should be automatically inducted into such programmes upon periodic examination of physical security by the competent governmental authority;

- Targeting the entity, not the transaction: Border management procedures should be designed to focus on risk of the trusted transit operator ending the transaction-by-transaction review;

- Regional certification: Customs authorities within regional schemes should agree to accept a single trusted transit operator application for all the entities the applicant may list in the regional community and to recognize such status granted in partner countries as applicable in all member countries;

- Coordinated border management: Trusted transit operator status should be granted on coordinated grounds by relevant border management agencies to avoid duplicative procedures at borders;

- Assurance of uninterrupted transit: Consignments from trusted transit operator traders to trusted transit operator traders through trusted transit operator logistics providers should not be interrupted by any agency for any reason except in the case of clear evidence of a threat or violation. Assurance of uninterrupted transit should be adopted as a basic feature of all trusted transit operator programmes and be supported by verifiable public metrics.

Source: Adapted from International Chamber of Commerce Draft policy position paper on authorized economic operators (forthcoming).

An inland freight terminal or dry port in the landlocked country or in the transit country along the transit corridor and physically linked to the transit seaport through adequate transport systems (see box 6.1);

A regulatory scheme allowing the uninterrupted transit of goods based on a trusted transit operator scheme that would need to be adopted at the regional or bilateral level (see box 6.2);

A logistics operator scheme ensuring the smooth integration of the different stakeholders and various stages of the transit chain, including public and private players. Wherever transit corridors and corresponding corridor management authorities exist, these would constitute the natural counterpart for the design and development phase of the transit belt system. Corridor authorities could contact traders, logistics operators and shipping lines to design an economically viable system. This may require formalization through bilateral or regional instruments.

D.   CONCLUSIONS

Thanks to the Almaty Programme of Action, the past 10 years have brought considerable progress in terms of knowledge and practical solutions to improve the access of landlocked countries to sea shipping services. Detailed field research has shed light on the rationale and high complexity of transit operations, their fragmentation resulting from stakeholders' individual interests and sometimes the conflicting relationships linking business and the public sector.

Paradoxically, while one of the most important advances in the analysis was achieved by applying a systemic supply chain approach to transit operations, applied solutions have remained partial, affecting only some stages of the transit chain. Improvements have mostly benefited well-

established and better-structured administrations such as customs or port authorities. These have benefited from modern technologies, improving both management techniques and processes equally, through privatization in ports or the ASYCUDA programme in customs. In most cases, however, other sectors, notably land transport industries and ancillary services central to the efficiency of transit operations, i.e. customs brokers and freight forwarders, lag far behind.

The time has come to design a new transit system paradigm for landlocked countries enabling them to operate along more reliable transit supply chains. The transit belt system approach would involve the design of a system open to all transit cargo, based on a trusted transit operator scheme guaranteeing uninterrupted seaport–hinterland transit and vice versa. The proposed approach would not only ensure reliability of the transit operation but would also bring higher quality services and lower traffic with higher volumes, thereby reducing the carbon footprint.

The 10-year Review Conference on the Implementation of the Almaty Programme of Action to be convened in 2014, as decided by the General Assembly in its resolutions 66/214 and 67/222, offers a good opportunity to include the design of such a paradigm in a new global framework for transit transport cooperation for landlocked and transit developing countries in the next decade and to ensure improved access of landlocked developing countries to international maritime transport services.

Transit systems can learn best practices from other transport and logistics systems, such as the maritime industry or mineral ore value and transport chains and combine their own experience to develop reliable and predictable transit logistics chains to increase the shipping connectivity of landlocked developing countries.

REFERENCES

Arvis JF, Carruthers R, Smith G and Willoughby C (2011). Connecting landlocked developing countries to markets: Trade corridors in the 21st century. Direction in Development. World Bank. Washington, D.C.

Arvis, JF, Raballand G and Marteau J (2007). The cost of being landlocked: Logistics costs and supply chain reliability. Direction in Development. World Bank Policy Research Working Paper 4258. June. World Bank. Washington, D.C.

Collier P (2007). Africa's economic growth: Opportunities and constraints. *African Development Review. 19(1):6–25. April.*

Faye M, McArthur J, Sachs J, and Snow T (2004). *The challenges facing landlocked developing countries. Journal of Human Development. 5(1):31–68. March.*

Fitzmaurice M and Hartmann O (2013). *Border Crossing Monitoring along the Northern Corridor.* SSATP (Africa Transport and Policy Programme). Working Paper 96. The International Bank for Reconstruction and Development/World Bank. Washington, D.C. April.

Hansen P and Annovazzi-Jakab L (2008) (UNCTAD) Facilitating cross-border movement of goods: A sustainable approach. In: *The Global Enabling Trade Report 2008. World Economic Forum. Geneva, Switzerland.*

International Chamber of Commerce (forthcoming). Draft policy position paper on authorized economic operators.

Kunaka C, Tanase V, Latrille P and Krausz P (2013). *Quantitative Analysis of Road Transport Agreements (QuARTA). World Bank. Washington, D.C.*

Limao N and Venables AJ (2001). *Infrastructure, geographical disadvantage, transport costs and trade. World Bank Economic Review. 15: 451–479.*

Maersk (2011). Daily Maersk: Introducing absolute reliability. Press release. 9 September.

OHRLLS (2013). *The Development Economics of Landlockedness: Understanding the Development Costs of Being Landlocked. OHRLLS. New York.*

Quintiq Inc. , (2013). Available at http://www.quintiq.com/industries/mining.html?keyword=%2Bcopper%20%2Btransport&matchtype=b&creative=33464640814&gclid=CJ--p7yKk7gCFUxe3godISEAuw (accessed 11 November 2013).

Rubiato Elizalde JM (2001). *Mejores prácticas de transporte intermodal en las Américas: estudio de casos de exportaciones del Mercosur al NAFTA.* Economic Commission for Latin America and the Caribbean. Series Natural Resources and Infrastructure, No. 33. United Nations publication. Sales No. S.01.II.G.154. Santiago.

UNCTAD (2013) *The Way to the Ocean: Transit Corridors Servicing the Trade of Landlocked Developing Countries. Transport and Trade Facilitation Series No. 4.* UNCTAD/DTL/TLB/2012/1. United Nations. New York and Geneva.

World Bank. 2013. *Improving Trade and Transport for Landlocked Developing Countries.* World Bank contributions to implementing the Almaty Programme of Action. A report preparing the ten-year Comprehensive Review. World Bank. Washington, D.C.

STATISTICAL ANNEX

Annex I. World seaborne trade by country group (Millions of tons)

Area	Year	Goods loaded			Total goods loaded	Goods unloaded			Total goods unloaded
		Oil & gas		Dry cargo		Oil & gas		Dry cargo	
		Crude	Petroleum products and gas[a]			Crude	Petroleum products and gas[a]		
Developed economies									
North America	2006	22.2	86.4	436.8	545.4	501.0	155.7	492.1	1 148.7
	2007	24.9	91.3	516.7	632.9	513.5	156.1	453.1	1 122.7
	2008	24.1	119.0	549.4	692.5	481.3	138.9	414.3	1 034.5
	2009	23.9	123.8	498.5	646.1	445.2	132.0	306.4	883.6
	2010	25.5	126.9	530.1	682.5	465.2	113.7	331.0	909.9
	2011	24.3	154.4	599.4	778.0	413.0	113.9	368.6	895.5
	2012	26.0	148.4	626.8	801.2	410.5	114.1	360.8	885.4
Europe	2006	100.9	235.8	768.6	1 105.2	535.6	281.9	1 245.2	2 062.7
	2007	96.9	253.3	776.6	1 126.8	492.2	262.2	1 154.7	1 909.2
	2008	88.2	261.5	751.1	1 100.8	487.9	273.0	1 213.1	1 974.0
	2009	78.1	236.0	693.8	1 008.0	467.9	281.8	935.0	1 684.6
	2010	93.7	266.3	735.1	1 095.1	484.2	280.6	1 044.1	1 808.9
	2011	77.9	269.8	748.7	1 096.3	457.9	336.5	1 049.7	1 844.1
	2012	78.9	271.0	798.4	1 148.3	463.7	318.1	1 067.2	1 849.0
Japan and Israel	2006	0.0	10.0	153.1	163.1	219.3	84.4	559.6	863.3
	2007	0.0	14.4	161.2	175.7	213.3	88.5	560.9	862.6
	2008	0.0	21.0	162.0	183.0	254.7	92.8	548.8	896.2
	2009	0.0	19.3	139.8	159.0	190.7	102.3	417.0	710.0
	2010	0.0	24.7	148.4	173.1	191.1	109.6	480.4	781.2
	2011	0.0	17.4	146.8	164.2	187.1	113.6	478.1	778.8
	2012	0.0	15.5	164.0	179.5	192.9	124.6	508.4	825.9
Australia and New Zealand	2006	9.9	4.2	632.7	646.8	26.2	13.5	50.2	90.0
	2007	13.3	4.0	656.3	673.6	27.0	17.3	51.7	96.0
	2008	16.7	3.8	718.5	739.1	27.3	19.2	56.7	103.2
	2009	12.9	4.8	723.4	741.1	21.5	13.8	60.8	96.1
	2010	16.7	4.3	893.6	914.6	24.8	18.7	60.9	104.5
	2011	15.3	10.4	918.2	943.9	27.5	17.3	69.0	113.9
	2012	16.7	12.5	1 004.8	1 033.9	30.5	16.8	71.1	118.5
Subtotal: developed economies	2006	132.9	336.4	1 991.3	2 460.5	1 282.0	535.5	2 347.2	4 164.7
	2007	135.1	363.0	2 110.8	2 608.9	1 246.0	524.0	2 220.5	3 990.5
	2008	129.0	405.3	2 181.1	2 715.4	1 251.1	523.8	2 233.0	4 007.9
	2009	115.0	383.8	2 055.5	2 554.3	1 125.3	529.9	1 719.2	3 374.4
	2010	135.9	422.3	2 307.3	2 865.4	1 165.4	522.6	1 916.5	3 604.5
	2011	117.5	451.9	2 413.1	2 982.5	1 085.6	581.3	1 965.4	3 632.3
	2012	121.6	447.3	2 594.0	3 162.9	1 097.7	573.7	2 007.5	3 678.8

Area	Year	Goods loaded			Total goods loaded	Goods unloaded			Total goods unloaded
		Oil & gas		Dry cargo		Oil & gas		Dry cargo	
		Crude	Petroleum products and gas[a]			Crude	Petroleum products and gas[a]		
Developing economies									
Economies in transition	2006	123.1	41.3	245.9	410.3	5.6	3.1	61.9	70.6
	2007	124.4	39.9	243.7	407.9	7.3	3.5	66.0	76.8
	2008	138.2	36.7	256.6	431.5	6.3	3.8	79.2	89.3
	2009	142.1	44.4	318.8	505.3	3.5	4.6	85.3	93.3
	2010	150.2	45.9	319.7	515.7	3.5	4.6	114.0	122.1
	2011	132.6	42.0	330.5	505.0	4.2	4.4	148.1	156.7
	2012	136.6	41.1	364.4	542.1	3.8	4.0	141.4	149.2
North Africa	2006	117.4	63.8	77.2	258.5	6.0	13.3	142.0	161.3
	2007	116.1	61.8	80.2	258.1	7.5	14.6	155.4	177.4
	2008	113.2	61.3	77.2	251.8	11.3	16.1	151.1	178.5
	2009	101.1	64.9	71.3	237.3	12.2	14.3	156.2	182.7
	2010	94.4	65.5	76.2	236.1	11.3	14.4	171.1	196.8
	2011	73.7	40.9	83.0	197.7	8.2	14.9	128.0	151.1
	2012	108.5	42.4	90.0	240.8	9.0	15.4	134.4	158.8
Western Africa	2006	110.6	12.6	39.8	162.9	5.4	14.2	62.4	82.0
	2007	110.1	10.3	46.5	166.9	7.6	17.1	67.8	92.6
	2008	111.8	9.1	54.2	175.1	6.8	13.5	61.5	81.8
	2009	104.4	10.5	41.4	156.2	6.8	10.8	66.2	83.8
	2010	112.1	13.5	56.0	181.5	7.4	12.8	92.3	112.5
	2011	115.0	18.1	57.4	190.5	5.1	15.5	87.7	108.3
	2012	111.9	18.4	64.3	194.6	5.7	16.6	91.5	113.8
Eastern Africa	2006	11.8	1.1	29.0	42.0	2.1	7.7	18.2	28.0
	2007	13.6	1.2	23.3	38.1	2.1	8.3	19.8	30.3
	2008	19.7	0.8	27.8	48.2	1.8	7.9	23.8	33.5
	2009	19.0	0.6	18.3	37.8	1.7	9.2	24.4	35.3
	2010	19.0	0.5	29.5	49.1	1.9	8.6	26.3	36.8
	2011	20.0	1.0	16.7	37.7	1.4	9.6	39.0	50.0
	2012	22.0	1.1	16.8	39.9	1.5	10.4	42.1	54.0
Central Africa	2006	114.0	2.6	6.3	122.8	2.1	1.7	7.3	11.2
	2007	122.7	2.6	7.8	133.1	2.8	1.9	7.7	12.3
	2008	134.2	5.8	9.0	149.0	1.7	2.8	8.9	13.5
	2009	129.3	2.0	8.5	139.7	1.9	2.7	10.9	15.5
	2010	125.3	7.2	9.7	142.1	1.4	2.3	8.3	12.0
	2011	129.3	6.0	9.3	144.7	1.4	3.8	12.5	17.8
	2012	127.3	6.8	11.4	145.4	0.9	4.4	14.2	19.4

Area	Year	Goods loaded				Goods unloaded			
		Oil & gas		Dry cargo	Total goods loaded	Oil & gas		Dry cargo	Total goods unloaded
		Crude	Petroleum products and gas[a]			Crude	Petroleum products and gas[a]		
Southern Africa	2006	0.0	5.9	129.9	135.8	25.6	2.6	39.1	67.4
	2007	0.0	5.9	129.9	135.8	25.6	2.6	39.1	67.4
	2008	0.3	6.2	136.0	142.5	23.4	3.1	42.8	69.3
	2009	0.3	5.1	131.5	136.8	22.0	2.7	44.8	69.4
	2010	0.3	5.4	139.5	145.1	20.8	2.3	35.7	58.8
	2011	0.0	2.5	150.7	153.2	21.7	2.5	26.8	51.0
	2012	0.5	3.9	162.1	166.5	18.9	5.0	37.9	61.7
Subtotal: developing Africa	2006	353.8	86.0	282.2	721.9	41.3	39.4	269.1	349.8
	2007	362.5	81.8	287.6	732.0	45.7	44.5	289.8	380.0
	2008	379.2	83.3	304.2	766.7	45.0	43.5	288.1	376.6
	2009	354.0	83.0	271.0	708.0	44.6	39.7	302.5	386.8
	2010	351.1	92.0	310.9	754.0	42.7	40.5	333.7	416.9
	2011	338.0	68.5	317.2	723.7	37.8	46.3	294.1	378.2
	2012	370.1	72.6	344.6	787.3	35.9	51.7	320.1	407.7
Caribbean and Central America	2006	108.4	34.6	73.5	216.6	18.5	42.1	101.5	162.2
	2007	100.4	32.4	75.2	208.1	38.8	44.5	103.1	186.5
	2008	89.1	41.0	84.4	214.5	35.7	47.0	103.5	186.2
	2009	75.1	27.4	71.0	173.4	33.6	46.8	87.2	167.6
	2010	75.9	29.3	81.3	186.5	34.7	51.4	99.4	185.5
	2011	80.1	31.7	89.0	200.8	35.7	47.5	121.2	204.4
	2012	75.0	33.9	98.3	207.2	37.7	49.8	126.0	213.5
South America: northern and eastern seaboards	2006	110.8	49.1	499.5	659.4	16.9	10.3	116.2	143.5
	2007	120.2	47.8	530.7	698.7	19.9	10.8	125.3	156.1
	2008	112.6	40.5	560.2	713.2	22.7	13.9	128.3	165.0
	2009	119.0	38.8	524.4	682.2	19.6	14.5	94.8	128.9
	2010	123.5	42.6	620.6	786.8	17.5	11.4	144.2	173.1
	2011	126.7	36.3	661.6	824.6	22.2	13.1	163.2	198.5
	2012	125.6	40.8	681.0	847.4	25.0	13.8	159.1	197.9
South America: western seaboard	2006	32.1	10.2	112.4	154.8	14.1	7.7	45.9	67.8
	2007	31.6	10.5	118.3	160.4	17.2	8.7	47.5	73.4
	2008	32.9	11.5	136.0	180.4	15.8	9.0	60.9	85.7
	2009	31.7	7.8	134.7	174.2	11.1	12.3	52.0	75.4
	2010	42.1	13.2	144.0	199.3	17.6	12.0	60.6	90.1
	2011	47.1	15.5	151.3	213.9	13.2	13.3	78.9	105.4
	2012	50.1	16.9	165.6	232.6	14.8	15.8	96.6	127.1

Annex I. World seaborne trade by country group (Millions of tons) (continued)

Annex I.   World seaborne trade by country group (Millions of tons) *(continued)*

Area	Year	Goods loaded				Goods unloaded			
		Oil & gas		Dry cargo	Total goods loaded	Oil & gas		Dry cargo	Total goods unloaded
		Crude	Petroleum products and gas[a]			Crude	Petroleum products and gas[a]		
Subtotal: developing America	2006	251.3	93.9	685.5	1 030.7	49.6	60.1	263.7	373.4
	2007	252.3	90.7	724.2	1 067.1	76.0	64.0	275.9	415.9
	2008	234.6	93.0	780.6	1 108.2	74.2	69.9	292.7	436.8
	2009	225.7	74.0	730.1	1 029.8	64.4	73.6	234.0	371.9
	2010	241.6	85.1	846.0	1 172.6	69.9	74.7	304.2	448.7
	2011	253.8	83.5	901.9	1 239.2	71.1	73.9	363.4	508.3
	2012	250.7	91.6	944.9	1 287.2	77.5	79.4	381.6	538.5
Western Asia	2006	729.1	158.1	151.0	1 038.2	27.0	50.3	296.5	373.8
	2007	753.7	155.2	179.5	1 088.5	34.4	51.2	344.4	430.0
	2008	714.0	159.8	181.9	1 055.7	30.6	54.5	349.8	434.9
	2009	717.0	135.8	172.4	1 025.2	22.3	53.1	320.1	395.6
	2010	720.4	152.7	183.8	1 056.9	30.2	55.6	343.7	429.6
	2011	737.4	147.9	212.1	1 097.4	22.3	54.6	365.3	442.2
	2012	784.0	153.6	229.1	1 166.7	20.9	59.2	397.4	477.5
Southern and Eastern Asia	2006	132.3	102.5	922.6	1 157.3	411.3	104.0	1 482.0	1 997.4
	2007	128.1	104.7	959.7	1 192.5	455.0	106.9	1 674.7	2 236.7
	2008	130.7	103.0	943.0	1 176.7	420.5	124.3	1 811.2	2 356.0
	2009	107.6	115.2	823.7	1 046.5	498.8	126.1	2 034.0	2 659.0
	2010	128.7	111.8	964.0	1 204.5	514.5	143.2	2 198.7	2 856.4
	2011	112.5	110.1	952.2	1 174.7	546.7	154.0	2 357.2	3 057.9
	2012	64.9	114.9	955.8	1 135.6	571.9	163.8	2 563.1	3 298.7
South-Eastern Asia	2006	59.8	96.5	721.3	877.6	114.4	94.4	326.8	535.6
	2007	56.4	98.2	779.0	933.6	131.3	102.6	363.0	596.9
	2008	58.1	75.8	837.3	971.2	114.6	108.0	348.5	571.0
	2009	47.7	94.7	840.3	982.7	115.2	90.7	332.0	537.9
	2010	58.4	73.7	701.0	833.2	107.0	134.2	311.0	552.3
	2011	66.1	130.2	858.3	1 054.6	128.8	119.5	360.4	608.7
	2012	55.8	129.1	889.6	1 074.5	121.0	118.5	380.5	620.0
Subtotal: developing Asia	2006	921.2	357.0	1 794.8	3 073.1	552.7	248.8	2 105.3	2 906.8
	2007	938.2	358.1	1 918.3	3 214.6	620.7	260.8	2 382.1	3 263.6
	2008	902.7	338.6	1 962.2	3 203.6	565.6	286.8	2 509.5	3 361.9
	2009	872.3	345.8	1 836.3	3 054.3	636.3	269.9	2 686.2	3 592.4
	2010	907.5	338.3	1 848.8	3 094.6	651.8	333.1	2 853.4	3 838.2
	2011	916.0	388.2	2 022.6	3 326.7	697.8	328.0	3 082.9	4 108.8
	2012	904.7	397.5	2 074.5	3 376.7	713.8	341.5	3 340.9	4 396.2

Annex I.   World seaborne trade by country group (Millions of tons) *(continued)*

| Area | Year | Goods loaded | | | Total goods loaded | Goods unloaded | | | Total goods unloaded |
| | | Oil & gas | | Dry cargo | | Oil & gas | | Dry cargo | |
		Crude	Petroleum products and gas[a]			Crude	Petroleum products and gas[a]		
Developing Oceania	2006	1.2	0.1	2.5	3.8	0.0	6.7	6.2	12.9
	2007	0.9	0.1	2.5	7.1	0.0	7.0	6.5	13.5
	2008	1.5	0.1	2.6	4.2	0.0	7.1	6.7	13.8
	2009	1.5	0.2	4.6	6.3	0.0	3.6	9.5	13.1
	2010	1.5	0.2	4.8	6.5	0.0	3.7	9.7	13.4
	2011	1.6	0.2	5.3	7.1	0.0	3.9	9.6	13.5
	2012	1.6	0.8	6.6	9.0	0.0	4.6	8.6	13.3
Subtotal: developing economies and territories	2006	1 527.5	537.1	2 765.0	4 829.5	643.6	355.1	2 644.3	3 642.9
	2007	1 553.9	530.7	2 932.6	5 020.8	742.4	376.3	2 954.3	4 073.0
	2008	1 518.0	515.1	3 049.6	5 082.6	684.9	407.2	3 097.0	4 189.1
	2009	1 453.5	502.9	2 842.0	4 798.4	745.3	386.9	3 232.1	4 364.2
	2010	1 501.6	515.6	3 010.5	5 027.8	764.4	452.0	3 500.9	4 717.3
	2011	1 509.4	540.4	3 247.0	5 296.8	806.7	452.1	3 750.0	5 008.8
	2012	1 527.2	562.5	3 370.6	5 460.3	827.3	477.2	4 051.2	5 355.7
World total	2006	1 783.4	914.8	5 002.1	7 700.3	1 931.2	893.7	5 053.4	7 878.3
	2007	1 813.4	933.5	5 287.1	8 034.1	1 995.7	903.8	5 240.8	8 140.2
	2008	1 785.2	957.0	5 487.2	8 229.5	1 942.3	934.9	5 409.2	8 286.3
	2009	1 710.5	931.1	5 216.4	7 858.0	1 874.1	921.3	5 036.6	7 832.0
	2010	1 787.7	983.8	5 637.5	8 408.9	1 933.2	979.2	5 531.4	8 443.8
	2011	1 759.5	1 034.2	5 990.5	8 784.3	1 896.5	1 037.7	5 863.5	8 797.7
	2012	1 785.4	1 050.9	6 329.0	9 165.3	1 928.7	1 054.9	6 200.1	9 183.7

Source: Compiled by the UNCTAD secretariat on the basis of data supplied by reporting countries, as published on the relevant government and port industry websites and by specialist sources. Figures for 2012 are estimates based on preliminary data or on the last year for which data were available. Historical statistics on world total volume of international seaborne trade are available electronically at http://stats.unctad.org/seabornetrade.

[a] Including LNG, LPG, naphtha, gasoline, jet fuel, kerosene, light oil, heavy fuel oil and others.

Annex II. (a) Merchant fleets of the world by flags of registration, groups of economies and types of ship, as at 1 January 2013 (Thousands of GT)					
	Total	Oil tankers	Bulk carriers	General-cargo ships	Containerships	Other types
DEVELOPING ECONOMIES OF AFRICA						
Algeria	757	11	88	66		592
Angola	170	10		10		150
Benin	1					1
Cameroon	327			1		326
Cape Verde	35	3		13		19
Comoros	686	113	93	373	4	102
Congo	1					1
Côte d'Ivoire	2	1				1
Democratic Republic of the Congo	9	1		0		7
Djibouti	7	3		0		3
Egypt	1 171	149	595	140	52	236
Equatorial Guinea	16	4		4		8
Eritrea	12	2		10		1
Ethiopia	160	27		133		
Gabon	211	0		5		205
Gambia	11					11
Ghana	22	2		4		16
Guinea	4					4
Guinea-Bissau	2			1		1
Kenya	9	1				8
Liberia	127 109	39 100	36 834	1 573	40 386	9 216
Libya	753	522		8		224
Madagascar	22	4		12		6
Mauritania	1			0		1
Mauritius	104	43		0		61
Morocco	254	5		12	47	190
Mozambique	19			11		8
Namibia	8			5		3
Nigeria	2 120	299	10	10		1 801
São Tomé and Principe	20			19		1
Senegal	9	0		1		8
Seychelles	337	293		4		40
Sierra Leone	1 157	166	172	488	222	110
Somalia	1			0		0
South Africa	70	12		0		58
Sudan	25			21		3
Togo	536	267	41	166	20	42
Tunisia	359		17	88		254
United Republic of Tanzania	4 774	4 360	67	271	38	39
DEVELOPING ECONOMIES OF AFRICA Total	**141 290**	**45 397**	**37 917**	**3 453**	**40 767**	**13 756**

Annex II. (a) Merchant fleets of the world by flags of registration, groups of economies and types of ship, as at 1 January 2013 (Thousands of GT) *(continued)*					
	Total	Oil tankers	Bulk carriers	General-cargo ships	Containerships	Other types
DEVELOPING ECONOMIES OF AMERICA						
Anguilla	1			1		
Antigua and Barbuda	10 934	38	949	4 044	5 596	306
Argentina	350	200	14	53		83
Aruba	0					0
Bahamas	54 511	18 433	10 370	826	1 550	23 332
Barbados	1 023	144	397	223	73	185
Belize	1 638	92	367	856	30	293
Bolivia (Plurinational State of)	322	42	201	63	5	10
Brazil	2 303	971	241	201	308	582
British Virgin Islands	7			1		6
Cayman Islands	3 592	298	859	4		2 431
Chile	549	238	160	67	30	55
Colombia	85	5		46		33
Costa Rica	5			2		3
Cuba	30	0		23		7
Curaçao	1 297	117	40	146	6	988
Dominica	1 143	353	691	40		60
Dominican Republic	99	80		14		5
Ecuador	239	205		5		30
El Salvador	0					0
Falkland Islands (Malvinas)	10			0		10
Grenada	1			1		1
Guatemala	1	0				1
Guyana	34	6		16		12
Haiti	1			1		
Honduras	470	89	17	242	2	121
Jamaica	161		81	20	58	2
Mexico	1 336	638	109	40		549
Netherlands Antilles	5					5
Nicaragua	2	1		0		1
Panama	227 754	34 016	116 085	6 918	34 451	36 285
Paraguay	54	4		36	7	7
Peru	269	186		17	12	53
Saint Kitts and Nevis	898	183	228	287	16	185
Saint Vincent and the Grenadines	3 505	66	952	1 101	193	1 194
Suriname	5	2		3		0
Trinidad and Tobago	45	3		1		42
Turks and Caicos Islands	1			0		1

Annex II. (a) Merchant fleets of the world by flags of registration, groups of economies and types of ship, as at 1 January 2013 (Thousands of GT) *(continued)*						
	Total	Oil tankers	Bulk carriers	General-cargo ships	Containerships	Other types
Uruguay	64	7		8		48
Venezuela (Bolivarian Republic of)	1 111	450	100	194	5	361
DEVELOPING ECONOMIES OF AMERICA Total	**313 853**	**56 865**	**131 861**	**15 500**	**42 341**	**67 285**
DEVELOPING ECONOMIES OF ASIA						
Afghanistan	2					2
Bahrain	534	81	33	1	255	164
Bangladesh	1 049	44	678	265	28	34
Brunei Darussalam	542	5		6		531
Cambodia	1 731	54	202	1 310	28	137
China	44 223	8 166	22 928	3 421	5 221	4 487
China, Hong Kong SAR	77 904	14 243	44 474	2 015	14 479	2 692
China, Macao SAR	2					2
China, Taiwan Province of	2 338	142	1 156	106	801	131
Democratic People's Republic of Korea	701	61	47	547	11	36
India	9 534	4 734	2 746	560	269	1 226
Indonesia	10 776	2 361	1 330	2 658	1 233	3 194
Iran (Islamic Republic of)	1 492	156	126	448	631	131
Iraq	92	18		23		50
Jordan	73			52		21
Kuwait	2 473	1 886	46	7	313	221
Lao People's Democratic Republic	0			0		
Lebanon	133	0	14	109	5	3
Malaysia	7 817	2 577	140	325	466	4 308
Maldives	83	7		61	7	7
Mongolia	426	42	169	167	12	35
Myanmar	164	3		139		22
Oman	27	2		2		23
Pakistan	391	175	177	13		26
Philippines	4 711	283	2 400	789	296	943
Qatar	903	303	70	1	235	295
Republic of Korea	11 149	781	6 530	1 148	1 037	1 652
Saudi Arabia	1 157	377		220	172	388
Singapore	58 090	20 411	16 507	1 207	11 379	8 586
Sri Lanka	173	8	58	71	16	20
Syrian Arab Republic	111		12	96		3
Thailand	3 040	886	894	400	218	643
Turkey	6 858	1 268	3 056	1 567	541	426
United Arab Emirates	990	203	64	70	247	405

Annex II. (a)   Merchant fleets of the world by flags of registration, groups of economies and types of ship, as at 1 January 2013 (Thousands of GT) *(continued)*

	Total	Oil tankers	Bulk carriers	General-cargo ships	Containerships	Other types
Viet Nam	4 512	925	978	1 871	147	590
Yemen	221	17		5		199
DEVELOPING ECONOMIES OF ASIA Total	**254 420**	**60 220**	**104 837**	**19 684**	**38 045**	**31 635**
DEVELOPING ECONOMIES OF OCEANIA						
Cook Islands	330	0	190	110	5	25
Fiji	30			9		21
French Polynesia	14			11		3
Guam	1					1
Kiribati	290	48	30	102	4	107
Marshall Islands	85 443	32 263	31 405	972	7 428	13 375
Micronesia (Federated States of)	9			8		1
New Caledonia	4			2		2
Northern Mariana Islands	0					0
Papua New Guinea	115	2		73	21	19
Samoa	11			9		2
Solomon Islands	5			2		2
Tonga	42	3		31		9
Tuvalu	1 438	618	219	125	3	473
Vanuatu	2 225	4	1 115	34	25	1 046
DEVELOPING ECONOMIES OF OCEANIA Total	**89 956**	**32 937**	**32 958**	**1 488**	**7 487**	**15 086**
DEVELOPED ECONOMIES						
Australia	1 612	85	136	141		1 251
Austria	0					0
Belgium	4 532	987	1 691	203	99	1 551
Bermuda	11 503	1 256	2 067	17	513	7 649
Bulgaria	357	8	246	83		20
Canada	2 831	632	234	1 001	15	950
Cyprus	20 464	3 364	10 085	1 087	4 434	1 493
Denmark	11 530	2 931	166	455	6 788	1 191
Estonia	290	10		22	3	256
Faroe Islands	218	36		56	24	102
Finland	1 737	338	118	766	10	505
France	6 197	1 975	178	266	2 117	1 660
Germany	15 053	372	442	337	13 354	548
Gibraltar	2 451	447	236	682	520	566
Greece	42 569	24 129	13 844	363	2 232	2 002
Greenland	5			3		3
Iceland	16	0		1		15
Ireland	177	0	75	71		30
Isle of Man	13 759	5 931	4 686	394	618	2 130
Israel	291	3		11	268	9

Annex II. (a) Merchant fleets of the world by flags of registration, groups of economies and types of ship, as at 1 January 2013 (Thousands of GT) *(continued)*					
	Total	Oil tankers	Bulk carriers	General-cargo ships	Containerships	Other types
Italy	18 098	4 579	4 309	2 750	861	5 598
Japan	15 732	2 691	4 897	1 801	100	6 244
Latvia	152	7		16		129
Lithuania	354	1	64	194	10	85
Luxembourg	1 498	209	58	456	166	609
Malta	44 113	13 697	18 966	2 181	4 707	4 562
Monaco	0					0
Netherlands	7 759	297	471	3 424	1 169	2 397
New Zealand	172	64		31	14	64
Norway	17 112	4 208	3 648	616	42	8 597
Poland	102	6		37		58
Portugal	1 131	310	86	150	33	553
Reunion	2					2
Romania	141	8		73		60
Slovakia	33			28		5
Slovenia	3					3
Spain	2 792	588	8	237	53	1 906
Sweden	3 243	337	17	1 161		1 728
Switzerland	714	51	511	82	56	14
United Kingdom	19 417	1 485	2 092	1 256	10 243	4 341
United States	11 279	2 244	264	2 573	2 530	3 669
Spain	522	37	1	48	5	431
Sweden	417	56	1	90	–	270
Switzerland	39	4	21	9	2	3
United Kingdom	1 346	104	38	181	186	837
United States of America	3 462	71	9	158	66	3 158
DEVELOPED ECONOMIES Total	**279 438**	**73 283**	**69 593**	**23 027**	**50 978**	**62 557**
TRANSITION ECONOMIES						
Albania	63			62		1
Azerbaijan	768	250		131		386
Belarus	34		31			3
Croatia	1 382	591	629	36		126
Georgia	321	17	39	226	6	33
Kazakhstan	104	53				51
Montenegro	51		43	6		2
Republic of Moldova	480	9	57	366	8	40
Russian Federation	6 052	1 478	296	2 453	63	1 762
Turkmenistan	75	29		9		37
Ukraine	595	23		357		215
TRANSITION ECONOMIES Total	**9 924**	**2 451**	**1 094**	**3 646**	**76**	**2 657**
Unknown flag	**2 652**	**414**	**28**	**361**	**11**	**1 839**
World total	**1 091 534**	**271 568**	**378 287**	**67 159**	**179 706**	**194 814**

Annex II. (b) Merchant fleets of the world by flags of registration, groups of economies and types of ship, as at 1 January 2013 (Thousands of DWT)						
	Total	Oil tankers	Bulk carriers	General-cargo ships	Containerships	Other types
DEVELOPING ECONOMIES OF AFRICA						
Algeria	739	17	150	66		507
Angola	312	16		13		283
Benin	0					0
Cameroon	655			2		653
Cape Verde	28	4		18		5
Comoros	937	218	159	454	5	101
Congo	0					0
Côte d'Ivoire	10	1				9
Democratic Republic of the Congo	11	2		1		8
Djibouti	7	5		1		1
Egypt	1 722	255	1 075	139	63	190
Equatorial Guinea	13	7		3		4
Eritrea	14	3		10		0
Ethiopia	223	42		181		
Gabon	404	0		5		399
Gambia	3					3
Ghana	25	4		5		16
Guinea	6					6
Guinea-Bissau	1			1		
Kenya	7	2				5
Liberia	198 032	71 083	67 047	2 058	47 298	10 545
Libya	1 408	989		12		408
Madagascar	26	6		15		5
Mauritania	1			1		0
Mauritius	135	76				59
Morocco	128	7		11	55	55
Mozambique	21			15		6
Namibia	3			2		1
Nigeria	3 600	485	13	15		3 086
São Tomé and Principe	27			26		1
Senegal	5	0		2		3
Seychelles	585	529		4		53
Sierra Leone	1 521	254	280	607	251	128
Somalia	1			0		0
South Africa	63	17		0		45
Sudan	28			26		1
Togo	832	484	65	228	24	31
Tunisia	367		26	48		292
United Republic of Tanzania	8 815	8 291	105	350	49	20
DEVELOPING ECONOMIES OF AFRICA Total	**220 716**	**82 799**	**68 922**	**4 318**	**47 745**	**16 932**

Annex II. (b) Merchant fleets of the world by flags of registration, groups of economies and types of ship, as at 1 January 2013 (Thousands of DWT) *(continued)*					
	Total	**Oil tankers**	**Bulk carriers**	**General-cargo ships**	**Containerships**	**Other types**
DEVELOPING ECONOMIES OF AMERICA						
Anguilla	1			1		
Antigua and Barbuda	14 142	57	1 565	5 207	7 057	255
Argentina	533	351	24	77		81
Aruba	0					0
Bahamas	73 702	34 105	17 754	845	1 801	19 198
Barbados	1 485	220	686	305	107	167
Belize	2 196	148	591	1 112	44	300
Bolivia (Plurinational State of)	536	67	370	87	7	6
Brazil	3 232	1 569	398	247	398	621
British Virgin Islands	2			1		1
Cayman Islands	4 310	552	1 368	6		2 384
Chile	804	399	262	64	38	40
Colombia	115	9		62		44
Costa Rica	2			1		0
Cuba	40	1		32		7
Curaçao	2 133	169	74	212	9	1 670
Dominica	2 037	618	1 301	61		57
Dominican Republic	166	149		16		1
Ecuador	364	343		6		15
El Salvador						
Falkland Islands (Malvinas)	6			1		5
Grenada	1			1		0
Guatemala	1	1				0
Guyana	42	8		19		14
Haiti	1			1		
Honduras	645	161	28	350	2	104
Jamaica	224		128	24	72	1
Mexico	1 835	1 054	195	21		565
Netherlands Antilles	4					4
Nicaragua	3	1		1		0
Panama	350 506	62 112	212 504	9 131	38 183	28 576
Paraguay	56	6		42	6	1
Peru	403	302		21	15	66
Saint Kitts and Nevis	1 231	292	374	323	19	222
Saint Vincent and the Grenadines	4 919	103	1 563	1 496	252	1 505
Suriname	7	3		3		0
Trinidad and Tobago	26	4		1		21
Turks and Caicos Islands	0			0		0

Annex II. (b) Merchant fleets of the world by flags of registration, groups of economies and types of ship, as at 1 January 2013 (Thousands of DWT) *(continued)*

	Total	Oil tankers	Bulk carriers	General-cargo ships	Containerships	Other types
Uruguay	43	10		11		22
Venezuela (Bolivarian Republic of)	1 679	783	175	308	6	407
DEVELOPING ECONOMIES OF AMERICA Total	**467 431**	**103 599**	**239 361**	**20 092**	**48 014**	**56 365**
DEVELOPING ECONOMIES OF ASIA						
Afghanistan	2					2
Bahrain	640	154	44	2	280	160
Bangladesh	1 656	80	1 137	368	38	33
Brunei Darussalam	449	7		8		434
Cambodia	2 319	82	324	1 780	36	98
China	68 642	14 104	39 654	4 490	6 274	4 120
China, Hong Kong SAR	129 806	26 115	81 416	2 662	16 473	3 140
China, Macao SAR	2					2
China, Taiwan Province of	3 487	210	2 130	152	926	68
Democratic People's Republic of Korea	1 008	100	82	782	14	30
India	15 876	8 569	4 908	799	345	1 254
Indonesia	14 267	3 894	2 303	3 362	1 629	3 080
Iran (Islamic Republic of)	1 965	263	218	601	774	109
Iraq	110	28		31		51
Jordan	61			53		8
Kuwait	4 169	3 510	78	7	330	244
Lao People's Democratic Republic	2			2		
Lebanon	142	1	23	108	6	3
Malaysia	10 508	4 588	243	433	585	4 660
Maldives	124	15		92	9	7
Mongolia	643	73	277	235	16	42
Myanmar	182	5		163		15
Oman	14	3		2		10
Pakistan	693	322	321	18		31
Philippines	6 417	441	3 927	1 057	352	641
Qatar	1 224	546	116	1	266	295
Republic of Korea	17 720	1 308	12 087	1 693	1 304	1 328
Saudi Arabia	1 421	659		214	185	362
Singapore	89 697	36 893	30 164	1 455	13 408	7 779
Sri Lanka	239	15	99	94	17	14
Syrian Arab Republic	169		19	149		2
Thailand	4 811	1 590	1 435	584	287	914
Turkey	10 215	2 185	5 279	1 783	683	285
United Arab Emirates	1 287	341	86	77	271	511

Annex II. (b) Merchant fleets of the world by flags of registration, groups of economies and types of ship, as at 1 January 2013 (Thousands of DWT) *(continued)*

	Total	Oil tankers	Bulk carriers	General-cargo ships	Containerships	Other types
Viet Nam	7 284	1 532	1 631	3 092	193	835
Yemen	442	28		4		410
DEVELOPING ECONOMIES OF ASIA Total	**397 695**	**107 662**	**188 000**	**26 353**	**44 701**	**30 977**
DEVELOPING ECONOMIES OF OCEANIA						
Cook Islands	479	0	302	148	6	23
Fiji	15			6		9
French Polynesia	10			9		1
Guam	0					0
Kiribati	367	81	47	131	4	103
Marshall Islands	140 016	59 377	57 022	1 230	8 761	13 626
Micronesia (Federated States of)	8			7		1
New Caledonia	4			3		0
Northern Mariana Islands	0					0
Papua New Guinea	138	3		91	29	15
Samoa	10			9		0
Solomon Islands	3			2		1
Tonga	47	3		40		4
Tuvalu	2 351	1 123	361	163	5	698
Vanuatu	2 887	6	1 832	37	29	983
DEVELOPING ECONOMIES OF OCEANIA Total	**146 335**	**60 595**	**59 564**	**1 877**	**8 833**	**15 465**
DEVELOPED ECONOMIES						
Australia	1 947	133	193	132		1 489
Austria						
Belgium	6 913	1 906	3 278	127	122	1 479
Bermuda	12 378	2 316	4 016	7	539	5 501
Bulgaria	483	11	383	76		13
Canada	3 371	1 035	371	1 362	15	589
Cyprus	31 706	5 854	18 161	1 329	5 300	1 063
Denmark	13 860	4 781	326	270	7 577	906
Estonia	75	16		15	3	41
Faroe Islands	219	52		72	30	64
Finland	1 338	569	180	426	14	150
France	7 434	3 655	344	123	2 342	971
Germany	17 128	567	856	260	15 100	346
Gibraltar	2 829	660	408	745	635	380
Greece	75 424	45 278	26 134	330	2 448	1 234
Greenland	4			3		1
Iceland	11	0		1		9
Ireland	244	0	113	103		28
Isle of Man	22 629	10 638	8 821	441	627	2 103
Israel	318	5		14	294	5
Italy	20 612	7 865	7 886	1 626	961	2 273

Annex II. (b) Merchant fleets of the world by flags of registration, groups of economies and types of ship, as at 1 January 2013 (Thousands of DWT) *(continued)*					
	Total	**Oil tankers**	**Bulk carriers**	**General-cargo ships**	**Containerships**	**Other types**
Japan	20 409	5 013	9 020	2 798	100	3 478
Latvia	72	9		22		42
Lithuania	289	2	94	129	14	51
Luxembourg	1 601	329	97	219	194	762
Malta	68 831	24 647	33 978	2 476	5 291	2 440
Monaco						
Netherlands	8 712	462	813	4 309	1 359	1 769
New Zealand	166	98		23	17	28
Norway	20 974	7 443	6 125	506	47	6 854
Poland	75	9		33		34
Portugal	1 225	564	149	202	40	270
Reunion	1					1
Romania	149	11		61		76
Slovakia	46			40		6
Slovenia	1					1
Spain	2 572	1 017	11	198	66	1 281
Sweden	1 887	511	21	688		667
Switzerland	1 144	80	865	106	79	15
United Kingdom	21 095	2 320	3 899	980	11 206	2 690
United States	12 353	3 669	435	2 761	2 767	2 723
DEVELOPED ECONOMIES Total	**380 526**	**131 525**	**126 974**	**23 011**	**57 186**	**41 830**
TRANSITION ECONOMIES						
Albania	93			92		1
Azerbaijan	684	355		131		197
Belarus	58			55		2
Croatia	2 269	1 092	1 096	43		39
Georgia	442	29	61	314	7	31
Kazakhstan	128	91				37
Montenegro	77		70	6		1
Republic of Moldova	566	16	102	410	10	27
Russian Federation	6 784	2 112	422	2 783	66	1 401
Turkmenistan	92	41		10		41
Ukraine	607	40		400		167
TRANSITION ECONOMIES Total	**11 801**	**3 777**	**1 807**	**4 189**	**83**	**1 945**
Unknown flag	**4 279**	**786**	**44**	**504**	**14**	**2 931**
World total	**1 628 783**	**490 743**	**684 673**	**80 345**	**206 577**	**166 445**

Annex II. (c) Merchant fleets of the world by flags of registration, groups of economies and types of ship, as at 1 January 2013 (Number of ships)						
	Total	Oil tankers	Bulk carriers	General-cargo ships	Containerships	Other types
DEVELOPING ECONOMIES OF AFRICA						
Algeria	111	9	4	12		86
Angola	49	8		15		26
Benin	5					5
Cameroon	16			4		12
Cape Verde	39	3		18		18
Comoros	272	17	4	138	1	112
Congo	5					5
Côte d'Ivoire	9	2				7
Democratic Republic of the Congo	13	1		1		11
Djibouti	14	1		1		12
Egypt	384	39	17	35	3	290
Equatorial Guinea	28	3		7		18
Eritrea	9	1		4		4
Ethiopia	10	1		9		
Gabon	24	1		10		13
Gambia	8					8
Ghana	42	2		8		32
Guinea	1					1
Guinea-Bissau	9			7		2
Kenya	23	2				21
Liberia	3 144	749	819	140	1 001	435
Libya	91	12		7		72
Madagascar	39	4		23		12
Mauritania	5			2		3
Mauritius	26	2		1		23
Morocco	85	1		7	6	71
Mozambique	25			11		14
Namibia	6			2		4
Nigeria	374	65	1	16		292
São Tomé and Principe	18			15		3
Senegal	21	1		3		17
Seychelles	24	8		6		10
Sierra Leone	392	54	12	221	9	96
Somalia	4			1		3
South Africa	71	5		2		64
Sudan	17			3		14
Togo	101	10	3	63	4	21
Tunisia	59		1	13		45
United Republic of Tanzania	198	50	6	82	6	54
DEVELOPING ECONOMIES OF AFRICA Total	**5 771**	**1 051**	**867**	**887**	**1 030**	**1 936**

	Total	Oil tankers	Bulk carriers	General-cargo ships	Containerships	Other types
DEVELOPING ECONOMIES OF AMERICA						
Anguilla	2			2		
Antigua and Barbuda	1 302	6	39	774	403	80
Argentina	148	27	1	17		103
Aruba	1					1
Bahamas	1 446	270	322	161	53	640
Barbados	133	10	16	71	4	32
Belize	829	64	23	447	6	289
Bolivia (Plurinational State of)	92	14	5	53	1	19
Brazil	619	47	11	66	13	482
British Virgin Islands	20			3		17
Cayman Islands	174	6	27	3		138
Chile	172	14	8	41	3	106
Colombia	94	7		25		62
Costa Rica	10			2		8
Cuba	39	1		14		24
Curaçao	127	6	1	48	1	71
Dominica	117	16	16	28		57
Dominican Republic	27	1		6		20
Ecuador	80	37		7		36
El Salvador	2					2
Falkland Islands (Malvinas) [a]	3			1		2
Grenada	6			3		3
Guatemala	6	1				5
Guyana	52	4		31		17
Haiti	3			3		
Honduras	645	100	1	332	1	211
Jamaica	26		4	4	9	9
Mexico	525	38	4	20		463
Nicaragua	5	1		1		3
Panama	8 580	955	2 772	1 601	734	2 518
Paraguay	47	4		26	2	15
Peru	78	10		2	1	65
Saint Kitts and Nevis	246	41	12	99	2	92
Saint Vincent and the Grenadines	1 046	21	51	340	21	613
Suriname	10	3		5		2
Trinidad and Tobago	104	1		3		100
Turks and Caicos Islands	3			1		2

Annex II. (c) Merchant fleets of the world by flags of registration, groups of economies and types of ship, as at 1 January 2013 (Number of ships) *(continued)*						
	Total	Oil tankers	Bulk carriers	General-cargo ships	Containerships	Other types
Uruguay	44	4		6		34
Venezuela (Bolivarian Republic of)	244	20	2	38	2	182
DEVELOPING ECONOMIES OF AMERICA Total	**17 107**	**1 729**	**3 315**	**4 284**	**1 256**	**6 523**
DEVELOPING ECONOMIES OF ASIA						
Afghanistan	3					3
Bahrain	232	5	2	4	5	216
Bangladesh	269	61	27	111	4	66
Brunei Darussalam	81	3		17		61
Cambodia	785	31	18	628	7	101
China	3 727	526	778	805	193	1 425
China, Hong Kong SAR	2 221	323	1 014	228	319	337
China, Macao SAR	1					1
China, Taiwan Province of	328	28	29	65	27	179
Democratic People's Republic of Korea	265	33	3	198	2	29
India	1 385	117	76	378	15	799
Indonesia	6 293	477	57	1 943	175	3 641
Iran (Islamic Republic of)	552	14	5	246	18	269
Iraq	75	5		10		60
Jordan	25			9		16
Kuwait	137	24	2	17	4	90
Lao People's Democratic Republic	1			1		
Lebanon	50	1	2	38	1	8
Malaysia	1 539	169	6	210	35	1 119
Maldives	69	16		38	2	13
Mongolia	168	31	9	73	3	52
Myanmar	85	5		44		36
Oman	39	2		9		28
Pakistan	50	5	6	3		36
Philippines	1 383	203	72	589	18	501
Qatar	106	7	3	3	11	82
Republic of Korea	1 894	310	145	448	88	903
Saudi Arabia	286	31		14	3	238
Singapore	3 339	743	348	139	345	1 764
Sri Lanka	77	10	5	16	1	45
Syrian Arab Republic	63		1	48		14
Thailand	755	239	44	128	19	325
Turkey	1 365	197	114	514	40	500
United Arab Emirates	547	41	4	78	4	420

Annex II. (c)   Merchant fleets of the world by flags of registration, groups of economies and types of ship, as at 1 January 2013 (Number of ships) *(continued)*

	Total	Oil tankers	Bulk carriers	General-cargo ships	Containerships	Other types
Viet Nam	1 772	118	58	1 337	22	237
Yemen	32	4		3		25
DEVELOPING ECONOMIES OF ASIA Total	**29 999**	**3 779**	**2 828**	**8 392**	**1 361**	**13 639**
DEVELOPING ECONOMIES OF OCEANIA						
Cook Islands	106	1	12	57	1	35
Fiji	40			17		23
French Polynesia	16			10		6
Guam	3					3
Kiribati	96	24	3	41	1	27
Marshall Islands	2 064	639	742	77	238	368
Micronesia (Federated States of)	17			13		4
New Caledonia	12			2		10
Northern Mariana Islands	1					1
Papua New Guinea	130	4		67	6	53
Samoa	9			4		5
Solomon Islands	20			13		7
Tonga	40	3		21		16
Tuvalu	216	45	11	43	1	116
Vanuatu	421	1	37	10	1	372
Liberia	33897	37681	4310	39910	5721	121519
Malta	18682	4661	3134	15417	3223	45117
Marshall Islands	24941	7175	1749	31527	10662	76054
Panama	106605	33779	24151	36082	14143	214760
Saint Vincent and the Grenadines	1260	81	1959	181	540	4020
DEVELOPING ECONOMIES OF OCEANIA Total	**3 191**	**717**	**805**	**375**	**248**	**1 046**
DEVELOPED ECONOMIES						
Australia	502	7	6	73		416
Austria	1					1
Belgium	216	13	21	23	4	155
Bermuda	168	24	26	1	13	104
Bulgaria	95	10	16	21		48
Canada	634	30	11	99	1	493
Cyprus	1 030	103	279	179	212	257
Denmark	663	133	3	105	98	324
Estonia	83	7		5	1	70
Faroe Islands	76	3		29	3	41
Finland	281	12	6	102	1	160
France	547	42	2	77	27	399
Germany	781	42	7	93	272	367
Gibraltar	304	61	6	136	39	62
Greece	1 551	458	258	197	35	603

Annex II. (c) Merchant fleets of the world by flags of registration, groups of economies and types of ship, as at 1 January 2013 (Number of ships) *(continued)*					
	Total	Oil tankers	Bulk carriers	General-cargo ships	Containerships	Other types
Greenland	8			5		3
Iceland	26	1		5		20
Ireland	88	1	8	30		49
Isle of Man	422	131	78	64	9	140
Israel	39	5		3	5	26
Italy	1 506	192	99	155	21	1 039
Japan	5 379	1 108	82	2 090	1	2 098
Latvia	58	8		9		41
Lithuania	71	1	5	35	1	29
Luxembourg	174	14	3	22	7	128
Malta	1 794	420	543	398	114	319
Monaco	1					1
Netherlands	1 250	28	12	605	64	541
New Zealand	91	5		13	2	71
Norway	1 593	123	98	306	2	1 064
Poland	172	9		18		145
Portugal	249	14	3	48	6	178
Reunion	7					7
Romania	152	10		17		125
Slovakia	18			15		3
Slovenia	8					8
Spain	522	37	1	48	5	431
Sweden	417	56	1	90		270
Switzerland	39	4	21	9	2	3
United Kingdom	1 346	104	38	181	186	837
United States	3 462	71	9	158	66	3 158
DEVELOPED ECONOMIES Total	**25 824**	**3 287**	**1 642**	**5 464**	**1 197**	**14 234**

Annex II. (c) Merchant fleets of the world by flags of registration, groups of economies and types of ship, as at 1 January 2013 (Number of ships) *(continued)*

	Total	Oil tankers	Bulk carriers	General-cargo ships	Containerships	Other types
ECONOMIES IN TRANSITION						
Albania	68			65		3
Azerbaijan	306	51		35		220
Belarus	7		1			6
Croatia	264	20	22	53		169
Georgia	192	8	4	107	2	71
Kazakhstan	94	8				86
Montenegro	14		2	3		9
Republic of Moldova	142	4	3	121	2	12
Russian Federation	2 324	386	21	859	10	1 048
Turkmenistan	59	7		4		48
Ukraine	492	16		139		337
ECONOMIES IN TRANSITION Total	**3 962**	**500**	**53**	**1 386**	**14**	**2 009**
Unknown flag	**1 088**	**113**	**2**	**326**	**3**	**644**
World total	**86 942**	**11 176**	**9 512**	**21 114**	**5 109**	**40 031**

Source: Clarkson Research Services.

For additional data and years see http://stats.unctad.org/fleet

Note 1   All propelled sea-going merchant vessels of 100 GT and above, excluding inland waterway vessels, fishing vessels, military vessels, yachts, and offshore fixed and mobile platforms and barges (with the exception of FPSOs and drillships).

[a]   A dispute exists between the Governments of Argentina and the United Kingdom of Great Britain and Northern Ireland concerning sovereignty over the Falkland Islands (Malvinas).

Country or territory of ownership	Antigua & Barbuda			Bahamas			China			China, Hong Kong SAR		
	Number of vessels	1 000 dwt	%	Number of vessels	1 000 dwt	%	Number of vessels	1 000 dwt	%	Number of vessels	1 000 dwt	%
Belgium	–	–	–	12	167	0.2	–	–	–	36	2 482	1.9
Bermuda	–	–	–	82	11 418	15.5	–	–	–	16	1 804	1.4
Brazil	–	–	–	12	991	1.3	–	–	–	–	–	–
Canada	–	–	–	41	3 530	4.8	–	–	–	13	477	0.4
China	–	–	–	11	93	0.1	2 665	66 936	98.2	1078	74 189	57.2
China, Hong Kong SAR	6	74	0.5	–	–	–	21	667	1.0	269	15 769	12.2
China, Taiwan Province of	–	–	–	–	–	–	3	201	0.3	46	4 196	3.2
Cyprus	3	30	0.2	2	11	–	–	–	–	18	1 099	0.8
Denmark	12	75	0.5	53	909	1.2	–	–	–	49	3 432	2.6
France	–	–	–	13	543	0.7	–	–	–	1	58	–
Germany	1 103	13 118	92.9	22	956	1.3	–	–	–	18	1 237	1.0
Greece	4	73	0.5	193	14 070	19.1	–	–	–	35	1 983	1.5
India	1	8	0.1	4	76	0.1	–	–	–	–	–	–
Indonesia	–	–	–	1	12	–	1	3	–	5	117	0.1
Iran (Islamic Republic of)	–	–	–	–	–	–	–	–	–	17	722	0.6
Italy	1	7	0.1	11	867	1.2	–	–	–	–	–	–
Japan	–	–	–	93	7 149	9.7	1	46	0.1	102	5 411	4.2
Kuwait	–	–	–	–	–	–	–	–	–	–	–	–
Malaysia	–	–	–	4	87	0.1	–	–	–	10	533	0.4
Monaco	–	–	–	17	1 028	1.4	–	–	–	–	–	–
Netherlands	22	126	0.9	20	2 115	2.9	–	–	–	1	4	–
Norway	13	73	0.5	185	4 086	5.5	–	–	–	34	1 930	1.5
Oman	–	–	–	1	82	0.1	–	–	–	–	–	–
Republic of Korea	–	–	–	4	306	0.4	–	–	–	26	797	0.6
Russian Federation	5	31	0.2	6	121	0.2	–	–	–	1	8	–
Saudi Arabia	–	–	–	18	5 283	7.2	–	–	–	–	–	–
Singapore	1	11	0.1	20	601	0.8	3	149	0.2	68	5 058	3.9
Sweden	–	–	–	9	400	0.5	–	–	–	–	–	–
Switzerland	2	29	0.2	2	117	0.2	–	–	–	9	337	0.3
Thailand	–	–	–	3	305	0.4	–	–	–	1	5	–
Turkey	11	61	0.4	5	122	0.2	–	–	–	–	–	–
United Arab Emirates	1	2	–	41	1 582	2.1	–	–	–	10	702	0.5
United Kingdom	8	72	0.5	128	3 529	4.8	–	–	–	13	612	0.5
United States	8	29	0.2	115	3 284	4.5	–	–	–	66	6 032	4.6
Viet Nam	–	–	–	1	2	–	–	–	–	–	–	–
Total Top 35	1 201	13 818	97.8	1 129	63 842	86.7	2 694	68 002	99.7	1 942	128 993	99.4
Other owners	63	277	2	214	9 825	13	–	–	–	17	708	1
Unknown Owners	6	30	–	2	2	–	22	173	–	1	36	–
Total of flag of registration	1 270	14 126	100	1 345	73 670	100	2 716	68 176	100	1 960	129 737	100

REVIEW OF MARITIME TRANSPORT 2013

Annex III. True nationality of the 20 largest fleets by flag of registration, as at 1 January 2013 *(continued)*

Country or territory of ownership	Cyprus			Denmark (DIS)			Germany			Greece		
(Flag of registration)	Number of vessels	1 000 dwt	%	Number of vessels	1 000 dwt	%	Number of vessels	1 000 dwt	%	Number of vessels	1 000 dwt	%
Belgium	8	43	0.1	–	–	–	–	–	–	–	–	–
Bermuda	1	300	0.9	–	–	–	–	–	–	–	–	–
Brazil	4	13	–	–	–	–	–	–	–	–	–	–
Canada	24	772	2.4	–	–	–	–	–	–	–	–	–
China	12	417	1.3	–	–	–	1	13	0.1	1	12	–
China, Hong Kong SAR	5	292	0.9	–	–	–	2	135	0.8	–	–	–
China, Taiwan Province of	–	–	–	–	–	–	–	–	–	–	–	–
Cyprus	183	6 178	19.5	–	–	–	1	75	0.4	–	–	–
Denmark	5	16	–	348	12 688	92.6	5	19	0.1	1	12	–
France	7	16	–	–	–	–	–	–	–	–	–	–
Germany	153	2 539	8.0	1	105	0.8	396	16 642	97.6	–	–	–
Greece	190	12 702	40.1	5	214	1.6	1	40	0.2	825	69 645	92.6
India	13	808	2.6	–	–	–	–	–	–	–	–	–
Indonesia	–	–	–	–	–	–	1	42	0.2	–	–	–
Iran (Islamic Republic of)	–	–	–	–	–	–	–	–	–	–	–	–
Italy	7	19	0.1	2	91	0.7	2	1	–	–	–	–
Japan	11	523	1.7	–	–	–	–	–	–	3	149	0.2
Kuwait	–	–	–	–	–	–	–	–	–	–	–	–
Malaysia	–	–	–	–	–	–	–	–	–	–	–	–
Monaco	–	–	–	–	–	–	–	–	–	7	1 050	1.4
Netherlands	64	623	2.0	–	–	–	1	8	–	–	–	–
Norway	47	314	1.0	9	65	0.5	1	2	–	–	–	–
Oman	–	–	–	–	–	–	–	–	–	–	–	–
Republic of Korea	–	–	–	–	–	–	–	–	–	–	–	–
Russian Federation	44	2 155	6.8	–	–	–	1	5	–	1	1	–
Saudi Arabia	–	–	–	–	–	–	–	–	–	1	1	–
Singapore	7	214	0.7	–	–	–	–	–	–	–	–	–
Sweden	4	12	–	22	396	2.9	2	3	–	–	–	–
Switzerland	4	145	0.5	–	–	–	1	43	0.3	–	–	–
Thailand	–	–	–	–	–	–	–	–	–	–	–	–
Turkey	2	22	0.1	–	–	–	–	–	–	–	–	–
United Arab Emirates	14	171	0.5	–	–	–	–	–	–	–	–	–
United Kingdom	44	2 490	7.9	3	142	1.0	–	–	–	24	3 600	4.8
United States	4	14	–	–	–	–	–	–	–	7	611	0.8
Viet Nam	–	–	–	–	–	–	–	–	–	–	–	–
Total Top 35	857	30 797	97.3	390	13 702	100.0	415	17 029	99.9	870	75 081	99.8
Other owners	61	862	3	2	4	–	2	23	–	3	4	–
Unknown Owners	1	5	–	–	–	–	–	–	–	12	125	–
Total of flag of registration	919	31 665	100	392	13 707	100	417	17 052	100	885	75 209	100

| Annex III. | True nationality of the 20 largest fleets by flag of registration, as at 1 January 2013 *(continued)* | | | | | | | | | | | |

Flag of registration Country or territory of ownership	Isle of Man			Italy			Japan			Liberia		
	Number of vessels	1 000 dwt	%	Number of vessels	1 000 dwt	%	Number of vessels	1 000 dwt	%	Number of vessels	1 000 dwt	%
Belgium	–	–	–	–	–	–	–	–	–	1	179	0.1
Bermuda	13	3 704	16.4	–	–	–	–	–	–	10	2 525	1.3
Brazil	–	–	–	–	–	–	–	–	–	20	3 182	1.6
Canada	1	21	0.1	–	–	–	–	–	–	1	31	–
China	–	–	–	1	13	0.1	2	12	0.1	92	6 972	3.5
China, Hong Kong SAR	–	–	–	–	–	–	–	–	–	2	335	0.2
China, Taiwan Province of	–	–	–	–	–	–	4	10	0.1	114	12 446	6.3
Cyprus	–	–	–	–	–	–	–	–	–	23	1 066	0.5
Denmark	53	778	3.4	4	44	0.2	–	–	–	5	188	0.1
France	–	–	–	12	42	0.2	–	–	–	2	231	0.1
Germany	48	1 059	4.7	9	57	0.3	–	–	–	1 298	65 927	33.3
Greece	63	6 433	28.4	7	436	2.1	–	–	–	618	42 583	21.5
India	–	–	–	–	–	–	–	–	–	7	524	0.3
Indonesia	–	–	–	1	5	–	2	9	0.1	2	214	0.1
Iran (Islamic Republic of)	–	–	–	–	–	–	–	–	–	–	–	–
Italy	1	82	0.4	673	19 098	93.5	–	–	–	24	1 058	0.5
Japan	16	2 267	10.0	6	375	1.8	738	17 216	99.3	113	9 159	4.6
Kuwait	–	–	–	–	–	–	–	–	–	–	–	–
Malaysia	–	–	–	–	–	–	–	–	–	3	7	–
Monaco	–	–	–	1	40	0.2	–	–	–	22	2 399	1.2
Netherlands	–	–	–	–	–	–	–	–	–	76	2 229	1.1
Norway	58	1 431	6.3	1	13	0.1	2	73	0.4	32	1 236	0.6
Oman	–	–	–	–	–	–	–	–	–	–	–	–
Republic of Korea	4	563	2.5	–	–	–	2	5	–	6	623	0.3
Russian Federation	–	–	–	–	–	–	–	–	–	92	8 350	4.2
Saudi Arabia	–	–	–	–	–	–	–	–	–	–	–	–
Singapore	3	166	0.7	–	–	–	–	–	–	45	4 231	2.1
Sweden	1	37	0.2	1	7	–	–	–	–	1	134	0.1
Switzerland	–	–	–	2	16	0.1	–	–	–	13	511	0.3
Thailand	–	–	–	–	–	–	1	3	–	–	–	–
Turkey	–	–	–	7	56	0.3	–	–	–	19	375	0.2
United Arab Emirates	–	–	–	–	–	–	–	–	–	75	9 225	4.7
United Kingdom	130	5 354	23.7	1	1	–	–	–	–	120	7 369	3.7
United States	–	–	–	5	74	0.4	–	–	–	89	5 852	3.0
Viet Nam	–	–	–	–	–	–	–	–	–	2	71	–
Total Top 35	391	21 895	96.8	731	20 277	99.2	751	17 328	100.0	2 927	189 231	95.6
Other owners	17	724	3	6	153	1	2	2	–	166	8 577	4
Unknown Owners	–	–	–	2	5	–	2	5	–	4	204	–
Total of flag of registration	408	22'619	100	739	20 435	100	755	17 334	100	3 097	198 012	100

Annex III. True nationality of the 20 largest fleets by flag of registration, as at 1 January 2013 *(continued)*

Flag of registration / Country or territory of ownership	Malta			Marshall Islands			Norway (DIS)			Panama		
	Number of vessels	1 000 dwt	%	Number of vessels	1 000 dwt	%	Number of vessels	1 000 dwt	%	Number of vessels	1 000 dwt	%
Belgium	4	41	0.1	2	67	–	–	–	–	5	325	0.1
Bermuda	3	206	0.3	36	5 783	4.1	4	678	3.8	18	3 633	1.0
Brazil	–	–	–	7	1 381	1.0	5	15	0.1	26	2 517	0.7
Canada	3	168	0.2	17	752	0.5	–	–	–	10	251	0.1
China	18	594	0.9	25	1 380	1.0	–	–	–	838	31 057	8.9
China, Hong Kong SAR	–	–	–	13	424	0.3	–	–	–	153	6075	1.7
China, Taiwan Province of	–	–	–	10	1 868	1.3	–	–	–	413	17 424	5.0
Cyprus	34	1 448	2.1	45	2 748	2.0	–	–	–	16	757	0.2
Denmark	30	1 081	1.6	11	585	0.4	10	289	1.6	55	2 204	0.6
France	8	545	0.8	5	997	0.7	–	–	–	10	52	–
Germany	111	2 661	3.9	261	11 918	8.5	–	–	–	29	2 506	0.7
Greece	510	33 856	49.2	496	32 524	23.2	2	152	0.8	491	23 229	6.6
India	2	162	0.2	10	820	0.6	–	–	–	49	2 467	0.7
Indonesia	1	13	–	4	112	0.1	–	–	–	47	1 380	0.4
Iran (Islamic Republic of)	36	3 475	5.1	–	–	–	–	–	–	8	74	–
Italy	50	1 377	2.0	8	721	0.5	–	–	–	33	701	0.2
Japan	13	818	1.2	90	6 558	4.7	–	–	–	2 481	158 909	45.4
Kuwait	10	1 309	1.9	5	323	0.2	–	–	–	6	276	0.1
Malaysia	–	–	–	16	600	0.4	–	–	–	27	518	0.1
Monaco	8	165	0.2	42	3 348	2.4	–	–	–	9	569	0.2
Netherlands	19	320	0.5	28	931	0.7	1	5	–	42	1 240	0.4
Norway	95	1 213	1.8	88	6 184	4.4	455	15 769	87.2	79	3 079	0.9
Oman	6	1 912	2.8	6	1 911	1.4	–	–	–	17	2 229	0.6
Republic of Korea	5	25	–	105	12 344	8.8	–	–	–	572	42 544	12.2
Russian Federation	73	656	1.0	9	349	0.2	1	5	–	44	667	0.2
Saudi Arabia	–	–	–	4	93	0.1	3	112	0.6	21	836	0.2
Singapore	3	136	0.2	106	7 319	5.2	–	–	–	238	8 327	2.4
Sweden	5	78	0.1	4	92	0.1	25	669	3.7	8	198	0.1
Switzerland	29	515	0.7	18	472	0.3	1	44	0.2	192	12 127	3.5
Thailand	–	–	–	2	93	0.1	–	–	–	19	126	–
Turkey	296	9 645	14.0	95	5 539	4.0	–	–	–	148	1 785	0.5
United Arab Emirates	2	15	–	46	1 309	0.9	–	–	–	180	3 898	1.1
United Kingdom	63	1 310	1.9	31	1 858	1.3	5	213	1.2	76	3 192	0.9
United States	24	673	1.0	252	20 666	14.8	4	105	0.6	121	4 500	1.3
Viet Nam	–	–	–	–	–	–	–	–	–	45	1 032	0.3
Total Top 35	1 461	64 417	93.6	1 897	132 067	94.3	516	18 054	99.8	6 526	340 703	97.4
Other owners	232	4 357	6	119	7 867	6	9	26	–	503	8 130	2
Unknown Owners	7	25	–	3	67	–	1	6	–	81	1 001	–
Total of flag of registration	1 700	68 798	100	2 019	140 002	100	526	18 086	100	7 110	349 833	100

Annex III.	True nationality of the 20 largest fleets by flag of registration, as at 1 January 2013 *(continued)*											
Flag of registration	Republic of Korea			Singapore			United Kingdom			United States		
Country or territory of ownership	Number of vessels	1 000 dwt	%	Number of vessels	1 000 dwt	%	Number of vessels	1 000 dwt	%	Number of vessels	1 000 dwt	%
Belgium	–	–	–	13	719	0.8	–	–	–	–	–	–
Bermuda	–	–	–	7	374	0.4	3	487	2.3	–	–	–
Brazil	–	–	–	15	5 131	5.7	–	–	–	8	23	0.2
Canada	–	–	–	–	–	–	–	–	–	5	81	0.7
China	–	–	–	40	3 582	4.0	3	208	1.0	–	–	–
China, Hong Kong SAR	–	–	–	6	63	0.1	4	44	0.2	–	–	–
China, Taiwan Province of	1	79	0.5	85	4 196	4.7	5	352	1.7	–	–	–
Cyprus	–	–	–	13	234	0.3	–	–	–	–	–	–
Denmark	–	–	–	170	13 742	15.4	42	1 937	9.2	24	1 257	10.7
France	–	–	–	18	522	0.6	35	2 565	12.2	–	–	–
Germany	1	122	0.7	29	691	0.8	65	1 966	9.4	5	202	1.7
Greece	–	–	–	29	828	0.9	2	75	0.4	1	47	0.4
India	1	52	0.3	36	2 229	2.5	2	27	0.1	–	–	–
Indonesia	2	5	–	49	858	1.0	–	–	–	1	6	–
Iran (Islamic Republic of)	–	–	–	–	–	–	–	–	–	–	–	–
Italy	–	–	–	6	286	0.3	8	166	0.8	–	–	–
Japan	5	178	1.0	158	9 582	10.7	1	151	0.7	–	–	–
Kuwait	–	–	–	–	–	–	–	–	–	–	–	–
Malaysia	–	–	–	57	5 624	6.3	–	–	–	–	–	–
Monaco	–	–	–	8	219	0.2	1	19	0.1	–	–	–
Netherlands	–	–	–	1	1	–	20	208	1.0	–	–	–
Norway	–	–	–	129	3 380	3.8	38	689	3.3	1	20	0.2
Oman	–	–	–	–	–	–	–	–	–	–	–	–
Republic of Korea	764	16 624	96.5	12	334	0.4	1	141	0.7	–	–	–
Russian Federation	–	–	–	6	300	0.3	–	–	–	–	–	–
Saudi Arabia	–	–	–	3	17	–	–	–	–	–	–	–
Singapore	2	19	0.1	1 090	32 711	36.6	1	16	0.1	11	623	5.3
Sweden	–	–	–	15	338	0.4	28	232	1.1	–	–	–
Switzerland	–	–	–	–	–	–	1	37	0.2	–	–	–
Thailand	2	6	–	35	983	1.1	–	–	–	–	–	–
Turkey	–	–	–	5	220	0.2	1	5	–	1	1	–
United Arab Emirates	–	–	–	15	217	0.2	–	–	–	2	4	–
United Kingdom	–	–	–	13	481	0.5	415	10 448	49.9	5	772	6.6
United States	–	–	–	17	590	0.7	6	111	0.5	766	8 640	73.9
Viet Nam	2	12	0.1	–	–	–	–	–	–	–	–	–
Total Top 35	780	17 098	99.2	2 080	88 453	99.0	682	19 883	94.9	830	11 677	99.8
Other owners	4	53	–	43	921	1	32	1 063	5	5	8	–
Unknown Owners	23	82	–	2	6	–	1	1	–	3	13	–
Total of flag of registration	807	17 233	100	2 125	89 381	100	715	20 947	100	838	11 698	100

Annex III.	True nationality of the 20 largest fleets by flag of registration, as at 1 January 2013 *(continued)*					
Flag of registration / Country or territory of ownership	Total, Top 20 Registries		Others		Grand Total	
	Number of vessels	1 000 dwt	Number of vessels	1 000 dwt	Number of vessels	1 000 dwt
Belgium	81	4 023	164	4 705	245	8 729
Bermuda	193	30 913	17	1 983	210	32 896
Brazil	97	13 253	213	2 900	310	16 153
Canada	115	6 083	236	3 139	351	9 222
China	4 787	185 478	526	4 601	5 313	190 079
China, Hong Kong SAR	481	23 877	85	448	566	24 325
China, Taiwan Province of	681	40 772	133	3 488	814	44 260
Cyprus	338	13 646	37	278	375	13 924
Denmark	877	39 256	114	1 459	991	40 715
France	111	5 571	298	5436	409	11 007
Germany	3 549	121 707	284	4 072	3 833	125 779
Greece	3 472	238 888	223	5 963	3 695	244 851
India	125	7 174	617	15 267	742	22 441
Indonesia	117	2 777	1 413	12 525	1 530	15 301
Iran (Islamic Republic of)	61	4 271	168	11 046	229	15 317
Italy	826	24 474	58	869	884	25 343
Japan	3 831	218 491	160	5 324	3 991	223 815
Kuwait	21	1 908	55	4 993	76	6 900
Malaysia	117	7 368	497	9 747	614	17 115
Monaco	115	8 839	11	319	126	9 158
Netherlands	295	7 812	912	8 860	1 207	16 673
Norway	1 267	39 556	641	6 436	1 908	45 992
Oman	30	6 134	4	5	34	6 139
Republic of Korea	1 501	74 306	75	790	1 576	75 096
Russian Federation	283	12 646	1 444	6 739	1 727	19 384
Saudi Arabia	50	6 342	137	1 466	187	7 808
Singapore	1 598	59 579	290	4 573	1 888	64 153
Sweden	125	2 597	214	3 848	339	6 445
Switzerland	274	14 392	56	1 259	330	15 651
Thailand	63	1 521	352	4 576	415	6 097
Turkey	590	17 832	990	11 259	1 580	29 091
United Arab Emirates	386	17 124	313	2 349	699	19 474
United Kingdom	1 079	41 443	158	8 862	1 237	50 305
United States	1 484	51 180	459	7 098	1 943	58 278
Viet Nam	50	1 117	791	6 846	841	7 963
Total Top 35	29 070	1 352 349	12 145	173 527	41 215	1 525 876
Other owners	1 500	43 584	3 677	38 999	5 177	82 583
Unknown Owners	173	1 785	557	3 512	730	5 297
Total of flag of registration	30 743	1 397 718	16 379	216 037	47 122	1 613 756

Source: Compiled by the UNCTAD secretariat on the basis of data provided *by* Clarkson Research Services.

Note: Cargo-carrying vessels of 1,000 GT and above.

Annex IV.   Containerized port traffic (Alphabetical order)

Country/territory	2010	2011	Rank 2011 (2010)		2010	2011	Rank 2011 (2010)
Albania	86 875	91 827	112 (113)	Honduras	619 867	655 199	68 (67)
Algeria	279 785	295 733	90 (89)	Iceland	192 778	193 500	99 (96)
Antigua and Barbuda	24 615	26 018	123 (123)	India	9 752 908	9 979 224	14 (15)
Argentina	2 021 676	2 159 110	41 (42)	Indonesia	8 482 636	8 966 146	16 (17)
Aruba	130 000	137 410	106 (107)	Iran (Islamic Republic of)	2 592 522	2 740 296	35 (35)
Australia	6 668 075	7 011 581	21 (20)	Ireland	790 067	763 280	60 (59)
Austria	350 461	370 437	77 (77)	Israel	2 281 552	2 394 000	39 (39)
Bahamas	1 125 000	1 189 125	52 (53)	Italy	9 787 403	9 529 351	15 (14)
Bahrain	289 956	306 483	87 (87)	Jamaica	1 891 770	1 999 601	43 (43)
Bangladesh	1 356 099	1 431 851	49 (48)	Japan	18 098 346	19 417 757	7 (7)
Barbados	80 424	85 008	114 (114)	Jordan	619 000	654 283	69 (68)
Belgium	10 984 824	11 034 037	13 (13)	Kenya	696 000	735 672	62 (61)
Belize	31 919	34 200	122 (122)	Kuwait	991 545	1 048 063	57 (57)
Benin	316 744	334 798	84 (84)	Latvia	256 713	305 339	88 (90)
Brazil	8 138 608	8 536 262	18 (18)	Lebanon	949 155	1 034 249	58 (58)
Brunei Darussalam	99 355	105 018	109 (109)	Libya	184 585	195 106	97 (98)
Bulgaria	142 611	150 740	103 (104)	Lithuania	294 954	311 766	86 (86)
Cambodia	224 206	236 986	94 (95)	Madagascar	141 093	149 135	104 (105)
Cameroon	285 070	301 319	89 (88)	Malaysia	18 267 475	20 139 382	6 (6)
Canada	4 829 806	5 058 741	28 (28)	Maldives	65 016	68 722	118 (118)
Cayman Islands	40 281	42 577	121 (121)	Malta	2 450 665	2 444 981	37 (37)
Chile	3 171 959	3 450 401	33 (34)	Mauritania	65 705	69 450	117 (117)
China	130 290 443	143 896 697	1 (1)	Mauritius	332 662	350 624	82 (82)
China, Hong Kong SAR	23 699 242	24 384 000	4 (4)	Mexico	3 693 956	4 080 434	30 (32)
China, Taiwan Province of	12 736 855	13 473 418	11 (10)	Morocco	2 058 430	2 083 000	42 (41)
Colombia	2 443 786	2 402 742	38 (38)	Mozambique	254 701	269 219	91 (92)
Congo	338 916	358 234	81 (81)	Myanmar	190 046	200 879	95 (97)
Costa Rica	1 013 483	1 065 468	56 (55)	Namibia	256 319	107 606	107 (91)
Côte d'Ivoire	607 730	642 371	70 (69)	Netherlands	11 345 167	12 072 696	12 (12)
Croatia	137 048	144 860	105 (106)	Netherlands Antilles	93 603		127 (111)
Cuba	228 346	246 773	92 (93)	New Caledonia	90 574	95 277	111 (112)
Curaçao		90 000	113 (127)	New Zealand	2 463 278	2 516 706	36 (36)
Cyprus	349 357	360 652	80 (78)	Nicaragua	68 545	72 452	116 (116)
Denmark	709 147	753 035	61 (60)	Nigeria	101 007	106 764	108 (108)
Djibouti	600 000	634 200	71 (70)	Norway	330 873	349 733	83 (83)
Dominican Republic	1 382 680	1 461 492	48 (47)	Oman	3 893 198	3 632 940	32 (30)
Ecuador	1 221 849	1 081 169	54 (51)	Pakistan	2 149 000	2 193 403	40 (40)
Egypt	6 709 053	7 737 183	19 (19)	Panama	6 003 298	6 911 325	22 (22)
El Salvador	145 774	154 083	102 (103)	Papua New Guinea	295 286	313 598	85 (85)
Estonia	151 969	197 717	96 (102)	Paraguay	8 179	8 645	125 (125)
Finland	1 247 521	1 326 840	50 (49)	Peru	1 534 056	1 814 743	45 (45)
France	5 346 800	5 362 900	26 (25)	Philippines	4 947 039	5 264 086	27 (27)
French Guiana	47 512	50 220	120 (120)	Poland	1 045 232	1 214 034	51 (54)
French Polynesia	68 889	72 816	115 (115)	Portugal	1 622 247	1 758 167	46 (44)
Gabon	153 657	162 415	101 (101)	Qatar	346 000	365 722	79 (80)
Georgia	226 115	239 004	93 (94)	Republic of Korea	18 542 804	20 833 508	5 (5)
Germany	14 821 767	17 218 712	8 (9)	Romania	556 694	662 796	67 (72)
Ghana	647 052	683 934	66 (66)	Russian Federation	3 199 980	3 448 947	34 (33)
Greece	1 165 185	1 973 864	44 (52)	Saint Helena	650	687	126 (126)
Guadeloupe	165 665	175 108	100 (100)	Saint Lucia	52 479	58 539	119 (119)
Guam	183 214	193 657	98 (99)	Saint Vincent and the Grenadines	18 852	19 927	124 (124)
Guatemala	1 012 360	1 070 065	55 (56)	Saudi Arabia	5 313 141	5 694 538	25 (26)

Annex IV.	Containerized port traffic (Alphabetical order) (continued)		
	2010	2011	Rank 2011 (2010)
Senegal	349 231	369 137	78 (79)
Singapore	29 178 500	30 727 702	3 (3)
Slovenia	476 731	589 314	73 (73)
South Africa	3 806 427	3 990 193	31 (31)
Spain	12 613 016	13 837 160	10 (11)
Sri Lanka	4 000 000	4 262 887	29 (29)
Sudan	439 100	464 129	75 (75)
Sweden	1 390 504	1 515 217	47 (46)
Switzerland	99 048	104 694	110 (110)
Syrian Arab Republic	649 005	685 998	65 (65)
Thailand	6 648 532	7 171 394	20 (21)
Trinidad and Tobago	573 217	605 890	72 (71)
Tunisia	466 398	492 983	74 (74)
Turkey	5 574 018	5 990 103	24 (24)
Ukraine	659 541	696 641	64 (64)
United Arab Emirates	15 176 524	16 780 386	9 (8)
United Kingdom	8 590 282	8 920 679	17 (16)
United Republic of Tanzania	429 285	453 754	76 (76)
United States	42 337 513	42 999 149	2 (2)
Uruguay	671 952	861 164	59 (62)
Venezuela (Bolivarian Republic of)	1 226 508	1 162 326	53 (50)
Viet Nam	5 983 583	6 335 437	23 (23)
Yemen	669 021	707 155	63 (63)
Grand Total	540 816 751	580 022 280	

Annex V.	UNCTAD Liner Shipping Connectivity Index (Alphabetical order)									
Country or territory	2004	2005	2006	2007	2008	2009	2010	2011	2012	2013
Albania	0.40	0.40	0.40	2.28	1.98	2.30	4.34	4.54	0.53	4.43
Algeria	10.00	9.72	8.70	7.86	7.75	8.37	31.45	31.06	7.80	6.91
American Samoa	5.17	5.30	4.86	6.28	6.44	4.60	4.85	4.56	4.39	4.19
Angola	9.67	10.46	9.46	9.90	10.22	11.31	10.71	11.27	13.95	13.80
Antigua and Barbuda	2.33	2.56	2.43	3.76	3.82	2.66	2.40	2.40	2.41	2.43
Argentina	20.09	24.95	25.58	25.63	25.70	25.99	27.61	30.62	34.21	33.51
Aruba	7.37	7.52	7.53	5.09	5.09	3.52	5.34	6.21	6.03	6.30
Australia	26.58	28.02	26.96	26.77	38.21	28.80	28.11	28.34	28.81	29.87
Bahamas	17.49	15.70	16.19	16.45	16.35	19.26	25.71	25.18	27.06	26.41
Bahrain	5.39	4.34	4.44	5.99	5.75	8.04	7.83	9.77	17.86	17.90
Bangladesh	5.20	5.07	5.29	6.36	6.40	7.91	7.55	8.15	8.02	7.96
Barbados	5.47	5.77	5.34	5.79	5.36	4.75	4.20	5.85	4.82	5.18
Belgium	73.16	74.17	76.15	73.93	77.98	82.80	84.00	88.47	78.85	82.21
Belize	2.19	2.59	2.62	2.61	2.32	2.30	3.95	3.85	9.99	10.32
Benin	10.13	10.23	10.99	11.16	12.02	13.52	11.51	12.69	15.04	14.28
Bermuda	1.54	1.57	1.57	1.57	1.57	1.57	1.57	1.57	1.57	15.92
Brazil	25.83	31.49	31.61	31.64	30.87	31.08	31.65	34.62	38.53	36.88
Brunei Darussalam	3.91	3.46	3.26	3.70	3.68	3.94	5.12	4.68	4.44	4.61
Bulgaria	6.17	5.61	4.47	4.83	5.09	5.78	5.46	5.37	6.36	5.89
Cambodia	3.89	3.25	2.93	3.25	3.47	4.67	4.52	5.36	3.45	5.34
Cameroon	10.46	10.62	11.41	11.65	11.05	11.60	11.34	11.40	13.44	10.85
Canada	39.67	39.81	36.32	34.40	34.28	41.34	42.39	38.41	38.29	38.44
Cape Verde	1.90	2.28	2.76	2.45	3.63	5.13	3.69	4.24	4.48	4.12
Cayman Islands	1.90	2.23	1.79	1.78	1.78	1.76	2.51	4.03	4.07	1.34
Chile	15.48	15.53	16.10	17.49	17.42	18.84	22.05	22.76	32.98	32.98
China	100.00	108.29	113.10	127.85	137.38	132.47	143.57	152.06	156.19	157.51
China, Hong Kong SAR	94.42	96.78	99.31	106.20	108.78	104.47	113.60	115.27	117.18	116.63
China, Taiwan Province of	59.56	63.74	65.64	62.43	62.58	60.90	64.37	66.69	66.62	64.23
Colombia	18.61	19.20	20.49	21.07	21.64	23.18	26.13	27.25	37.25	37.49
Comoros	6.07	5.84	5.39	5.51	5.15	5.00	5.74	7.14	5.17	5.21
Congo	8.29	9.10	9.12	9.61	11.80	11.37	10.45	10.78	12.57	15.82
Costa Rica	12.59	11.12	15.08	15.34	12.78	14.61	12.77	10.69	14.13	14.00
Côte d'Ivoire	14.39	14.52	12.98	14.98	16.93	19.39	17.48	17.38	16.45	17.55
Croatia	8.58	12.19	10.47	12.33	15.36	8.48	8.97	21.75	21.38	20.44
Cuba	6.78	6.51	6.43	6.71	6.12	5.92	6.57	6.55	5.96	5.77
Curaçao (until 2010 Netherlands Antilles)	8.16	8.23	7.82	9.22	8.56	8.57	7.97	8.14	6.59	8.14
Cyprus	14.39	18.53	17.39	18.01	11.81	13.31	16.20	17.12	16.02	16.39
Democratic Republic of the Congo	3.05	3.03	2.66	2.68	3.36	3.80	5.24	3.73	4.05	4.01
Denmark	11.56	24.25	25.39	22.10	26.49	27.68	26.76	26.41	44.71	38.67
Djibouti	6.76	7.59	7.36	10.45	10.43	17.98	19.55	21.02	16.56	20.29
Dominica	2.33	2.51	2.33	2.40	2.31	2.73	1.88	2.08	2.08	1.59

Annex V.	UNCTAD Liner Shipping Connectivity Index (Alphabetical order) *(continued)*								
Country or territory	2004	2005	2006	2007	2008	2009	2010	2011	2012	2013
Dominican Republic	12.45	13.95	15.19	19.87	20.09	21.61	22.25	22.87	23.72	25.57
Ecuador	11.84	12.92	14.17	14.30	13.16	17.09	18.73	22.48	23.05	21.74
Egypt	42.86	49.23	50.01	45.37	52.53	51.99	47.55	51.15	57.39	57.48
El Salvador	6.30	7.32	8.07	7.90	8.67	10.34	9.64	12.02	8.75	8.36
Equatorial Guinea	4.04	3.87	3.76	3.36	3.86	3.73	4.37	3.68	4.54	4.02
Eritrea	3.36	1.58	2.23	0.00	3.26	3.26	0.02	4.02	4.17	4.02
Estonia	7.05	6.52	5.76	5.78	5.48	5.71	5.73	5.84	5.43	6.44
Faroe Islands	4.22	4.40	4.43	4.45	4.20	4.20	4.21	4.20	4.21	4.21
Fiji	8.26	8.32	7.24	7.35	10.31	8.74	9.44	9.23	12.39	12.05
Finland	9.45	10.16	8.58	10.70	9.72	10.15	8.36	11.27	15.51	9.34
France	67.34	70.00	67.78	64.84	66.24	67.01	74.94	71.84	70.09	74.94
French Polynesia	10.46	11.14	8.91	8.60	9.01	8.39	8.88	8.59	10.86	9.90
Gabon	8.78	8.76	8.72	8.57	8.93	9.16	8.55	7.97	9.23	8.95
Gambia	4.91	6.13	4.80	4.74	4.97	7.53	5.38	5.24	7.81	5.89
Georgia	3.46	3.81	2.94	3.22	4.03	3.83	4.02	3.79	4.99	4.17
Germany	76.59	78.41	80.66	88.95	89.26	84.30	90.88	93.32	90.63	88.61
Ghana	12.48	12.64	13.80	14.99	18.13	19.33	17.28	18.01	17.89	19.35
Greece	30.22	29.07	31.29	30.70	27.14	41.91	34.25	32.15	45.50	45.35
Greenland	2.32	2.32	2.27	2.27	2.36	2.27	2.27	2.30	2.30	2.30
Grenada	2.30	2.52	3.37	4.09	4.20	4.13	3.71	3.93	4.04	4.59
Guam	10.50	10.52	9.56	8.73	8.56	8.57	8.78	8.76	8.41	7.85
Guatemala	12.28	13.85	18.13	15.40	15.44	14.73	13.33	20.88	20.07	20.28
Guinea	6.13	6.89	8.71	8.47	6.41	8.32	6.28	6.21	7.42	8.06
Guinea-Bissau	2.12	5.19	5.03	5.22	5.34	3.54	3.50	4.07	4.31	4.00
Guyana	4.54	4.37	4.60	4.51	4.36	4.34	3.95	3.96	4.06	4.31
Haiti	4.91	3.43	2.91	2.87	3.44	4.40	7.58	4.75	5.08	5.12
Honduras	9.11	8.64	8.29	8.76	9.26	10.68	9.09	9.42	10.03	10.73
Iceland	4.72	4.88	4.75	4.72	4.72	4.73	4.70	4.68	4.68	4.66
India	34.14	36.88	42.90	40.47	42.18	40.97	41.40	41.52	41.29	44.35
Indonesia	25.88	28.84	25.84	26.27	24.85	25.68	25.60	25.91	26.28	27.41
Iran (Islamic Republic of)	13.69	14.23	17.37	23.59	22.91	28.90	30.73	30.27	22.62	21.30
Iraq	1.40	1.63	4.06	2.61	1.20	5.11	4.19	4.19	7.10	5.69
Ireland	8.78	9.66	8.18	8.85	7.64	7.60	8.53	5.94	12.99	12.68
Israel	20.37	20.06	20.44	21.42	19.83	18.65	33.20	28.49	31.24	32.42
Italy	58.13	62.20	58.11	58.84	55.87	69.97	59.57	70.18	66.33	67.26
Jamaica	21.32	21.99	23.02	25.50	18.23	19.56	33.09	28.16	21.57	25.32
Japan	69.15	66.73	64.54	62.73	66.63	66.33	67.43	67.81	63.09	65.68
Jordan	11.00	13.42	12.98	16.46	16.37	23.71	17.79	16.65	22.75	22.68
Kenya	8.59	8.98	9.30	10.85	10.95	12.83	13.09	12.00	11.75	11.38
Kiribati	3.06	3.28	3.05	3.06	3.06	2.85	2.86	3.11	2.91	2.91
Kuwait	5.87	6.77	4.14	6.22	6.14	6.54	8.31	5.60	6.60	7.12
Latvia	6.37	5.82	5.10	5.87	5.52	5.18	5.98	5.51	5.45	4.07

Country or territory	2004	2005	2006	2007	2008	2009	2010	2011	2012	2013
Lebanon	10.57	12.53	25.57	30.01	28.92	29.55	30.29	35.09	43.21	43.16
Liberia	5.29	5.95	4.55	4.50	4.25	5.49	5.95	6.17	8.11	5.88
Libya	5.25	5.17	4.71	6.59	5.36	9.43	5.38	6.59	7.51	7.29
Lithuania	5.22	5.88	5.66	6.83	7.76	8.11	9.55	9.77	9.55	5.84
Madagascar	6.90	6.83	8.31	7.97	7.82	8.64	7.38	7.72	11.80	11.85
Malaysia	62.83	64.97	69.20	81.58	77.60	81.21	88.14	90.96	99.69	98.18
Maldives	4.15	4.08	3.90	4.75	5.45	5.43	1.65	1.62	1.60	8.12
Malta	27.53	25.70	30.32	29.53	29.92	37.71	37.53	40.95	45.02	49.79
Marshall Islands	3.49	3.68	3.26	3.06	3.06	2.85	2.83	3.08	2.91	2.91
Mauritania	5.36	5.99	6.25	7.90	7.93	7.50	5.61	5.62	8.20	6.53
Mauritius	13.13	12.26	11.53	17.17	17.43	14.76	16.68	15.37	23.86	24.72
Mexico	25.29	25.49	29.78	30.98	31.17	31.89	36.35	36.09	38.81	41.80
Micronesia (Federated Sates of)	2.80	2.87	1.94	3.13	3.85	3.85	3.43	3.62	3.58	2.17
Montenegro (until 2009 Serbia and Montenegro)	2.92	2.92	2.96	2.96	3.20	0.02	4.48	4.04	1.35	2.35
Morocco	9.39	8.68	8.54	9.02	29.79	38.40	49.36	55.13	55.09	55.53
Mozambique	6.64	6.71	6.66	7.14	8.81	9.38	8.16	10.12	9.82	10.23
Myanmar	3.12	2.47	2.54	3.12	3.63	3.79	3.68	3.22	4.20	6.00
Namibia	6.28	6.61	8.52	8.37	11.12	13.61	14.45	12.02	15.18	15.50
Netherlands	78.81	79.95	80.97	84.79	87.57	88.66	89.96	92.10	88.93	87.46
New Caledonia	9.83	10.34	9.00	8.81	9.23	8.74	9.37	9.17	9.41	9.23
New Zealand	20.88	20.58	20.71	20.60	20.48	10.59	18.38	18.50	19.35	18.95
Nicaragua	4.75	5.25	8.05	7.89	8.91	10.58	8.68	8.41	8.23	8.30
Nigeria	12.83	12.79	13.02	13.69	18.30	19.89	18.28	19.85	21.81	21.35
Northern Mariana Islands	2.17	2.20	1.85	2.86	3.76	3.76	3.43	3.65	3.44	1.37
Norway	9.23	8.31	7.34	7.80	7.91	7.93	7.93	7.32	5.31	5.28
Oman	23.33	23.64	20.28	28.96	30.42	45.32	48.52	49.33	47.25	48.46
Pakistan	20.18	21.49	21.82	24.77	24.61	26.58	29.48	30.54	28.12	27.71
Palau	1.04	1.04	1.87	3.07	3.79	3.79	3.43	3.62	3.58	2.17
Panama	32.05	29.12	27.61	30.53	30.45	32.66	41.09	37.51	42.38	44.88
Papua New Guinea	6.97	6.40	4.67	6.86	6.92	6.58	6.38	8.83	6.86	6.61
Peru	14.79	14.95	16.33	16.90	17.38	16.96	21.79	21.18	32.80	32.84
Philippines	15.45	15.87	16.48	18.42	30.26	15.90	15.19	18.56	17.15	18.11
Poland	7.28	7.53	7.50	7.86	9.32	9.21	26.18	26.54	44.62	38.03
Portugal	17.54	16.84	23.55	25.42	34.97	32.97	38.06	21.08	46.23	46.08
Puerto Rico	14.82	15.23	14.68	15.96	15.62	10.92	10.65	10.70	13.67	9.71
Qatar	2.64	4.23	3.90	3.59	3.21	2.10	7.67	3.60	6.53	3.35
Republic of Korea	68.68	73.03	71.92	77.19	76.40	86.67	82.61	92.02	101.73	100.42
Romania	12.02	15.37	17.61	22.47	26.35	23.34	15.48	21.37	23.28	25.73
Russian Federation	11.90	12.72	12.81	14.06	15.31	20.64	20.88	20.64	37.01	38.17
Saint Kitts and Nevis	5.49	5.32	5.59	6.16	6.19	3.08	2.84	2.66	2.67	2.58
Saint Lucia	3.70	3.72	3.43	4.21	4.25	4.25	3.77	4.08	4.55	4.93

Annex V.	UNCTAD Liner Shipping Connectivity Index (Alphabetical order) *(continued)*									
Country or territory	2004	2005	2006	2007	2008	2009	2010	2011	2012	2013
Saint Vincent and the Grenadines	3.56	3.58	3.40	4.34	4.52	4.13	3.72	3.95	4.02	4.10
Samoa	5.44	5.33	5.09	6.50	6.66	4.62	5.18	4.56	4.39	4.19
São Tomé and Principe	0.91	1.28	1.57	1.64	2.54	2.38	3.33	2.13	2.28	6.87
Saudi Arabia	35.83	36.24	40.66	45.04	47.44	47.30	50.43	59.97	60.40	59.67
Senegal	10.15	10.09	11.24	17.08	17.64	14.96	12.98	12.27	13.59	11.08
Seychelles	4.88	4.93	5.27	5.29	4.49	4.90	5.16	6.45	6.50	8.08
Sierra Leone	5.84	6.50	5.12	5.08	4.74	5.56	5.80	5.41	7.40	5.15
Singapore	81.87	83.87	86.11	87.53	94.47	99.47	103.76	105.02	113.16	106.91
Slovenia	13.91	13.91	11.03	12.87	15.66	19.81	20.61	21.93	21.94	20.82
Solomon Islands	3.62	4.29	3.97	4.13	4.16	3.96	5.57	5.87	6.07	6.04
Somalia	3.09	1.28	2.43	3.05	3.24	2.82	4.20	4.20	4.34	4.20
South Africa	23.13	25.83	26.21	27.52	28.49	32.07	32.49	35.67	36.83	43.02
Spain	54.44	58.16	62.29	71.26	67.67	70.22	74.32	76.58	74.44	70.40
Sri Lanka	34.68	33.36	37.31	42.43	46.08	34.74	40.23	41.13	43.43	43.01
Sudan	6.95	6.19	5.67	5.66	5.38	9.28	10.05	9.33	12.75	8.42
Suriname	4.77	4.16	3.90	4.29	4.26	4.16	4.12	4.16	4.48	4.91
Sweden	14.76	26.61	28.17	25.82	30.27	31.34	30.58	30.02	49.45	42.32
Syrian Arab Republic	8.54	11.84	11.29	14.20	12.72	11.03	15.17	16.77	15.64	16.53
Thailand	31.01	31.92	33.89	35.31	36.48	36.78	43.76	36.70	37.66	38.32
Togo	10.19	10.62	11.09	10.63	12.56	14.42	14.24	14.08	14.07	14.76
Tonga	3.81	4.75	4.45	4.07	4.23	3.99	3.73	3.72	3.37	3.17
Trinidad and Tobago	13.18	10.61	11.18	13.72	12.88	15.88	15.76	17.89	18.90	17.26
Tunisia	8.76	7.62	7.04	7.23	6.95	6.52	6.46	6.33	6.35	5.59
Turkey	25.60	27.09	27.09	32.60	35.64	31.98	36.10	39.40	53.15	52.13
Ukraine	11.18	10.81	14.88	16.73	23.62	22.81	21.06	21.35	24.47	26.72
United Arab Emirates	38.06	39.22	46.70	48.21	48.80	60.45	63.37	62.50	61.09	66.97
United Kingdom	81.69	79.58	81.53	76.77	77.99	84.82	87.53	87.46	84.00	87.72
United Republic of Tanzania	8.10	8.59	8.71	10.58	10.46	9.54	10.61	11.49	11.07	11.10
United States	83.30	87.62	85.80	83.68	82.45	82.43	83.80	81.63	91.70	92.80
United States Virgin Islands	1.77	3.00	3.22	3.76	3.81	3.70	3.32	3.39	3.34	3.37
Uruguay	16.44	16.58	16.81	21.28	22.88	22.28	24.46	24.38	32.00	31.37
Vanuatu	3.92	4.48	4.41	4.34	4.36	4.22	3.75	3.70	3.88	3.42
Venezuela (Bolivarian Republic of)	18.22	19.90	18.62	20.26	20.46	20.43	18.61	19.97	18.93	18.90
Viet Nam	12.86	14.30	15.14	17.59	18.73	26.39	31.36	49.71	48.71	43.26
Yemen	19.21	10.18	9.39	14.28	14.44	14.61	12.49	11.89	13.19	19.00

Source: UNCTAD, based on data provided by CI-Online and Lloyds List Intelligence.

Note: For more details see: http://stats.unctad.org/lsci

QUESTIONNAIRE

Review of Maritime Transport

In order to improve the quality and relevance of the Review of Maritime Transport, the UNCTAD secretariat would greatly appreciate your views on this publication. Please complete the following questionnaire and return it to:

Readership Survey
Division on Technology and Logistics
UNCTAD
Palais des Nations, Room E.7044
CH-1211 Geneva 10, Switzerland
Fax: +41 22 917 0050
E-mail: rmt@unctad.org

Thank you very much for your kind cooperation.

1. What is your assessment of this publication?

	Excellent	Good	Adequate	Poor
Presentation and readability	☐	☐	☐	☐
Comprehensiveness of coverage	☐	☐	☐	☐
Quality of analysis	☐	☐	☐	☐
Overall quality	☐	☐	☐	☐

2. What do you consider the strong points of this publication?

   _____

   _____

3. What do you consider the weak points of this publication?

   _____

   _____

4. For what main purposes do you use this publication?

   Analysis and research   ☐   Education and training   ☐

   Policy formulation and management ☐   Other *(specify)* _____

   _____

   _____

5. . How many people do you share the *Review of Maritime Transport* with or disseminate it to?

   Less than 10   ☐   Between 10 and 20   ☐   More than 20   ☐

6. Which of the following best describes your area of work?

Government	☐	Public enterprise	☐
Non-governmental organization	☐	Academic or research	☐
International organization	☐	Media	☐
Private enterprise institution	☐	Other (specify)	☐

_____

_____

7. Personal information

Name (optional): _____

E-mail: (optional): _____

Country of residence:_____

8. Do you have any further comments?

_____

_____

_____

_____

***

HOW TO OBTAIN THIS PUBLICATION

Sales publications may be purchased from distributors of United Nations publications throughout the world.
They may also be obtained by writing to:

United Nations Publications Sales and Marketing Office
300 East 42nd Street, 9th Floor, IN-919J
New York, New York 10017
United States of America

Tel: +1 212 963 8302
Fax: +1 212 963 3489
E-mail: publications@un.org

https://unp.un.org/